MW00579450

DEAR FRIENDS

A Prophetic Journey Through Great Events of the 20th Century

DEAR FRIENDS

A Prophetic Journey Through Great Events of the 20th Century

Rabbi Jacob Pressman

KTAV Publishing House, Inc.
Hoboken, NJ

Publications by Rabbi Jacob Pressman

The Hebrew Alphabet
Paintings by Joe Rose
Copyright 1988 Triton Publishing Co.
Library of Congress
ISBN: 0-9620948-0-3

✡✡✡✡✡

This Wild and Crazy World
by
Rabbi Jacob Pressman
Registered in 1999
With the United States Copyright Office
Library of Congress, #TXu755-199.

✡✡✡✡✡

Dear Friends
by Rabbi Jacob Pressman
Registered in 2001
With the United States Copyright Office
Library of Congress,
TXu-1-002-705

Distributed by
KTAV Publishing House
900 Jefferson Street
Hoboken, New Jersey 07030

LOVINGLY DEDICATED

This volume is lovingly dedicated
to my Woman of Valor, Margie,
my partner and match in all things;
to our son, the rabbi, Daniel,
who became a rabbi despite my advice
and is a better rabbi than ever I was;
to our son, Joel, who fulfilled
my secret wishes to be a teacher,
performer, musician and conductor;
and to our daughter, Judy,
as lovely as the dawn
who fulfilled my dream of Aliyah;
to my dear mother, Dora, and father, Solomon
who gave me free rein to be myself,
never denigrating, always praising;
and to all my teachers along the way,
who molded my heart and mind.

TABLE OF CONTENTS

PREFACE

Dear Friends,

With the salutation "Dear Friends" I have introduced almost 4,000 sermons over the past 60 years. I use it now to introduce this volume drawn from those sermons which historic events, significant personalities, and the yearnings in my soul demanded preaching. The sermon has been variously the voice of the prophet, laying bare the social ills of the times; the voice of the priest, teaching the rules and regulations of the times; and the voice of the commentator, reacting to the significant events of the times. My sermons reflected each of these functions at one time or another.

In their commentary, these sermons recorded the history-making events and movements of a given moment. Ever since reading Rabbi Sabato Morais' sermon on President Abraham Lincoln's Emancipation Proclamation, I have realized that the rabbinic response to great moments is frozen for posterity in the rabbi's message. As I reviewed the incredible speed and variety of events to which I have reacted over the past 50 years, I concluded that there might be some value in compiling a representative sampling of sermons.

It will be noted that my reaction to a given situation was sometimes later proven misguided for lack of information only made available subsequently. The sermon after V-J Day (Victory over Japan) failed to grasp the full horror of the atom-bombing of Hiroshima and Nagasaki, which, arguably, might have been avoided and victory attained without setting the stage for the international missile mania ever since. The sermons were simply colored by the emotions of a point in time without the hindsight of later years.

That hindsight is reflected in the introductions I have written. These confess the mistakes in judgment I made as shown in later revelations of the truth of the matter or the true conduct of individuals reported. However, these sermons reflect all we knew at the time.

These sermons should also reveal a difference in attitude, and, perhaps, even wisdom between the 20-year old and the 80-year-old preacher except that during those 60 years the world has changed so rapidly and so radically that cumulative wisdom was always challenged by unprecedented circumstances for which there had been no experience. For example, "Samson in the Ghetto" (1944) with its description of the Battle of the Warsaw Ghetto, does not relate to the granting of autonomy to the Palestinians in the Gaza Strip and Jericho in 1994 anymore than the parade of German tanks and troops down the Champs Elysees in 1944 related to a similar parade in 1994 in celebration of Bastille Day.

What I offer here is the truth of the moment, the crisis of the moment, the reaction of the moment, which are, in their way, more accurate of the temper of the time than subsequent historic records. They convey some of the excitement, anxiety, fear and exultation which the crisis pulpit conveyed as no other source could.

My hope is that it reminds my contemporaries of our response to well-remembered experiences and gives those who came later some insight into what was preoccupying the pulpit. Today, the pulpit speaks more in the voice of the priest: teaching, expounding the classical texts and commenting on the weekly portion. I suggest that it might be useful if the pulpit also reacted to the contemporary scene a bit more elaborately and in more permanent form for the edification and instruction of future generations.

Rabbi Jacob Pressman

GRATEFUL ACKNOWLEDGMENTS

Since the following sermons were all written in solitude, I find it fascinating that it has taken so many people to get them into print. If I deserve any credit in creating them, which is questionable, they would still be slumbering in my files were it not for a platoon of individuals who have given them new life in this volume. Forgive me if I wax verbose and maudlin. That is what writers do.

Please assume the words, "I am grateful to..." before each of the following. That will save paper.

My trophy bride of 60 years, Marjorie Steinberg Pressman who urged me for years to publish some of my sermons, and whose insistence and perseverance in the face of my obstreperousness compelled me to follow through. I would not have done so without her patient support, her critical expertise, her love of synagogue life, and her contagious sense of righteous indignation,

Our son, Rabbi Daniel Pressman, who gave the rabbinate, and me personally, the greatest of compliments: his choice of the rabbinate as his life's work, attesting to his respect for the calling, and his willingness to risk the comparisons with his father. He has distinguished himself as a caring, effective rabbi and *mensch*. Most of all, he has published, which I have not, and thus inspired me to publish at last myself.

Dr. Laurence Kaplan, a friend and congregant who approached me a few years ago and said, "Rabbi, I have loved and learned from your sermons for years. You must publish them." He then volunteered thousands of dollars to cover the costs which would be incurred, and when I delayed he came to my home, took the 60 heavy loose-leaf notebooks from my shelves, carted them off to be copied so they could be scanned letter by letter as if they were being retyped, bought the computer equipment required by the process, and ran interference for me with my publisher. It is correct to say, this publication is the result of his efforts for almost three years.

A series of congregations: Beth Am Israel in Philadelphia, the Forest Hills Jewish Center in New York, Sinai Temple and Temple Beth Am in Los Angeles where the members had to listen to me as I preached.

Temple Beth Am, in particular, where I have been Senior Rabbi and Emeritus for 52 years, presented me in concert on my 80th birthday, and dedicated a substantial part of the proceeds to my publication fund. Its rabbis and members have encouraged me always.

A series of wonderful women who have handled the endless computer work involved: Susan Bogorad who created a database for all 4000 sermons, volunteering her time and her enthusiasm; Natalie Stanger, who did the bulk of the organization and word processing, and Carol Schwalberg, who performed much of the editing with a professional eye.

Before them, a succession of secretaries who typed sermons over the years, including Florence Gritz, Mona Altman, Rachael Ferrier and Marilyn Grobeson.

KTAV Publishing House, whose CEO Bernard Scharfstein has undertaken to publish this book, for his enthusiastic ideas, patience and wise counsel have guided me in all the challenging steps of accomplishing my goal.

For the photos from which the cover was designed, I must acknowledge and thank the following: Photo of Henrietta Szold – courtesy of Hadassah, The Women's Zionist Organization of America. Photos of Rabbi Abraham Joshua Heschel, Prof. Louis Finkelstein and Rabbi Simon Greenberg – Women's League for Conservative Judaism Archives. Photo of Rabbi Mordechai Kaplan – courtesy Prof. Mel Scult. Photos of Winston Churchill, Martin Luther King, Jr., Golda Meir, Prince Ibn Saud and Franklin Delano Roosevelt – Getty Images, Inc./Hulton Archive.

I must make special mention of our son, Joel, who almost daily fielded my questions about the computer, and gave me hands-on guidance with it. He formatted and printed the photo-ready copy by means of which this was printed, and gave me many wise editorial suggestions. He also created the concept of the book jacket as well as the flattering bio.

Special appreciation to Kevin Hummer of BoldFace Design for his artistic input in finalizing the design of the book jacket.

As I mentioned above, it is fascinating to review how many people it has taken to get me this far. I guess it takes a village to raise a book of sermons. Now if only a couple of people read it, our work would be justified.

Rabbi Jacob Pressman, January 2002

THE RENAISSANCE RABBI

To the hundreds of thousands who know Rabbi Jacob Pressman, he is the "Renaissance Rabbi," renowned for his preaching, his singing and piano playing, his ability as designer, painter, calligrapher, his witty song parodies which, thanks to the Internet, have appeared at Seders world-wide, and for his leadership on so many crucial issues in the Jewish community and the larger community.

His formal education is impressive: after graduating Phi Betta Kappa and Magna cum laude from the University of Pennsylvania, he earned degrees as Master of Hebrew Literature, Rabbi, Doctor of Hebrew Letters and Doctor of Divinity from the Jewish Theological Seminary of America. We who love his sermons and become energized when he begins with "Dear Friends" will not be surprised to learn he also won a Public Speaking prize at the Seminary. Another degree, Doctor of Humane Letters, was awarded to him by the University of Judaism, of which he was among the founders and its first Registrar.

A Hebrew School principal while still a teenager, Rabbi Jack served a pulpit in Forest Hills, New York, before moving to California where he ultimately became Rabbi of the Temple he has served since 1950, Temple Beth Am in Los Angeles.

As early as 1944 he was reporting the true magnitude of the Holocaust to his congregation in Forest Hills and recruiting masses of uncommitted Jews as active Zionists demanding a Jewish State for the survivors. He was for years one of the most powerful speakers on behalf of Bonds for Israel, helping to raise millions and millions of dollars in bonds. He was perhaps the first Rabbi in town to listen to survivors and lead them in memorial services. He succeeded in having Beth Am erect the first memorial to the Six Million in the Kotel-like wall in its sanctuary.

Beyond the myriad day-and-night duties of leading Temple Beth Am and ministering to its membership, Rabbi Jack was instrumental in helping to initiate in 1964 the "Save Soviet Jewry" national movement, which did indeed save many Soviet Jews by enabling them to emigrate to Israel, the United States and other countries. Serving with him on that committee were Theodore Bikel, and Rabbi Abraham Joshua Heschel, among others. He marched with Martin Luther King, Jr. in Montgomery, Alabama in 1965. As founding first president of the Beverly Hills Maple Center in Beverly Hills, he helped to create a counseling center which has helped thousands of young and old and has become a model for other organizations nationally. His efforts and strong beliefs in the need for more intensive Jewish education paved the way for now-thriving Jewish day schools in Los Angeles, from nursery through high school, including Herzl Schools, Akiba Academy and the school named in his honor, the Rabbi Jacob Pressman Academy.

When Rabbi Jacob Pressman became Rabbi Emeritus in 1985, fortunately for us he never consulted Webster about the meaning of "Emeritus." He may have retired from official duties at Beth Am, but he continues to participate in High Holiday services with his much-anticipated classic benediction and his sermon. He became a circuit rabbi in Santa Clarita, conducting bimonthly services for a congregation without a rabbi. He remains active in Bonds for Israel, the University of Judaism, the Bureau of Jewish Education, Friends of Sheba Medical Center and the Jewish Federation Council. His amusing parodies are the highlights of celebrations of special friends.

Several years ago he embarked upon a new career by writing a weekly column for the Beverly Hills Courier. There we can read his latest thoughts and observations about the human condition. Because we identify with his observations we enjoy his expositions which are invariably astute, succinct, amusing and perceptive, and written in poetically inspired prose. A volume of many of those delightful and thoughtful columns is scheduled to be released in 2002

These thoughts and facts on Rabbi Jacob Pressman cannot possibly capture the man and his influence on so many. To get to know some measure of the man as a spiritual leader, read these sermons. They will hint at the quiet moments, counseling loved ones mourning their lost relatives. They will show you the same humor and warmth which filled the hospital rooms he visited, giving comfort to the sick. And they will show you a rabbi with a unique ability to capture the crucial issues of his time and to tell his congregation not what they wanted to hear, but what they needed to hear.

Working on this volume took far longer than it should have, because the temptatiom was too great not to stop, read and re-read every chapter. I am sure you will see why.

Joel D. Pressman
Loving son and typesetter

CHAPTER ONE
The Decade Which Changed the World

The ten years from 1938 to 1948 were undoubtedly the most transforming decade in the social history of the human race. From the rapid rise of Fascism, to the rape of a continent and the decimation by genocide of almost the entire European Jewish population, to the bloodiest of wars against civilians as well as the military, to its abrupt conclusion with the dropping of the atom bomb which can never more be aborted, to the shifting of populations, the creation of new national boundaries, the United Nations, and, for us, the declaration of the Third Jewish Commonwealth.

Throughout the Thirties I had listened to my rabbi, Morris S. Goodblatt, at Congregation Beth Am in Phildephia, warn of the rise to power of a dangerous man named Adolph Hitler, the peril his intentions posed to Jewish survival, and the urgent need of a homeland for the embattled Jews of Europe. I drank in his words, and repeated them as well as I could to a Youth Congregation of some 250 teenagers for whom I served as rabbi from 1938 to 1941. Many of my talks on those Sabbaths were unscripted, but I had the opportunity to express the burden of my opinions in a composition in English class at the University of Pennsylvania, titled herein, "Prologue: Is Zionism the Answer?"

In February, 1944, in the middle of my junior year, Dr. Louis Finkelstein, Chancellor of the Jewish Theological Seminary, sent me to serve as interim rabbi at the Forest Hills Jewish Center in Queens, New York. Many of my sermons reflected the events of the day reactively and proactively. When the American press was not too concerned with the plight of Jews but rather with the bigger picture of World War II which was not going to well for us, I spoke again and again about the Battle of the Warsaw Ghetto, the raging anti-Semitism which spilled over from Europe to our very doorsteps, the conferences of the big world powers as they reflected upon our Jewish survival, the infamous White Paper which cost millions of Jewish lives, the birth of the United Nations, and ultimately the rebirth of Israel complete with the attack of the Arab nations against Israel, a war which rages still today. The pulpit was the second line of defense.

PROLOGUE: IS ZIONISM THE ANSWER?

This sermon predates my preaching days. It was written when I was still a student and sometimes an acting rabbi. I was 18 years old and a sophomore at the University of Pennsylvania.

My English professor, Dr. Longaker, assigned us an informal argument. I chose to draft an argument for Zionism as the only answer to what was generally referred to as the Jewish Problem: namely, that the Jewish people had too long been the object of discrimination and persecution in land after land.

That was an unusual subject then. America was isolationist and the university had strong restrictions against the matriculation of Jews.

Nevertheless, I chose this subject because the American Jews were apprehensive about the rise of Hitler and debated among themselves how best to cope with rising anti-Semitism. There existed a small pro-Zionist number, a small and vocal anti-Zionist number and general apathy among the rest.

I was pleased when my professor commented: "This is a capable, well thought-out piece of work. But can Jewish Palestine assimilate more than a few thousand additional immigrants a year? Is it adequate in space and resources? Is the Arab threat sufficiently dispelled?"

In spite of his personal reservations, he gave this essay an "A". I believe it set the stage for my subsequent decision to enter the rabbinate and the years of preaching which followed. It is incredible to realize that only 10 years later, after this essay was written, there was a Jewish state, and a sadly-decimated Jewish world.

MAY 10, 1938

Ever since Theodore Herzl founded the Zionist movement in 1897, Jewish people everywhere have asked the question, "Is Zionism the answer?" After considering long I have come to the conclusion that it is.

Many people misunderstand the purposes of Zionism. Its ambition is clearly stated in the first paragraphs of its formally declared program: "Zionism aims at establishing for the Jewish people a publicly and legally assured home in Palestine." To what is Zionism the answer? It seems to me that Zionism attempts to answer for the Jewish people the questions; Where shall we go? What shall we do?

At present I am a student at the University of Pennsylvania enjoying the privileges of a scholarship and sharing equality of opportunity with my fellow students. My country has been good to me; I enjoy the benefits of its facilities for culture and entertainment, for physical, mental and moral development. Why, then, should I trouble myself with such questions as Where shall we go? What shall we do? Is Zionism the answer?

True, I am content here in America, and, indeed, almost all American Jews share this contentment. We, however, represent only one-quarter of the scattered race. There are twelve million Jews all over the world who lack the opportunities we have found in America. Their position is unstable. In many countries economic and social persecution and sometimes even loss of life threaten them. It is of them I am thinking when I say that Zionism is the answer.

The story of the situation of the Jews in Germany has become old news. There is nothing I can add to paint a more touching picture of their plight than that which the sketchy reports of the press have already suggested. Were Germany the only country where such oppression exists the picture might not be so black. Poland and Rumania must not be forgotten. In Poland the non-Aryan child must not sit on the same side of the classroom as the more fortunate student. Over a million people are suffering the indignities of discrimination and occasional physical injury. Rumanian King Carol has recognized what he calls a problem.

Russia's attack on all religion has brought anguish to the men to whom religious practices were as dear as life. Now daily out of Austria come reports of new persecution there. Faint rumblings of trouble are beginning in Sudetan Czechoslovakia. It is the problem of the people suffering in these countries I am considering when I argue for Zionism in the light of the pressing need for some solution to their problem.

My friends often say to me, "But if the Jews would assimilate, lose their Jewish identity, cease to set themselves apart and follow an outmoded faith, surely the problem would be solved. Surely there would be no need for Zionism." To them I always point out the lessons that history has taught us.

Two thousand years ago, the Children of Israel tried to assimilate. They were living as one nation at that time in their little country, Palestine. When the Hellenistic culture that spread over all of Asia Minor reached Palestine the rich young men thought it fashionable to give up their Judaism for the thrilling new civilization out of Greece. These attempts sowed the seeds of the destruction of the nation, for when conflict arose between the pious and the Hellenist, Rome stepped in and gobbled up the land, scattering its inhabitants. Assimilation had caused our first down fall.

Some of our people wandered to Spain, and there, from 1200 to 1492, prospered in the period we call the golden age in Spain. They became famous in medicine, science, mathematics and letters, but in 1492 came their downfall. They were driven out. Assimilation had failed.

If assimilation fails, how about complete withdrawal into ourselves, non-association with our neighbors without leaving the land altogether to journey to Palestine? In the ghetto we were secluded and withdrawn, but such a life was unbearable. We stood still while all the world was progressing, learning, creating a new civilization. What a relief it was when the ghetto gates were finally thrown open, when the Jew was free to breathe the air of emancipation, live like a man with his neighbors and learn the wisdom of the modern age. We tried seclusion, but without success.

Once again we attempted assimilation. We lived in Poland and Russia, and felt that we were safe at last. Then in 1880 began the pogroms and persecution such as we had forgotten existed in the world. We fled in droves to a refuge in the New World where we found security and hard work. Many, however, remained in Germany, and prided themselves that they were Germans, not Jews. They wrote, invented and studied as Germans. They believed themselves secure. Nothing could ever happen to them. But an Austrian house painter arose and achieved a power and fearfulness greater than any man since Napoleon, and the German Jews suffered, non-Aryan blood was traced back three and four generations. Those who had assimilated were forced to embrace their religion once more.

My interpretation of these historical events is that neither assimilation nor ghetto seclusion has ever served to answer the questions, Where shall we go? What shall we do? Our people in Europe must have an answer to these questions, however, they must have an adequate, workable plan; and they must have it immediately. Surely England, France, and the United States cannot absorb them safely, even though the United States recently made a generous offer of hospitality. Palestine seems to be the only answer.

Many people say that Zionism will not provide a satisfactory solution. They say the plan is not workable. They must be ignorant of the true situation, for it is working now. From what was a stony barren waste, the chalutzim or pioneers have created fertile farm land. Palestine has opened its arms to thousands of refugees from various countries where oppression has sprung up. Almost two million Jews have made a home for themselves there. The best proof that it can work, then, is that it is working.

Will this plan which sounds so simple now continue to operate? Recently England stated that she would restrict the land open to colonization to one-tenth of the Palestine of Biblical times. True, the statement came as a blow to the hopes of those who believe in Zionism, but will it shatter their plans? I do not think so. I believe that an unprecedented movement like this one, in which a people is trying to move back to its land not by aggression or armed conflict but by dint of hard work, saving and buying back the land piece by piece, must go on by virtue of the oneness, the honesty and the daring of its purpose.

If Zionism is the answer, will it answer the problem immediately, completely, and satisfactorily? I cannot say yes to any part of this question. Immediate solution of the problem is out of the question. It will be a hundred years or more before Palestine can absorb as many people as it has to. It cannot answer the problem completely because, in my opinion at least, Palestine would not be able to support all the people who might wish to come back to it. It has no oil of its own, no coal nor any too plentiful lumber supply. The Jordan, however, tumbles down to the Dead Sea with a tremendous force, and already engineers are planning to harness it for the power the country so sorely needs. Zionism cannot solve the problem in an ideal way because of the presence of the Arabs who, very rightly, refuse to forsake their land. I do not claim too much for Zionism, but I doubt that anyone can devise a better plan.

Night falls over Tel Aviv, the only Jewish city in the world. As the stars brighten, bonfires leap up to meet them from streets named after the lovers and builders of Zion. Jewish boy scouts pass in the street carrying their blue and white flags. Schoolgirls sing a Hebrew song. The broad shouldered young chalutzim, who have made the stony land bear fruit and have cleared the swamps, dance together in the square. Farmers, professors, little children, everyone speaks the living Hebrew tongue. There is promise here: a promise of a home and a chance to hold up their heads again for those suffering oppression and privation; a promise of inspiration to those of us who have found happiness and opportunity in lands where reason, not blind tyranny, rules. There is proof here: proof that Zionism is the answer.

SAMSON IN THE WARSAW GHETTO

It has been charged that American Jews did not do enough to save the Jews trapped in Europe from genocide. In rebuttal, many insisted that we did not know what was actually happening.

Both allegations are not entirely justified by the facts. We knew a great deal, but not everything. This sermon states that we were helpless to do anything but give money. We protested, we petitioned, we screamed *"gewald!"*, but it was not enough.

I cite the following sermon as evidence of the degree to which we were informed. The newspapers ran banner headlines in the early forties blaring, "TWO MILLION JEWS KILLED BY HITLER" and later "FOUR MILLION JEWS SLAIN." The Polish Jewish local media printed reams of information smuggled out of Europe. Few Americans believed it. There are Holocaust revisionists even today. I tried to do my part through sermons like this.

APRIL 24, 1944

Dear Friends,

The Philistines captured Samson, and put out his eyes, and bound him with fetters of brass, and he did grind in the prison house. And the Philistines gathered together to hold a celebration. And they called for Samson out of the prison house and made sport of him. Then Samson called upon the Lord, and said, "Lord God, remember me, I pray Thee, and strengthen me only this once that I may be avenged of the Philistines. Let me die with the Philistines." And Samson pulled with all his might on the two supporting pillars of the Philistinian temple, and down fell the temple, killing all inside. So those he killed in death were more than those he killed in life." (Judges 16:21, 23, 25, 28, 30)

The night of April 19, 1943 was the first Seder night. That night last year, most of us were at the Seder table, recalling the freeing of the slaves in Egypt, not suspecting what was happening that very Seder night in the Warsaw ghetto, not dreaming that a tragic and glorious chapter was being written there, not knowing that the spirit of the ancient hero Samson had arisen once more.

On April 19, 1943 and for many days thereafter, the pomp and pride and military might of the German army was humbled and made ridiculous before the world by the ragged, weary, poorly armed and half-starved Jews of the Warsaw ghetto. As battles are scaled in this war, it was not a tremendous military venture. Casualties were not in the millions. The results were predetermined by the German possession of planes, tanks and heavy artillery, and yet, one of history's greatest moments was written there in blood in an epic of heroism.

April 19, 1943 was the climax of a chain of events the like of which has never been equaled for cruelty and savagery. Before this war there were over three million Jews in the country of Poland. In 1939, Warsaw had the largest Jewish community of any city in Europe, 375,000. Today there are scarcely 20,000 Jews left in all of Poland and these are being exterminated daily by the thousands.

In the fall of 1939 the Germans marched into Warsaw and the reign of terror began for the Jews. The Germans, indulged in unbridled anti-Semitism, beating Jews in the streets, stripping them of possessions and looting synagogues. In November of 1939, the German authorities advised the Jewish Council of Warsaw that a ghetto would be established. In April, 1940, an epidemic of typhus broke out in the Jewish quarter of Warsaw because of the crowded conditions there. The German authorities thereupon declared it a "closed, contaminated area" saying "it had been found necessary to construct a wall about the Jewish quarter because it was a breeding place of disease."

The epidemic was only an excuse to enclose the Jews in the ghetto for in August of 1940 a decree was published ordering all Jews coming to Warsaw from other parts of Poland to reside within the walled section. Those Jews who lived in other parts of Warsaw had to move into the walled area, and non-Jews were to move out. These non-Jews, of whom there were about 90,000, were given until November 15. On November 16, the ghetto was closed without warning, and all supplies of food to it were stopped. A black market arose, and Germans shot on sight any Jews or Poles attempting to smuggle food into the ghetto. A story is told of a little Jewish boy who was caught trying to smuggle in a bag of food; he was dropped into a sewer.

Four hundred and fifty thousand Jews were by now crowded into the dirtiest and most neglected part of the city, where half that number had lived before. The number of people per room soared to eight, even ten, resulting in disease and filthy conditions. The mortality rate was high because of starvation, overcrowding, and appalling sanitary conditions causing epidemics of spotted fever, typhus, typhoid and tuberculosis. During the entire severe winter of 1941-1942, there was no heating in the ghetto. The death rate reached 13 per cent. The birth rate dropped to nothing, but the population remained about the same because Jews were constantly being shipped in from the Western European countries. Around the whole teeming, disease ridden, starving ghetto were brick walls, seven feet high, with broken glass cemented on top, and barbed wire fences.

The Jews were dying, but not fast enough to satisfy German requirements. When Heinrich Himmler visited Poland in March 1942, he gave orders that 50% of the Jews of Poland were to be exterminated by the end of the year. Execution by machine-gun began, and in a month 700,000 Polish Jews were massacred. Apparently bullets were either too slow or too costly a means of extermination for the Germans so other methods were substituted. Poison gas was used at Chelm; electrocution at Belzec where tens of thousands of Jews from the provinces of Lwow, Lublin, and Kielce were murdered..

The liquidation of the Jews of Warsaw began in July, 1942. On July 17, the Jews were registered. Beginning July 20, flying squads of German police drove through the streets looking for educated Jews. They killed the better-dressed Jews on sight. One non-Jewish doctor lost his life this way, although he had official permission to perform his medical duties in the ghetto. On July 21, the whole Jewish Council was arrested, but while some members were kept as hostages, most of them were released, including the Chairman, M. Czerniakow.

The next day, July 22, an order was read to the Jewish Council commanding that it supply from six to ten thousand persons daily for what the Germans called "resettlement to the East." The notices which were posted read that families would be allowed to go together, could take all their valuables with them and would all be resettled in places where they would find peaceful work. On the evening of July 23, the German police again called on Czerniakow, chairman of the Jewish council, and asked that the first contingent of Jews be raised to 10,000 and 7,000 every day thereafter. Shortly after they left, Czerniakow committed suicide, thus registering his protest in the only way left at his disposal.

The first group of volunteers for resettlement was to report on Stawski street. We are told that tens of thousands actually lined up voluntarily that first day, a thought to craze the mind: thousands of people going voluntarily to their death, yet not knowing what was to happen. Day after day thousands reported voluntarily. False letters arrived from those who had left, describing how well things were going for them in their new localities. By the sixth day news seeped back to the ghetto that those being resettled were actually going to their death, and the volunteers ceased coming.

The German police were forced to step in. They blocked off streets and apartment houses and forced all the inhabitants into the streets. Those who were slow in coming or hid or tried to escape were shot. All the infirm, old, and crippled were taken to the Jewish cemetery, shot and buried. Those remaining were then taken to the railroad siding near Stawski Street and packed into boxcars. They choked for lack of air since the cars were sealed from the outside, and sometimes the floors were covered with chlorine and quicklime which emitted noxious fumes when wet down by urine. Sometimes those standing were forced to take off their shoes so their legs and feet might be burnt. Many fainted and vomited from the heat and the stench. Some died, their bodies still standing pressed between the tightly-packed, half-conscious men, women, and children. Sometimes they were able to see the stations they passed and realized they were on their way to the notorious extermination camp of Treblinka.

At Treblinka, the railway line ran alongside a platform specially built for unloading the human cargo. Upon arrival the cars were rapidly emptied, the living separated from the dead. The half-conscious men, women, and children were lined up separately and told to strip for a bath. For some diabolical reason which we shall probably never learn, the Germans had posted a sign to encourage the people, "Do not worry about your fate. You are all going to the east to work. Men will have work and women housework. You should deposit all your valuables and money in the cash desk here. You will get a receipt, and after you have had your bath and been disinfected, you will get everything back."

When everyone had stripped, the clothes were taken away and sorted, and the valuables confiscated. Here, the whole farce of reassuring the victims ended, and they were driven terrorized down a long path into a one-story brick building. They were driven inside, slipping and falling on the wet terra-cotta floor. They could not get up as new groups were driven in and piled upon them. Children were thrown in over the heads of the prostrate people. At last, the doors were closed and sealed and the nature of the chamber was revealed. It was a steam chamber. From the nearby boiler rooms live steam was forced into the mass of human bodies. They died of slow strangulation, literally boiled to death. The cries died down completely and in fifteen minutes all was still.

The doors were opened but not one body fell out. Due to the steam, all the bodies had been fused into a homogeneous mass cemented together with the perspiration of the victims. Cold water had to be sprayed on the mass before the bodies could be separated and removed for burial. A bulldozer dug long craters and into them the bodies were piled. Such was the process of resettlement.

In August of 1942, all the children from the schools and orphan homes were deported, and it is feared they went to Treblinka. In January of 1943, no more than 40,000 Jews remained in the ghetto, but somehow with the new year a new spirit of resistance began to stir. The Jews began to receive arms from the Polish underground. The Allied successes in North Africa filtered through to them and they were given new courage to fight for life and freedom. On the 18th and 19th of January the Germans began anew their deportation program, and this time the newly-formed fighter unit of Jews met the Gestapo with guns in their hands.

Three months passed between this first resistance and the great battle of Passover. Imagine the tremendous courage of these people during those months. After more than three years of demoralizing persecution they were still able to organize and prepare themselves politically, militarily and spiritually for the incomparable, historic act. Imagine arming 3,000 men under the eyes of the Gestapo, organizing leadership, dividing the city into defense sections and digging tunnels for communication with the part of the city outside the Ghetto walls. All this took tremendous courage, self-sacrifice, imagination, and will-power. It took dignity, pride and faith that something good would come of it to organize and plan a war that was doomed before it began.

About midnight on the first Seder night, April 19, 1943, six German tanks rumbled into the ghetto. They threw a blockade around one of the streets they were going to empty for deportation as usual. But this night was not as usual. Symbolically, the Jews chose the anniversary of the deliverance from Egypt to rise, to pit their tortured, broken, starving numbers against the well-fed and fully-armed Nazi slave-drivers. The Germans were met with bullets and bombs and perished in the flames of their own exploded tanks. All able-bodied men and women were armed. Large houses were turned into forts. Every street had its arsenal. Trenches were dug, cellars used as shelters. Children were used as messengers and to bring food and water.

The Nazis withdrew. Next morning the Jews stormed the nearby arsenals and supply houses, taking ammunition, foodstuffs and Nazi army uniforms. They outfitted their most Aryan-looking members as Nazi soldiers and raided the Pawiak jail, releasing several thousand Jews and Poles to help them fight. Day after day, the Nazis raided and shelled the ghetto, but despite flame and casualties, the defenders held. The Gestapo and the military were puzzled as to who should handle the situation. Finally, half a division of German soldiers was called up. German planes showered incendiary bombs on the ghetto.

As the Germans mined and exploded house after house and burned their way into the ghetto, the defenders sold each inch of ground dearly. Tanks and panzer divisions faced only rifles, machine guns and home-made bombs, but the battle continued for days and weeks. Five weeks passed and the Jews were still resisting, The ghetto was in flames. The Jews sent messengers to the Polish underground of Warsaw, urging them to begin a revolt of the entire city, but the Poles refused so the Jews held out alone.

The ghetto ran out of food and water. The dead piled up. Epidemic raged. Sick and feverish, the defenders stuck to their guns. On the forty-second day the Nazis surrounded the last building whose occupants still held out. It was a four story building, each of its floors a fortress. The Nazis fought their way into the building and upward floor by floor. For eight hours the fight raged until by evening the last defenders were on the roof. They were members of Hechalutz, the Zionist pioneer movement. They erected their flag on that roof and there it waved until late that night when suddenly firing ceased from the building. For a moment the flag disappeared. After a few moments something wrapped in blue-and-white crashed to the street. It was the last defender, who jumped to his death wrapped in the flag.

Thus ended the battle of Warsaw, but its heroism touched off numerous uprisings in other ghettos throughout Poland: Bialystok, Lodz, Treblinka, Paniatov and many others. Their message got through to the world. They cried out to us, "In the name of the millions of murdered Jews, in the name of all those who were burned, tortured, and slaughtered, in the name of those who are still fighting heroically though condemned to certain death in an unequal struggle, we call to the world to listen to us today. Our Allies must finally realize that a tremendous historic responsibility will fall upon those who remained passive, in the face of the unbelievable Nazi crime against a whole people whose tragic epilogue we witness today. The desperate heroism of the people of the ghetto must stir the world to an action equal in greatness to the movement." It is to our eternal shame that the call from the flames of the ghetto remained unanswered by the world. At least the Jewish brethren of these martyred dead have responded. We have mourned for them, and we mourn for them tonight.

But there must be something more we can do. In the face of the odds they had against them, would we have been as brave? I wonder. And then I asked myself, How can we American Jews show our admiration for them and our response to their last request? And I suddenly realized sadly, we have but one way, immediate and concrete, by supporting the current United Jewish Appeal. Our money can rehabilitate whatever remnant of Jewry is left when the Nazis retreat, as it has already done in North Africa and Sicily. It can strengthen Palestine so that if and when some of our people escape to it, they can be received. It can help train and rehabilitate those who are saved in whatever new home they seek. We can keep faith with the martyrs of the ghetto by spending our money to save the remnant as unselfishly as they spent the only thing they had to give, their lives.

Yes, a year ago the spirit of Samson entered into the ghetto. Shattered in body but unbroken in spirit, the Jews rose to their full height and faced their tormentors. Like Samson, they had been imprisoned and chained, tormented and made a sport and a mockery. And like Samson, too, they called upon the Lord and said, "O Lord God, remember us, we pray thee, and strengthen us only this once that we may be avenged of the Philistines. Let us die with them together!" And the Lord gave them strength so that the grandeur of their martyrdom might inspire us with new spirit and courage. And they fought and they died, but their enemies died with them!

Let us rise to hallow their memory.

THE WAR AGAINST THE JEWS RAGES ON

On Yom Kippur, 5705, when the full story was being told of the slaughter of millions of Jews in Europe, the America First Committee, an isolationist movement opposed to American participation in the battle against the Nazis, had as one of the planks in its political program the sterilization of all of the Jews in America.

The mood of the congregation was one of depression. Some American Jews reacted to the horror reports with panic, with fear that their own lives were in jeopardy because of the possibility that Hitler might still prevail. Some were in denial, burying their heads in the sand of indifference and refusing to believe the evidence. Some degenerated into self-hatred. "It must be our own fault!"

The sermon addresses these reactions and proposes positive alternative.

SEPTEMBER 27, 1944

Dear Friends:

The Lord is my light and my salvation; whom shall I fear?
The Lord is the stronghold of my life, of whom shall I be afraid?
When evildoers came upon me to eat up my flesh,
Even my adversaries and my foes, they stumbled and fell.
Though a host should encamp against me my heart shall not fear.
Though war should rise up against me even then will I be confident.

In these words from Psalm 27 which we read this morning we hear assurance at a time when assurance is needed. We said on *Rosh Hashanah* that the coming year holds great promise of victory for the United Nations, that the future had a brighter look than it has had for a long time. All that is true.

But the war between the United Nations and the remaining nations who are our enemies is not the only war going on. There is another war, a war that began before this one. A cruel and bloody war. A one-sided war. A war the cause of which is so elusive we cannot put our finger on it. A war which will continue after V-day. That is the war against the Jews, the twentieth century version of which we have all experienced in our lifetime.

In this war against the Jews, we Jews are not winning. No, we are suffering the most humiliating, the most crushing defeat in all our long history of battle for survival. We have experienced an astounding number of casualties, millions of dead Jews whose exact identity now is known only to the methodical German butchers and to God. We have lost more than human casualties. We have lost as well our feeling of security in every country in which we still live. We have lost our peace of mind. And we have lost those of our number whose cowardly reaction to the danger has been to abandon their people and repudiate their Jewish identity. No matter what happens from now on, we have suffered a terrible defeat.

Now as we face the future, there are no signs to reassure us. On the contrary, we have every reason to believe that the war against us will grow ever more violent. Our enemies have done their work well. They have demonstrated irrefutably that one may harm the Jews and not be punished for it. They have prepared a way for open demonstration against the Jew at the earliest possible excuse for an opportunity.

Tragic reports began to appear in the newspapers recently, telling of the atrocities committed against the Jews of Europe. We half-hoped that the American public would be aroused, its sympathies would become articulate, its indignation would take practical form. We hoped in vain. There are still those who refuse to believe the evidence. There are still those who consider those outrages to be Hitler's only redeeming acts. Of course there are a few who have been aroused on our behalf, but they are mighty few indeed.

The very day after the public announcements in Dublin of the documented evidence of the slaughter factories, here in our own land the America First Committee suggested the sterilization of the Jews of America as one of its political planks.

In the face of such depressing events, lacking assurance that the war against the Jews will even come up for consideration at the peace conferences that will take place one day, it is with heavy heart that we repeat today the words of the Psalmist: "Though a host should encamp against me, my heart shall not fear; Though war should rise up, against me, even then will I be confident."

We Jews have reacted to this war against us in several different ways. One immediate reaction when we feel the hot breath of our enemies on our necks is panic. The world is treated to the comic spectacle of Jews on the run. Some of us are quite honestly afraid, and who can blame us, but we react by disclaiming our Jewishness and accomplish nothing.

Some Jews refuse to take to their heels and beat a cowardly retreat. Instead they play the ostrich, burying their heads in the sand of indifference and refusing to hear or see what is going on. Having tender stomachs, they will not be informed of the sufferings of their fellow Jews and refuse to believe that anyone could mean them harm. And so, when their windows are broken, when their children are attacked on the streets, they are shocked and bewildered.

One particularly bitter reaction is that the Jew upon learning that he has strong enemies, takes to hating the fact that he is a Jew. He cannot bear to be on the losing side, even if temporarily. He takes refuge in changing his name to something that sounds as if it belongs on the winning side. He cuts off a little bit of his nose to spite who knows what. But with all his trimming and clipping of his Jewish characteristics, he can never completely divorce himself from the fact that he is a Jew. His enemies know it, and he knows it. What a hard lot it is to live with something you hate, particularly when that something happens to be yourself.

None of these spontaneous, irrational reactions can help the Jew win his war. Nor will oversensitiveness help calm his jumpy, nervous excitement every time he is called a name or reminded of his religious preference by his non-Jewish neighbor. "Don't wear your Judaism as a tag," said a writer recently, "but stamp it on your heart."

No, the challenges of this war against us must be met bravely, intelligently and optimistically. We must react with resourcefulness so as not to be totally destroyed by it. The path ahead for us if we would wrest any kind of victory out of this new battle of ours, is threefold: Our survival depends on the victory of liberalism in the world, on our ability to live an attractive and meaningful Jewish life, and on the establishment of a Jewish national homeland in Palestine.

The first of these three requirements: the triumph of equality and tolerance and social justice in the world, we discussed on the first day of Rosh Hashanah. We said then and repeat today that the Jew has no place in reaction for he is the first target of reaction.

The Jew, on the contrary, stands for that which is progressive, that which is ethical, that which is for the greatest good of the majority of the people. That is why anyone who manifests any liberal tendencies is immediately labeled a Jew by the reactionaries, for they know that the Bible of the Jews and the teachings of the Rabbis have pointed the way for the eventual establishment of a heavenly kingdom of equality and justice and love here on earth.

Secondly, we can bring dignity and joy to our Jewish life even in the face of attacks from without if we imbue it with meaning and intensity.

This aspect of our survival, which was expounded on the second day of *Rosh Hashanah*, can turn defeat into victory here in America.

It begins with the establishment of more intensive Judaism in the home, with the very *mezuzah* on the door which announces with quiet dignity that here lives a Jew proud of his identity. But it must not stop at the door. The Jewish spirit must pervade the home, shine from the pages of books which are opened, sparkle on the table where the Sabbath and the festivals are welcomed. The Jewish spirit must be nourished by education, not merely education for bar mitzvah, but education in the formative adolescent years, and education for the adult.

But the third path we must follow in order to win our battle is the path that leads to the establishment of a home for the Jewish spirit in Palestine. There is some confusion among us, that it is possible to be a complete Jew, a religious Jew, and yet have no hand in the restoration of Zion. I say confusion, for if anyone holds that belief he has failed to listen to what his mouth has said. The Jew who disclaims any national identity for the Jews and insists we are only a religious group has either never read the prayer book or never understood it. Nine times on this Yom Kippur day we say, "O may our eyes witness Thy return to Zion. Blessed art Thou O Lord, who restorest Thy divine Presence unto Zion." Every time we rise to recite the *Shema Yisrael* we say "*Ohev amo Yisrael.* Blessed art Thou O Lord, who lovest Thy people Israel."

Whenever we read the Torah we chant, "Father of compassion favor Zion with Thy goodness and help us to rebuild the walls of Jerusalem." Every *bar mitzvah* boy who reads the Haftarah chants "Be merciful unto Zion, for it is the home of our life." And if there be any here who insist that Palestine is not one of the most important answers to our problem, then let him not read the Haggadah, and let him not recite when the Shofar is sounded this evening, "*L'shanah ha'ba-ah b'Yerushalaim!* Next year in Jerusalem" for he would be committing the grave sin of expressing a prayer he did not honestly mean.

No, the religious Jew, who understands what he is praying, who understands the one hope, the one goal that sustained the Jewish people through all manner of persecution and despair, that Jew is a Zionist in his heart. But unfortunately, as we wage a war for our survival, it is not enough for us to have in our ranks people who are Zionists at heart but not at hand. The hour calls for personal participation in the Palestinian renaissance, for feeling what Palestine means. Many of our American soldiers who have visited the Holy Land write that they intend to return there some day. More of us must think in terms of visiting and sending some of our youth to study there. The times demand that we be organized, articulate, active Zionists.

The picture of European life today is far worse than the most pessimistic among us have guessed or realized. One-half of Europe's Jews have been physically wiped out. Those who are left are economically ruined, a Jewry destitute, with no political identity and no cultural expression, with all its great centers such as Warsaw and Vilno completely destroyed.

In France, German propaganda has wrought its influence in a country which was comparatively free from anti-Jewish feeling. President Benes of Czechoslovakia says the return of Jews to his country will create a problem of anti-Semitism. Where are these people to go? Do you see any indication that America is going to welcome them with open arms?

Palestine today holds the key to the solution, if not of the entire problem, at least of much of it. But Palestine is being denied us and its doors are temporarily closed in our faces. Our behavior has given the British and the Americans the right to say, "Why should we give Palestine to the Jews? Some Jews want Palestine and some refuse to have any part of Zionism."

It is time that we all identify ourselves as Zionists through the Zionist Organization of America and present a united front so that those who hold the fate of Palestine in their hands can see where we stand. It is the duty of every Jew who prays in the words of his *Machzor* for the restoration of Zion, of every Jew who thrills to the heroic struggle of our ancestors throughout the centuries of their exile sustained only by the belief that God would one day restore to us our ancient homeland, of every Jew who feels the slenderest thread of kinship binding him to the homeless Jews of the world to become a Zionist in action, a Jew not only ready to fight the unequal struggle against our enemies, but willing to don the uniform of Zionism to do so.

We mentioned earlier that *Yom Kippur* concludes with the exclamation, "Next year in Jerusalem." There is a beautiful parable which attempts to explain the inclusion of this phrase and which sums up all we have said today.

It concerns a certain king whose daughter reached the age of marriage. Many noblemen asked for her hand in marriage, but she spurned them all until her father vowed to give her to the first man he would meet on the road. The first man was a villager to whom the princess was soon married.

The groom took his royal bride to his village, where she worked hard as an ordinary villager's wife. The villagers made sport of her.

She wrote the king daily, complaining of her lot until he came to visit her. The village was decorated for the visit. The princess was garbed once again in her royal clothes.

When the king arrived, the princess said, "Father, do not believe what you see. This is only a show."

The king turned to the husband and said, "Is my daughter being mistreated? Don't you realize she is a princess?"

The poor villager said with tears in his eyes, "But what can I do? I cannot give her the comforts of life. But you are a king, take me yonder to your palace and let me live in comfort, and I will treat your daughter as befits a princess."

The King in our story is meant to be God, and his daughter, the Torah and the Jewish way of life. In the hands of the tormented Jew in exile, the Torah is neglected, and we do not understand the Jewish way of life. And when the month of Elul comes, announcing the approaching visit of the Lord on the High Holidays, we begin to repent until the shofar on *Rosh Hashanah* announces the arrival of the court of the Lord. On *Yom Kippur*, the Holy presence comes in our midst and sees us all humble and fasting and clothed in white, crowding the synagogues to honor the Torah and live intensively our Jewish life for one day. But then *Neilah* comes and it is time for the Lord to depart. The Torah cries out to him and says, "This is all a temporary thing, as soon as you leave, they all neglect me."

And when the Lord faces Israel with this accusation, Israel pleads, "But Lord, I am a poor people, with no land of my own, who dwells among people who revere not thy Torah and is thus not able to render it due honor. But you Who art the king, bring me up to thy holy land and establish me there with the social, economic and spiritual opportunity to lead a Jewish life." And so at the conclusion of *Neilah* we all say, "Next year in Jerusalem."

This is only an ancient parable, but our devotion on these solemn days need not be our only visit to the house of worship, our special efforts on these days need not be sham and pretense. We can strive to give all peoples everywhere the social and economic and spiritual opportunity to lead a better life, and we can make of our Jewish life a year round effort to preserve and enrich our great heritage. We can labor openly and bravely to bring to fulfillment the oft-repeated prophecy of the restoration of Zion. Armed with such positive weapons of the spirit, we can never be defeated as a people no matter how great the odds. With the Psalmist we say:

"Though a host should encamp against me my heart shall not fear. Though war should rise up against me even then will I be confident." (Psalm 27:3)

When the shofar sounds this evening, let it fill us with new hope to shout defiance to the enemies of God who carry on this unholy war against us, as we say:

"I shall not die, but live! And declare the works of the Lord!"

THE WHITE PAPER SPELLS DEATH FOR JEWS

Fast forward from my warning of 1938. My worst fears were realized over the next six years of unbridled Nazi terror against Jews. Already 4,000,000 Jews at least were slaughtered and millions more were in jeopardy.

The very first time I rose to preach as rabbi of a congregation was March 31, 1944 at the Forest Hills (N.Y.) Jewish Center. I had labored over a report on a symposium in the February 1944 issue of The Contemporary Jewish Record *in which 11 of the outstanding young Jewish writers and critics of the day were asked if there was any relationship between their Jewishness and their work.*

The answers of people like critic Louis Kronenberger, novelist Howard Fast, poet Muriel Rukeyser and the others were discouraging. They questioned the value of their Jewish heritage and claimed it had no relationship to their work and little to themselves. All this, bear in mind, while their Jewish brethren were being slaughtered in Europe.

At the last moment, suddenly realizing that the British White Paper of 1939 had trapped all but a few Jews who wished to settle in Palestine and had consigned the rest to Hitler's death camps, I hastily prepared and preached the following sermon.

It was the first of what were to be a great number of sermons relating to the yearning for, the establishment and survival of the Third Jewish Commonwealth. Sadly, it documents the duplicity of leaders we believed to be our friends: Franklin Delano Roosevelt and Winston Churchill.

It was heart breaking for me to preach. In today's violence and jeopardy for the State of Israel, it is even more heartbreaking for me to reread. But it must be told.

MARCH 31, 1944

Dear Friends:

For tonight I had planned to discuss a symposium recently published in *The Contemporary Jewish Record*, but in the light of the history making significance of this day I am compelled to talk of another, more pressing matter. This is March 31, 1944, the day of the crushing of a 2,000-year-old aspiration, the day of awakening from a dream of 27 years. That dream and that hope were for the rebirth of Zion, for the establishment of a Jewish national homeland in Palestine.

This is March 31, 1944. One week from tonight we shall be seated at the Seder table and conclude the Haggadah with the age-old note of optimism: "Next year in Jerusalem." Perhaps we had best not express that wish next week. Perhaps we should strike it from the pages of the Haggadah, for this is March 31, 1944, the last day upon which Israelites may enter the land of Israel. **According to the terms of the British White Paper of 1939, after today no more Jewish immigrants may enter Palestine except with the consent of the Palestine majority, which means the Arab population there, who outnumber the Jews two to one.**

It is already April 1 in Palestine, the first day Jewish immigration is barred by the British White Paper. Palestine is armed and seething. An era has passed, and a new one begun for the Jewish people. On such a day, have we the right not to talk of Zion, or, indeed, to talk of anything else?

If there are any among us who are not lovers of Zion, let them ponder tonight what is to become of our beleaguered brethren who have looked to Palestine as their sole refuge, the only possible avenue of escape for them. They tonight, this minute, are watching the dawn of April 1 in Europe, a dawn which brings no promise, no hope!

As for the many among us who have labored zealously for the fulfillment of God's promise to let us rebuild our homeland, let us take stock of the situation on this day and seek renewed strength to continue our efforts in the face of mighty opposition. Let us bear in mind the words of the man who created modern Zionism, Theodore Herzl, who said, "If you will it, it is not a dream."

Last Sunday, we heard President Roosevelt's statement to the Zionist leaders who visited him, "I have never approved of the Paper of 1939 to stop Jewish immigration to Palestine. When future decisions are reached, justice will be done to those who seek a Jewish national home." But tonight the picture is very different. This country, upon whose influence we had depended to strengthen our cause, has reversed its stand. This Tuesday our president told the Press, he could find no fault with the opposition of the United States Army "to continuation of Jewish immigration into Palestine."

Herzl said, "If you will it, it is no dream." Yet the events of the past 27 years appear tonight to have been merely that, a dream.

Twenty-seven years ago, on November 2, 1917, it seemed that Herzl's words had indeed come true. The Balfour Declaration was made by the

British Government. The words of the declaration are familiar to all of us, "His Majesty's government view with favor the establishment in Palestine of a national home for the Jewish people, and will use their best endeavors to facilitate the achievement of this object..."

The Balfour Declaration was not a purely British formulation of policy. It was for many months the subject of long and earnest negotiations between the principal Allied powers. In 1918, the French and Italian governments issued parallel statements in support of the declaration.

President Wilson said, "I am persuaded that the Allied nations, with the fullest concurrence of our government and our people, are agreed that in Palestine shall be laid the foundations of a Jewish commonwealth."

The Prime Minister of England said, "The notion that Jewish immigration would have to be artificially restricted in order to ensure that the Jews should be a permanent minority never entered into the head of anyone engaged in framing the policy."

On July 24, 1922, the Council of the League of Nations unanimously ratified the mandate for Palestine, which was then offered to Great Britain. At the same time the United States Senate and House of Representatives passed a joint resolution stating that this country favored the establishment in Palestine of a national home for the Jewish people.

What grand assurances, what a sparkling future for Zionism! The Palestine contemplated in the mandate included the land on both sides of the Jordan. Jewish energy began to pour into the effort. Funds, pioneers, enthusiasm were abundant. But through all these bright days, no one chose to bring home to the Arab population of Palestine the fact that the Balfour Declaration was an inter-Allied policy and a part of international law. The Mufti of Jerusalem, Haj Amin al-Husseini, was very bitter against both British and Jews. It was he, by the way, who joined Hitler in Berlin when this war broke out. In May, 1921, there were riots by the Arabs, and the result was the temporary suspension of Jewish immigration.

The appeasement policy went into action. In 1922 a White Paper, sponsored by Winston Churchill, declared that "the terms of the Balfour Declaration do **not** contemplate that Palestine as a **whole** should be converted into a Jewish National Home," but that such a home should be established **in** Palestine. Thereupon all of Palestine east of the Jordan, that is, all of Transjordan, was closed by administrative decree to Jewish immigration, virtually half the territory.

Between the years 1922 and 1929 the building up of Palestine grew. Then in 1929 the Grand Mufti spread rumors that the Jews were preparing to attack the Moslem holy places and proceeded to incite riots against the Jews. A British commission was sent to investigate and laid blame for the riots on Jewish immigration and Jewish land purchases. A second commission was dispatched, and it reported that Palestine could absorb only 200,000 additional settlers. (It has since received more than 300,000.) As a result of all this, the Passfield White Paper was issued in 1930, cutting down Jewish immigration, forbidding Jews to settle any land other than vacant land they already possessed, and declaring, rather irrelevantly and without justification, that "the creation of a Jewish national home is not meant to be the principal feature of the Mandate!"

In 1936 the Arabs precipitated new riots. The Peel commission, which England sent to investigate, suggested dividing what was left of Palestine into two parts, giving the Jews a state in the northwest section and the Arabs a larger state in the south and east. Although dissatisfied with the small area given them, the Jews voted to accept the plan, but the Arabs refused.

Matters continued in this vague state until 1939. Early in that year the British government declared it is not part of their policy that "Palestine shall become a Jewish state," and finally issued the MacDonald White Paper. (This document was condemned by the Mandates Commission of the League of Nations which declared in June, 1939, in its last session, that the policy of the White Paper is entirely the reverse of that which the commission had intended for the Palestine Mandate.)

The terms of the White Paper were as follows: first, a Palestinian state would be set up in which the Jews would remain a permanent minority of one-third of the population (not quite what Lloyd George had said in 1918). Second, Jews could purchase land only in a very tiny area. Third, immigration would be completely stopped after March 31, 1944.

Since this last white paper was issued, we have waged a tireless fight to have it abrogated. During this trying period we have seen a vociferous, if tiny, Jewish anti-Zionist group arise who have injured the cause of Zionism to a considerable extent. They maintain that all Jews do not hope for the establishment of a Jewish national homeland in Palestine. Not content to remain merely uncooperative, they have advertised their views to such an extent as to confuse the rest of the world. Gentiles who might help us are forced to ask, "Do you people or don't you people want Palestine?"

The anti-Zionists maintain that the Jewish people is a religious group only, and on those grounds they combat all efforts to secure a homeland.

Have they then forgotten what we recite during the religious service at the Passover table, "Next year in Jerusalem?" Have they forgotten that we recite the same fervent wish at the conclusion of the services on the most sacred day of the year, on *Yom Kippur*? Do these self-styled religious Jews never say grace that they do not know we read: "And rebuild Jerusalem the Holy city speedily in our day?" Can they fail so utterly to realize the significance of the prayer we recite in the *Amidah*, "O, may our eyes witness Thy return to Zion, Blessed art Thou, O Lord who restorest Thy divine presence to Zion."

The love of Zion and the hopes of rebuilding it weave a steady pattern through all of Jewish history and through all the practices and prayers of our faith. Tonight, once again we recited *V'techezenah,* "O, may our eyes witness Thy return to Zion." Tonight, on the eve of a new period in our history, we reaffirmed our faith in the restoration of Zion, some of us, I imagine, without thinking very much about it.

What is the future of Zionism from the vantage point of this evening? Our primary task from now on is to redouble our efforts. Like Commodore Perry, at this blackest of all hours, we declare, "We have not yet begun to fight!"

We have been told that though Britain may not abrogate the White paper, perhaps it will let us get around it. I believe it is not fitting and proper that we should have to steal into the Promised Land through loopholes like so many thieves in the night, not when so many great statesmen gave us their sacred assurance of our God-given right to be there, not when the Mandate, ratified by almost every nation in the world, begins with the words, "Whereas recognition has hereby been given to the historical connection of the Jewish people with Palestine and the grounds for reconstituting their national home in that country." How dare great nations treat serious promises so lightly! How dare they make such a mockery of the written pact in the name of appeasement or expediency!

When our president made his statement on Tuesday that he found no fault with the army's opposition to further Jewish immigration into Palestine, he also said that the White Paper was a civilian matter, to be worked out in the future when there is a more permanent peace. "When future decisions are reached," he said, "justice will be done to those who seek a Jewish national home."

I fear that by the time future decisions are reached, the only justice we shall be able to accord those who are now seeking refuge in Palestine, will be a decent burial. If we stand pat and wait for a more permanent peace, the problem of those Jews seeking a national home will have already been decided by the Nazis!

The White Paper, issued on the eve of this war, is not a civilian matter. War has been waged against the Jews of Europe, brutally one-sided war against frightened unarmed people, a war that has taken a toll of millions. That casualty list is no civilian matter, and yet that casualty list is so huge because no concerted effort was made by neutral or powerful nations to get the victims out of Europe and into Palestine. The shattering of the program of Zionism is no more a civilian matter than the possible bombings of Rome, of which we have read a great deal lately. It appears that the prayers of the Catholics and the pressure of their leaders may be sufficient to change the course of the war so that Rome may be saved for humanity. It will be most interesting to observe whether the military expediency which necessitates the sustaining of the White Paper and the condemning of four million innocent souls to annihilation will also necessitate the bombing of Rome.

Now it becomes very clear what our course must be. It does not lie in giving up the fight or in postponing it for the duration, nor does it lie in rioting in Palestine. We must hammer at the governments of England and our own country to execute justice now, not eulogies later. We must confront them with their own promises to us. We must challenge them with the tremendous services Jews everywhere, and particularly in Palestine itself, are rendering the cause of the United Nations in this war. We must insistently remind them of the folly of appeasement! Yes, and we would do well to recall the promises of God to Israel that we would one day be restored to our homeland.

Tonight, we wonder: is this the fruit of years of labor on behalf of Zionism? Was it for this we gave of our money and our time and our devotion to be thus disappointed? Is this the end? No. This is **not** the end! Our work must continue, our faith in the fulfillment of God's promise never fail! This is only a hurdle blocking our way to the goal. We may have to go under it or over it or around it or we may have to tear it down with whatever weapons are available, with our bare hands, if necessary, but pass it we shall! We have not poured our love into Zion only to give up the results. We have not wrested a garden out of the desert sands only to be told now it is not for us.

This obstacle in our path is only temporary. In the words of Herzl, if we will it, and work for it, with hope and not defeat in our hearts, it will prove to be no dream, but a reality.

Let us recall to ourselves and to the nations of the world, the noble prophecy God put in the mouth of Isaiah, that we shall not only build a Jewish homeland in Palestine, but that we shall also dwell therein:

> *"And they shall build houses and inhabit them. And they shall plant vineyards and eat the fruit of them. They shall not build and another inhabit; They shall not plant and another eat. They shall not labor in vain, nor bring forth for calamity. And all this shall transpire in Zion."* (Isaiah 65: 21-23)

Amen.

TO THE BIG THREE, OPEN THE GATES OF PALESTINE

At this moment in time, with hopes of winning the war rising, the American Jewish community was in confusion as to what to ask of Roosevelt, Stalin and Churchill who were soon to meet. Should the Jewish survivors, if any, be returned to their original homes? Should we wait for divine intervention in the form of some miracle? Should we stridently demand the tearing up of the infamous White Paper barring Jews from Palestine? The Jewish community in the United States was divided as to the path to take.

In this sermon I vigorously called for the opening of Palestine as the only viable answer.

JANUARY 26, 1945

Dear Friends:

It is the beginning of Spring, and the warm sun promises the coming summer to the green valleys and sunny beaches of Palestine. While we shiver and complain and scarcely dare to stir outside our homes even to attend religious services, in just a few days, on next Monday, it will be *Chamishah Asar B'shvat*, the fifteenth day of the Hebrew month of *Shevat*, the new year of the trees, the day for the planting of young trees by young people in *Eretz Yisrael*. On such an occasion, can we fail to think about a Jewish national homeland?

An American Jewish Conference was held recently. There has been strife and controversy within the ranks of the leadership of American Zionism. Two overzealous youths assassinated a British Colonial Office official, were brought to trial before an Egyptian court and condemned to death. By their act, they have evoked miles of words from statesmen, writers, and puzzled people everywhere. At such a turbulent time as this, can we fail to talk about a Jewish national homeland?

The President of the United States goes soon to meet with the leaders of Britain and Russia to discuss these weighty matters. Can we desist from praying for his personal safety and the success of his mission? We have cause to believe that the knotty questions of saving Jews in Europe and the future of Palestine will form part of the agenda to be discussed. That being the case, can we fail to petition for a Jewish national homeland?

The situation of the majority of our Jewish brethren today is strikingly similar to what it was 3,500 years ago as described in the portion of the Bible we read tomorrow morning. The Israelites had marched out of Egypt and were encamped at the shores of the Red Sea when suddenly they lifted up their eyes and beheld the Egyptians coming toward them with horses and chariots, to slaughter them or to take them back into captivity. There our ancestors stood, confused; before them the sea, behind them the pursuing Egyptians. They were distracted by fear and further demoralized by divided counsels. In that time of emergency, what cries must have filled the air, what shouted suggestions as to how to proceed.

Our Rabbis paint the picture for us in a few words. They say,Israel on the shores of the sea was divided into four factions: One faction said, "Let us drown ourselves in the sea." One said, "Let us go back to slavery." One said, "Let us fight the Egyptians, though we shall surely lose." And the fourth said, "Let us cry out against them to the Lord," to which the Lord answered, "Wherefore criest thou out unto me? Speak unto the Children of Israel, and let them go forward! Forward, to the promised land, to *Eretz Yisrael.*"

Do we not stand once again today in the same bitter situation? Breathing hot on the necks of most of our Jewish brethren is the 20th century Pharoah and the hordes of our enemies, and before them, a vast sea of seemingly impassable proportions stretches between them and the road to the same promised land, to the same *Eretz Yisrael.*

The hordes of our enemies are at our backs despite the ever mounting victories of the armies of liberation. We are beginning to realize all too slowly that for the majority of European Jewry there is no liberation from the bitter feelings surrounding them. James G. McDonald, prominent administrator of refugee rehabilitation for many years, surveyed the European scene with a pessimism born of a realistic attitude. He foresees that of 30,000,000 people displaced by the war in Europe, probably 95 percent will be able to return to their own homes and resume their interrupted lives.

But for the million or more homeless Jews, there will be few welcome mats spread. Possibly France, Holland, Belgium, Norway, Denmark and Luxembourg will be ready to receive the Jewish people exiled from these countries yet even in these lands we can expect a repetition of the tangled problems arising from the requests of Jews for the return of their businesses and homes confiscated by the Nazis and sold to their non-Jewish neighbors.

How welcome would you feel and how long would you want to live in a country where you could pass your home or your shop, the product of a life's labors and know that the present owner looks upon you with suspicion and your government is reluctant to do anything about it?

Even under such adverse conditions, only a small number of Europe's Jews would be welcomed back, for in Germany, Poland, Hungary, Rumania, Bulgaria and Czechoslovakia the life of returning Jews would be just as difficult in peacetime as it had been during the war. Surveying these difficulties, Mr. McDonald comes to the inevitable conclusion, "Palestine offers incontestably the primary hope for the solution of the problem of Jewish refugees."

The conclusion which emerges inescapably from a realistic resume of 25 years of intergovernmental dealings with refugees and from a realistic appraisal of the world situation is that in Palestine, and only there, can the mass of Jewish refugees hope to be welcome and to be assisted to integrate themselves in the life of the community. Only in Palestine will most of them feel they have returned home."

Among our own leaders there is shaping up a unanimity of opinion on the Palestine question. At the recent American Jewish Conference, the majority voice clearly spoke out for American Jewry's support of all efforts to reopen the doors of Palestine as a national homeland. Even the organizations not committed by their purposes to a Zionist philosophy showed themselves completely sympathetic to the movement.

Mr. Henry Monsky, president of B'nai Brith, echoed the opinions of all when he said, "Where in the whole of the universe, other than Palestine, do we find a community with its arms outstretched to receive their brothers in ever-increasing numbers?" Yes, to receive them in a community psychologically conditioned to absorb them with enthusiasm and with a deep interest in their welfare!

Apparently, we are ready to see eye to eye on this truth: that the majority of our European brethren cannot go back whence they came, that behind them forever lie their homes in the midst of the Egyptians of today, and there is no turning back.

But if Egypt lies behind our brethren, what lies before them? Once again it is the sea, and not only a figurative sea, but the sea itself as well.

The first and mightiest difficulty of all those that lie in our path as did the Red Sea of old, is one we seem prone to forget: the White Paper of 1939, which limits Jewish immigration into Palestine, is still in force. And while it is still in force many who might be able to arrive at the shores of

Palestine in crowded, rotting hulks of ships will be turned back, Turkey will feel justified in refusing passage through its territory of Jews seeking haven in Palestine, and terrorism may well inflame minds tormented by the knowledge that not even in the land of Israel can Israel find sanctuary. While the White Paper is in force there is no passing through the sea to the promised land.

Moreover, even the slim encouragement of passage of a Congressional resolution favoring Jewish hopes in Palestine is denied us. Not only is this small source of comfort denied us, but unfortunately it has become a bone of contention over which important Zionist leaders have engaged in public argument. See how great is our anxiety and the desperation, that our leaders must be divided over mere shreds of encouragement, over a paper reaffirming what both our houses of Congress declared more than 20 years ago, that this country favors the establishment of a Jewish national homeland in Palestine.

Finally, as the mighty developments in international politics and military campaigns occupy the minds of the public and leaders as well, when the fate of nations and governments and millions of people is being shaped, we see a tendency to minimize the importance of what happens to a few million Jews and their tiny speck of a homeland. Indifference to our problem, even more than active opposition to us, is perhaps the greatest obstacle lying in our path.

And so, standing as we do betwixt and between, we have fallen into the same confusion as did our forefathers at the shores of the Red Sea. We have some who are very generous with the lives and futures of others and say, **נפול בים**, "Let them drown in the sea. We can do nothing for them. Let them cease to be a source of embarrassment and reproach to us."

We have some who suggest, **נחזור למצרים**, "Let them return back to Egypt." Let them try to live in hostile Europe blinding themselves to the impossibility of such a course.

One faction which suggests, **נעשה מלחמה כנגדן**, "Let us wage war for our demands." Let us fight terror with terror and frighten the world into giving us a land. I fear, the world is not frightened easily by us, only aroused to anger against all of us for acts of terror by a few of us.

There is a faction which urges, **נצווח כנגדן**, "Let us cry out to the Lord against them." Let us hope for a miracle, and meanwhile let us sit by the sea and wait for divine intervention.

This last reaction the Lord has already rejected as long ago as the Exodus, saying, **מה תצעק אלי** "Wherefore does thou cry out to me?"

דבר אל בני ישראל ויסעו "Speak to the children of Israel and let them go forward."

The one faction proposing a plan for action today, the majority faction in modern Israel, is the Zionist movement which says, "Let nothing stop us, let us go forward!" How are we to go forward? Not by despairing, or turning back, or throwing bombs or wringing our hands, but by systematically, persistently pressing our cause, declaring our Zionist aims, buying land in Palestine, and building, eternally building, the ranks of organized Zionism in this country until they represent all of American Jewry.

In more specific terms, we must do the following: we must before next week, begin to pour letters and telegrams into Washington, to the President himself, urging the necessity for considering the situation of the Jews at the forthcoming Big Three conference. We must say to them, in effect: "Remember us! We have been patient, but the time has come to do something about us, to open the barriers before us that we may walk on secure ground to our promised land, promised by God, and promised, gentlemen, by you yourselves."

Every family which can be stirred by any methods of appeal, should write or telegraph the White House within the next few days, expressing congratulations to the President upon the undertaking of a fourth term, hope for his safety and insistence upon a consideration of the fate of the Jewish people when he meets with Britain and Russia.

Moreover, we must make *Chamishah Asar B'Shevat* an occasion for determined optimism, by planting trees in Palestine, by renewing membership in the Zionist organizations and by making those memberships count. It is imperative that we all become Zionists, but affiliation alone is not enough.

Knowledge, study of what Zionism always has been and is today–these will give meaning and value to that affiliation. Making our demands vocal and to the point, acting with optimism and assurance that our requests are just and possible of fulfillment, strengthening the ranks of the Zionist movement and learning through study what the movement means. These things will help Israel to overcome the obstacles lying before her and escape the dangers from behind.

Yes, the Israelites saw their prayers answered at the shores of the Red Sea, for the Bible tells us, "And the Children of Israel went into the midst of the Sea upon the dry ground."

The rabbis were puzzled by this statement and asked, "If they went into the sea, then why does it say upon dry ground? And if they went on dry ground, then why does it say into the midst of the sea?"

This teaches that Israel plunged into the sea until the water reached to their very noses and they were about to drown. Even then they took another step forward, and at that moment the waters parted and they continued across the Red Sea on dry land.

Today, for us, the situation looks very dark, and yet the only direction for us is forward, the only direction Jewish life can take with hope of overcoming its difficulties is the direction of Palestine. The situation opens its barriers only if we take an attitude of hope and continue to march forward even when the water seems to have mounted to our very lips. This *Chamishah Asar* buy trees in *Eretz Yisrael*, write to your President and ask him to remember us. Unite with your fellow Jews in the Zionist movement and do all these things with the knowledge confirmed by our history, that when you move in the direction of the promised land, even the seas must eventually open up.

מה תצעק אלי דבר אל בני ישראל ויסעו

"Wherefore criest thou out unto me," saith the Lord, "Speak to the Children of Israel, and let them go forward!"

HITLER IS DEAD ...MAY HIS NAME BE BLOTTED OUT!

The reported suicide of Hitler did not generate an enormous amount of emotion in an emotionally drained community. The armies of Russia, England, France and the United States were converging on Berlin, and the war was virtually all over in Europe, although continuing against Japan.

When we received the news about Hitler, I used the sermon as a springboard to discuss the Jewish illiteracy of the American Jew, saying, "Now that Hitler is dead our greatest remaining enemy is our own ignorance of what we are and what we can be." In view of the ongoing menace of anti-Semitism in the United States, in Europe with a special problem in Russia, and the ultimate Arab terrorism against Israel and Jews anywhere, I was undoubtedly exaggerating when calling our own ignorance our greatest remaining enemy. The fact remains that this ignorance has within it the seeds of our own self-destruction, and in the past fifty years we have addressed it with a considerable degree of success.

MAY 4, 1945

Dear Friends:

We have just lived through another exciting, incredibly eventful week. Peace rumors fill the air. Mussolini is dead. The San Francisco Conference shows encouraging as well as disappointing signs. Hitler is dead politically and may be dead in fact. Coincident with the death of Hitler, the man whose success has caused so much ruin and devastation in our Jewish ranks, I gained still more respect for the Jewish facility of self-expression.

You see, I had read the *New York Times*, which had charming family portraits of Hitler and lengthy articles on him much in the same way it had on the late Roosevelt; I had read other news items elaborating on the event, now so unimportant; I had even chuckled over the Illinois Legislature which had passed a resolution commending Hitler's suicide as the one decent thing he had ever done and rebuking him for doing it ten years too late. But the most fitting remark made anywhere was made in a Jewish newspaper, the *Morning Journal,* on the front page a streamer headline,

הטלער איז טויט ימח שמו וזכרו

"Hitler is Dead May His Name and His Memory be Blotted Out." There was a picture of him and above the picture the withering observation, "*A Schene, Rene Kapara.*" There is no English equivalent. If you don't know, ask your neighbor.

The only trouble with asking your neighbor may be that your neighbor might not know either, for it is an undeniable truth today that, Jewishly, the Jewish adult in America is uneducated. He may be, and usually is, a skilled laborer, a good businessman, a brilliant lawyer, a celebrated physician, a benign philanthropist, a gifted artist, and in every way a gentleman; but he is unfamiliar with his people's past, its current history, its literature, its religion or its philosophy. He belongs to many a Jewish organization and supports sundry Jewish causes, but that hardly helps dispel his ignorance. He is swamped with letters, circulars and pamphlets which in no way contribute to his enlightenment for all this literature tells a weary tale of budgets, deficits, misery, persecution, hatred, intolerance, and defense, all calculated to appeal to his heart, but rarely to cultivate his mind. At best he is willing to take a certain pride in the fact that his ancestors were great scholars and his people were in the past pious and learned.

Many of us tend to believe that in the past all Jews received a thorough Jewish education. That is not quite true. In all generations, there were Jews who were ignorant of their literature and their lore, and there were always all the gradations from ignoramus to extraordinary scholar. The battle against ignorance is as old as Judaism itself.

In the past, however, even the most untutored Jew had a detailed, practical knowledge of Jewish law because in it he lived and moved and had his being. The Sabbath and the Festivals, the prayer book and the Torah, the customs at birth, marriage and death, these and a thousand other aspects of Jewish life were absorbed from living. Yiddish and the other vernaculars spoken by Jews were enriched by hundreds of Hebrew words and idioms so that even the most uneducated Jew unconsciously used quotations from the Bible and the Talmud, the prayer book and Rashi, and so enriched his life with the ethical and religious insights of Judaism.

Moreover, Jewish life in the past was marked by a deep respect for Jewish learning. Each man in the community took his position in the group according to the level of his knowledge of the Torah, not according to his trade or his means. Therefore scholarship among Jews became not the specialty of the few but the avocation of the many. Long before the creation of modern educational science Jews discovered the basic truths that adults are teachable, that study is enjoyable and that learning is a life-long process.

Today we no longer live in an all-Jewish atmosphere, and Jewish law is more honored in the breach than in the observance. Jews still love learning and pursue it at all the schools and universities so that we have untold numbers of Jews who possess a high level of general culture, but unfortunately, most of them are Jewishly uninformed. Jewish ignorance is not new, as we have seen, but in the past at least it was accompanied by a sense of humility, a recognition of one's limitations. Today, however, Jewish ignorance is all too often accompanied by a sense of pride or, at best, of complacency. It is by no means rare to meet Jews who regard their total lack of Jewish knowledge as a sign of modernity. They actually think they are very modern if they know nothing of the great Jewish culture which countless generations have preserved for them, often at tremendous personal sacrifice.

Out of this lack of knowledge, so often accompanied by a lack of respect for Jewish values, have come the psychic disorders of so many modern Jews: their lack of spiritual roots, their sense of homelessness, their failure to achieve dignity and poise, their defenselessness and bewilderment whenever they are attacked.

What can remedy the situation? What might help the Jewish adult? The simple and trite, but none the less basic and inevitable answer, is education. If a Jew is to find something to compensate him for ceaseless martyrdom, if he is to sense the grandeur as much as the pain of his destiny, he must know Judaism. Memberships and contributions will avail him little if he is devoid of Jewish content. Today the wheels of Jewish continuity are impelled by the momentum of yesterday. How about tomorrow? Tomorrow what will provide the motive power? What outside their heritage can urge Jews on, can comfort them in their misery and steel them to survive?

Too many Jews are ready to unload their burdens upon their children, believing that it is enough if their children know something about Judaism. A whole generation of Jews delights to justify its own ignorance by exclaiming, "We do not need the synagogue and the Hebrew school for ourselves, but our children need them." We are gradually beginning to realize that what we do not need for ourselves, our children do not want either. It is pure folly to send a child to Hebrew school to learn a language nobody can help him with at home, to learn customs he never sees practiced at home, to be taught to be more observant than his parents. The spiritual and cultural needs of the adult do not differ in essence from the spiritual and cultural needs of the child, anymore than physical needs do. Education and Jewish life for children is splendid, but it is painfully limited if not paralleled by education and Jewish life for adults.

Unfortunately, however, adult education has not yet been fully integrated with the synagogue program as a whole.

If American Jewry is to be worthy of the tasks entrusted to it by destiny, it will require a rebirth of the spirit, an enrichment of the mind. In that process of revitalization, no American Jew has the right to call himself cultured unless he possesses at least ten elements of Jewish knowledge: a knowledge of the basic fundamentals of Hebrew reading; a knowledge of functional Hebrew; those Hebrew words which can never be adequately translated, words like *Shabbat, Mazal Tov, Kosher, Kapara*, and hundreds of others; a familiarity with Jewish customs and ceremonies, their meaning and history; an interpretation of the basic Jewish religious ideas; a survey of Jewish history; a knowledge of the Bible; a conception of the Talmud and its literature; an appreciation of modern Hebrew and Yiddish literature; an understanding of Zionism; and finally, an understanding of the contemporary Jewish scene.

Here at our center this year, we have continued to broaden the basis of adult education initiated so early by Rabbi Bokser, long one of the leaders in this work in America, and who recently presented the idea at a Boston education conference. Out of the initial 65 persons who registered for courses this year we are able to award 54 certificates, representing for some as many as four courses taken this year. Two classes began the study of Hebrew starting with the alphabet, and one of those classes, after only 14 hours of actual class work, can read from the prayer book, sing some of the songs, and find the place in the Haggadah. Another albeit tiny group undertook advanced Hebrew grammar and read in Hebrew stories by David Frischman and Yehudah Leb Peretz. The course in Bible was a source of fruitful study for a large group of students. Surely in a congregation whose membership alone represents 1,200 adults it is not too much to expect that 100 will rise to accept adult education as a religious duty superseding all other, for have not the rabbis taught us that all the religious commandments are important: ותלמוד תורה כנגד כלם "The study of the Torah is equal to all the other commandments put together."

We must make it clear once again that for an adult Jew to continue to study is not merely a matter of personal pleasure and self-development, it is rather a primary duty placed upon him as a follower of the Jewish religion. His failure to study is not only a grievous personal sin of omission, but a menace to the entire Jewish community.

From whom can the world at large acquire knowledge of and respect for Judaism? Shall it be from the thousands of Jews in New York who shout themselves hoarse at the World Series games when they coincide with our holiest days? Shall it be from the Jewish students at universities or the soldiers who cannot tell an *aleph* from a corkscrew, and often prefer the corkscrew? What can we have of Jewish life if our leaders of national organizations know nothing of Jewish history or of the roots of the anti-Semitism they fear so much? What can the level or complexion of synagogue, lodge or Zionist district be if they are composed of Jews who are strangers to Judaism?

Now that Hitler is dead, our greatest remaining enemy is our own ignorance of what we are and what we can be. Therefore, let us labor together steadily to build here and everywhere academies of learning so that the cultured American can also be a cultured Jew. And let us do so with a sense of consecration, of religious obedience to the ageless advice given us in the book of Proverbs: ראשית חכמה, קנה חכמה ובכל קנינך קנה בינה "Wisdom is the principal thing, therefore, get wisdom; and with all thy getting, get understanding."

V-J DAY: JAPAN SURRENDERS

On Wednesday, August 15, 1945 we gathered in the synagogue to add some quiet moments of prayer to the revelry in the streets. We came to give thanks that the carnage was over and our boys were coming home. I note that I did not refer to "our girls," although we had many women in service, such as The WAVES, and the WACS and those who served with the Medical Corps. It was an inexcusable omission, which I would never commit today.

The congregation who came that day included some gold star parents, meaning those whose sons were never coming home. I raised the question of whether we were ready for peace, with all the emotional, economic and political unknowns it would bring.

I am astonished at myself that there was no mention of the dropping of atomic bombs upon Hiroshima and Nagasaki and the human cost of that expedient. My only tangential reference to the bombings was: "The terrible devilish new weapons we have devised are sheathed at the moment."

Clearly neither I nor those I was addressing had fully absorbed the enormity of the horrible genie we had unleashed. For me the horror was brought home years later when I stared into the crater, now a park, in Nagasaki and viewed the photographs in the museum, so reminiscent of photographs of the Holocaust and yet, in an indirect way, also the consequence of Hitler's madness.

AUGUST 15, 1945

Dear Friends:

For the past 24 hours we have attempted to react adequately to the enormous bounty of peace which has fallen to our lot. Emotions long pent up were unleashed with a fury of primitive raw noise. But noise does not measure up to the greatness of the hour. We found noise to be futile and so we reveled and danced in the streets, but even Bacchanalia was unavailing. For when the revelry and the noise stops, then we can hear what we could not hear over the laughter and the bells. We hear the throb in our hearts. We hear the soft weeping of those who have lost their dear ones so that the world might know peace again and the weeping does not stop, but mounts higher and higher until we seek a different mode for reacting to this hour. We turn to God and we pray.

During the past 24 hours, millions of words have spilled from thousands of lips, repeating a worn-out phrase about winning the peace and promising us a brave, new world. Well, my friends, the world is not so brave. It is tired and broken and old. Nor are its inhabitants suddenly metamorphosed by the coming of peace into something better than they were before the war ever began. The only thing that is different, the only thing that is new, is time. Every second is a precious new opportunity to do better, to purge our souls of greed and self-interest and to labor to bring about the ideals which spurred us on during the war. The triumph of destruction does not bring us peace. Nothing brings us peace, but the triumph of principles.

One might suppose from all the celebration, that everyone is eager for peace. But is that really so? Is the man who will have no job on Monday really eager for the peace? Is the man who this instant fears the collapse of his business enterprise really eager for the peace? When were there more lavish carousels, more riotous living, more loud laughter: during the ten years of depression from 1929 to 1939 or during the six war years from 1939 to 1945? Will each one of us now say in his innermost soul, "I prefer, I welcome peace, even if it brings poverty. I reject, I hate war, though it brings wealth!"

This is not a matter of economics. This is a matter of religion, of faith! We have a world to rebuild, a world, which save for these Western shores is shattered, starving, broken. Perhaps we can effect its restoration without lowering our own standard of living. I have great faith that we can, we will! But whether we can or cannot should not matter. If we are truly religious, if we are worthy to be true disciples of Moses and our God, all that must matter is that the world is now at peace! Men have ceased, officially, from killing one another. The terrible, devilish new weapons we have devised are sheathed for the moment.

Our boys are coming home and, save for the risks of daily living, we know that they will be alive! We no longer tremble when a familiar battleground or vessel or plane is mentioned in the news. Is there a greater blessing than life? Our religious faith teaches us that there is no greater blessing.

Our boys are coming home. Our sons whom we worried about trusting with the car have been piloting planes over thousands of miles of lonely ocean. Our boys about whom we worried if they sneezed, have spent days and slept nights in mud-filled holes. They have traveled the globe. They have killed, but not for pleasure. They have performed a thousand tedious, monotonous, menial jobs, and now they are coming home to the humdrum, petty, beautiful life of peace.

God grant us the plain, ordinary common sense to treat them properly, which means to treat them normally, neither to overwhelm them with irksome attentions nor to show ourselves ungrateful for all they have given up, for all they have suffered, for the chunk of their life war has bitten off and spat out into oblivion. God grant us the skill to provide them with schooling, with recreation, with work and with faith. This Jewish community is proceeding even now with its plans to provide them at home with the kind of recreational and religious life they learned on the field of war.

Our boys are coming home. Some will stride through the door, healthy, happy men. Some will walk more slowly, more haltingly, those whose sacrifice has been their limbs. Some will have to be led wherever they go, those whose offering has been their sight. And some, well, their bodies lie in poppy fields, in volcanic ash, on the floor of the sea. In their resting places, there is no discrimination. A wooden cross stands beside a star of David, a symbol of the world they died to create. Their bodies will not return, but already their sweet memory lies enshrined in the heart of mother and father, their souls rest with their creator.

And so we come to pray for peace, for peace that is enduring because it is endurable for all peoples, for peace which in its simplest terms will mean that never, never, again will we have to rise and turn toward God's Torah and chant אל מלא רחמים, *El Mole Rachamim,* Oh God, so full of mercy for boys who have died for peace.

ZIONISTS, GET ON YOUR FEET!

When the concentration camps were liberated by the Allied armies, the survivors, homeless and unwelcome everywhere, were herded into displaced persons camps. These were worse, if such a thing were possible, than their former prisons. This sermon describes their wretched situation and protests Great Britain's refusal to open the doors of Palestine to them.

We held a protest rally which featured Dorothy Thompson, an influential newspaper columnist, as guest speaker. It was attended by thousands of people in Queens, New York. I railed out against the American Council for Judaism which was publicly opposing a Jewish state and also the majority of Jews who were not making their voices heard. We had hoped and prayed there might be some Jewish survivors of Hitler's Final Solution who might go to our promised and re-promised land, but now everything was threatened.

At the end of this speech, a thousand people rose to their feet and waved cards of enrollment in the Zionist cause.

OCTOBER 7, 1945

Dear Friends,

I was prepared to say much of what Miss Thompson has already told you, but too often I have been victimized by repetitive and anti-climactic speeches, which have completely ruined the effect of the impact of the principal address. I shall not so victimize you tonight.

Nor will I repeat the customary stale jokes about the difficulty of following the eloquence of Miss Thompson. It is not difficult. On the contrary, I find my task infinitely easier because she not only excited the imagination of all present, but she inspired this speaker as well.

Miss Thompson has painted for you a three-dimensional picture of the land, once a desert, which has sprung alive under the loving attentions of an inspired pilgrim people. This Palestine, object of our prayers, goal of our dreams, target of our recent labors, this oasis of devotion and planning, how pleasant it would be to dwell at greater length on the positive side of the picture, to envision what could yet be built thereon. How tempting is the prospect of sketching in the mind's eye what this land could be, a land such as Dr. Walter Lowdermilk predicted only recently, "Once the great undeveloped resources are properly exploited, twenty to thirty million people may live decent and prosperous lives where a few now struggle for a mere existence."

Yes, it would be pleasant, but unfortunately, the vision has been darkened, the dreams have been shattered, and imagination has been frozen by the current betrayal of all our hopes. For a few short weeks ago, as expected by a few, but like a bolt from the blue for the majority of us, the following statement was issued by the leaders of American Zionism:

"News of the utmost gravity has reached us concerning the policies to be pursued by the British government in regard to Palestine. Despite the unequivocal resolution adopted by the Labor Party Conference last May, in favor of the opening of Palestine to unrestricted Jewish immigration and the establishment there of a Jewish majority; despite further the appalling conditions of those Jews in Europe who survived the Nazi massacres and for whom there is no hope except among their own people in Palestine, the new Labor government from which so much has been expected, apparently intends to continue, with slight modifications, the infamous policy of the Palestine White Paper and to restrict Jewish immigration there to a trickle."

The knife, so skilled already at stabbing us in the back, so recently withdrawn to raise our hopes and tantalize us with rumors of success, the knife has plunged back into the old wound, still gaping, still bloody. So much had been expected from Britain, too much, perhaps, and so little had been forthcoming.

No, I cannot dwell on the positive side, and I almost hesitate to speak of the negative side of our present and future. You have heard and read so much of it that you have reached the point where you can casually pass over new pictures of bodies piled high and seek out the baseball scores and other more important items. They are only the anonymous bodies of European Jews, there are so many millions of those bodies, so many thousands of such pictures that what matter a few more?

What can I tell you that you have not heard? What fresh horror will move you? I was almost ready to say I know of none, when I received the report rendered by eight medical students from this country who toured the concentration camp at Belsen four weeks after the British army took over there. I am going to read to you from their report because it reveals the utter unspeakable conditions to which Jews have been plunged.

There are parts which are embarrassing to people who have never lived in such camps, but let us pocket our Emily Post for a few minutes and read and hear this brief excerpt from a dispassionate, scientific report rendered by medical men and remember, these are our people being described. These are the people about whom some of you have been receiving telegrams reporting that your entire families have been exterminated.

They are you and I, their shame is our shame, their fate our fate, the indifference to them is the indifference that could tolerate the same treatment for you and me.

The men describe their visit to Camp #1 in Belsen, Germany: "About a quarter of a mile from the camp, the stench that we were to know so well became obvious. Smells such as this are indescribable but in it were compounded the stinks of feces, decaying flesh, burning rags and the warm, sour, acrid scent of human sweat.

"Then we saw the camp for the first time, half a square mile in area, it held 28,000 persons. To call this 'overcrowding' would be grossly to understate the case. They lived in the wooden huts already mentioned, 'blocks' as they called them.

"They were all dilapidated and falling apart, roofs holed, windows broken, floor boards collapsed and drains stopped up. No light, no water; in many huts, no beds or bedding of any kind. And under these conditions lived not 40 people as one might expect in a full E.M.S. hut of this size, but in my own hut, for example, 580! Some huts housed even more, some less.

"It was impossible for anyone to lie down at full length, there being no room. Instead they had to stand or huddle up on top of one another on the floor, the sick, the starved, the dying and the dead, all one huge, wretched, seething mass of disease-riddled, vermin-infested, stinking humanity.

"The stench in these huts was almost more than we medical students, brought up as we are to meet bad smells unflinchingly, could bear. And little wonder, for universally the floors were carpeted, literally, with a thick, glutinous layer of weeks-old excreta. The reason?

"Weeks before, such sanitary arrangements as were provided in the huts had become defunct and yet the S.S. guards, knowing this as they must have done, had forbidden the inmates to defecate or micturate outside the huts on pain of death, should they be caught disobedient. There was no alternative, then, and in any case the majority of the people had become too apathetic to care or else too weak to move so that they would remain where they were, saturated time and time again by their own excretions.

"This lack of shame, this apathy, this regression to sheer animality was evident on all sides. Men and women would walk around the camp stark naked, cold as it was, and think nothing of it; they would sit side by side on the latrines and gaze on passers by unblushingly, expressionlessly. Before long we ceased to marvel at the sight of emaciated figures crawling out of their huts with eating bowls in their hands which they had just used as bedpans, emptying them down the nearest latrine, wiping them on the filthy rags which served them as clothing and then returning to their huts to take their meals from these self same bowls. They would pick up any small object they found lying about the camp no matter how useless, worthless or filthy, bits of wood, cigarette ends, rags, it made no difference, and carry them off as though they had stumbled upon some invaluable prize.

"And when food was brought round to the huts, those who were strong enough would fall upon it like packs of wolves and fight for every morsel they could obtain, thinking only of themselves and caring nothing for those who could not move and who consequently went without, all gibbering unintelligibly in high-pitched tones the while like a swarm of angry monkeys.

"I have not described the thick, black malodorous mud through which we had to wade on wet days and the fine, poisoned, yellow dust which billowed everywhere on dry ones. I have not described the endless tangles of barbed wire nor the refuse heaps all around nor the confusion of races - Polish, Hungarian, Russian, German, Czech, French, Dutch - representatives from every country.

"Meanwhile we had to supervise the distribution of the food in person to ensure that the very weak and very ill did not have their portions appropriated by the fitter inhabitants, a heavy undertaking for one man with 400 to 600 patients (as we now called them) in his care.

"We were assisted in this by fit internees (i.e. those who could walk and talk) and by Hungarian soldiers who had formerly been camp guards and who were now in our service as general laborers, and hindered by repeated breakdowns in the water supply which seemed always to occur just at the time when the food was being prepared.

"Preparation and distribution of meals was in the hands of Army officers and Rowsell and Tizard, in addition to looking after their huts, had the thankless task of making up thousands of liters of Bengal Famine Mixture, protein hydrolysate, etc., every day."

To these animal depths human beings have been depressed, our brethren, our fellow Jews. Can the survivors live again among those neighbors who tolerated these things? Dare they live again among such people? What is the alternative? Palestine, as Miss Thompson described it to us, as we envision it, could save the remnant and recapture their self-respect and fortify ours.

But the doors are barred by treachery and of more immediate concern to us, they are barred by our own lethargy, our own laziness, our own stubbornness, they are barred by the fact, the hard, cold, statistical truth, that there are 5,000,000 Jews in America and there are 300,000 Zionists. No wonder Britain can ask us, why clamor for Palestine if all the Jews do not want it? No wonder on the very same day which reported that wonderful mass protest last Sunday night at Madison Square Garden, the newspapers could carry the following statement by those whom Dr. Silver so aptly branded "shell-shocked Jews," Jews so frightened by what happened to others in Europe that they turn tail and run, tossing over their shoulders as a sacrifice of appeasement the remaining survivors in Europe and the future of the Yishuv in Palestine.

No wonder they reported to the press at that crucial moment when we were trying to present a united front:

"Lessing J. Rosenwald, president of the American Council for Judaism, declared in a statement issued last night that attempts were being made by holding mass meetings and other propaganda devices to foster the erroneous impression that all Jews were united in support of the Zionist plan to establish Jews as a nation and to make Palestine a Jewish commonwealth.

"This is simply not true," he said. "No one possesses the authority or the right to speak in the name of all Americans of Jewish faith.

"On behalf of the American Council for Judaism, an organization of Americans of Jewish faith who oppose Jewish nationalism, refuse to participate in a political organization of Jews, and oppose the creation of a Jewish state, we call attention to the divergence of opinions among Jews on this subject. We draw public attention to our program which seeks to maintain the only identity of Jews as individual adherents of a Jewish religion. We seek one thing only for Jews; a status of equality of rights and obligations throughout the world.

"As to Palestine and its status, Mr. Rosenwald said the Council urged aid for immigration into that country from political objectives and consistent with Palestine's sound economic development and political well-being without discrimination or privileges for any group.

"We favor the earliest possible acquisition of self-government in Palestine in which all, Moslems, Christians and Jews, fulfilling requirements of citizenship shall participate equally.

"We deem it particularly important to draw attention to the fact that an overwhelming body of American Jews hold this view by virtue of their

principles as Americans of Jewish faith. We reject all those self-appointed spokesmen who presume to make their partisan claims in the name of all Americans of the Jewish faith."

And nobody can contradict them because hundreds of thousands who are Zionists at heart are not enrolled Zionists. And when our friends in high places are prevailed upon to help us they are confused and confounded by the carpings of the American Council for Judaism and their misguided cohorts.

What can we do? There is only one thing you and I can do. We can, we must stand up and be counted as Zionists. Give the Zionist statesmen numerical support and encouragement. Throw the lie back in the teeth of those who say the majority of Jews don't want Palestine!

From here on every loyal Jew becomes a soldier in the army of Jewish liberation! We have no draft for our army. We are all volunteers, But we are volunteering in a militant demand that Eretz Yisrael shall open its doors without quotas to every driven, hunted, homeless soul who can get there. *Eretz Yisrael* will be ours, we have prayed for it, worked for it. Let us not lose it because we are too lazy to stand on our hind legs and declare ourselves as Jews.

Men, join the Z.O.A. Ladies, join the day or the evening groups of Hadassah. Now, tonight, by tearing off the right hand stub from your ticket and passing it to the ushers. I want to see who are the soldiers and who are the brave.

I want you to get on your feet and show me our enemies are wrong and at least here, in Forest Hills, Rego Park and Kew Gardens, we are united for Palestine.

Get on your feet, all Zionists, old and new! Tear off that right-hand stub, pass it to the usher and then get on your feet as a Zionist. Theodore Herzl said, "If you will it, it is no dream!" We will it and we will have it!

A PASSIONATE CALL FOR A HOLOCAUST MEMORIAL DAY

World War II was over. The death camps, the slave labor camps, the crematoria had been opened by the triumphant Allied Forces. The enormity of the Holocaust was beginning to dawn even on the skeptics. For this sermon, I used the title "Let It Snow" not only because it was a snowy December Shabbat, but because the expression is used fatalistically when we feel there is nothing we can do about the weather. I wanted to make the congregation consider how we must not accept the Holocaust fatalistically but memorialize it properly and insure that it never happens again.

I suggested that there should be a special day of mourning and remembering annually, even as we have a fast day on the tenth of the month of Tevet, Asarah b'Tevet, to recall the day when the Babylonians began their siege against Jerusalem in 586 B.C.E. which ended with the rape of Judea and the exile of its inhabitants. We still remember that tragic moment with fasting and prayer.

Should we do no less for the tragedy of the Holocaust which claimed six million Jewish lives and millions more? Fearful that the world would lapse into denial and forgetting, I preached what turns out to be rather prophetic, with both revisionism and commemoration increasing in intensity over the years to where Yom Hashoah is a fixed date in our official Jewish calendar world-wide.

DECEMBER 17, 1945

Dear Friends:

It seems that the title given tonight's remarks was "Let it Snow." There is an inevitability about the falling of snow, the play of all the elements, to which man has become resigned. When a man says "Let it snow. What can I do about it?" he is not being a fatalist. But when a man approaches the problems of society with the same resignation, with the same feeling of being unable to do anything about it, he is being a fatalist. The Jew has often been obliged to adjust his life in the face of forces stronger than he, but fatalism has played no part in Jewish thinking. Jewish thinking follows this line: the control of the destiny of mankind lies in the hands of man. Man is not eternally doomed to squalor, to sickness, to bloodshed, to ignorance. By his own efforts he can elevate and educate himself and he can bring peace and security to all society. This is Jewish thinking. This is the optimism that has characterized Jewish survival all these centuries, despite many reversals and many tragic blows to our people.

One such tragic blow was commemorated today. Today was the tenth day of the Hebrew month of *Tevet*, the fast day of *Asarah b'Tevet*, which commemorates the day when the Babylonians began their siege against Jerusalem in 586 B.C.E. The siege ended in the fall of Jerusalem and the exile of the Jews to Babylonia. That was indeed a calamity which we can only measure if we translate it into current terms. Imagine, and it will not be too much of a strain upon the imagination, that Tel Aviv, Jerusalem, all the model villages, the port of Haifa, in fact, all of Jewish Palestine were destroyed by an enemy of Israel. Imagine that the 600,000 Jews now living there were forcibly exiled to a strange land. Imagine that, and you begin to get a picture of the calamity that befell Israel in that ancient day which we commemorate on *Asarah b'Tevet*.

How has Israel reacted to that ancient tragedy? By declaring a fast day, by prescribing that special Biblical passages be read. By adding to the prayers of Israel additional poetic works which explain the blow as a just punishment for the sins of the people or of the nation as a whole. So has it always been with the Jewish people. Many and varied have been the tragic experiences which have befallen us, but each and every one of them has been recorded in our history and remembered by new memorial dates, by new prayers, by new penitential hymns.

Tisha b'Av, the ninth day of the month of Av, commemorates several events: the day in ancient Egypt when it was decreed that Jews might not leave Egypt and enter the land of Palestine; the day when the Temple was destroyed both the first and the second time; the day Bethar was conquered and Jerusalem plowed under by the Romans. What a mournful collection of events are remembered on *Tisha B'Av!* And how are they remembered? Not with frenzied promises of revenge! Not with cries of resentment against the Lord! They are remembered by reading from the Bible the sad verses of the Book of *Eicha*, the Book of Lamentations. They are remembered by reading the poetical productions which were begun in Gaonic times and continued for centuries. These poems of lament, stressed the belief that trouble and distress grow out of the sins of man; that only penitence can revoke the severe decrees and that help can come only after sincere repentance has been rewarded by forgiveness.

That belief was applied to the greatest blow the Jewish people suffered:

the destruction of the Temple and the fall of Jerusalem which resulted in the dispersion of the people in exile. The people believed that only through repentance and wholehearted return to God could redemption come. But despite this belief, the pain of that national calamity was felt so intensely that instinctively the poets broke forth in lamentations, recalling the lost glory, the brutality of the Babylonians and the Romans, the devastation of the holy city, the massacre of hundreds of thousands of men, women and children; the desecration of all sacred things, the burning of the Holy Scriptures and the torture of the sages.

Thus have we reacted to national tragedy by searching ourselves for the fault, by pouring out our hearts in prayer, by emphasizing the need for self-purification that we might be worthy of the forgiveness of God. Compare the Jewish reaction to disaster with that of some other nations. A recent example is Germany, the Germany which came out of the first World War defeated but resentful, consumed with a desire for revenge, fired with the lust for conquest which finally led only to another defeat for her. If a nation like Germany were to declare a fast it would be a fast of self-castigation for not having been brutal and cunning enough to win the war. It would not be a fast for the sins of Germany which brought about the war. With Israel, when we fast, as on *Asarah b'Tevet*, as on *Tisha b'Av*, as on the seventeenth of *Tammuz*, we fast so that we may search our souls and discover the sins and where we have been wanting in our spiritual perfection.

The traditional way of Israel in commemorating our tragedies is the proper way: we appoint a special day of the year in which to search our soul for the blemish which must have resulted in our calamity, we enrich our lives with new works of creation, we give charity to those who are in need, and we pray for forgiveness and guidance. Unfortunately, all of Israel's tragedies have not taken place in the dimness of antiquity. From day to day during the past dozen years our newspapers have chronicled the blackest chapter yet in the history of our people. Only today, we read the final, official German report of the enormous crime which the Nazis committed during those years.

The figure is out, it is 6,000,000 Jews massacred. And as we repeat that figure in this moment there is no gasp of horror or surprise. We all knew that the massacre was taking place. We have heard or thought of little else during the last few years. Here, in our own lifetimes, virtually before our very eyes, has been enacted the most terrible scene in all the long drama of Jewish suffering.

How have we reacted? What new fast day have we imposed upon ourselves? What new works have poured from the suffering heart of our people? What new sins have we searched for and found blackening the heart of humanity? What great resolutions have fired us to a more intense, a more meaningful, a more religious Jewish life? What change has taken place in your very being and in mine because 6,000,000 Jews were murdered in cold blood? None, absolutely none! Oh, of course, we have given a few extra dollars to charity because we were touched with pity and because we could afford them. Of course, when telegrams came reporting that members of our immediate families were among those 6,000,000 anonymous corpses, we were properly heartbroken.

But more basic, more far-reaching than these effects, what change has taken place in the moral fiber of American Judaism, of American Jews? Has there been an effective and lasting rededication to Jewish ideals, to a Jewish way of life? No, there has not! There has been one visible product: the strengthening of fear in the hearts of American Jewry, fear that something of the sort might conceivably happen here. And fear, my friends, is not the most commendable of human qualities..

Are you sometimes pricked by a troubled conscience which demands that something constructive come out of all the misery of recent years? Are you sometimes desperate for a way of wresting a blessing from the curse that laid a heavy hand upon our people in Europe? Then examine the example of *Asarah b'Tevet*, of *Tisha b'Av*, of those fast days by which we have remembered our past tragedies.

First of all, their example teaches the necessity of setting aside a day, a time for remembering. In all the dizzy whirl of our life, we need specific times for remembering. Otherwise, the rush of events keeps us from thinking about the very things we should remember. After all the months and years of torture our people endured in Nazi Europe, surely at least one day must be set aside so that we may meditate upon and learn something from their terrible experience. Someone, somewhere will have to set aside such a day. If I were ever to be asked for a suggestion it would be the day, when after holding out for 42 days in pitched battle against the might of the Nazi army, the last Jews died fighting in the battle of the Warsaw ghetto. Shattered in body, but unbroken in spirit, the Jews in that ghetto, that nightmare of our time, rose to their greatest height and faced their tormentors.

Such a day should be set aside to take its place alongside *Asarah b'Tevet* and *Tisha b'Av*. But those days are marked by more than our merely fasting. They are marked by study and by creativity. On these days the poetic creations of inspired minds are read and the holy books are studied. A beauty and a way of life are sought so that out of the ruins may be created a better world.

Surely there is need for such a reaction today. It is not enough that we are moved to pity and to charity by the concentration camps and the yawning graves of Europe. We must be moved to something which is actually easier, but which we, American Jews, seem to find more difficult. Study of the great treasures of Judaism, study of its practices, study of its beliefs so that we may incorporate them in to our daily lives.

Give me the Jew who will look across the waters at the graveyard of European Jewish scholarship and say he wants to learn the Hebrew tongue, and I will have found the Jew to whom the meaning of these past years has been brought home. Give me the Jew who wants to study the Bible, who wants to feel and understand the beauty of the prayer book, who wants to be intelligently informed about the works of the rabbis, and I will have found the Jew who wants to impart immortality to those inert figures dead and dying. Unfortunately, it is easier today to find the man who is willing to give a dollar than it is to find the man who is ready to give an hour to Jewish study and to Jewish living.

Not only must we have a day of remembrance, a new dedication to study, but most pressing and most important of all, we need a rededication to religious Jewish life. We need a religious revival, one which will not only fill the synagogues with people, but which will fill the people with a zeal, with a drive, with a missionary enthusiasm to bring the lessons of Jewish living home to their Jewish neighbors. You, the members of this congregation, who say "Let it snow," and mean that nothing can deter you from living a Jewish life, from offering up your prayers in the company of your fellow worshipers. If you feel so touched, if you feel in the slightest measure affected by the reports you have read in your newspapers this very evening, you must be bold and confident in urging a more intensive Jewish life upon your neighbors.

Never before was the world so gravely in need of a truly religious way of thinking and of living. We cannot hope to convert the whole world to our way of thinking, but we certainly can aspire to influence our fellow Jews. And this we can urge upon them: synagogue, service and study. Synagogue, which includes worshiping together and community life; service, which includes works of charity and mutual assistance; and study, which means study at home or in the company of your friends or in classes provided by your synagogue.

We shall not let the memory of this latest tragedy in Israel fade into oblivion without deriving from it some measure of good. We never have permitted such a waste in the past, as our fast days testify. Israel's history is a long chain of building upon ruins, bringing beauty and light out of darkness and devastation, a chain that goes back to the classical Biblical story of Jacob. You must remember that on that night before Jacob was reunited with his brother Esau, he wrestled through the night with a strange and mysterious adversary, an adversary who wounded Jacob seriously upon the thigh. But in the morning Jacob was victorious and would not let his adversary go before he blessed Jacob. And the blessing was that Jacob's name became Israel, meaning one who has struggled with God and with man and has prevailed.

For these many years the children of Jacob have been wrestling in the night with a strange and powerful adversary. Grievously have we been wounded. But despite our wounds, we can wrest a blessing from this experience, a blessing which we can bring about by resolving that the martyred dead of this and every generation shall not go unremembered; by resolving that we will perpetuate and enrich the treasury of Israel's heritage by teaching it to our children and by meditating upon it and learning it ourselves; and by resolving that Jewish life and the Jewish faith shall have a rebirth in our day.

Six million Jews have died, but 10,000,000 remain and call out beyond the grave, "We must never forget the dead!"

We shall seek, not vengeance but rededication to prayer, to study and to virtuous living. So long as one Jew lives and remembers and studies and prays to God for a world in which all men shall be free, the Holocaust will be remembered.

SAN FRANCISCO, OPEN YOUR GOLDEN GATE

The prospect that the forthcoming meeting of 48 nations of the world in the San Francisco Opera House could spell the dawn of a congress of nations united for peace and the common welfare seemed to the Jews to be the fulfillment of Biblical prophecies of the end of war and the coming together of all people. It was a prospect particularly appealing to the modern Jew who had suffered so much and so long as the scapegoat of a fragmented and fractious world.

This sermon goes so far as to claim of the nascent United Nations, "It is not a political affair, but a religious matter involving the fate of all of God's creatures."

We wondered: would the United States fail to ratify the United Nations' constitution and join the organization? After all, the U.S. had failed to join the League of Nations at the outset, which contributed to its ineffectiveness and ultimate dissolution. We prayed to the Lord to bless the delegates to the United Nations with wisdom, discretion and success.

APRIL 27, 1945

Dear Friends:

Lord of the Universe, Father of Humanity! We invoke Thy blessing upon the delegates of the United Nations as they assemble to shape the instruments of peace. We pray Thee to bestow Thy spirit upon them, that they may be conscious of the sacredness of their task. Illuminate their minds with the light of Thy truth. Sensitize their spirits to the sorrows of the world and to the cry of all the victims of war and persecution. Be Thou with them in their counsels, that their deliberations may be in Thy spirit, their decisions in Thy service and their actions in Thine honor, and that through them Thy kingdom on earth may be enhanced. Amen

These are world-shaking and soul-shaking days. How is it possible to live through them and remain unchanged? How has it been possible for us to receive the shocking news of the death of the world leader, our late president? How has it been possible for us to sit still in our chairs and read that the armies of Russia have fought 2,000 miles across Europe, and the armies of this nation and Canada have fought 3,000 miles across Western Europe and that these two Armies have met in the heart of Germany and henceforth will fight side by side? How has it been possible for us to look at photographs of naked, hunger-shriveled bodies, bodies that were once our fellow Jews or our fellow human beings of whatever extraction, stacked one atop the other like so many pieces of lumber?

How has it been possible for us to look and then turn to our tables and eat the feasts that are the commonplace American meal? How has it been possible for us to continue about our daily tasks, realizing that out in San Francisco there has begun an assembly which has it within its grasp the means of uniting the nations of the world in a peace we can bequeath our children or sow the seeds of disunity which could mean the suicide of the human race? How is it possible?

The answer must be either that we fail to begin to appreciate the magnitude of what is transpiring before our very eyes, when each day is more momentous than a whole year or a whole lifetime in ages past or else we have simply grown so calloused, so inured to tragedy, horror and great decisions that we are unimpressed. Therefore it is vital that at a time like this, when the armies of East and West have met, when the statesmen of East and West are meeting, and when, meanwhile, the Jewish people in Europe are either stateless, starving, or unburied, it is vital that we force ourselves to think about these matters.

Let us turn our eyes first to the West, to San Francisco. The meeting that is taking place there now is not a political affair, but a religious matter involving the fate of all of God's creatures. It is another step on the road toward the building of a Messianic era on this earth when all the nations will dwell together in harmony as envisioned by our prophets of old. It is another step on the road that began with Ten Commandments which set the pattern for human relationships, that continued with the Magna Carta of England, the Constitution of our United States and the League of Nations that followed out of the First World War.

President Roosevelt trod that road and met with the leaders of the other great nations and laid the groundwork for future cooperation. Then in September of 1943 the United States House of Representatives passed the Fulbright Resolution, which marked the first time the American people through their legislative body pledged themselves to an international organization. In October of 1943 Secretary of State Hull, with a rough draft of a declaration in his pocket, traveled 25,000 miles by air and sea to confer with Foreign Minister Eden and Commissar Molotov in Moscow.

At the end of that conference the three nations and China pledged themselves to cooperate for peace as they had done for war. They issued a declaration that said the governments of the United States, the United Kingdom, the Soviet Union and China "recognize the necessity of establishing a general international organization open to membership by all states, large and small, for the maintenance of international peace and security."

The House of Representatives had agreed to such an organization, and the State department was working toward it, but the Senate was the body which would have to accept such a treaty by a two-thirds vote. How did the Senate feel? This time the Senate passed the Connally Resolution by a vote of 85 to 5, stating, "That the United States, acting through its constitutional processes, join with free and sovereign nations in the establishment and maintenance of international authority with power to prevent aggression and to preserve the peace of the world." We were then ready for diplomatic conversations to develop proposals for such an organization.

Late in 1944 the four nations already mentioned, with Secretary of State Stettinius as chairman, gathered at Dumbarton Oaks and evolved the proposals which are now being considered by representatives of 46 nations at San Francisco. We should all be familiar with the broad outlines of these proposals for they mean our future happiness or our future distress .

The proposals call for a General Assembly with one vote each of all the member nations. This assembly can call for the study of international problems and recommend better ways for nations to work together. This Assembly will elect six non-permanent members of the Security Council and all the members of the important Economic and Social Council.

The Economic and Social Council of 18 members elected by the General Assembly, would be concerned with such matters as the Bretton Woods monetary proposals. It would try, in other words, to prevent worldwide depressions and make sure that new methods and materials for the production of goods are available to all peoples. Peace can best be maintained by guaranteeing economic security to every nation.

The second group working with the General Assembly would be the Security Council. It would be its business to settle any threats to peace that might develop between nations. It would consist of one representative each from the United States, Great Britain, the Soviet Union, China and France as permanent members, plus one representative from each of six member states chosen for two-year terms by the General Assembly.

If a problem can be settled on the basis of international law, it will be taken before a World Court, the third agency working with the General Assembly. If the disagreeing nations are willing to settle it with the help of a third power, the Council will provide an arbitrator. Should the nation refuse to settle a dispute peacefully, the Security Council may take whatever means seem necessary to prevent war. It may invoke economic sanctions or it can call instantly upon armed forces of member nations acting as a police force.

An assembly and an economic and social council to iron out difficulties which lead to friction between nations. A world court to settle disputes by law. A security council to prevent war either by peaceful means or by armed might if necessary. These are the Dumbarton Oaks Proposals being considered by the United Nations in San Francisco. These we must support and by raising a great ground-swell of public opinion, leave no doubt on the part of our senators that the American people want an international organization to maintain peace.

At the present moment, the picture looks promising. There is but one discordant note which we as Jews feel most keenly but which we protest not only as Jews, but as Americans. Turkey, Egypt, and Saudi-Arabia have declared war on Germany in order to obtain seats at the San Francisco Conference, but the Jewish people, who have been at war with Hitler longest of all, the people who have given one and a half million fighting men to the Allied cause and who have sustained 6,000,000 casualties, will have no seat at the Conference.

When peace comes, the Poles, the Czechs, and the Dutch will be free and go home. They will rightfully sit in the council of nations. But for hundreds of thousands of Jews who have survived the Hitler slaughter, the future holds little promise. They are naked, hungry, sick.

The poison of anti-Semitism which the Nazis left behind, has made them literally homeless. Their eyes are turned to the ancient homeland of their people, Palestine, the land promised us time and again, the land which we are rebuilding.

Palestine has room to spare for the Jews who seek entry into it, but, and this is a situation so intolerable that it cries out to the heart of humanity, these Jews whose only hope lies in Palestine cannot enter Palestine.

The United Nations are now meeting, standing on the threshold of victory, and we plead for one word of reassurance from them, that there will be full justice for the Jews of Europe and that Palestine will be a free and democratic Jewish commonwealth. We know this conference has not been called to consider individual cases but rather to set up the machinery. Is it too much to ask that we have one vote, one seat - no more than has Saudi-Arabia or Turkey or Egypt who, by their very inactivity during the most trying moments of this war, cost the United Nations hundreds of thousands of lives? This Sunday at two o'clock, at the Lewisohn Stadium, the Jews of New York will assemble in mass demonstration to plead for these things, not in the name of mercy, but in the simple name of justice.

While we plead for justice, we must be prepared to act in our own behalf until justice is forthcoming. Hardened as we are to the stories of Nazi bestiality, casually as we may stare at pictures of our stiffened, starved brethren being buried in the conquered concentration camps, we cannot shut our ears to the clamor of the Jews still living, the displaced Jews of Europe, roving the countryside, near starvation, no government ready to help them because they are not constituents of any European government.

We cannot close our eyes to the fact that though they may be free from the Gestapo, they are not free from the ravages which follow: economic, social and political collapse and chaos in Europe. We cannot rely on the governments of Europe. We cannot depend solely upon UNRRA because it does not operate in neutral or occupied countries nor in liberated countries unless invited by their governments with the approval of military authorities. It is up to us to see to it that those who survived Hitler do not fall victims of hunger, hopelessness and disease. By years of shame and sorrow and torture they have earned the right to a bit of security and a crumb of happiness. For 12 long years we have awaited the moment when we could lift our brethren out of the depths of misery and despair, since we cannot lift the dead from their graves. This year once again, the New York area has united its Jewish causes under the United Jewish Appeal, and in Forest Hills we assemble next Wednesday evening to open the floodgates of our generosity.

Our generosity is being sorely taxed these days. Ever so many people have told me recently that they are becoming impatient with all the demands made upon them: taxes, Red Cross, clothing, blood, Federation, Allied Appeal. When will it end, they want to know.

It will end, only when we have given enough. It will end only when the United Nations put a stop to wars. It will end only when poverty and misery, persecution and starvation, isolationism and selfishness are banished from the earth. Until that time, those of us whom God has spared must share our good fortune with those whom man has afflicted. None of us will ever become as destitute by giving as are those who are now asking out of dire need.

Life has ceased to be a loose network of dissociated events. The death of our president, the junction of the two great Allied armies, the attempts of our people at organized self-help and the historic meeting at

San Francisco are all a part of the same struggle upward by man, upward out of the mud and slime and blood of man-made misery to the sunshine of divinely inspired peace and happiness. It must come. We cannot go on as we have, eternally suffering, eternally fighting, eternally callous to the misery of our neighbors. "Have we not all one Father? Hath not one God created us all? Why do we deal treacherously every man against his brother, profaning the covenant of our fathers?"

Our path is not clear but we know at least where next our steps must turn. Tonight we thank the Lord for the miracle of the union of the armies of the United Nations. On Sunday afternoon we shall assemble as Jews and as Americans to entreat the world for a speedy hearing of our cause. On Monday, Tuesday and every day thereafter we shall follow eagerly the ups and downs of conference of the nations as they grapple with the tremendous problem of creating international order out of centuries of international anarchy. And on Wednesday we shall demonstrate that we do not stop with asking the world to help the Jewish people, but we are eager to help ourselves and are ready to bring hope into the lives of Jews everywhere.

At this hour we turn our faces westward, westward to San Francisco and we exclaim, "Open Thy Golden Gate, the gate that leads to a reign of peace on this exhausted earth, the gate to unity within a brotherhood of nations, the gate to justice for all oppressed peoples everywhere. To the delegates there assembled we offer a guide, the words of Zechariah, who when facing a world of dispute and dissension proclaimed the way to everlasting peace:

לא בחיל ולא בכח כי אם ברוחי אמר ה צבאות

"Not by might, nor by power, but by the spirit of the Lord."

ISRAEL IS BORN, WHITTLING BEGINS

We in the Diaspora were glued to the news media during the unbelievable days of the establishment of the Third Jewish Commonwealth, which proudly called itself Israel. We were devastated by the immediate outbreak of attacks against her on all sides. As the fortunes of the battle between Israel and her neighbors bent on destroying her swung back and forth, after months of bloody battle, Israel's victory on the field of battle astonished a world which expected the fledgling state to be destroyed.

Israel had pushed back her enemies and appeared to be capable of overrunning them. The United Nations watched silently as Israel was attacked; but now voices were raised demanding that Israel declare a truce. Crocodile tears were shed for the "poor Arab refugees" who had fled their homes with full expectation of returning to an Israel destroyed and ripe for pillaging.

Each time the tide of war swept Israel's way, the cry of truce went up again. England and China offered a resolution threatening economic sanctions against Israel if she did not withdraw from hard-won territory. Canada, France, Belgium and even the United States were ready to vote for it.

In that climate I called the attention of the congregation to a shameful world which would not even permit the people who had survived the Holocaust to have a home to call their own.

NOVEMBER 5, 1948

Dear Friends:

This year, if I mention the date, November 2, I feel certain that everyone will recognize it as the date of the great surprise when the majority of American voters went to the polls and voted for one candidate, although they were convinced that everyone else was voting for another. In so doing they confirmed our basic American faith in the right of every man to his own opinion in his own land.

Now that the excitement has abated somewhat, however, we may be able to recognize November 2 as the anniversary of a great event in Jewish history, an event to which we must pay some attention these days: the issuing of the Balfour Declaration 31 years ago.

Thirty-one years is a long time to wait for a home and yet a very brief span in the history of nations. Thirty-one years ago on November 2, Lord Arthur James Balfour, Minister of Foreign Affairs in the British government, sent the following letter to Lord Rothschild, a message meant for all the Jews that is now known as the Balfour Declaration. "His Majesty's Government view with favor the establishment in Palestine of a national home for the Jewish people, and will use their best endeavors to facilitate the achievement of this object..."

His Majesty's government has succumbed to failure of memory since that day, however, perhaps as a result of old age and decay; because yesterday, November 4, 31 years later, in the Security Council of the United Nations, Britain led in demanding that the new State of Israel surrender its recently won positions under the threat of sanctions.

Thirty-one years after pledging to do all in its power to facilitate the achievement of a national home for the Jewish people in Palestine, Britain is doing all in it power to prevent such a happening.. no surprise. The surprise of this week, second only to the results of the national elections in America, is that the United States delegate to the Security Council voted with Britain and seven other powers against little Israel. This service is not the occasion for us to try to explain the first surprise, we shall leave that to the political observers with their great hindsight. This service should be the occasion for us to try to explain the second surprise and to interpret its consequences.

The history of recent events leading up to yesterday's action by the United Nations Security Council is an interesting one, if a man could repeat it without bursting a blood vessel. When Lord Balfour issued his declaration back in 1917, the Jewish people, the Arabs and all the nations who were later to band themselves into the League of Nations, believed that Palestine, including Transjordan, would be developed by the Jews as their national home. Since that day, however, Transjordan was stolen by the British and made into an Arab state over which they set a king, Abdullah, whom they provided with an army, weapons and an annual cash stipend.

Various plans for dividing the remainder of Palestine were offered by British commissions of investigation, while Jewish immigration was hampered and Arab immigration encouraged. With British blessings, the loose groups of Arabs in the surrounding lands were organized into the Arab League.

Finally, at the tables of the United Nations a partition plan was devised and passed on November 29 of last year, giving Israel a few square miles of Palestine plus the Negev or desert country to the south. Acting on this recommendation the State of Israel was declared on May 15 of this year. Immediately the Arab states to the North, South and East attacked. Transjordan's British-trained and British-directed troops attacked; Egypt's British-trained and British-equipped troops under cover of British Spitfire planes attacked; Syrian troops attacked.

While the Arab troops were on the march against Israel there was no voice raised in protest. The moment it became clear that Israel was holding the line successfully and driving the Arabs back and that panic-stricken Palestinian Arabs were fleeing from Jewish Palestine, the hue and cry went up. "Truce," cried the United Nations. "Woe unto the poor Arab refugees," cried great humanitarians all over the world who had watched Jews rot in detention camps even after the war and had held their tongues.

The new State of Israel, eager to be just and law-abiding, acceded to the truce and lived behind a blockade while the Arabs continued to arm. Count Bernadotte came to Palestine to observe the uneasy truce and came up with the plan of further crippling Israel by taking away the Negev, four-fifths of all of the state of Israel and internationalizing Jerusalem and Haifa. Bernadotte was assassinated by irresponsible extremists and immediately acclaimed a martyr for peace and his plan approved.

On October 14, Egyptian troops began firing on Israeli convoys to the Negev colonies. What do you suppose the Israeli soldiers did? They threw the Egyptian troops out of the Negev. Nor was that done without considerable loss of Jewish life and property. Once again, the moment it became clear that the Jews were winning, instead of losing, the cry of truce went up. United Nations mediator Ralph J. Bunche ordered both sides to cease fire on Friday, October 22, at noon. The order did not include a request for the withdrawal of troops. Such a withdrawal was to follow direct negotiations between the Jews and Arabs.

Now we come to the interesting part of the story. Last week Britain and China recommended to the United Nations Security Council, in a joint resolution, that they force Jewish troops in the Negev to withdraw to the position they held on October 14. If the Jewish troops did not withdraw, a seven-nation committee was to be appointed to consider punishing Israel with economic sanctions. This proposal met with immediate approval. Canada, France, Belgium and the United States were ready to vote for the proposal.

It took a telephone call from President Truman to Secretary of State Marshall to prevent the vote. Yesterday, the vote was taken, and the United States and eight other powers voted in favor of a resolution demanding that Israel surrender its recently won positions in the Negev under the threat of sanctions. Only the Soviet Ukraine opposed the motion.

And so the cycle, begun on November 2, 1917, took a complete reversal on November 4, 1948. This turn of events is of great interest to us for many reasons. It interests us as Jews because of what it may mean for the State of Israel. It interests us as Americans because our country voted in favor of the motion.

It interests us as Jews who have labored and contributed and prayed for a Jewish homeland. What will this new proposal mean? Apparently the Israeli government is not too concerned, for we hear that Aubrey Eban, Israeli representative in Paris, is not protesting too loudly. The motion calls for withdrawing both Israeli and Egyptian troops, not the evacuation of Jewish settlements in the Negev. If the United Nations guarantees the safe conduct of Israeli convoys bringing food and supplies to the Negev colonies until the final question of Bernadotte's plan is settled, well and good. David Ben-Gurion has said, "We will never retreat to the positions held on October 14."

Our second point of interest stems from the fact that America voted for the resolution, two days after the election, and four days after Truman specifically asked Marshall to oppose the move demanding sanctions. Here is a question which American citizens will demand to have answered. Did President Truman phone Marshall again, telling him it is now safe for our United States delegate to vote against Israel? Or did Marshall go ahead on his own, without consulting the president, as he has done before? Either way we must voice our indignation and our protest.

For there is a third point of interest in this entire matter and that is the first time the United Nations assembled to consider invoking economic sanctions is now, against the struggling State of Israel.

There have been times when the nations of the world were morally bound to blockade economically the aggressor nations of the world. The nations of the world should have invoked sanctions of all types immediately against Mussolini when he went conquering, against Hitler, against Franco, against Hirohito when Japan was chewing up China. Ah, but did they? No, they did profitable business with the aggressors and permitted wars to break out.

Here, at last, the nations of the world have summoned enough courage to speak of economic sanctions in brave, blustering terms. Against whom? Against the Arabs who turned aggressor toward the Jews time after time? Perish the thought! The sanctions are to be leveled against the Jews and the Arabs if they do not withdraw their troops. The Arabs have withdrawn because Israel kicked them out and so the sanctions will be against the Jews.

What will happen, then? I am certain that you are as concerned as I am over the future of the State of Israel and that you realize that without the Negev, Israel will become a good intention, not a nation. Well, then, it is well for us to understand that the Israeli people now in the Negev will never retreat from it alive. Down there in that desolate patch of wilderness, a guerrilla army whose average age is 18 years is holding and will continue to hold the Negev as long as life is left in them. Platoons of young boys hold those wild and lonely sites with a tenacity rarely matched in human history. When the leader of one of these tiny bands was asked when he would return to Tel Aviv, he answered, "When we can go from here to Tel Aviv by automobile, not by night and not by planes, but by auto and in full daylight."

Recently, a young woman, actress, author and lecturer whom some of you have heard, Helen Warren, visited the Negev, and this is what she wrote one week ago: "We drove constantly further into the desert and passed settlements, some completely destroyed, some still holding out. In the baked clay-like soil, we could still see the tracks of British tanks that had advanced on some of the settlements together with the Egyptians.

"The most harrowing desolation and stunning fortitude in the Negev is at the young settlement of X…, a settlement started a few years ago right at the Egyptian border by boys and girls between the age of 17 and 20. X…has been the scene of a major attack from the Arabs twice. Today the Egyptians sitting a few yards away content themselves with occasional sniping. I was shocked to discover every building had been razed by shelling from the enemy.

"The place appeared barren and abandoned, but as we came nearer, a shaggy young head appeared suddenly from a hole in the ground. Then suddenly from a different place in the ground came another, then another. One by one the boys and girls alone on the border had watched their buildings crumble, their comrades die and held back the furious Egyptian onslaught with 14 rifles, one projectile weapon and some Molotov cocktails. It had been the Corregidor of the Middle East.

"Those who survived at first were too shocked to do anything. Everything had been lost in the fighting but their lives and the ground on which they had lived for two years. All their equipment for living was smashed. But then, little by little, as one girl put it, 'Like Robinson Crusoe we began to try to live again.' They dug themselves into the ground. Today they are all living under the earth they loved, like moles. From the depth of a superhuman resilience they created their settlement, bit by bit, under the ground. They have a kitchen and a hospital. They have sleeping rooms with bunks one on top of the other. They have a headquarters and are still busy constructing downward. They have one cup of water for all their needs each day; four on Friday so they can wash.

"Do you imagine that this settlement and the few dozen like it in the Negev are ever going to retreat from their positions after having thrown back the attacking Arabs at such a high cost? Never while they live! The United Nations will never starve Israel out of the Negev with sanctions. To drive Israel out of the Negev they will be obliged to kill every last boy and girl living above the desert clay or within it. The Negev is irrevocably in the State of Israel, and if there is a spark of decency and justice lift in the rest of the world, we shall not rest until that reality is recognized by international law."

It is a long way from the Balfour Declaration to the spirit of resistance in the foxholes of the Negev, and yet one has developed slowly and inexorably from the other. In the next few months, far from surrendering to weariness and disinterest after the political settlement of November 2, let us remain alert, informed and vigilant to keep faith with the young State of Israel. We must see to it that the United Nations and our country keep faith, and that Jews may pour out of the dread displaced persons camps of Europe and Cyprus into the blessed sanctuary of Israel and there live in peace in accordance with the faith of our fathers.

CHAPTER TWO
The Rocky Road to Jewish Survival

A distressing realization dawned upon us that the age-old plague of anti-semitism did not disappear either with the end of the Holocaust or with the establishment of the State of Israel. It has been with us before, during and after those extraordinary days. I gave it a new name: Hatelerism.

Hatelerism resurfaced in the Arab world during World War II when the Grand Mufti of Jerusalem sat it out in Berlin, and the Arabs did nothing to impede the swift conquest of North Africa by "The Fox," German General Rommel. It was given new expression by King Ibn Saud of Saudi Arabia, with whom President Roosevelt was cozying up even before the end of the war.

Russian Hatelerism simply intensified after the war, and terrorism under the auspices of one nation or another was expressed by the murder of Israeli athletes at the Olympic games in Munich, the massacre at Lod Airport, and the taking of hostages in Entebbe.

Saddam Hussein emerged as iron-fisted dictator of Iraq and represented another threat to the State of Israel. The old heinous practice of using the Jew as scapegoat was tried in crisis after crisis from Argentina to Japan, to the consternation and huge disappointment of those of us who wistfully hoped that Hatelerism was buried with Hitler.

It was not to be.

HATELERISM
ANTI-SEMITISM FROM HAMAN TO HITLER

World War II was over. With Hitler crushed and discredited, one might expect that the principal victims of the infamous plan he so clearly stated in "Mein Kampf" might at last rest easy. Hitler and his crew of anti-Semites gone, we Jews by and large breathed a sigh of relief and believed we were on the threshold of a new day of brotherly love among all people.

Somehow, I could not rest easy. My grasp of history and my reading of the recent events, including the peak of 141 specifically anti-Semitic organizations in the United States alone in 1941, made me look sharply at the undiminished anti-Semitism persisting even after the war. I felt the need to remind my euphoric flock of the long and tragic record of persecution of our people, not to depress them but to alert them.

In general the thrust of my preaching has been to accentuate the positive of our long and glorious record. I do not subscribe to what is called "the lachrymose history of the Jewish people." Nevertheless, there are times when we cannot let down our guard, and post-World War II was such a time. The embittered and the bereaved among our neighbors often blamed America's costly participation in World War II upon the Jews for whose sake they claimed America fought while American Jews managed to stay out of uniform. Forgotten was the attack upon Pearl Harbor. Ignored were the Stars of David among the crosses on the military cemeteries.

It was a time for nudging our people to stay awake. It is still that time.

OCTOBER 19, 1945

Dear Friends:

There is a four-line jingle in English literature which reads as follows:

I do not love thee, Doctor Fell,
The reason why I cannot tell;
But this alone I know full well,
I do not love thee, Doctor Fell.

This little poem, I suspect, is patterned after a line by the Roman writer, Martial, who said, "I do not like thee, Sabidius. I cannot say why. All I can say is this: I do not like thee."

Currently, a great many young Jews who attained their social majority during the war years and a great many older Jews who have only recently interested themselves in Jewish affairs have come to the shocking conclusion that there are people in this world who do not like Jews. Particularly from some of my friends who served in the past war I have learned that they have made this – what is to them, new – discovery. They had an idea that the rabbis were blissfully unaware of the existence of anti-Semitism. They tell me, "You don't know how serious the situation is." And they add, "It is up to you rabbis to do something about it. That is your real job, to fight this growing anti-Semitism."

Nor are those who have not served in the military any less surprised. I saw that in the alarm registered when earlier this month the Christian Fronters made a new bid for recognition and support on Springfield Boulevard in Jamaica, Long Island. One might imagine that this monster had just sprung up from the nether world; one might imagine it had not reached a peak of 141 specifically anti-Semitic organizations in these United States in 1941; it had not a 300-year-old history on this continent.

One might imagine Jewish blood has not been shed violently in every land in Europe, North Africa, and the Middle East since the moment the Israelites escaped from Egyptian slavery 3,165 years ago. But to those who are aware of the long history of the hatred of the Jew as well as to those newly awakened to its existence, there are two terrible questions remaining unanswered: Why? Why do they not love us? Why are we chosen to suffer? Why are we the eternal scapegoats? And how? How do we protect ourselves? How shall we behave in the face of hatelerism, a new term for describing bigotry and prejudice in any form. To answer these two questions in a year of continuous discussion would be difficult. To do so in half an hour is impossible. Nevertheless I shall try, at the risk of being sketchy in my analysis and giving partial answers.

The great question is "Why?" Why do men hate, and more specifically, why have Jews been hated? In order to find the answer we must, at the outset, differentiate between true causes and mere excuses for persecution, excuses used to mislead, to explain away acts for which there is no valid justification. To understand the difference as well as to review again the antiquity of hatelerism, let us touch the high spots or rather, the lowest depths to which outbursts of violence have exploded against us.

We need go back no further than the year 70 C.E., when Jerusalem was destroyed by the Romans and the Jews were driven into exile, thrown to the lions, enslaved, forced to tear each other to ribbons in gladiatorial combat and butchered by the tens of thousands. What excuse did the

Romans offer for that atrocity? Believe it or not, they claim in their histories that the Jews were plotting to overthrow the Roman empire. That is as plausible as stating that Coney Island plans to conquer and rule the United States.

That was the Roman excuse for its actions. But that was not the true cause of the Roman destruction of the Jewish people. The Romans feared, as another great empire fears today, that the Jews might enlighten their oppressed neighbors in the Middle East and that the Middle East would free itself from Western domination. This Roman fear was aggravated by rumors which were prevalent throughout the ancient world that out of Palestine would come a Messiah to bring liberation to all oppressed peoples. Therefore Rome was careful to seek out and crucify every Jew who claimed or was credited with messianic powers. So this flimsy excuse was used to cover the cause of preservation of empire.

A quite different excuse was used by Mohammed in the early seventh century when his new faith, Islam, cut itself off from the Judaism which had originally inspired Mohammed to declare himself the true prophet of the God of Israel. The Jews in Arabia, from whom Mohammed learned the biblical tradition, refused to recognize him as God's chosen prophet. In 625 the people of Mecca severely defeated Mohammed's troops. Mohammed was wounded, and his cause temporarily suffered a set-back.

Enraged and frustrated, Mohammed turned against the Jews and there ensued a series of massacres in which a flourishing Arabian Jewry was reduced to poverty in wealth and numbers from which it never recovered. Mohammed claimed he had restored the true religious cult as it had originally existed under that first preacher of Islam, Abraham, father of Ishmael and Isaac. What excuse did Mohammed offer for the massacres and looting? He claimed the angel Gabriel had told him in a dream that the Jews were plotting against his life.

Simultaneously, in Spain, the Jews were suffering for quite different reasons. There, the pagan Visigoths and Suevi had accepted Christianity and there was no one left against whom the spirit of intolerance could be exercised - no one but the Jews. Some 90,000 Jews were forced to accept the sacrament. When they continued to practice Judaism secretly, they were subjected to all manner of torture.

During the Eleventh, Twelfth and Thirteenth centuries, England was the site of hatred directed against the Jews. The excuse offered for violence: the accusation of ritual murder. In 1144 in Norwich, far from the Jewish quarter, a dead Christian boy was found. The Jews were accused, and a former Jew, a convert named Theobald, told the court that once a year Jews had to sacrifice a Christian in scorn of Christ. In 1189, some Jews went to Westminster Abbey to congratulate Richard upon his coronation. They were pushed by the crowd within the fence, and that was a signal for rioting. A mob set fire to Jewish homes in London and pillaged and murdered for 24 hours. The rioting spread throughout England, and particularly to York, where 500 Jews were trapped in a castle and all were slaughtered or committed suicide. In 1210, every Jew in England was put in prison and had his wealth investigated. One Abraham of Bristol had one tooth pulled out every day for seven days until he turned over all his wealth. Every other Jew lost an eye during the pogrom. In 1218, every Jew was ordered to wear a white badge. So it went, with six more ritual murder accusations providing the excuse.

The cause was something else again. The Jews, forced into money lending by the confiscation of their lands, held notes from the barons and lords of England. The king of England could confiscate these debts from the Jews and use them as a weapon against the barons who were often as strong as he was. The barons, therefore, at regular intervals, incited the uneducated mobs into violence on trumped-up excuses of murder. They killed the Jews and took back their notes of indebtedness. Eventually, in 1290, all Jews were expelled from England. Many perished in the English Channel.

In France, in 1242, 24 carts of volumes of the Talmud were publicly burned in a square in Paris. In 1288, in Troyes, a man visited the rabbi's house on the seventh day of Passover and secreted a corpse there. The body was found and a charge of ritual murder raised against the community. Thirteen people, including the rabbi, his wife, daughter-in-law and grandson were burned at the stake. The Jews suffered in France until 1306 when they were expelled. The excuses I have told you. The reason? The king could take the property of the murdered and use the money.

In Germany, there were regular massacres on the charge of ritual murder. In Spain, the picture was slightly different. There, the clergy and the monarchy were fired with a religious zeal to convert every Jew by force if need be. Preachers inflamed the mobs in every city with furious passions which resulted in attacks upon Jews in the streets, the burning of homes and the stealing of all kinds of property. Jews were confined to ghettos, restricted from virtually every trade, forbidden to shave or cut their hair and forced to wear a long, drab mantle. Finally the Inquisition was introduced by the authority of Pope Sixtus IV, empowering Spain's monarchs to inquire as to the religious beliefs of all their subjects. Queen Isabella and King Ferdinand appointed Tomas de Torquemada as inquisitor general in 1485. In the name of forcing Jews to convert to a truer faith, he burned 8,800 Jews at the stake and punished 96,504 Jews by torture, life imprisonment and the confiscation of goods. In 1492, the Jews were expelled from Spain, and 300,000 people were forced to wend their way along hostile roads, attacked, hungry, and diseased, to the seashore where they crowded into all manner of boats. Many drowned or died of plague.

Meanwhile the Black Death, that terrible plague which carried off one-third of Europe's population, gave rise to a different excuse for murdering the Jews. As the dread disease raged through Europe, the Jews, because of their natural abstemiousness, their hygienic habits and ritual and their segregation, were somewhat less exposed to the ravages of the disease. So they were accused of poisoning the wells and rivers which supplied Europe's drinking water – no small feat to perform unobserved. Why didn't the Jews die from that poison? Because it was made from spiders, lizards, frogs, human flesh, the hearts of Christians mixed with the dough of sacred hosts –and Jews were magically immune. Does this excuse sound fantastic, implausible? Maybe so, but because of it, in Strasbourg, the city council brought the whole Jewish community of 1,800 souls to the cemetery on a Sabbath and burned them all alive, then ordered all documents of indebtedness to the Jews destroyed and their money distributed. The same happened in 60 large and 150 small communities in Europe. The treasures of the Jews made Gentile or Christian people rich. So the cause, the true cause peeps through the black mumbo-jumbo of the excuse.

The Jews, in lending money to the lower nobility, enabled them to resist the efforts of the cities to obtain their independence from their petty rulers, so the common people hated the Jews to start with, and used the plague excuse to murder them. The result was the opposite of what they expected, for they thus freed the nobility from its indebtedness to the Jews and strengthened them a little while longer.

I cannot dwell upon subsequent persecutions in Poland, Russia, Rumania, Italy and almost everywhere else. They should be known to you, however, even if it involves reading a book of Jewish history. But I must point out the terrible example which you do know, only too well, the example of Germany. Was the excuse there that the Jews refused to assimilate, refused to embrace Christianity?

On the contrary, it was just the opposite! Hitler accused the Jews of polluting the pure Nazi blood stream by becoming too much like their

German neighbors by assimilating themselves too readily into the society around them. Hitler persecuted those who had the slightest strain of Jewish ancestry for the crime of becoming like the Germans though they were not Germans.

So we see the wheel of excuses has made a complete turn. For centuries, the Jew was accused of being different. Once he tried not to be different, he was accused of trying to be the same. The Jew has been accused of poverty and filth, of capitalism and oppression of the poor. He has been accused of plotting to rule the world, of poisoning and murdering his neighbors, and lately, of cowardice and weakness far beneath the pure Aryan level; he has been accused of rejecting Christianity and of embracing it; of clannishness and of pushing himself in where he is not wanted.

By their very contradictions, you must see that these are only excuses. The justifications attempted to explain acts of villainy against us which are based on deeper causes, and these are first of all, anti-Semitism itself. It exists and has existed. It is a fact. It has a history, which I have sketched for you. It is what Rabbi Milton Steinberg calls "a prejudice in search of a pretext."

Prejudices are transmitted from father to son. From the moment a child hears at home, at church, in a classical play or a story that a Jew is or was something to hate, prejudice has been planted which a lifetime cannot always eradicate.

Second, anti-Semitism is the product of economic disturbances, from the English barons who owed Jews money to the European kings who used the Jews as a handy source of revenue, to the tradespeople and city-dwellers who hated the Jews for lending to the feudal barons, to the impoverished Germany which spawned Hitler. Economics has played a great and terrible role in anti-Semitism. Produce a society in which no man wants, no man hungers, and no man envies, and you will have a society without hatred of Jew or any other people provided you can deal with the third factor: namely, that anti-Semitism is the result of certain psychological factors: hatred of what is different, suspicion of the unknown, dislike of the unlike.

Finally, anti-Semitism is the product of deliberate scheming and planning in which the Jew is used as a scapegoat to conceal some more far-reaching plot against humanity. This was so in many of the instances I have cited. It was classically so in the case of Nazism. It was so in Nazi-inspired attempts to split the population of America.

I have not mentioned something that you might have had in mind. I have not laid blame upon the Jews themselves. Some Jews believe that since the world complains against us, there must be something wrong with us, and they go about in mortal fear of every Jew who achieves success, of every Jew in public office, of every Jew who does not act in accordance with the rules of Emily Post. To tell our fellow Jews that they must make their way inconspicuously through life's side streets, that there is something distasteful about them and they must constantly reform themselves is to ask innocent people to behave like criminals. This is not the answer to the problem of Hatelerism because it is merely pandering to the excuses and does not strike at the causes.

What then is there for us to do? First of all, let me state unequivocally: it is not the Jews who make anti-Semitism, and it is not the Jews, no matter how we behave, who can eliminate it. It is a cancer which has been growing ever larger and feeding on the moral tissues of civilization. No operation on us will remove that cancer. It is up to the rest of mankind to remove it from its own body. This it can do first by self-education. The perpetuation of Hatelerism is a process of education, as we have pointed out. It must be eliminated by education. The truth must be told in churches, schools and around the dinner table. The excuses offered against us must be unmasked as attempts to fool people and betray their very own interests. It must be eliminated by working with Christians for common goals so that they may discover the true nature of the Jew and not perpetually envision the caricature of us our enemies have created. This cannot be done through formal goodwill meetings but by natural, spontaneous labors side by side for the same good purposes.

It must be eliminated by making this world a place of opportunity for all men. A society which eliminates poverty and insecurity can also eliminate group hatreds and tensions. These things all men can do, Jews and Christians.

But there are some things we Jews can do for ourselves. We must resist anti-Semitism tooth and nail. The French writer Corneille said "He who allows himself to be insulted deserves to be!" Thank the Lord, in this land the law forbids violence and pillaging, even against the Jews, and it is our duty to invoke that law whenever we are wronged, to be militant in defense of our rights and vigilant not only on our own behalf but on behalf of human freedom. Every Jew must protect the democratic freedoms which are his, or someday they will be taken away not only from him but from his Christian neighbor as well. This then is our program against Hatelerism: no appeasement of our enemies. Bring them to justice before they gain strength over our prostrate bodies and destroy American democracy altogether.

Secondly, anti-Semitism is not created by Jews so let us stop blaming ourselves and one another for it. If we want to be polite, refined, dignified, let us do so not because of what our neighbors will think, but because it is right to be all those things.

Thirdly, once we have exerted ourselves to the utmost and attempted everything in our defense within our strength, let us stop thinking about it. This is no life if we go about all day obsessed with a feeling of impending disaster. Let us use the same energy in strengthening our inner resources, in strengthening Judaism, in learning more about the positive side of our past and our future. Let us aspire to that inner fortitude as convinced, active, informed Jews, the fortitude which sustained our Polish brethren in the ghettos, but for want of which some of our German brethren had no inner strength with which to meet and understand their misery. Hatelerism must eventually perish, or humanity will perish. It must always be our belief that the fate God has in store for humanity is not damnation but salvation, that the kingdom of God is not an empty phrase, but a goal that can be achieved, when the lion shall lie down with the lamb, and man will achieve for himself peace of mind and of body. Then this world will be a little bit of Heaven.

Let this be the motto of every Jew as he faces a future which may witness the further growth of Hatelerism before it is finally eradicated.

לא אמות כי אחיה ואספר מעשה יי

"I shall not die, but live, and declare the works of the Lord."

ANOTHER REPLY TO IBN SAUD

On March 10, 1945, when it was becoming evident that Hitler was losing, President Franklin Delano Roosevelt's so-called friend, King Ibn Saud of Saudi Arabia, addressed an obsequious letter to him, expressing his pleasure at how the war was going and launching into a diatribe against the Jews, including those Jews still imprisoned and dying in Hitler's concentration camps.

He wrote to Roosevelt, "The Jews are preparing to create a form of Nazi-Fascism within sight and hearing of the democracies and in the midst of the Arab countries." The President answered him, addressing him as "Great and good friend" and in no way refuting any of the King's outrageous lies.

I took the occasion of the twenty-eighth anniversary of the Balfour Declaration to address quite a different reply, citing facts and history which may now have been forgotten. The sermon is richly documented and carries greater meaning in view of today's realities in the Middle East.

NOVEMBER 2. 1945

To His Majesty, Abdul Aziz bin Abdur Rahman al Feisal al Saud,
King of Arabia:

This reply is sent on the twenty-fifth anniversary of the Balfour Declaration and is a supplement to the reply you received from the late President of this republic, Franklin Delano Roosevelt. We cannot address you as he did, as "Great and good friend." You are no friend of ours, and when we say "ours," we mean all the United Nations.

You may recall that on March 10, 1945 you wrote a long, repetitious, flowery, cunning, and completely misleading letter to the late president. This letter, your excellency, is an Arabian tapestry of vicious lies, diabolical half-truths and veiled but meaningless threats such as would have delighted the warped mentality of the late but unlamented Joseph Goebbels.

We can hardly believe that from the pen of your excellency could come ought but pearls of truth. So we must assume that the councilors by whom you are surrounded have deliberately misinformed you, and we shall endeavor to reveal the true facts to you. We hope some of our own people will also hear these facts for, verily, your letter did perplex and confound great numbers of us. Some of our people, traditionally lovers of the truth, have exclaimed, "If the facts as stated by Ibn Saud be true, then there is no validity to our Zionist claims." And so, lest they and you continue a moment longer in confusion, we hasten to set matters aright.

We know that you must be a lover of the truth, but unfortunately some people cannot handle the truth without scratching it. Hear then a classification of the various statements in your letter. You wrote the late president, first, that you delight at the triumph of those principles in defense of which war was declared. We were unaware that you knew a war had been declared. You certainly did not participate except to hamper the allies and give aid and comfort to Germany.

Next you said, "The Jews are preparing to create a form of Nazi-Fascism within sight and hearing of the democracies and in the midst of the Arab countries, as well as in their very heart and in the heart of the East which has proved itself loyal to the Allied cause in these critical times." Jewish Nazi-Fascism? Eastern loyalty to the Allied cause? My dear King, so that you may punish your false councilors, these sentences comprise an outrageous lie.

Next you said, "The Arabs have a natural right in Palestine which needs no explanation. We have on separate occasions mentioned to your Excellency, as we have many times to the British Government, that the Arabs have inhabited Palestine since the beginning of history, and that they have, throughout the ages been its masters and enjoyed overwhelming numerical superiority. We will now make a brief reference to Palestine's history. The earliest recorded history of Palestine begins in the year 3500 B.C., its first inhabitants being the Canaanites, an Arab tribe which emigrated from the Arab peninsula and had its abode in the lowlands, hence the name Canaanites."

Dear King, there is not a truth in the whole paragraph, nor in the next one you wrote which we shall quote so you may recall it. "This history of Palestine, an Arab country, shows that the Arabs were its first inhabitants and that they dwelt there...and ruled it alone, or with the Turks for a period of about 1,300 years, whereas the disjointed reign of the Jews did not exceed 380 confused and sporadic years. No Jewish rule has existed in Palestine since 332 B.C."

King Saud! Is it possible, that you, the ruler, of a great land, know less about history and anthropology than the average American high school student? Can you have meant it when you wrote: "The Jews were merely aliens who had come to Palestine at intervals and had then been turned out over 2,000 years ago." Jews aliens in Palestine, Ibn Saud? If so, where are they not aliens?

But of the Arabs you said, "The Arabs are not aliens in Palestine, and there is no intention to bring any of them from other parts of the world to settle there." You said this, knowing that there has been a 100 per cent increase in immigration of Arabs into Palestine since World War I.

You said further, "To bring these scattered people, put them in countries already occupied and do away with the original inhabitants is an act unparalleled in human history." Do you imply, after you call the Arabs the original inhabitants, that the Jews mean to "do away" with them? We plan no such act, but as for such an act being unparalleled in history, let me remind you of that glorious age in Arabian history, when in the seventh and eighth centuries of the common era, the Arabs conquered an empire greater than ever held by the Nazis and left the bloodiest trail of murder, rape, and looting that the world has ever known. Now you have a parallel.

Let us go on with your letter. You wrote concerning the Jews, "These people began their vile work by wronging the government that had treated them kindly and sheltered them, namely, the British government. Their assemblies declared war on Britain and organized dangerous military formations. This, then, is the way they have behaved with the Government which has treated them so kindly." And you go on to predict that if unchecked, we will massacre the Arabs, stir up trouble between the Arabs and the Allies, conquer all the surrounding countries and eventually attack Britain. These statements, in American parlance, are the payoff. This, then, is your letter in brief. This is the letter that was published in American newspapers without comment. This is the letter we search in vain to discover a grain of truth, a semblance of decency, only to find nothing but lies, clever lies, malicious lies, lies that must be refuted with the facts that are open to any casual visitor to any public library.

At the risk of boring you, King Saud, let us have some truths for once, to brush the cobwebs of doubt from our minds, doubts which threaten all Jews, Zionists and non-Zionists, with the suspicion of universal plotting, intended violence and false demands. Let us do what you suggested in your letter, "make a brief reference to Palestine's history," and if you wish to stake all on who lived there first, so be it.

Some 20,000 years ago, at the time of our last Ice Age, Arabia enjoyed a temperate climate, well-fitted for habitation. Its vegetation, found in fossils, resembled that of wet, tropical Africa and its inhabitants were a dark, Hamitic, Negroid type who probably mingled freely with the Abyssinians in Africa by a land bridge that made the Red Sea an inland lake, and which later submerged to form the shallow straits of Bab al Mandab.

As the ice cap receded, Arabia became hot and dry. Its rivers turned to rocky ravines and it became one of the hottest and most rainless parts of the earth's surface. About 3000 B.C.E., an invasion of Armenoid people from the North streamed down the Palestine coast into Egypt and down the east side of the Syrian desert into northern Arabia, mingling with the Negroid people already there. These people were the ancestors of the Canaanites. They were not Arabs at all. In vain have we searched the most anti-Semitic histories of Palestine for an early mention of the Arabs. Over and over again, we find in those same anti-Semitic sources, however, that to the Canaanites, the Arabs were known as the people of the East. All the hostile tribes who dwelt outside Palestine, the Ishmaelites, Edomites, Midianites, Horites, Ammonites and Moabites, these may have been Arabs, but they were not Canaanites. They were the enemies of the Canaanites and they dwelt to the east and south of Palestine, never in it.

The Canaanites were not members of what we call the Semitic peoples, of which the Arabs are one. Archeological discoveries show that the shape of the skull indicates a people not of the Semitic race. The same conclusion may be drawn from the fact that they burned their dead since cremation was not a Semitic custom. So, King Saud, when you claim the Arabs lived in Palestine as early as 3500 B.C.E., you know not whereof you speak.

The first recorded appearance of Arabs on the scene was after the Israelites settled there and assimilated, not massacred, the Canaanite inhabitants. Then the pre-Arab tribes we mentioned already formed a coalition against the Israelites. All during the period of the early judges, they tried to conquer Palestine, but were turned back. Thus, dear King, you are wrong about who lived in Palestine first. Just how far wrong will come as a blow to you when we inform you.

First, however, we must continue our history so you may join the millions who already know that the Jews lived in Palestine longer than 380 years. Call in your royal mathematicians, seat them on your royal rugs and with the aroma of your inseparable comrades the royal goats wafted on the desert breeze, let them add the true number of years we spent in that land. Your own Koran accepts the presence of Abraham, Isaac and Jacob in the land some 3,500 years ago, but we shall count only from the return of the Israelites from Egypt in 1220 B.C.E. even though archeology reveals the continued presence of Israelites in Palestine while their brethren were coming in from the desert.

Israel was ruled by the judges until the kingship of Saul, and thereafter by its kings until the exile into Babylonia in 586 B.C.E. So far we have at least 650 undisputed years of occupation of Palestine. After an exile of 50 years, during which time a remnant still lived in Palestine, the Israelites began to return, and after a while, always with a Jew as governor, Persia permitted virtual autonomy in Palestine. During this period the Bible was assembled, rabbinic literature developed as oral tradition, and we enjoyed a golden age of culture in Palestine. In 332 B.C.E., the Greeks, under Alexander, conquered Palestine, thus giving us at least another 200 years of occupancy. You, great king, discount the next period, during which we were ruled by the Greeks, but we do not. They maintained only a garrison in our land, but we elected our own high priest, who was the political and spiritual leader of the Jews, and we enjoyed another Golden Age until the Macabbees threw off the Greek yoke and ruled alone until the Romans intruded and finally conquered us in the year 70 of the common era. This gives us another 400 years in the land.

Nor did Jews leave the land of Palestine even then. For centuries, Palestine continued to be predominantly Jewish. The Jerusalem Talmud originated there as did the great academies of learning. The great sages Akiba, Ishmael, Judah ha-Nasi dwelt there and taught great truths which were copied by the church fathers of the struggling Christian sect. Here we have another 500 years.

It was not until 637 of the Common Era that the Arabs, embarked on their bloody war of conquest, invaded Palestine. That year, O Truth-loving King, is the accurate date of the entry of Arabs into Palestine, an entry by force, as alien conquerors, which resulted in the desolation that has gripped the land ever since. To loosen the death-producing grip of the Arabs, the Christian world launched crusade after crusade.

All the while there were Jews in the Holy Land. There were Jewish academies there, which engaged in correspondence with the Western world. As early as the Tenth, Eleventh and Twelfth Centuries, the harried Jews of Western Europe sought to flee there. Maimonides, Meir of Rothenberg and Jehudah Halevi turned their faces eastward. Why? Because there were no Jews there? No! Because Palestine was and always has been the Jewish homeland.

In 1517, 400 years before the Balfour Declaration, the Turks conquered Palestine, thus giving them, if we follow your reasoning, as much right to that land as have the Arabs. But the Turks neglected the land shamefully, and not until the Zionist movement repeopled the land with its original inhabitants did the land flower once again.

Add up the years, Ibn Saud, and tell me, where did you ever get the figure 380 for the number of years Jews have inhabited their land? For your information, the true figure is an unbroken residence of 3,500 years of which 1050 were years of self-government and another 500 were years of autonomy under foreign emperors to whom we paid tribute. On the Arab side of the ledger, the Arabs ruled Palestine by the sword for approximately 900 years and have lived there at all for only 1,300 years, not 5,500 as you claim in your truly remarkable letter.

Do you know what happened back in 1917? Have you any notion as to why the Balfour Declaration was made? During the first world war, Turkey and Britain became potential enemies. Britain and the Arabs, under Sherif Hussein, found it mutually beneficial to join forces. As an inducement to revolt, and you Arabs certainly require inducement, Britain offered the Arab people freedom from the Turkish Empire, and ownership of all their land with one small exception.

For one small piece of territory Britain had other plans. Syria was to go to the French, and Palestine was to become a Jewish homeland. This pleased the Arabs who received a tremendous reward for what turned out to be a very feeble effort, in which the Arabs did virtually nothing toward the defeat of Turkey. No Arab protest was raised then. In fact, Emir Faisal, the leading Arab figure of the time, worked with Chaim Weitzman, leader of the Zionists, in closest harmony.

And now you say in your letter that we plan to replace the Arabs in Palestine? The Arabs in Palestine are enjoying the fruits of a civilization which the Jews brought to them. That is why more Arabs than Jews have immigrated into Palestine than Jews since the Balfour Declaration. The British Colonial secretary said to the House of Commons in 1938, "The Arabs cannot say that the Jews are driving them out of their country. If not a single Jew had come to Palestine...I believe the Arab population would still have been around 600,000 instead of over one million. **It is because the Jews who have come to Palestine bring modern health services and other advantages that Arab men and women who would have been dead are alive today, that Arab children who would never have drawn breath have been born and grow strong."**

And by the way, where do you come off connecting the Zionist movement with Nazi-Fascism? Let me remind you, you sudden lover of the Allies, what happened during the war just over. In the summer of 1942 the British, for whose safety at the hands of the Jews you are so fearful, these same British were on their knees in Egypt.

Rommel had pushed the British back across North Africa and was poised for the blow that would deliver Egypt and the Arab world into his hands and assure the nightmare of a union between the Nazi-Fascists and Japanese in Asia. England needed friends as never before.

Did the Arabs rush to her defense? No, there were as many British soldiers policing the seething Arab world as there were facing Rommel. Egyptian Arabs were all smiles. In Palestine, the Arab aristocrats were telling the peasants, "Go and sell your land to the Jews and be quick about it, for in a month Hitler will be in Jerusalem and you will not only have your land back, but everything the Jews possess." The two honored guests of Adolph Hitler, the ex-mufti of Jerusalem and the ex-premier of Iraq were gleefully announcing their speedy return to the Arab world.

Did you rush to Britain's aid, Ibn Saud? No, you could not spare a single trooper, a single camel, a single donkey when Rommel stood at El Alemein. But the Jews of Palestine came to Britain's aid. They volunteered in the tens of thousands. One quarter of Montgomery's army at El Alemein was Jewish! The suicide garrison of Tobruk was almost all Jewish. The 500 Jewish engineers who laid the mine field at the southern tip of Montgomery's battle line were Jewish and only 43 came out of the encounter alive after keeping the enemy from turning the flank of the British army.

Is this the Arab friendship of which you boast, the fact that you kept a knife in the back of the Allies at the most crucial moment? Is this the Jewish enmity of which you speak, the fact that Palestine was the arsenal, the breadbasket, and the source of troops for the North African campaign which turned the tide of the war? Just some more of your lies, o Gracious King.

You lied that the Arabs have lived in Palestine for 5,500 years, when they have been there only since the seventh century. You lied that the Jews have only been there 380 years, when every schoolboy knows they have been there continuously since Abraham. You lied about our intentions against the Arabs and you lied about your friendship for the Allies. God spare the United Nations any more such friends as you, and speed your return to the truth.

Signed, The Jewish People, Zionists and Non-Zionists

P.S. By the way, just where do you come in, O King? Are you not in

Arabia, not in Palestine? By what right do you speak for Palestinian Arabs? Why did President Roosevelt extend you the courtesy of a reply, ambiguous and noncommittal though it might have been? Why is the Arab world of 7,000,000 square miles concerned over Palestine with its 10,000 square miles?

I'll tell you why. Because Jewish Palestine has brought a breath of fresh air into your musty and decadent empire. Because the freedom, prosperity, education and sanitation the Jews have brought is tempting to the trichoma-reddened eyes of the Arab peasants who have been kept in virtual serfdom by the feudal lords of the Arab world, and you and your fellow princes are fearful that they might wake up some day to the truth that you are their true enemy and not the Jewish people. Some day they may discover what the record shows, that in so-called Arab-Jewish riots, more Arabs are killed by Arabs than by Jews.

We are now a desperate people. Out of the flames of Europe has been born a determination to die on our feet rather than live on our knees. Do you realize what we are fighting for in Palestine? For the right of our people to come home, not for Palestine's Arabs to leave, but for Palestine's ancient people to return, to bind up their wounds, for each man to dwell under his vine and his fig tree. We repeat, with the late president, that no action will be taken which might prove hostile to the Arab people. We ask only the fulfillment of a promise made 28 years ago and accepted in good faith and of another promise made in the dawn of history to father Abraham, who is the patriarch of your faith and of ours:

"For all the land which thou seest, to thee will I give it and to thy seed forever. And I will make of thee a great nation. And I will bless them that bless thee, and him that curseth thee will I curse; and in thee shall all the families of the earth be blessed." (Genesis 13:15, 12:2-3)

Some day, and we pray God it will be soon, despite your best efforts to turn your tortured people's dissatisfaction against the Jews, they will arise, and overthrow you with your royal splendor wrung from their sweat, and freedom, and happiness will return to the birthplace of liberty and the cradle of the belief in one God.

THE IRON NOOSE TIGHTENS

Late in 1952 we became aware of trials in Communist Czechoslovakia against prominent leaders, the majority of them Jews. They were accused of Zionism, Titoism, Trotskyism, and American imperialism. Nine had been hanged, and thinly-veiled anti-Semitism was surfacing in Hungary, Rumania and other Russian satellite countries.

I felt a responsibility to alert my congregation to an ominous trend not yet generally perceived in all these disparate venues. The warnings I raised were soon to be born out by subsequent events. The first feeble cries of "Let my people go!" were being sounded.

Many American Jews took an indifferent position, some even took a vindictive stance against Jews behind the Iron Curtain "who had brought it on themselves by embracing Communism in the first place."

It is amazing to think that, since then, Jews left Russia by the hundreds of thousands, many to Israel, and today, one prominent refusenik, Natan Sharansky, is a power in the Israeli political system.

JANUARY 12, 1953

Dear Friends:

Tuesday evening of this week, in an atmosphere of gloom the members of our post-confirmation class sat and discussed the fate of the 2,400,000 Jews behind the Iron Curtain. These youngsters, 15, 16 and 17 years of age, had not yet been born when Hitler came to power 20 years ago and were too young to grasp fully the enormity of the tragedy which claimed so many millions of our people a decade ago.

For the first time in their life, they were experiencing that terrifying, bewildering and frustrating emotion which grips the heart with chilling fear when the news of the outbreak of attacks against Jews is heard. One of them asked me, "What is wrong with us that people can hate us so much that they will not hesitate to destroy us?"

As I tried in vain to reason away their fears and their self-criticism and pointed out how the victim of attack will often turn his accusation away from the attacker who cannot be reached and direct it against himself, I had a sense of impending events of great historical significance.

Once again the Jew seems to be the trigger used to set off great changes in human history. A kind of mystic thread weaved through that history these thousands of years, and wherever it twists, it seems the Jew has been an unwitting and unwilling, key to the fate of great movements and great empires.

The Jew was a slave when Egypt crumbled. The Jew was a captive when Assyria was overwhelmed by Babylonia. The Jew was an exile who was welcomed in by the Persian conquerors who displaced Babylonia. The Jew stood in the very no-man's land between the Seleucids of ancient Syria and the Ptolemys of Hellenistic Egypt. The Jew was at the birth of Christianity. The Jew was the inspiration for Islam and its first victim. The Jew was the buffer between the rising monarchs and the desperate lords of feudal Europe. The Jew was driven from Spain at the moment her empire began crumbling. The Jew was the first victim of Hitler, the scapegoat for the defeated Germans of World War I and the whipping-boy for Germany's march into World War II.

And now the Kremlin has suddenly reversed official Russian policy and lashes out at the Jew for the crime of his Jewishness. Behind the Iron Curtain a noose of iron has been coiled around the throat of 2,500,000 Jews. Everywhere Jews are wondering with fear in their hearts: will the noose tighten and repeat the oft-told story of Jewish martyrdom in our time, and what will it mean for the world?

A few weeks ago I called the attention of our congregation to the trials being conducted against 14 prominent Czech Communist leaders, 11 of whom were Jews. Nine of the 11 have already been hanged for the crimes of Zionism, Titoism, Trotskyism and serving the interests of American imperialism.

Since those trials, the tempo has been accelerating. We heard that in Hungary 62,000 Jews had applied for permission to leave for Israel. All over the Iron Curtain countries news reports of the trial were characterized by violent anti-Jewish language and attacks against the state of Israel, linking it with American imperialism. Czechoslovak papers called for the destruction of Zionism as a duty of the Czechoslovakian government.

Arrests began in other countries. In Rumania, former strong-woman Ana Pauker, soon to be tried for treason, began to be identified as Jewish. The security police in Prague arrested and sent some 200 alleged Zionists to concentration camps around Moravska-Ostrava without trial, and from the Czech radio came the outlandish and outrageous description of the Slansky gang, as it called the accused, "that their world culture and Hebraic self-advancement are but two sides of the same coin, both under the cover of Wall Street."

At first, then, it appeared that there was a move afoot with the Soviet satellite countries to discredit Zionism, to curry favor with the Arab nations and to shift the blame for internal weakness and economic problems to the international Zionist movement.

But then the emphasis moved toward outright anti-Semitism, in an attempt to discredit the Jew as a Jew, to prove him an untrustworthy element in Communist-dominated countries. In Odessa, six Jewish Soviet officials were arrested for violating Soviet laws and pilfering state property. Dr. Arieh Kubovi, Israeli Minister to Czechoslovakia and Poland, was ordered out of those countries. Employees in Czechoslovak governmental organizations began to petition for dismissal of all their Jewish colleagues. Wholesale deportation of Jews from Szeged, the second largest city in Hungary, began. Those fit for work were sent to slave labor camps in Russia while others were sent to concentration and labor camps in eastern Hungary.

Suddenly, in the beginning of this month, we received word from East Germany that a violent campaign was launched against what the Nazi-like propaganda termed "capitalist Jewry" and "agents of Zionism." On January 7, an order seizing all property of Jewish families who had not returned to East Germany was issued, thus confiscating several hundred millions of dollars of property. The flight of Jews from Communist Germany to the West was suddenly cut off, trapping some 2,500 Jews in East Germany.

All over the Soviet-dominated part of the world anti-Jewish feeling was mounting higher and higher. Then, on January 13, the fantastic story of a Jewish plot against the lives of top Soviet leaders came from Moscow, when nine doctors, the majority of them Jewish, were arrested. They were accused of killing Andrei Zhdanov, one of the top members of the Politburo and considered a likely successor to Stalin, who died in 1948. They were also charged with bringing about the death, in 1945 through false diagnosis, of Alexander Sherbakov, head of the political administration of the Soviet army. *Izvestia*, the Soviet newspaper gloated, "The unmasking of the band of doctors and poisoners constitutes a crushing blow against the Anglo-American warmongers. Their agencies were caught and rendered harmless, the true face of the slave-owners and cannibals of United States and England now stands revealed."

All over the civilized world grave concern was felt. Last Friday mass arrests of Jews in Moscow were reported. Any Jews suspected of having had any contact with people abroad at any time were taken into custody, and it is feared they may be exiled to Siberia.

Last Sunday Jewish homes in East Berlin were raided by Communist police authorities and Jews were deprived of their identity documents, so that they could not leave their homes. A concentration camp has been set up in Thuringia, where freezing weather, starvation rations and electrified fences mock the victory of the Allied powers against the Nazis eight years ago.

The plea of the Jewish Agency was the cry of Jews everywhere, "Let the millions of Jews not be hostages without letting them out of the trap. Permit them to leave for the land which is waiting for them."

This reasonable appeal was seconded by the Zionist Organization of America last Sunday: "Whether or not they (the Communist governments) deliberately seek to restore the pogrom as an instrument of national policy, they are unleashing forces of hatred which may soon be uncontrollable. We call upon them to halt their present policy, while there may still be time to avert a major catastrophe. Moreover we declare, that if the so-called Jewish bourgeois elements and cosmopolitans are undesirable to those who dictate the policies of the Soviet bloc, they should be permitted to emigrate to Israel. Indeed, the Zionist movement would gladly undertake to carry out such a transfer en masse, if only the countries within the Soviet Orbit would agree to it. Let them go to Israel, where they will be warmly welcomed."

So matters rest tonight. Once again in our generation we are pleading for the release of Jewish hostages being ground inexorably between the millstones of deliberately fanned hatred and impassable walls. Once again we are fearful to the point of hysteria that Jewish blood will be shed, if not in one great mass murder, then in long, torturous years of slave labor, starvation and exile. No wonder that our young people are bewildered, frightened and full of questions as to how such things can happen.

Now why do I bring these matters to your attention? Because I know you too are concerned and apprehensive there are some cautions I would give you and some lessons we must learn. The cautions I would give have to do with our own personal reaction. I have detected an appalling reaction in some quarters. There are Jews who are very self-righteous and feel that this terrible iron noose represents the deserved punishment of those Jews who made themselves a part of Communist Russia, little realizing that for many there was no choice, and for others it seemed to promise the end of the very anti-Jewish crimes we are now bemoaning.

There are other Jews who feel that the present situation has opened the eyes of Communist sympathizers outside Russia to the true duplicity of the Soviet regime and they may well be right.

There are still other Jews who in their heart of hearts are saying, "If these Jews suffer, it will prove to the Western world that Jews are not really Communists, and therefore my own position is more secure!" This is not only a cruel and a vicious reaction but a misleading and misguided one.

The attacks against Jews in Communist countries for the crime of being capitalist sympathizers will not prevent attacks against Jews in capitalist countries for being Communist sympathizers. Such a result would have to be based upon reason and logic. Anti-Semitism is not today and has never been reasonable and logical. It has always been a blind and blinding hatred of the Jew seeking any pretext to result in murderous action, and it is the same kind of hatred today. Despite the fact, now clearly established, that Jews are considered unsafe risks in Communist leadership, the tempo of accusations against Jews as being unsafe risks in Western lands is still accelerating. No good comes to Jews anywhere when Jews suffer elsewhere, and there is no comfort for us here in the death of Jews at the hands of the Kremlin.

These are the cautions I would give. Now as to the lessons, hard, bitter lessons we must learn at, I pray, not too great a cost in human misery. The big question in the mind of many people who have concerned themselves little with affairs in Russia and her satellites is, "How could these lands which professed to outlaw anti-Semitism and protect the Jews in their very constitutions, suddenly produce so violent and vindictive a campaign against Jews?"

And the answer comes now out of the terrifying black lines of the news dispatches: the anti-Semitism of the Slavic peoples was not arrested by the Communist regime. It simply became a part of Soviet policy, a platform of the party line, to suppress that anti-Semitism. Had the people of those lands actually been taught the lessons of brotherly love, of the dignity and the rights of man had they washed from their hearts the black stains of hatred still there from the pogroms of the turn of the twentieth century, the flames now threatening to consume the Jews could not have been fanned alive so precipitously.

But there were no such lessons. There was simply a national discipline. To be loyal was to tolerate the Jews. The moment the party policy shifts, the moment to be loyal means to attack the Jews, all the latent smoldering, deep-rooted prejudices flare up with even greater force than ever before. That has happened in these last two months. And it has taught us, that the totalitarian climate is not safe for Jews, be its name fascism, Nazism, or Communism. The only climate in which Jews may live and work in security is the democratic environment in which the rights and the dignity of every human being are held sacred, in which there is freedom of thought and expression, freedom to worship, freedom from want and from fear. Wherever we live, we must work for that kind of society, not only for our own security, but for the good of the world.

Until we achieve that kind of world, what is going to happen? I fear, my friends, that we must prepare for days of trial ahead. The Iron Noose is drawing tighter and may very possibly claim its victims before our very eyes while we stand impotently by and are unable to help. Protestations are being made before the United Nations, but they fall on deaf ears. And I do not believe the western world is prepared to go to war to save the Jews now trapped, any more than it was prepared to go to war to save the six million from Hitler. I believe it holds two and a half million more Jewish lives expendable rather than risk the many millions more who would surely die in this atomic age. Therefore our one slender hope rests upon the whim of the Kremlin. A policy so swiftly reversed could be reversed again with equal swiftness. This is admittedly a slender hope indeed, but upon that slender thread hangs the fate of all those Jewish lives. And if not, then Russia has nailed the first peg in her own coffin.

Let us pray as fervently and earnestly as we ever have that the march of recent events will be reversed and these lives will be spared not because they are Jewish lives, albeit far estranged from us, but because, as human beings innocent of the charges leveled against them, they evoke our pity. May God spare them and rescue them from the pit, for if they are saved it will mean a change of heart by their enemies which will mean hope for all mankind. Every day let us pray for their lives, morning and night, for our generation has endured more than its share of martyrdom, and the soil of the earth calls not for more blood or human sacrifice, but for the plowshare and the pruning fork to bring peace and plenty to a weary world.

JUNE 6, 1944 AND 1967

As I faced the congregation on Friday evening, June 6,1967 for the Sabbath service, I was emotionally drained and yet riding high on adrenaline for the lightning Six Day War of June, 1967, had come to a stunning, triumphant end for Israel. Earlier, on Tuesday of that week, the Israeli soldiers broke through to the Western Wall of the ancient Temple, and the war was essentially over.

I was obsessed all that week with the contrast between June 6, 1944, and June 6, 1967, a mere 23 years apart but light years distant in their impact upon the Jewish people. My euphoria must have been apparent to the congregation as I tried to engrave those dates on their memory.

JUNE 9, 1967

Dear Friends,

June 6, 1944, was D-Day, when the greatest armada ever assembled in all of history crossed the English Channel to launch the assault against Nazi-fortified Europe at Normandy. After long, hard, bloody and bitter battles this landing led to the ultimate collapse of Hitler and the opening of the death camps where the starved and tormented remnants of European Jewry languished.

June 6,1967, this past Tuesday, was the day which marked the end of the Six Day War for all practical purposes, when the first Israeli soldiers reached the Western Wall of the Temple Mount in Jerusalem and blew the shofar there in thanksgiving and in triumph.

The world, had settled down in resignation to watch helpless little Israel be ground up by enemies on three sides and spat into the sea on the fourth. Suddenly the world sat up and cried out that mighty Israel had become a relentless and efficient military machine with the world's best air force. They cried that this mighty Israel should cease and desist forthwith and spare the totally demoralized and beaten enemy troops she dominated.

What a contrast! In June 1944, the Nazi murderers were accelerating the speed of genocide. In dozens of camps, some of which are scratched into Temple Beth Am's memorial wall, and all of which are seared into our memories, our Jewish brothers and sisters lay stacked like firewood: the living, the dead and the half alive. There seemed no hope whatsoever of stopping Hitler before he carried out his repeated threat to murder every last Jew in Europe and cast his eyes westward in the hope of repeating his carnage here.

How vividly do I recall on D-Day, I was the rabbi of the Forest Hills Jewish Center in Queens, New York. We had known an invasion of Europe would be launched, but we didn't know if it would be in time to save any of our people. Our congregational honor roll of sons and daughters in military service was long and punctuated with the gold stars which marked the names of youngsters who would never come back.

Week after week I received telegrams which I was to carry to the home of a member family. Then I attempted to ease the incredible pain of parents who were first learning that their beautiful soldier was dead.

In Jamaica, Long Island, I stood with aging members of the Jewish War Veterans of America, listening to brown-shirted Americans screaming epithets against Jews. They claimed that it was the Jews who kidnapped the son of the pioneer airman, Charles Lindbergh, ground up his flesh and used it for *haroset*.

So it was with full awareness of what D-Day would mean in terms of new telegrams and new gold stars, but also with the slim hope that Hitler might be stopped before he poisoned the world that we gathered on that Tuesday, June 6, 1944, in our synagogue and prayed with a fervor I have rarely felt since until Tuesday, June 6, 1967, when the tide of battle was turned by the repossession of the Western Wall in Jerusalem.

Again and again we assembled in prayer this week, volunteered our money and our persons. We sat every spare moment glued to the radio and the television. Would the Arabs, as they had constantly boasted, complete the work of total extermination of the Jews which had been initiated by Adolph Hitler? We agonized for our Israeli brethren, many of whom had been among the tattered survivors of the Holocaust. Now they were under attack again in the very land of their refuge.

But when that Shofar sounded at the regained wall, when Ben Gurion tore down the street sign that said in three languages "Wailing Wall" and proclaimed, "No more wailing here!," suddenly the self-respect and self-confidence which had lain dormant for 1897 years were reawakened, and we wore them like an invisible badge of pride.

What a contrast between those two June 6ths! In 1944 we were either the objects of insane hatred, of pity or of horror over what had happened to us, of despair that of the 16 million Jews in the world only 10 million survived, three million of them in Russia. In 1967, there was talk of a mighty military machine, little David beating up on poor oversized Goliath, begged by the U.N. to stop and not cut off the giant's head.

It was reminiscent of the contrast between the slaves who left Egypt and were fearful of the mighty peoples of Canaan and of the armies of Joshua 40 years later, who struck terror into the hearts of the Canaanite tribes. Then, 1944, it was the storming of the cliffs of Normandy to save the remnants of our people, and to save the rest of the western world, too, because, unchecked, Hitler might have been in New York and in Los Angeles. Now it was the moment of reaching the Western Wall, the Kotel, for which we had dreamed and prayed so long. It was not only an unbelievable military victory, but a psychological, religious and political victory as well.

It is Shabbat morning now in Israel, and I can just imagine people running to exercise their right for the first time since 1948, to pray at the Kotel. Placing their hands against the stones cold from the night air, and replacing the morning dew with human tears, they must surely be breaking into the blessing in which we can actually join them because it is 1967 and not 1944. We can say with astonishment of heart and an overflowing measure of gratitude:

ברוך אתה יי אלהינו מלך העולם, שהחינו וקימנו והיגיענו לזמן הזה

Blessed art Thou, O Lord our God, King of the Universe, who hast kept us alive and sustained us, and enabled us to reach this great moment in time!

THE MASSACRE AT LOD AIRPORT

Tuesday, May 30, 1972, the bubble of euphoria which followed the enormous military and moral victory of the Six-Day War was burst when three Japanese mercenaries sprayed the crowded Lod Airport terminal near Tel Aviv with machine gun bullets and grenades, slaughtering 26 persons and wounding another 81.

The first opportunity to react to this outrage was during the Sabbath eve service when I not only responded bitterly to the tragic turn of events but was moved to place this latest atrocity alongside the many others which preceded it. Our hopes that this was the last straw which would break the back of terrorism by reason of a universal outcry against it were soon dashed by the slaying of 11 of Israel's top athletes at the Munich Olympics.

JUNE 2, 1972

Dear Friends

In the portion of the Haftarah this morning, the Prophet Zechariah speaks to the generation of Israelites who have returned to their homeland after two generations of exile in Babylonia. The rebuilding of Zion has not been easy. Their neighbors roundabout are hostile and life has been difficult. At that moment Zecharaiah arises to offer them hope and a program for overcoming their problems and their enemies. His program remains our ideal to this day: **לא בחיל ולא בכח, כי אם ברוחי אמר יי צבאות**, "Not by might nor by power, but by My spirit, saith the Lord of Hosts." (Zech. IV:6)

Today, 2,492 years later, the children of Israel have returned to their homeland after a hundred generations of exile in all four corners of the Earth. Again, the rebuilding of Zion has not been easy. Again, their neighbors roundabout are hostile and life has been difficult. Zecharaiah's program of not relying on armed conflict is again challenged, and this week in history has severly tested it again.

Five years ago this week, Sunday night, June 4, 1967–the days fall this year exactly as they did then–we listened to the late news and heard to our consternation that it was already eight o'clock Monday, June 5, in Israel and war had broken out in the Sinai Peninsula between Egypt and Israel; Jordan, Syria, Iraq, Lebanon joined the fray. By Saturday, June 10, it was all over. All the while, Israel fought alone. The United Nations was silent after having triggered the war by withdrawing its peace-keeping mission at Egypt's demand. The Catholic Church was silent. The friendly nations did nothing and the enemy nations screamed death to the Jews.

Five years have elapsed. Nasser is gone, but Sadat rules in Egypt, an Egypt rearmed and better equipped by far than in 1967. Arab voices call for holy war. The Koran is invoked to vilify the Jew. In April, King Feisal of Saudia Arabia, addressing foreign journalists, blamed the Jews for every misfortune of history. He said the Jews were responsible for the Crusades, the Mongolian invasion, World War I, World War II and the war between India and Pakistan. He then accused us of an eternal conspiracy to dominate the world. He said we created Communism, imperialism, the rotary clubs and Freemasonry, and reminded the world that Jews are still using Gentile blood in the baking of matzot.

Sadat, not to be outdone, quoted the Koran in which Mohammed describes the Jews as "a mean and treacherous people." This is the Sadat who, in 1942, acted as a go-between for two Nazi agents who came to his home in Cairo dressed as British officers to establish a spy center there for Hitler. This is the Sadat who, in 1953, was one of the officers who advised Nasser on how to wage war against the Jews.

That is when the scurrilous "Protocols of the Elder of Zion," a European anti-Semitic classic became a standard work of Arab socialism. It was in that year, 1953, that Sadat was quoted in a Cairo weekly, to the effect that if Hitler suddenly rose from the dead, he would say to him, "Dear Hitler, I welcome you back with all my heart...You are eternal and we shall not be surprised to see you again, or a second Hitler, back in Germany."

Today, he heads the Egyptian government, and his anti-Semitic tone has not softened. On April 25, this year, the birthday of Mohammed, Sadat spoke in these words, and I quote them not to dignify them but to establish the background for the infamous slaughter at the Lod Airport on Tuesday of this week:

"I declare here, on this anniversary, that the dreams and the elation from the conceit of victory which they now talk about and which they thought they achieved in 1967 and will continue to maintain forever. I tell them on this anniversary and from this place: we will not give up one inch of our territory and we will not negotiate with Israel under any circumstance and we will not bargain over any right of the Palestinian people...I promised you that last year. This year, I pledge to you that we will celebrate on the

next anniversary, God willing, and in this place with God's help, not only the liberation of our land but also the defeat of the Israeli conceit and arrogance so that they may once again return to the condition decreed in our holy book: 'Humiliation and abasement has been stamped on them'...We will not renounce this. The matter is no longer our honor, dignity and the message in which we believe. We shall turn them back to what they were. If they thought that they had suddenly secured some strength, we shall turn them back because strength does not come from weapons, as I have said, the strength of the individual, the strength of faith in the message, faith in ideology and faith in principle..."

The fanaticism demonstrated by this speech reached its most despicable expression when three Japanese-hired terrorists claimed their baggage at Lod Airport near Tel Aviv, opened their suitcases, assembled their sub-machine guns, took their grenades, and then in cold blood sprayed their bullets over arriving passengers and awaiting Israelis, indiscriminately slaughtering 26 and wounding over 81. Two of them then committed suicide, while the third is in custody. Twelve Puerto Rican Christian pilgrims along with Israelis and European Jews died there and in Tel Hashomer hospital. The Palestine Liberation Front takes credit and promises an escalation of such incidents. And Sadat said, "This proves that Israeli military supremacy is a myth."

This outrage extracted from Prime Minister Golda Meir a tearful burst of mournful eloquence I wish you to hear, since I have abused your ears with the lies and venom of Sadat. This Jewish grandmother rose before the Knesset in Jerusalem on Wednesday and spoke as follows:

"The Arabs in the terrorist organizations found a way, not only to kill and wreak bloodshed, but also to do so by emissaries. And all this in the name of war against imperialism. What did the Japanese who was apprehended say? 'World revolution.' We betide such 'world revolution' and local revolution, built on bloodshed and based on murder for its own sake.

"As soon as the news of what happened broke, joy broke out in Cairo and in Beirut as well over the 'great victory.' Dozens of people killed and scores of others wounded and there is no end to the rejoicing. Those who were unable to stand up against us on the battlefield are great heroes at hiding explosives in planes, at assaults on planes and passengers and in their readiness to blow up a plane with a hundred people aboard - as they did two years ago in the 'Swissair' disaster. This indeed takes great 'courage.' And if the little 'courage' needed for that is lacking, foreigners are recruited for the purpose; still, the joy is great...

"We shall do everything that can be done, but I have not the slightest doubt that unless other governments and airlines will cooperate and consider this as their concern, and not merely for our sake, the scourge shall remain to plague all."

And, indeed, Golda Meir is so right, because only a few hours ago, Western Airlines Flight 701 from Phoenix to Seattle was hijacked with a demand for money and the release of Angela Davis.

The frustration of these days make the recourse to violent retaliation and counter-retaliation a tempting release for all the pent-up anger and righteous indignation we legitimately feel. And still, across the bridge of centuries, in the voice of a young bat mitzvah comes Zechariah's gentle reminder:

לא בחיל ולא בכח, כי אם ברוחי אמר יי צבאות, "Not by might nor by power, but by My spirit, saith the Lord of Hosts." (Zech. IV:6)

There must come a time when the armaments stockpiled give way to arms outstretched in fraternal embrace. Every pistol shot, every cannon roar, every bomb fragmenting is a waste of the divine economy and the purpose of man and only delays the true final solution which is not death but life, not the power and might of armies, but the spirit of goodness and truth and love God has breathed into us.

This week has been another setback in the quest for a peaceful solution to man's dilemma. As it ends we pray that reason will break through the walls of hate that divide Vietnam and Korea, and the Middle East and the races of America. In the week that lies ahead let us renew our pursuit of true peace but for now, let our indignation give way to sympathy for those innocently and senselessly slain in Lod and Ireland and Vietnam and the dark recesses of this land and let us rise and say Kaddish for them all.

MURDER AT MUNICH

Again, in 1972, a grievous blow was struck against Israelis and the morale of Israel. Still reeling from the Lod massacre, but proud of the Israeli athletes who represented her at the 1972 Olympic games in Munich, the Jewish people everywhere were plunged into despair and rage by the capture and slaying of their finest. The ironic location of the tragedy in the city of Munich evoked bitter memories of the birth of the Nazi beast in that very place.

Before dawn Tuesday, September 5, 1972, Arab terrorists struck the Israeli dormitory in the Olympic village and by the end of another 23 hours, 11 athletes had been murdered.

That Shabbat, September 9, ushered in the Jewish year 5743. It was impossible to ignore the tragedy so in my sermon I attempted to place the awful moment in the context of the ongoing hostilities which have consistently challenged us. To American Jews searching for a constructive way to give economic and moral support to Israel, I recommended investment in bonds of the State of Israel .

SEPTEMBER 9, 1972

Dear Friends:

I need your prayers today, need them desperately, your prayers for me that I may have the wisdom and the words that this moment in history demands. I am emotionally wrung out, all but bankrupt in spirit. I have not yet recovered from the initial shock of my dear father's death three weeks ago today and from the exhaustion of the week of Shivah. My mother sits alone for the first time, and my responsibilities keep me from sitting next to her in the seat my father occupied since this building was dedicated, comforting her and letting her comfort me. I am tired of being strong for everybody and crave the luxury of being weak and dependent for once.

This was my mood when the first unbelievable news broke of the capture of the 11 Israeli athletes in Building 31 at the Olympic village, and the murder of the first two. Since Tuesday, I have stumbled in a daze because as it happens to everyone sometime, I have reached the end of my inner resources for this moment the very time when I know you, too, are dependent and need a spiritual lift from me. And so I say, "I need your prayers today, so that I can measure up to the staggering task that faces me in moving you to new heights of solidarity with our Jewish brothers everywhere, when they are cast down to such depths of sorrow and trouble!"

You will be reading such a prayer in the Musaf service: "Our God and God of our fathers, inspire the lips of those who have been appointed by Thy people the house of Israel to stand in prayer before Thee. Teach them what to say, instruct them what to speak. לאדם מערכי לב ומיי מענה לשון The preparation of the heart is the concern of man, but the gift of speech comes from the Lord."

Pray for me. Like every other rabbi in the world, my happy sermon ushering in the 25th year of the State of Israel, lies in the wastebasket, together with the shattered pieces of the pretty plastic bubble that was the 20th Olympic games. I wanted to speak of the beauty and the achievements of Israel as Margie and I saw them once again six months ago, with our own eyes and through the eyes of our children, Judy, Danny and Beverly.

But everything positive and hopeful has once again been vomited upon by the events of this week; all our pride in Israel's calm strength, her fantastic growth, her sacrificial absorption of 17,000 Russian Jews this year so far, her expectation that the figure will reach 30,000, her preparations for a joyful celebration of her first quarter century of rebirth! It is all spoiled, soured for a moment when our Rosh Hashanah exultation should be running over. I wanted so to share a message of pride and beauty and happiness with you, enough tears, enough fears.

Instead, my grieving friends, let me share the racing thoughts this week's events evoked in me. I turned my attention reluctantly toward Munich when this week began, reluctantly, because for me Munich evokes memories of the beer hall where Adolph Hitler ימח שמו came in September, 1919, to a rally of the German Worker's Party and conceived the idea of rising to power on a tide of condemnation of the Jews for Germany's World War I defeat and humiliation.

In November of 1923, in Munich, he tried (unsuccessfully) his first putsch or revolution to seize authority in the state of Bavaria. He chose Munich for a meeting with British Prime Minister Neville Chamberlain, French Premier Edouard Daladier and Italian Duce Benito Mussolini on September 29, 1938. There, the infamous dismemberment of Czechoslovakia was agreed to by England and France, and Hitler's first great bluff succeeded. Chamberlain returned to wave the paper agreement gleefully from the windows of 10 Downing Street and shouted, "I believe it is peace in our time." Instead, the agreement set the stage for World War II.

It was ten miles outside of Munich that the death camp of Dachau was established in 1933. It swallowed up hundreds of thousands of Jewish victims. Where the rows of prison buildings stood, all is neat and grassy now. It was to Dachau last week that the visitors to the Olympiad were invited to view the memorial there, to read the inscription: "For the dead, honor, for the living, a warning," to see the inscription on the monument, "Never Again" in four languages and hear the archbishop intone the names of all the other death camps, the same names we have on our memorial wall here.

Unfortunately, only 50 athletes out of the 122 national teams participating showed up at the memorial service, but then, as Britain's Olympic captain Lynn Davies said, "an emotional visit around a former concentration camp was not the best preparation for athletes on the eve of the games."

Anyway, this Munich was to be the site of clean, pure athletic competition for the next few days. It had very much to do with us in this very room today, as we shall see, again and again.

In only the first of the many bitter ironies of this week, however, that we all watched while Mark Spitz, an American Jew, broke seven world records and won seven gold medals. I looked at that strong, handsome, tanned body slashing through the water and heard the roar of the crowds that hailed him and I thought, "Thirty years ago, this boy might have huddled, his arm tattooed, his body a sick and bony bundle of rags on a wooden shelf in one of those Dachau blockhouses, as some of you in this room did, with no medals, no cheering crowds." I didn't know whether to gloat over his conquest of that whole Olympiad or be ashamed that he went there in the first place.

And then, it happened. At almost 5 a.m., Tuesday, the Arab terrorists scaled the Olympic Village fence, came to Building 31 and knocked. Dr. Weigel, the Israeli team physician, opened the door. The Arabs shot and instantly killed Moshe Weinberg, wrestling coach and Yosef Romano, the weight lifter, who tried to block their entry. The next 23 hours we all watched and listened, fearful and still hopeful. After all, the people who had administered Dachau and the other camps so efficiently could surely stop these gangsters somehow. But no, this time efficiency lost to savagery. At Furstenfeldbruck Airport the nine others died. The games marked time for one day and then resumed. Now the search for whom to blame goes on. Millions of words have been written and spoken, but the 11 men are dead.

I tried to analyze my own shock. Why was I so deeply distressed? This is neither new nor unexpected. It was in the shadow of Dachau, after all. Nor was it the first time Arabs have slaughtered Jews. What of the ambushing of buses in the 1920's and 30's? What of the nightly raids on the early border settlements? And the bloody attack of 1948? And the hundreds killed since by land mines and booby traps, in school buses, in the supermarket in Jerusalem, in the cafeteria at Hebrew University, the bus depot in Tel Aviv?

And how long ago did the Arab terrorists hijack great jets and, incidentally, how many times did the alert Israeli guards outwit them only to have the International Red Cross cry, "Foul play?"

Wasn't it only this past May 30 that three Arab-hired Japanese gunmen sprayed Lod Airport with bullets and left 26 dead, 80 wounded. There wasn't such great shock as this! Protests were feeble and self-seeking, as, for example, Pope Paul VI's message of consolation that expressed the hope that "people may return to being civilized and good and more Christian."

Why am I shocked, when at this very moment new and frightening developments face our brethren in Russia? Suddenly last month we learned that Russia has placed an incredible exit tax on educated Jews wishing to emigrate to Israel. Until now, each Russian Jew leaving lost his job first, and paid 940 rubles, about $1,000, for the privilege of leaving.

Now a price list has been set up which forces people with educational degrees to pay huge sums for exit, supposedly in repayment for the education they received, with a 35 to 45 percent special duty tax on top of it as a transfer surcharge. So a high school graduate must pay about $7,000, a science graduate $20,000, and a doctor or professor $36,000. The family of Victor Perelman, a Moscow journalist, applied for exit visas. He lost his job, and is being asked for more than $50,000 for the family, an obvious impossibility.

If such a ransom were paid it would have cost $100 million this year and $150 million next year. From Moscow Victor Perelman pleads, "Don't pay it. If these demands are met it will doom thousands of Russian Jews to wait as pariahs for ransom money from abroad." He writes it will affect future applicants. "Maybe we'll have a chance to go, but what will they say if we condemn them to years as unsold slaves because of the egotistic and hasty decisions on our part?" (*Observer*, 9-1-72, pg. 5).

Let me bring home what this means in an average family. A boy is now in high school. If he goes to college he is heading for a ransom cost of

$15,000 or more. If he goes to a technical school it will only be $8,000. If he enlists in the army instead of going on to college, his ransom will be much smaller, but then he cannot leave Russia for at least five years after finishing military service. What should he do?

Meanwhile, Jewish activists are being arrested, tried and convicted of various crimes or else declared psychotic and sent to mental institutions. Outside Potma prison in Siberia, a new large concentration camp is being built. Russian Jewry feels trapped.

Apparently Russians and Jews alike were waiting to see how forcefully the United States would press the Jewish issue during President Nixon's summit meeting with Brezhnev this past May. Apparently, too, it was not forceful enough because soon thereafter Russia adopted a harder line toward her Jewish citizens. There seems to be a feeling that the West doesn't care deeply about Jewish freedom within Russia and that Jewish unrest there can be crushed with impunity. The race is on, then, to see how many can get out and get to Israel before the mounting tide of anti-Semitism rolls over them.

So it comes back to Israel's capacity to absorb new immigrants, as many as humanly possible, and that possibility brings us back to this room again for nothing happens in Munich, in Moscow, in Lod or in Jerusalem that does not have its repercussions right here in these walls.

We had astonishing demonstrations of those repercussions during Israel Expo West,[1] touching, informative, and frightening. Remember the Jerusalem walls and gates we erected at our entrance? One night before Expo opened we walked out and saw little notes stuck in the chinks of the wall, just as our people do in the Kotel, the Western Wall, in Jerusalem.

There were prayers on them, prayers for peace, for love, for health, one even said, "Please God, send me a man," and it was signed. Elderly people came and stayed all day, saying rather wistfully, "This is probably as close as I'll ever get to Israel." The very outpouring of overflow crowds told the message of how deeply our people care about Israel.

And we learned an even more important lesson from Israel. It happened the last day of Expo. At four o'clock, a phone message came to the switchboard, "There's a bomb in the building. Die, Jew."

Suddenly, this wasn't imitation Israel. We were on her frontiers. We called the police and searched the building even as the crowds grew. At five the voice called again. "There's a bomb, and it goes off at nine." We

---

1. A week-long Israel Exposition attended by 50,000 people in our Temple.

asked the police, "Should we close down?"

"We can't advise you. That's your decision."

"We can't put 5,000 people on this pavement. Can we close off La Cienega and evacuate into the street?"

"No, you can't do that."

At 5:15 came the third call. "Nine o'clock."

Temple President Berg went out to inspect the telephone booths around La Cienega where someone might be watching and waiting, but there was no sign of anyone.

At six o'clock, the fourth call came. We took hasty council. Should we close down and cancel the Ron Eliran concerts which would bring 2,400 more people into these buildings?

A small group of officers discussed it. Could we take a chance with so many people's lives? To the lasting credit of our men, they said, "Rabbi, if we close tonight, why can't they threaten us into closing tomorrow night and Sunday morning and whenever they choose? This is an Israel fair. The Israelis live in constant jeopardy, but they keep going. Let's be like Israelis for once and not give in to threats!"

"But," they added, "you have to realize that while we're men enough to take responsibility for the decision, in the end the buck rests with you, Rabbi."

At eight o'clock I threw myself down on the steps by the Ark, and I prayed to God for an answer. I say it now, I say it just once and without embellishments. As I lay there in my head I heard the words, "Better to die on your feet than live on your knees."

I said, "We go. We stay open."

And something wonderful happened. In place of fear, a great peace, even happiness, came over the faces our people who knew the problem. Nobody left. We told Ron Eliran, the Israeli, and he just laughed and went on tuning up. At nine o'clock, one eye on my watch, I stood and announced the winners of our trip to Israel. At midnight we closed the greatest experience in our lives. We had lived by the courageous standards of the Israelis whom our Exposition had honored.

But there isn't that much difference between us. What happens to our people anywhere affects us. Once again, Wednesday evening, I learned that. All day people had been on the talk shows, offering consolation to Israel or spewing irrational hateful vicious lies. On my desk there appeared a strange package, brown paper crudely addressed to Rabbi, La Cienega. I opened it and inside was a smaller package, beautifully gift wrapped, and on it a little white card, in Arabic. I wasn't about to open it. I called the police. The men in the patrol car wouldn't touch it either and sent for the bomb experts. They came and opened my gift from the Arabs. It turned out to be human excrement wrapped in toilet tissue. What happened in Munich touched this building.

Yesterday the terrorists boasted they have men all over the United States and they will attack American Jewish leaders at will, as if the 11 dead, innocent athletes were not enough disgrace on their record.

My friends, there is no sure defence against such terror other than a self-respecting, courageous stand. The Russians may wish us quiet and unprotesting, the Arabs might wish us to vanish suddenly from the face of the earth, but we owe it to those who perished in the blood bath which began in Munich with Hitler and had its latest chapter in Munich with the terrorist members of Black September; we owe it to those brave Russian Jews who are staking their livelihood and their very lives on our ability to get them out somehow, we owe it to brave Israel that has restored our self-respect to us and taught us how to stand up to barbarians.

We owe it to Golda Meir, who has wept over every fallen Israeli as only a mother can weep, and just buried her own sister yesterday to crown her grief; and we owe it to the 11 souls represented by these 11 candles of mourning to put meaning into our mourning by establishing bonds with Israel as never before. What a hollow mockery it would be if we let them toss away their young lives without endowing their sacrifice with tremendous significance. Consul Carmel said it Thursday. "This is no more time for words. It is time for deeds."

Edmund Burke said it earlier and I want it to ring in your ears and your heart. "All that is necessary for evil to triumph is for good men to do nothing."

Today I implore you. Strike back against those who would love to see Israel falter and her friends fail her. Strike back not with bullets like those savages, but with bonds, bonds to help Israel stay afloat, bonds to help Israel defeat the poverty and unrest that plague some of her people, bonds to help Israel settle those Russian Jews who have already come, bonds to enable Israel to accept those who, God willing, will soon come, bonds to say to Israel, "We are here, under the נר תמיד , the Eternal Light which rivals the Olympic Torch."

Let us say that to Israel louder and clearer than ever before. I know you. You are good people, but if even good people do nothing, evil will triumph.

I began with a personal note. May I conclude with one. My dear mother, whom some of you know as a sweet lady, not too strong, who leaned heavily on my dear father, k'z ,has very little security, but she said to me, "This year, in spite of everything, I have to buy a bond. Israel needs all the help we can give!" And so, Mom, God bless you. I give you the honor of the first purchase, which will not be the largest one today, but in my opinion, the dearest. And may I follow you by buying a hundred dollar bond for each of the 11 victims of the Munich Massacre, and one more for a dear, sweet man I miss today, my dad.

One last observation. In that Olympic Village apartment where the Israeli team stayed, there was a distance walker named Shaul Lodany. When that early morning knock came at the door, instinctively, he fled out the back door and survived. Why? Because he remembered another morning knock on the door of his home in Hungary in 1944, when he was only eight. It was the Nazis, who entered, and took him and his entire family to Bergen-Belsen so when he heard the knock on the door in the dead of night, he knew and he fled.

The knock on the door that strikes fear into the Jewish heart, we heard it in Czarist Russia, in Nazi Germany, again in Communist Russia, and now in Munich. The day must come when a Jewish child can grow up without that built-in alarm device that says "*Run mi shlagt Yidden*. They are smiting Jews." Let us move toward that day by strengthening Israel with our bonds, Israel that has stiffened the backbone of Russian Jewry and given you and me a new defiant self-respect. We have wept enough this week. The time is here for us to act. Even those people among us who have never yet bought an Israel bond, isn't this the time to begin? Even those who have bought substantially before, isn't this the time to add more dollars for the Russian Jewry exodus?

I prayed earlier for the power to move you. If I have failed, let not Israel suffer thereby. Let those 11 silent candles kindle a fire within you and stir you to invest in life for our people over there and self-respect for ourselves here.

DO YOU KNOW WHAT, AMIN?
THE ISRAELI RAID ON ENTEBBE

On July 4, 1976, America's bicentennial Independence Day, the most memorable expression of defiance against tyranny was the "impossible" mission by Israel to Uganda. Israelis raided the airport, rescued 105 hostages taken by terrorists and flew them to the safety of Israel.

The world had known that their Air France flight had been hijacked by two German and two Arabs, and the world did nothing. Who could confront the cruel dictator, Idi Amin on his own land and snatch hostages under his very nose?

Israel could and did, and won the grudging admiration of much of the Western world. On this Yizkor, we reflected upon Israel's heroism and Israel's vulnerability and once again challenged Diaspora Jews to shoulder their share of the ongoing struggle of Israel to achieve true peace and security.

OCTOBER 4, 1976

Dear Friends:

Fascinating is the word for the Book of Jonah, four little chapters, 48 verses in all. It has fascinated more commentators than its total number of verses. What is the point of this book? Its point is that to be a Jew means to feel compelled to get involved with one's fellow-man. It means to care. It means to have a strong sense of one's own unique identity. The Jew has no difficulty knowing who he is.

The Book of Jonah begins with a powerful, unforgettable affirmation of identity. When Jonah, trying to escape his prophetic duty of confronting the city of Nineveh with an accusation of its collective wickedness, took a ship at Jaffa to run away to Tarshish, a terrible storm threatened to swamp the ship. The frightened sailors believed that Jonah had brought a curse upon the ship, and so they found and questioned him, and to all their questions he gave one answer. They asked, "מה מלאכתך, What is your profession?"

He answered, "עברי אנכי, I am a Hebrew."

"ומאין תבוא, Where do you come from?"

"עברי אנכי I am a Hebrew."

"מה ארצך From what land?"

"עברי אנכי I am a Hebrew."

"ואי מזה עם אתה From what people?"

"עברי אנכי I am a Hebrew."

"Who are you?"

"עברי אנכי ואת יי אלהי השמים אני ירא I am a Hebrew and I revere the Lord, God of heaven."

"I am a Jew," was his reply, "That is my profession! That is my people! That is my country!"

In a sense what you and I have affirmed by our presence here today is what Jonah affirmed, עברי אנכי "I am a Jew," and that affirmation has been sharpened by the swift events of these past few months. We have a new measure of time, we are no longer in the Hitler era, we are no longer in the post-World War II era. This is the era of post-Entebbe Israel, which has replaced post-Yom Kippur War Israel, which replaced post Six-Day War Israel.

The post-Entebbe era means it comes more easily, more proudly to say עברי אנכי "I am a Jew," because to be a Jew now means to be one of those who dared mightily. That audacious operation, first called "Operation Thunderbolt" but renamed "Operation Yonaton," has become the symbol of resistance to blackmail and terrorism.

It all began when an Air France liner was hijacked by terrorists (two German, Gabrielle Krock-Tiedemann and Wilfried Boese; and two Arabs from the Peoples Front for the Liberation of Palestine). The four were financed by Libya and welcomed by Uganda.

The world greeted the news with a yawn. The United Nations had better things to do than worry about a mere 105 Jews so they went back to speeches attacking Israelis and by association, Jews everywhere, as racists and voted another resolution condemning Israel and demanding she give back occupied territories.

But Jews could not yawn because there was one special element in this hijacking that struck at the freedom of Jews everywhere. When first captured, Air France Flight 139 had 253 persons aboard, but then some were released. The two Germans began to pass judgment by rule of thumb once again. They reviewed the passengers for Israeli and Jewish names and, with a jerk of the thumb, directed the Jews to one side to remain as hostages.

It was the selection of the concentration camps all over again. As one of the hostages, a concentration camp survivor, wrote in her diary, "I felt I was back 32 years ago. The Germans were giving their orders and waving guns. I could just imagine the shuffling lines of the Nazi concentration camp. I could hear the harsh cries, 'Jews to right,' and the world was still silent."

Once again it was Jonah (1:8,9) "עברי אנכי, Where do you come from? מה ארצך What is your land? ואי-מזה עם אתה And from what people?" And once again the answer was עברי אנכי, I am a Jew.

And then on July 4th, in the early dawn, the news flashed out: from under the very nose of Ugandan boss President Idi Amin, his captives had been rescued. It was "Mission Impossible" carried off in real life. It was electrifying.

Despite what the United Nations representatives said, the people of the world were excited and dared hope the time had come to end the reign of terrorism in travel.

My wife and I were in England a few days later. Even in that country which was overrun by Arabs buying up everything in sight, the people were ecstatic and outspoken. Let me share some of their letters:

A retired naval officer in Somerset wrote, "In this age of the mediocre, the soft option of self-preservation at all costs, your people have again personified courage, selflessness and daring, to make us lesser mortals gasp, and realize they too are men."

From Watsall came, "It must be a great comfort to the Israeli people to know that their government values them so highly as individuals. I am envious."

He undoubtedly had in mind the apologetic, half-hearted effort England made to demand the release of 75 year old Dora Block, a lady who held British citizenship together with her Israeli citizenship, a lady who had been ill in Uganda and was dragged screaming from her hospital bed to a forest where the cowardly Ugandans killed her and left her body to rot.

From Yorkshire, a Roman Catholic Sister of Mercy wrote, "I am a pacifist, but when violence is used, then I would rather it was the Israelis who used it, briefly, efficiently and with the least amount of violence possible."

And finally, from Aberdeenshire, "Should the Israeli resolution ever waver, I hope they will remember that the vast majority of people, as opposed to politicians, in this world support their actions against violence and blackmail 100 percent. The Israeli nation is an inspiration to us all."

Indeed, Israel has been an inspiration to us all and the post-Entebbe era has been marked by some wonderful news. First of all, her example seems to have put starch into the backbone of other nations. Egyptian paratroopers recaptured a hijacked Egypt lines; a Dutch plane was recovered from hijackers with the cooperation of Israel and Cyprus.

Then there was Israel's appearance at the Olympic games in Montreal last summer only days after the Entebbe incident. It would have been understandable if Israel had decided not to compete. There still hung over the Olympic games the black shadow of the murder in Munich of 11 Israeli athletes four years earlier. Now that the terrorist cause had lost face at Entebbe, perhaps they may have wanted to regain initiative by some murderous stunt at Montreal.

Nevertheless, a most popular expression in Israeli life is ואף על פי כן ולמרות הכל "Even though it is so, and in spite of everything," Israel sent a sizable contingent of athletes to Montreal. One of the thrills of my life was seeing the Israeli team come marching into the Olympic stadium and hearing the roar of spontaneous cheers that greeted their entry. And Israel was satisfied indeed that their soccer squad ranked eighth and that Esther Shachamorov-Roth, the only Israeli who had also been in the 1972 Olympics squad, came in sixth in the 100 meters swimming finale. As one lady at the supermarket enthused, "Just think of it - our Esther within three-tenths of a second of a gold medal."

Shortly after the major Olympics, there was an Olympiad for handicapped athletes in Toronto. There, too, Israel sent a delegation, being well-supplied with strong young veterans of their wars—40 wheelchair athletes, 17 amputees, six blind, who bore on their bodies the crippling evidence of their bravery. One Israeli paraplegic won the gold medal for featherweight weightlifting, but had to sleep over Friday night on a bench in the arena in order not to violate the Sabbath.

Another, Uri Bergman, whose legs are paralyzed, won the 100 meter free-style swim. Among six gold medals he earned, all were world records. In the 100-meter swim, he set a course record while beating Abdul Latif of Egypt, who came in second. When it came time for the awards, Uri appeared together with the third place winner, and the crowd wondered if the Egyptian would appear. There was an awkward pause, and then Abdul came out, stood next to Uri at attention as the flag for Israel was raised and the *Hatikvah* was sung. Then Abdul reached over and shook Uri's hand.

A little thing, perhaps, but to Israel, yearning for any sign of possibility of reconciliation with her hostile neighbors, it was a great moment.

But then, Israel was fifth in the Students Chess Olympics in Venezuela, and third in the Handicapped Olympiad, as I mentioned. Then there is one contest in which we placed first. The new Miss Universe is beautiful, *chenivdik* Rita Messenger of Tel Aviv University, Miss Israel.

There is still another contest in which Israel holds unchallenged leadership, and that is in humanity, compassion and genuine love of fellow man. Once again, Israel has demonstrated these qualities in what is popularly called the Good Fence between Israel and Lebanon. This is the fenced northern border of Israel. It was erected to keep out the murderous infiltrators who used to cross over into Israel from what only recently was called Fatah Land because it harbored the Palestinian terrorists. They came and bloodied Kiryat Shemoneh and Ma'alot and sniped at school busses and farmers in the field.

Now there are three openings in that fence. Since last April, some 7,000 Lebanese citizens, 4,000 Christians and 3,000 Moslems have crossed into Israel at Metulla, Dovev, and Hanita. Through the gates, which are opened each morning, stream the demoralized Lebanese seeking help in what used to be enemy territory. They are given a thorough security check and then proceed to the field infirmaries set up for their benefit.

Here are some typical cases. In the khaki-colored van, a doctor in lieutenant's uniform is working. He is on reserve duty and normally works at Chaim Sheba Medical Center at Tel Hashomer. Opposite him sits a slim woman in black with a small boy on her knee. The doctor prescribes medication for the boy's gastric infection, and then the woman, a Christian Arab, goes on to visit her father, who is in a hospital at Safed from a heart ailment.

Next comes in a man suffering from dizziness. He is the *mukhtar*, the head man, of a Moslem village 15 miles north of the Good Fence. Why has he come? He smiles and says, "Our own doctors have gone away and left us. A million people have left, including 60 percent of all Lebanese doctors. If it were not for the Israelis, we would simply die when we fell ill, but you see, Allah is kind."

Yes, Allah is kind, but Israel says, "עברי אנכי, I am a Jew," and a Jew is compassionate. So the Lebanese come. Hundreds are in Israeli hospitals, thousands treated in the border clinics. Since the Lebanese colleges are closed, some Lebanese are studying in Israel. Lebanese come through the Good Fence and buy food, fuel, water and medicine.

Recently, Gideon Rafael, Israel's ambassador to England received this note from a Lebanese nun, "I want to convey my grateful thanks to your country's generous hospitality and a promise of God's blessing of your people and country." We'll accept it!

The fence in the Golan along the Syrian border has opened a crack near Majdal Shams to permit Druze villagers in Syria to visit their relatives on the Israeli held side of the Golan Heights. And of course, Israel has maintained an open bridges policy with Jordan for the past nine years.

Parenthetically, Israel has sent agricultural task forces to England to show England how to cope with its current catastrophic water shortage. Israel says "עברי אנכי I am a Jew," descendant of the first עברי, Abraham, renowned for his hospitality and his compassion.

But post-Entebbe, while Israel's spirit is high, Israel's position in the world is still jeopardized by many problems. She is still groaning under the costs human and financial, of all her wars. Even the brilliant adventure at Entebbe cost a heavy price. Israelis are making great sacrifices. Taxes are the highest in the world, now close to 70 percent. Inflation continues at a rate of about 23 percent per year. Bread, milk and transportation costs are rising sharply. The government has had to cut back on health, education and welfare. Israel is fast running out of energy and water and must develop new sources of both. That takes money and lots of it.

Israel is managing its meager finances well. The creeping devaluation which saw the Israel pound drop from four to the American dollar, to six, eight, nine, ten, seems to be working, but cuts down on the purchasing power of the Israeli worker. Still it has made Israeli products cheaper for other countries to buy and her exports have risen 15 percent. Israel's imports have dropped ten percent this year because she can't afford it.

Israel must create new jobs for Russian and other immigrants. She must drill for oil and finance other explorations for energy sources. Next July, her products will enter the nine-member countries of the European Common Market duty-free, but she has to expand her export production in order to have goods to sell. It is an opportunity that must not be missed, for it could revolutionize the country's entire economic future.

And yet, almost half of her annual budget must go for defense, since Moscow is still, even now, pouring in arms, new MIG fighters and the most advanced tanks, to Egypt from Czechoslovakia, Algeria and the Soviet Union. Libya is receiving massive Russian arms and men, and the Soviet Mediterranean Fleet freely uses the ports of Bengazi and Tripoli.

Meanwhile, we are selling billions of dollars worth of arms to Iran and Saudi Arabia and there is lucky little Israel, always in the middle, forced to spend the pounds that should go to solve social problems and answer human needs on engines of destruction.

If that were not enough, the Arab economic boycott squeezes Israel in using petrodollars and threats of oil embargo to persuade companies even in these United States not to deal with Israel, and not to employ Jewish personnel of any nationality, including American Jews. Yet, Israel comes to us, not to beg, but to borrow, because she is proud, עברי אנכי.

We love Israel for what she is, but Israel cannot live on love alone. We owe it to her to give her help. We owe it to her to respond fervently ourselves to the questions Jonah was asked. And if we need a symbol in human scale, we owe it to some of her sons, including some of those who fell at Entebbe.

We owe it to Jean Jacques Maimoni, once of Morocco, who cheered the frightened hostages until he was fatally shot.

We owe it to Ida Borowicz, once of Russia, a pioneer in the struggle to emigrate to Israel and a proud new Israeli until she was fatally shot.

We owe it to Pascal Cohen, triumphant survivor of Hitler's concentration camps, and a free Israeli, until he was shot.

We owe it to Dora Block, citizen of Israel and England, a 75 year-old mother who was dragged screaming from her hospital bed in Uganda, murdered in cold blood and tossed into the forest.

We owe it to Lt. Colonel Yonatan Netanyahu, born in New York and raised in Israel, a wounded veteran of the Six-Day War and the Yom Kippur War; assigned to lead the commandos into the terminal, who was shot in the back by a Ugandan soldier as he stood on the tarmac next to the rescue plane, directing the hostages to safety.

We owe it to his father, a professor at Cornell, who came back to Israel for his son's honorable burial and never shed a tear, because pride strengthened a broken heart as he said, "עברי אנכי, I am a Jew."

We owe it to the commandos who were wounded, to the one who will go through life as a quadriplegic, paralyzed in both arms and both legs; a boy who was scheduled to be discharged on Friday, July second, but was asked to go on one more mission.

At *Sheloshim*, the memorial on the 30th day of the death of Lt. Col. Yonatan Netanyahu, a fellow combat officer spoke as follows:

"The tragedy of our nation is that it has had to fight for its survival, losing in the process not only the best of its present fighters and commanders, and the best of its future military leaders, but losing also the bearers of its spiritual future, poets, writers, thinkers and scientists.

"Belonging to a generation which has witnessed the tragedy of the Jews in Europe, the rebirth of Israel and the wars of Israel, our judgment is oppressed by the concentration of these events, the disasters and the triumphs. The short-sighted among us find it difficult to grasp the fact that from time immemorial, from Yonatan, the son of Saul, through Yonatan the Maccabee, to our own Yoni, the survival and the sovereignty of Israel have depended on the sword of Israel, wielded by a few of her sons and on the willingness of those sons to grasp this sword and raise its heavy burden.

"This was the Yoni of the history and philosophy books, Plato, Marx, Klausner and Raymond Aron. The Yoni who saw the history of Israel not as a collection of dry facts, but rather as a source of personal imperatives to action. The Yoni who raised from the ashes an armored battalion crushed beneath the weight of battle in the Golan Heights. And the calm, contented Yoni at home, with his pipe and his records, relaxing out of uniform.

"We saw him at peak moments of satisfaction and achievement, and we saw him take upon himself, not without a heavy heart and clenched teeth, the lonely command of the unit at the head of which he was to fall.

"Because above and beyond arms, men, training or experience, beyond the delicate balance between daring and circumspection, required for military planning and action, beyond all these qualities, it was the indomitable spirit of Israel that was on trial at Entebbe, and it was this that stood the test, despite the heavy cost.

"We can never bring Yoni the man back to life. But Yoni the symbol of our heritage, the spirit, the warm heart thirsty for knowledge, the faith in the rightness and value of the path he had chosen and the willingness to throw his life into the balance, all these are ours, if we wish, to adopt, to cherish, and to bequeath. If we fail to do this, we will have shirked the obligation which his death has placed on us."

The obligation which his death has placed on us, which all the dead have placed on us, which the decency and the sacrifice of the living have placed upon us, which our pride in a land that produces a Yoni Netanyahu and an Uri Bergman, a Rita Messenger and a Golda Meir, a people who pull off the most daring, courageous, and brilliant military operation of our time, but whose commemorative stamps quote the Talmud, "By three things is the world preserved, by **אמת**, truth, by **דין**, judgment and by **שלום**, peace" and produces a thing of beauty for its mail.

What is our obligation? Israel asks us at least to buy a bond, to lend her some of our own bounty and for our loan she will return us principal and interest and pride. She asks us and the spirit of Yonatan Netanyahu asks us, "Who are you?" It is now our turn, yours and mine to answer, as Jonah answered, "**עברי אנכי**."

THE POISED RATTLESNAKE

Yom Kippur of 1990 was an uneasy time. A few weeks earlier, on August 2, Saddam Hussein, the tyrannical dictator of Iraq, had invaded the oil-rich neighboring state of Kuwait with an eye to annexing it. The United Nations imposed economic and military sanctions against Iraq on August 9 and called for the use of force, if needed, on August 25.

We began to agonize over the vulnerability of the State of Israel, an easy target for Iraq's missiles, and the unknown nature or quantity of Hussein's arsenal of chemical, biological or atomic materials delivered by those missiles. American Jews were particularly fearful for Israel. The Allied anti-Iraqi governments strongly urged Israel not to engage in preemptive or retaliatory military actions against Iraq.

It was in such circumstances that I had to face my congregation on Yom Kippur. What could I possibly say beyond articulating their fears and calling for others to silence Hussein, whom I chose to demonize as the desert rattlesnake, poised to strike? It was not until January 17, 1991 that Operation Desert Storm was launched. Hussein was defeated in battle, but remains in power.

SEPTEMBER 29, 1990

Dear Friends:

The rattlesnake is poised to strike. The tragic nightmare of 1973 has robbed us of our sleep again. It is Yom Kippur, a day associated with atonement and hope of forgiveness of our sins, and instead that unseemly and unlikely combination of terms appears again: a Yom Kippur War.

Yes, we are at war. If we haven't said so, the rattlesnake himself has said so. On Tuesday evening we heard Saddam Hussein declare that the land, sea and air embargo against Iraq is tantamount to a state of war. We also heard him make that odious association of Zionism and neo-Nazism when he insisted the United States has been pressured into a form of neo-Nazism in its resistance to Iraq, by the so-called Zionist lobby.

Hussein's pan-Arab fantasy has no room in it for the toleration of a Jewish state in its middle, and his forked tongue reaches into these United States and draws you and me into the confrontation as part of that all-powerful Zionist lobby which he says manipulates our government. If Hussein wins out he will turn the attack against Israel and lead the holy war he has already proclaimed against Israel and against any Arabs who disagree. If he loses and must back off in the Gulf, he will escape humiliation and defeat by turning against Israel.

In Israel, Hussein has always been taken seriously. Israel kept warning the Western powers of Hussein's ambitions and is currently taking it more seriously even while declaring great confidence in the Israel Defense Forces to hold off Iraqi might once again. Still, as one average Israeli citizen confided to *New York Times* reporter, Joel Brinkley, "This man is a crazy dictator. He could send bombers here, suicide planes, missiles with chemical warheads. What is worrisome this time is that he is trying to incite the (Palestinian) population in the territories."

Already a month ago, Palestinians in several West Bank and Gaza cities held marches, flaunting Iraqi flags as they shouted, "Saddam, you hero, attack Israel with chemical weapons! We are with you until victory."

A painful corroboration of this concern comes from yet another source. The Chief Sephardic Rabbi of Israel, Mordechai Eliyahu, was asked a *halachic* question. "Is it permitted to shave one's beard in order to fit safely into a gas mask?" And the Rabbi answered, "Yes, you must shave your beard in this case so that the gas mask may help save your life."

I don't know why this little incident struck me so poignantly. It conjured up for me pictures of laughing Nazi soldiers cutting off the beards of aged and pious Jews in the early days of the Nazi horror. Hussein is making us perform on ourselves the indignity Hitler forced upon us.

In the light of what is happening at this very moment and the danger which awaits, there is undoubtedly no rabbi anywhere in the world this Yom Kippur who is not compelled to focus our already heightened attention upon what should be the Jewish response to Hussein.

Let me say at the outset that it cannot be love. He is our sworn enemy. Jews do not love the enemy. We are bidden to love our neighbor as ourself. We are told not to hate our neighbor in our heart. But we never believed God asks that we love our enemy. Last year, South African Archbishop Desmond Tutu visited the Arab prelate of Jerusalem and, while there, also visited the Holocaust memorial at Yad Vashem. His reaction was, "Jews should forgive the Nazis."

We Jews can't do that. We learn on this holy day that to be forgiven, one must admit wrongdoing and ask forgiveness. The hard-core Nazis never asked to be forgiven and their victims are dead and in no position to forgive them. We, Jews, are commanded by God in the Book of Deuteronomy (25:17-19) "*Zachor*! Remember what Amalek did unto thee by the way when ye came forth from Egypt...thou shalt blot out the very remembrance of Amalek from under heaven...*lo tishkach*, thou shalt not forget!"

At the most solemn moment of the conclusion of the Passover Seder we rise and we read from the Psalms (29:6,7; 69:25) and the Book of Lamentations (3:66) "Sh'foch Hamat'chah...Pour out thy wrath upon nations that do not know you...for they have devoured Jacob and laid waste his dwelling place...pursue them in anger and destroy them from under the heavens of the Lord."

Yes, I know. These harsh, unyielding, vindictive words sound out of place in these days when we have all been looking to a kinder, gentler world. How can I, a lover of peace, a teacher of kindness and mercy evoke these words even if they are part of our tradition? Believe me, I have agonized over my position in this new world and Jewish crisis, and I have found my answer in a teaching from that tradition which I must share with you. It was my son, Rabbi Daniel Pressman, who pointed it out. In a work called, "*Mishneh Kesef*," Joseph Kaspi wrote in medieval Spain, הרחמנות על הרעים אכזריות לטובים "Mercy to the wicked is cruelty to the good."

It must be clear to us by now that this swaggering, blustering tyrant, Saddam Hussein, armed to the teeth by so many governments who were more than kind, who were happy to sell to him, teach him the know-how, align with him in enormous stockpiling of conventional and forbidden instruments of destruction, have made possible his cruelty to the good.

This saying summarizes the original form of the teaching from the *Midrash (Kohelet Rabbah)* which says:

אמר ר שמעון בן לקיש, כל מי שנעשה רחמן
במקום אכזרי, סוף שנעשה אכזרי במקום רחמן

"Rabbi Shimmon ben Lakish said: 'Whoever shows himself merciful in circumstances when he should be cruel, in the end becomes cruel when he should be merciful."

This should have taught us two important lessons: If we make no moral distinctions in our actions, then we end up without a moral compass and will do great harm despite our good intentions. And second, if we do not put down evil when it first raises its head, then it will simply grow and grow and eventually good people will be hurt or destroyed.

The French who helped Saddam build the nuclear reactor which would have added nuclear bombs to his arsenal, the French who rushed to condemn Israel when Israel, fortunately, knocked out the reactor before it could get on line, the French denounced Saddam vigorously the other day when President Mitterand bespoke his outrage at the invasion of the French consulate. Germany, which supplied the hardware and the materials for the production of Iraq's poison gas stockpile, Germany joined the voices of condemnation. Russia, which sold Iraq all those huge Soviet tanks rumbling down the streets of Iraq and lined up on the border with Saudi Arabia, Russia, which provided Iraq with 8,000 military advisers and other specialists, and earlier this week refused to recall the last 1,000 with 150 still there; Russia which sold Iraq the helicopters, landing craft, surface-to-air missiles, night fighting equipment and spare parts it needed for its *blitzkrieg* of Kuwait, Russia which supplied Iraq with MiG 29 fighters with extended range kits and surface-to-surface missiles which are now facing Saudi Arabia and our troops, trained Iraq's general staff officers and helped organize its intelligence service over the past 30 years, Russia now accuses Iraq of carrying out an act of terrorism against the emerging new world order on August 2, which it called "Black Thursday" and suggested that the United Nations may have to use military force to stop that terrorism.

We, in the United States, showed our lack of moral compass in our lack of effort to restrain Saddam's cruelty. We did not protest vigorously when Saddam ordered his own Kurdish nationals massacred through poison gas weaponry. We supported him in his eight-year war against Iran which cost a million lives, hoping it might lead to gratitude and moderation. But all we did was feed his contempt for the West and encourage his latest adventure. "Mercy to the wicked is cruelty to the good."

William Safire wrote a column in the *New York Times* on August 10, called "Reading Saddam's Mind," in which he succeeded in conjuring up the tyrant's mentality as if Saddam himself were writing it. In it he has Saddam say, "A great leader, a new Saladin, is known for the enemies he makes. I now have the enemies I need. The Arabs in the streets are sick of weakness and cry out for a conqueror to wreak vengeance on the sheiks, the West, and the Jews... ah, my new enemy, the American. We will see how they like sitting in 110-degree tents in their poison gas gear. I hold 30 times as many American hostages as the Ayatollah ever did. America lost an eight-year war against an enemy one-tenth its size. Iraq won an eight-year war against an enemy triple our size. We'll see who is better prepared to bear the strain of oil blockage. If America cannot win a war in a week, it begins negotiating with itself.

"I have broadcast the meeting with Senator Dole's delegation telling me how he opposed the Israeli bombing of my reactor in 1981, assuring me that the Voice of America fired the writer who insulted my secret police. Weaklings all…I fooled the Americans and the Saudis by taking Kuwait. They fooled me by agreeing to base troops near the oil fields. Now it's my turn again. Let them dig in and sweat. I have the opportunity to launch the first surprise non-attack."

Saddam continues, "After inflation and recession, Bush will want to bring the boys home by election day."

"Mercy to the wicked is cruelty to the good." Because of America's obsession with Iran, we blinded ourselves to Saddam's despotism and unshakable ambition. Only weeks ago, one top State Department official was quoted as saying, "We see (Saddam) as engaged in menacing behavior, yes, but not as a menace. He's not Kadaffi, for instance, beyond hope of change." (*New Republic*, September 20-27, page 12)

How could we think that when, two years after the end of the Iran-Iraq war, Iraq was still spending ten billion dollars a year on armaments? How could we give her $3.5 billion in guaranteed loans and take Saddam's regime off the list of terror-sponsoring states?

The rabbinic teaching I have been quoting is about evil and how to handle it. What is moral? Which was more moral, Israel's bombing of the Iraqi reactor at Osirak in 1981 or the Western world's failure to protest Iraq's chemical assaults on Iran during their war? In terms of the number of innocent lives saved thereby, Israel's surgery was far more effective than the West's faith-healing.

In one sense, Saddam's move now may have been a bit premature. He moved before France had time to deliver a new guidance system for its long-range Condor II missile, to be part of his missile-delivery system for the nuclear warheads it would have been ready by 1995.

All of this is the worst possible scenario for the State of Israel. Saddam always has that trump card to pull out of his sleeve. Attack Israel. On June 18, he told an Islamic conference meeting in Baghdad, "We will strike at (the Israelis) with all the arms in our possession…Palestine has been stolen," he declared. He then asked the whole Arab world to "recover the usurped rights in Palestine and free Jerusalem from Zionist captivity."

We have every reason to be deeply concerned for Israel on this Yom Kippur. Already, even as tens of thousands of American boys and girls are sweating it out within range of Saddam's weaponry, we hear the stirrings of suggestions that the United States should reevaluate the importance of its ties with Israel. Sermons are being given by Christian leaders urging withdrawal of American troops and the call only gets louder day by day. Read the letters to the editor. Listen to call-ins on talk radio programs, and you will sense the first vibrations of once again dreaming that by sacrificing Israel we might bring peace to the Middle East and to the world, for that matter.

Sadly, I call to your attention the fact that the most primitive notions have still not disappeared from the world. Before the advent of Hebrew monotheism, ancient religion was dominated by the idea that an innocent person must be sacrificed in order to appease the angry gods. The innocent were sacrificed for the guilty. The human sacrifice was always an innocent child, a pure virgin, the best and most beautiful. Even in medieval times, we had vestiges of this in the person of the "whipping boy." If a young prince made mistakes in his geometry or Latin lessons, his "whipping boy" was flogged in his stead. I remember hearing in Hawaii the stories of casting a pure young maiden into the volcano to appease Pele, the god of the volcano. This would cause it to stop erupting and destroying homes. The Swiss playwright, Duerrenmacht, wrote a devastating piece of theater called "The Visit" in which a whole community is corrupted into offering up as a sacrifice the most beloved man in town. It is not a new idea, the innocent suffering for the guilty. Why do they suffer? Because "Mercy to the wicked is cruelty for the good."

Deeply concerned for Israel as I am, and I am sure you are, it is not the only concern. I worry every moment for the men and women in uniform who are now baking in the Arabian desert and facing an enemy seasoned in that type of terrain and that kind of warfare. I am sickened by the realization that on the verge of a new era of East-West cooperation to reduce the crushing burden of military expenditure and all the hopes which were raised may now come dashing down in the reality of the situation. Europe itself will not be in the mood to disarm itself if its Middle Eastern neighbors continue to build up their military strength and show no compunctions about adventuring into conflict no matter what the human cost. Here at home, our own military establishment is arguing, "You see, we can never let down our defenses because you can never tell when the weaponry we sell to others may be turned against us." And so, while Saddam or any other tyrant surfaces, our dreams of world disarmament, of turning our precious materials and labor to the nobler tasks of reducing homelessness and hunger, poverty and disease are crushed.

All of this leads to the question, "What to do about Saddam?" Every news analyst has an answer. People are stopped on the street and asked to share with the media what their advice is for President Bush.

To diffuse the crisis by diplomatic means and to leave the laboratories, plants, storage sites, ready and intact in their many remote desert installations and to leave Saddam Hussein intact and enraged by this temporary interruption of his grand plan is to set the stage for some other *blitzkrieg*, probably against Israel, by a still stronger Iraq armed with nuclear weapons. What to do?

My reluctant answer is the answer given by President Franklin Delano Roosevelt, "When you see a rattlesnake poised to strike, you do not wait until he has struck to crush him!" When an enemy points a pistol and says he will blow your head off, there is no high moral obligation to wait until he does.

A few months ago, Hussein made it crystal clear that he intended to use his tanks, planes and million-man army to control the Middle East and get rid of Israel. At that time, a massive embargo might have slowed him down. Before he blitzed Kuwait, confiscated its funds, got rid of much of its population, took hostages, ravaged Kuwait City and moved his tanks and troops to strategic positions, it would have been wise for this country to join with the State of Israel in massive, preemptive air strikes at the targets Israel knows so well. Yes, it would have cost Israeli lives, but not nearly so many as are now threatened by this blustering bully. That not having been done, it is my humble opinion that even now the 753 combat aircraft of Israel and whatever air forces and missile capacity the United Nations forces already possess could overcome the 513 combat aircraft of Iraq and neutralize the major military targets of Iraq proper.

Strange, inappropriate thoughts by a rabbi on this holiest of days. I heartily agree. They are not my first choice. But I prefer them to the words of panic and desperation we had to sound on Yom Kippur in 1973. Then the synagogues of Israel emptied out as its enemies chose a preemptive strike on the day they believed the Israelis were most vulnerable.

This Yom Kippur, time is not on our side, not on the side of the United States, not on the side of the United Nations force there, not on the side of Israel. At this point we are not fighting for cheap oil. We are fighting to prevent a wicked man from dominating a whole corner of the world and the energy source upon which the economy of the world depends. And, we are fighting to save Israel from its most adventurous, determined, avowed nemesis. To be merciful to him now, to let him step gracefully and unmarked from the trap of his own making is to be cruel to millions of innocents, including our American soldiers and the whole people of the State of Israel.

Call me a hawk. Call me what you will. But at least think carefully about the lesson we have learned at enormous cost: "Mercy to the wicked is cruelty to the good." Let the world learn this lesson…fast. Let it learn that no short-term goal, no perceived benefit, no temporary relief can remove either the taint or the danger of trafficking with murderers and despots. Let us learn to be tough when we have to be, so that the kinder values we espouse will be able to survive and flower without threat, in a world purged of monsters like Saddam Hussein.

SCAPEGOAT IN THE TWENTY-FIRST CENTURY?

In editing this sermon, I find it disheartening that the comprehensive analysis of the brokenness of society world-wide in this sermon is strikingly similar to an analysis of society as we ended the Twentieth Century. The situation may be worse today. Pollution, world-wide disease, large and small wars, famine, loss of moral values, and on and on seem substantially worse than at the time of this sermon.

The sermon assumes that individuals as well as governments may reverse the direction in which we are going. Modest efforts at combating substance abuse, violence and prurience in the entertainment media, poverty and disease have been initiated, but it seems we lose more ground than we gain. Our contention that a strong sense of partnership with the Creator in תקון עולם, *repair of the world, is the best foundation for a society with moral values seems the answer to our dilemma all the more today.*

OCTOBER 3, 1995

Dear Friends:

Is anybody thirsty? Not yet, right? I ask because I am considering the wisdom of Rabbi Chaim Sandzer of a little *shtetl* in Eastern Europe. One Yom Kippur day, the sexton (that's the *shamash*) came up and told the rabbi that a congregant, who was both wealthy and miserly (which, by the way, is how some people get wealthy) had fainted due to the fast and asked if he could give the man some water.

The rabbi said, "According to the law you can give him a spoonful of water."

A few minutes later the shamash reported to the rabbi that the man revived, but fainted again. He asked for more water.

This time the rabbi decreed differently. "Tell him that he can drink as much water as he requires provided he donates 100 guilders to charity for each spoonful of water."

As soon as the rabbi's ruling was told to the fainting congregant, his thirst disappeared and he felt sufficiently refreshed to continue with the Yom Kippur prayers. So, again I ask, "Is anybody thirsty yet?" We shall be together for approximately 24 hours, during which the richness of the prayers and poems in our *mahzor* give us water and food. The water, say the rabbis, is Torah. As they put it, אין מים אלא תורה. "The water we read about in our tradition is really Torah." As for food, where will you find as much food for thought as in the 276 pages of the Yom Kippur services?

For starters, for me, there is Psalm 27, which we recite at the end of the evening service throughout this penitential period. It is on page 24 and is read between two recitations of the mourner's Kaddish. The last two verses in particular have puzzled me and many, many people through the years.

לולא האמנתי לראות בטוב יי בארץ חיים "If I didn't believe I would see the goodness of the Lord in the land of the living." Then it goes on, קוה אל יי חזק ויאמץ לבך וקוה אל יי "Wait for the Lord. Be strong and let your heart take courage, yea, wait for the Lord."

Now, did you notice something? The verse says, "If I didn't believe I would see the goodness of the Lord in the land of the living…" And then something seems to be missing. Why doesn't it say what you would do if you didn't see the goodness of the Lord in the world? It doesn't say. Something is missing, perhaps deleted. Could it be that what is missing is the threat, "Then I wouldn't believe in God, if I didn't see his goodness in this world." The person's faith is at stake because what he sees in the land of the living is strife and evil, suffering and violence.

As the century draws to a close, we realize to our dismay, that the high hopes with which it began have one by one been dashed to the ground. One scarcely knows where to begin. In America, a veritable revolution has taken place in the way we do business. Large corporations are merging, and the question hangs heavy: Will monopoly eventually result in control of quality and price and new technologies downsize the numbers of workers making a living?

Sweatshops are developing with immigrants kept in virtual slavery within unsafe workplaces, scarcely eking out a living no matter how many hours they labor. Children and women of various ethnic groups, many not speaking English are the primary victims of the system.

A flood of immigrants, legal and illegal are pouring into our country, taking the undesirable jobs at the bottom of the work ladder, generating hostilities of group against group, resulting in vicious gangs and the growth of crime. Substance abuse is on the increase with addicts roaming the streets in a stupor.

Corruption threatens the political and police systems, which are frequently the captives of all-powerful business interests upon whose financial support they are increasingly dependent. The centers of big cities are deteriorating into a mix of ugly factories and unlivable housing for the poor.

The waters are being polluted by the noxious wastes of industry and a swelling population. The air is dark with the poisonous clouds of the exhaust of all kinds of combustion. Around the world people look more and more to the United States to police and resolve international tensions. Bloody civil wars pit brother against brother. The rich are getting richer and the poor are getting children.

Sound familiar? Discouraging? Well, take heart. I am not talking about the 1990's. I am talking about the 1890's. The one difference is that in the 1890's, people looked ahead to the Twentieth Century as the time when a more utopian world would be achieved.

In the 1990's we are not looking ahead to the Twenty-first Century with quite the same optimistic anticipation because we are beginning to get the message: human life, in every century, in every generation, in every year is confronted with the challenge of human frailty.

Our Torah confronted that frailty and described it as the struggle within each of us between the **יצר הטוב**, the good impulse, and the **יצר הרע**, the wicked impulse. In a way, there is a certain comfort in the realization that these are not the worst of times, any more than they are the best of times.

These **ימים נוראים**, days of awe, are the days appointed for us to take stock of ourselves and recognize that we have come to pray not only for a relief from our *tsarot*, our troubles, but also to acknowledge that we are part of the problem. Human frailty is our frailty. The sins of humanity are our sins.

How does each line of our confessional begin?

על חטא שחטאנו לפניך For the sin which we have sinned before you. "We," humanity collectively. How does the confessional conclude?

ועל כלם אלוה סליחות סלח לנו מחל לנו כפר לנו "For all these, O God of forgiveness, forgive us, pardon us, grant us atonement." The *Untaneh Tokef* prayer we read on Rosh Hashanah says, "In the Book of Life, **וחותם יד כל אדם בו** The seal of every man's hand is set thereto." If this is an imperfect world, it is our imperfect world and we are part of the imperfection.

Tonight I must share with you a strong apprehension I feel. We are approaching a dangerous moment in history, I have this eerie sensation that closing in all around us is a strange confluence of events which do not bode well for our welfare in the Twenty-first Century. It seems entirely possible that we, Jews, will once again be cast in the role of scapegoat about which we read tomorrow from the Torah. The events I refer to are basically unrelated to one another, but their surfacing at approximately the same time increases the hazard.

The Los Angeles County layoffs of civil servants, echoed in major population centers around the country, the downsizing of corporations leading to unemployment, the threat of the loss of medical care and the fear of reduction of Social Security benefits are all currently happening or being debated. Affirmative action, that emotionally charged issue, is under vigorous attack, and those benefiting from it are understandably fearful and resentful.

The strong Christian radical right push to turn this republic into a Christian state is heating up under the guise of political activity. Minister Louis Farrakhan is calling for a march of a million black men on Washington, D.C. for what he calls, interestingly enough, "a holy day of atonement and reconciliation."

It is scheduled for October 16, which just happens to be *Shemini Atseret*, our eighth day of solemn assembly at the end of *Sukkot*. The way I figure, we shall be reciting *Yizkor* about the same hour that the march assembles on the Washington Mall. This man, who was rightly described by Judge Stanley Crouch as a "racist, anti-Semitic, nut leader" will address a sea of faces in the same place where the late Reverend Martin Luther King, Jr. called for non-violence and brotherhood.

Farrakhan can be expected to use skilled rabble-rousing oratory to inflame tens of thousands of men who feel society has conspired against them to keep them in an inferior position. He will promise them the moon and offer a scapegoat at that gathering or something close to it, possibly you and me. The election fervor is heating up, and the radical right and the racist volunteer militia groups will be turning up the fire of the irresponsible rhetoric or campaigning. All of this happening in the next few weeks.

You may be thinking, Rabbi, what do you want us to do about it? Why are you troubling the serene atmosphere of Kol Nidre to talk about it? The first thing I want all of us to do is to pay attention, be informed and know the details of the danger. Remember that Kol Nidre, of all our Holy Days, is symbolic of times of peril for our people, going back to the time of the Inquisition when the Kol Nidre formula took on immediate significance. At that time, the Jews of Spain and Portugal were forced to choose between vowing to be a true Christian or suffering torture or even death by immolation at the stake. The Kol Nidre formula was used to annul all such vows in advance, Kol Nidre: All the Vows. This background of Kol Nidre makes it mandatory that we alert ourselves to any possible present danger.

The danger these days is not forced conversion. It is the risk of being used as a scapegoat one more time. The passage we read form the Torah tomorrow gave our vocabulary the term scapegoat. We shall hear once again how the High Priest, Aaron, in the wilderness was to select two goats, load upon one symbolically all the sins of all the children of Israel and drive it off into the desert. That goat was called the scapegoat, the one who suffers for the sins of others.

How many times since then have the Jewish people been used as a scapegoat, the one blamed and punished for the misdeeds of others? This Yom Kippur, I felt it important to raise the flag of caution by pointing out the several flash points, any one or more of which spell trouble.

I wonder if you have caught the new code words for referring to Caucasians and African-Americans? It is now the haves and the have-nots, a distinction which is actually not correct. There are haves and have-nots in all racial groups. In any case, another flash point is the economy. The perception of the have-nots is that the economy is better, but for them, unemployment is worse. They feel they are being manipulated by the Jewish media, Jewish Wall Street and the Jewish czar of the economy, Federal Reserve Chairman Alan Greenspan. If, in the ghettos and the barrios, there is hopeless depression, who do you think will be elected scapegoat?

The new Christian Right is using the religious stations on radio and television for the sale of videotapes and books and the religious and political podiums for gaining power by attacking political incumbents. President Clinton is the prime target at the moment. One videotape, being touted on Sunday morning broadcasts by Reverend Jerry Falwell and others, accuses Clinton of heinous crimes. It is called "The Clinton Chronicles." It accuses him of smuggling $100,000,000 of cocaine a month into Arkansas. A book of Christian poetry called, "The Perished Soul of America," calls Clinton "a draft-dodging, drug-inhaling, sodomy-protecting, shady-dealing, tax-raising, child-exploiting, baby-killing, feminist-pandering, gun-confiscating, military-reducing womanizer." The poem is dedicated to Jesus of Nazareth.

What I have quoted is symptomatic of the blurring of the lines, the crumbling of the wall of separation between church and state. If it goes, then a tiny two percent minority, the American Jewish Community, will have no protection.

Another example of the threat is to be found in a devil's brew of extremist militias, paramilitary organizations, skinheads, neo-Nazis, the resurgent Ku Klux Klan, racism, and religious bigotry. The Jew is the announced target of some of them and the hidden agenda of others. The arson attacks against a few synagogues here and there, the Molotov cocktail thrown at a temple in Corpus Christi, Texas, the swastikas painted on many synagogues, including ours more than once, are just a few of the 2,000 incidents reported last year.

These incidents are echoed by the bombing in London, the bloody destruction of the Jewish Central Building in Buenos Aires, Argentina and the car-bombing in front of a Jewish school in Lyon, France. As you know, had the school clock not been running two minutes slow, the bomb, timed to explode at the closing bell, would have taken the lives of many innocent children.

We are told that anti-Semitism is alive and very, very sick in Europe. We were in Budapest this past summer. Some of the Jewish leaders and even a non-Jewish guide reported that Jews living there are in fear of rising anti-Semitism.

In far-off Japan, a country with virtually no Jews, in recent years, there has been an inexplicable rise in anti-Semitism, inexplicable except if we recognize it as scapegoatism. Books attacking the Jews sell well in Japan. Two million copies warning that the Jews were about to buy up Japan and then destroy the nation by allowing blacks and Hispanics to take Japanese jobs, and to rape Japanese women. A member of the Japanese Parliament, Aisaburosaito, published a book, "The Secrets of Jewish Power to Control the World." The president of McDonald's, Japan, Ltd., Den Fujita, wrote, "If you can understand the Jews, you can understand the world, Japan, blueprint of Jewish conspiracy, Jewish business methods, controlling the economy of the world." Books accusing the Jews of everything, from Watergate to financing Hitler to controlling the world's food supplies abound in Japan and, of course, *The Protocols of the Learned Elders of Zion* is still published there. (Liberty, July-August, 1995, page 5)

The immediate presence of the Nation of Islam, the NOI, which ordinarily we do not notice, has come to public attention because the Federal government has made a deal with their so-called security agency to have them patrol and keep the peace in slums, depressed areas and crime-ridden locales. The Nation of Islam has public and private contracts in Chicago, Philadelphia, Pittsburgh, Atlanta, and Los Angeles, and headquarters in Washington, D.C.

In Baltimore, the checks were late for 30 NOI security guards. The manager told the crowd waiting for their pay, "The pay checks will be late today. Somebody tapped into the computer system and it was the Jews. The Jews put a virus in our computer."

It is baffling and it is frightening. Most insidious and dangerous of all is the orchestrated methodical campaign to infiltrate and take over local city councils, school boards and civic organizations.

So, as the century winds down and the future is not rosy, why do I say, "This is an imperfect world?" You know that. But when I add, "And we are part of that imperfection" and we pray, "We have sinned before you, forgive us, pardon us, grant us atonement." What are we doing? What are we talking about?

I believe the answer is to be found in the metaphor of the Midrash, "Humanity is being weighed on a balance scale, the kind with two pans suspended from it. On one pan is loaded all the goodness in the world. And on the other is loaded all the evil." You and I must choose on which pan we belong, and then each of us will tip the scales either in the direction of the good or the direction of evil.

The Jewish tradition about these Holy Days is that each and every one of us has the awesome responsibility and the freedom to determine which way the world goes. On this most spiritual of days we are forced to examine the state of the world and make our choice as to which direction it will take.

What are we going to do about the discouraging world report I merely touched on and you know very well without my reminding you? Remember the unfinished verse from Psalm 27? "If I didn't believe I would see the goodness of the Lord in the land of the living." I said that for some people the missing sentence would be, "Then I wouldn't believe in God." That is understandable. When we look at anything from the Holocaust to the atom bomb, there are those who have lost their faith. They are the ones who say, "God is dead." That interpretation is unacceptable to me and I hope it is to you. The missing verse has to be, "Then I wouldn't be rolling up my sleeves and working to change the world, and asking for the help of the Lord."

What shall we do about this old world of ours which is leaning so far to the side of evil? We have to make up our minds not to accept it as it is. Our motto has to be that simple but wonderful cry, "We're not going to take it any more!" If there are things to do which will tip the world to the side of the good, clean, beautiful place God has designed it to be, then by God we must do them and not simply wring our hands and be voices of doom and despair.

I don't pose as a man with all the answers. Believe me, you know them as well as I do, perhaps, better. Once we have said we are not going to take it any more, then we must attack the sources of misery head on and not stand helplessly by. First and foremost is the problem of poverty, hunger and homelessness in the world. If it is not insurmountable, governments and individuals can solve it. Our government, for one, has stored enough corn, grain, butter and cheese, (which you and I have paid taxes to subsidize for the farmers and then stored away to keep the prices up) to feed millions. The world is far too hungry for us to keep millions of acres unused and pay the farmers for crops they don't produce in order to keep prices up.

As for you and me, individuals can do wonders. We have created "Sova," the food bank to which we asked you to bring packages on your way here tonight. It feeds thousands. Mr. Mickey Weiss of this community, who retired from the food business, saw the big fruit and vegetable markets throw away huge amounts of perfectly good food which had not been bought. He set up a collection system to pick up that surplus and supply it fresh the same day to warehouses where the hungry come and are nourished.

Another man has set up a system of collecting surplus food from restaurants, You and I probably throw enough food down the garbage disposal to feed another family. Since there's no way we can redistribute it, then we must make atonement for this waste by finding ways to feed others.

I have only scratched the surface of what can be done. I took a big risk that somebody will go home and report that all Rabbi Pressman talked about was garbage disposals. Tell them the truth; he was making the difference between starvation and living.

Can we do anything about the homeless, the gangs, the crime, the unemployment? We can, government and individuals. The government is spending enough on defense, although it is not quite clear as to defense from what...enough to build and rebuild schools, train and employ teachers at attractive salaries, create college campuses and opportunities, upgrade job training and lick the substance abuse problems.

We could turn the downward trend of the inner cities and the rural areas around, and still have enough left over to keep American strong and safe from tigers. Corporations must be made to stop fattening their profits by turning people out on the streets without jobs. Now you and I do have a say in our government. You and I do have a say in business, big and small.

So why do we keep silent without even a note of protest?

We shall not solve these problems by governments taking a sterner and ever more penurious approach to them, and business refusing to see beyond the bottom line. Always, in human history, the have nots could not be starved and exploited forever. Instead, they tore down the society which denied them and then everybody had to start over again. It happened in ancient Rome. It happened in Teutonic Germany, in the decadent French monarchy. It happened in Czarist Russia.

In a society of people making a good living and having a stake in the community, we should be able to walk down the street at night, live in front of our homes and enjoy the friendship of our neighbors rather than hide behind walls. It can be done. It is not impossible. Neither is the ultimate elimination of homelessness, wars and disease.

But these wonderful things will never happen if you and I don't believe it and do whatever little we are able to do.

Besides, on Yom Kippur, at the heart of our service, we have a prophetic imperative. In tomorrow's Haftarah we read the Prophet Isaiah's challenge, "Is not this the fast that I, God, have chosen? To loose the fetters of wickedness, to undo the bands of the yoke, and to let the oppressed go free, and that ye break every yoke? Is it not to deal thy bread to the hungry, and that thou bring the homeless to thy house? When thou seest the naked that thou cover him, and that thou hide not thyself from thy fellow man?" (Isaiah 58:6-7)

Isn't it remarkable how much Isaiah thinks like me, or perhaps it is vice-versa? He was preaching the painfully simple truth that we don't have to take it. The world doesn't have to be a cesspool of pollution, violence and deprivation. It is up to each of us to get beyond his or her concern with self, beyond pessimism, beyond cynicism, and change something, anything, we can for the better.

A wise rabbi recently wrote: "To do that we are going to have to overcome the current cynical attitude toward moral values and goals where nothing is sacred. It is being hammered in on us from every direction and by much of the media that we do not believe in goodness, in wholesomeness, in a better future. To be in style today and not be square, you must believe that the family is at worst, oppressive, at best, boring. People who actually like family life are like the Brady Bunch: saccharine, white bread, clueless. All marriages are unhappy. Divorce is not the sad, difficult ending of a close, vital relationship. Divorce is liberation. A child who likes to read and learn is a nerd. A kid who is kind and thoughtful is a goody-

goody, Honest people are suckers. A person who works at a blue collar job is a stupid loser.

"If you make a lot of money you should spend it on fabulously expensive luxuries so everyone knows how successful you are. If you give to charity (and why should you?), do it as cynically and as self-servingly as possible. Religious people are all hypocrites and secret sinners. Businessmen are rapacious and greedy. Politicians are the scum of the earth. Everything is a joke. Every important person is a fair target for slander or ridicule." (Rabbi Daniel Pressman, "The Potter's Wheel," 1995)

A professor from Brown University wrote in the Columbia Journalism Review, "An unwholesome environment for young people at home and at school is producing a cynical attitude toward moral values and goals, a failure of spirit. The antidote for a failure of spirit would seem to be 'belief.' Cynics add nothing, do nothing and produce little that endures."

Judaism affirms that there is a higher meaning to human existence. We are partners with God in *Tikkun Olam*, repairing the world's brokenness. Judaism teaches us that it is the positive, "square" people who make the world worth living, who form the core of a healthy society, who believe there is goodness and there is Godliness. We don't have to wring our hands and watch the human race go down the drain.

My understanding of Psalm 27, which we add to the service at this season, is saying to us, "If I didn't believe that I can yet see the goodness of God in this world, I couldn't go on. I must see. I must do. I must believe. The breaches in the wholesomeness of the world can be, must be repaired, replaced or removed forever altogether."

That is the message of the last verse of that Psalm which should be translated, "Hope in the Lord. Be strong and let your heart take courage. Yea, trust in the Lord." And then roll up your sleeves and help God do something about it!

CHAPTER THREE
Disturbing Issues in Society

More than ever, today, it is clear that we live in one world, and what happens anywhere within it affects the Jewish people directly or indirectly. It is here that the Prophetic function of the pulpit expresses itself. During the years in which I had the privilege of exercising that function there were many issues, some of which are addressed in the following sermons.

By the 1950's it became clear that the relationships between the Black and White communities would be changing radically. At the same time, the development of the Cold War between Russia and the United States created a paranoia in both countries which saw a spy or a subversive under every bed as a Fifth Column in their midst. Here the ultimate expression of that paranoia was engendered by one Senator Joseph P. McCarthy, whose committee created the Loyalty Oath. It became a necessity to sign an oath attesting that the individual or organization being challenged was not nor had ever been a member of the Communist Party of America. The challenge even reached the Board of our synagogue.

The issue of integration of Blacks into the white schools, entertainment venues, and commerce raged. The war in Vietnam was hotly debated. Leaders who acquired huge followings in religion and politics were caught with their clay feet showing and were torn down from their pedestals. I referred to the 20th Century as a century of false prophets.

"BLACK BOY" BY RICHARD WRIGHT BLACK-JEWISH ALIENATION: A PROPHECY

In the last months of World War II, "Black Boy," an autobiography by Richard Wright called the attention of the white community to the festering hostility coming to the surface in the black community. The book sounded the alarm of coming confrontation between blacks and Jews, the blacks focusing their hatred against the most vulnerable element in the white community.

This was a prejudice which the majority of the Jewish community did not recognize at the time. Jews believed themselves to enjoy good relations with the blacks and were unaware by and large of the seething hostility which would surface only some 40 years later.

I called on the people before me to wake up and smell the time-bombs.

MARCH 16, 1945

Dear Friends:

The prophet Amos once rose and called the attention of the Jewish people to an acute social problem saying,

הלוא כבני כשיים אתם לי בני ישראל נאם "

"Are ye any better to me than the children of the Ethiopians, O children of Israel?" saith the Lord. (Amos, 9:7)

The same social problem, still acute, is the subject of "Black Boy," a recent autobiography written by a child of the Ethiopians, a Negro, Richard Wright. In his work, Mr. Wright, without sparing his own or his reader's feelings, paints the life of a Negro boy, growing from infancy to maturity refusing to sink to the level his society automatically establishes for him.

As I read the book and considered its significance to me as an American and as a Jew, the full weight of the cry of Amos burst upon me with tremendous impact: "Are ye any better unto me than the children of the Ethiopians, O children of Israel?"

And the only answer we can give with honesty at this time is, "No, the children of Israel are not any better nor any better off the exiled, persecuted children of the Ethiopians."

And it behooves us to sympathize with their state as it is important they sympathize with ours; to understand their plight, as they must understand ours. One important key at least to such an understanding, may be found in the reading of this new book by Mr. Wright. It enables us to compare the economic, social and psychological problems of the Jew and the Negro. The results of such a comparison are a revelation.

One need not read this book to know that both Negro and Jew suffer a limitation of economic opportunity. In "Black Boy," Mr. Wright merely succeeds in bringing it more forcibly to our attention. The central figure, Richard, who is Mr. Wright himself, describes his attempts to climb out of the poverty, the squalor, the illiteracy of his environment.

He aspires to be a writer, but his superstition-ridden grandmother condemns writing as the work of the devil. His white employers dismiss his dreams with a curt, "You'll never be a writer. Who on earth put such ideas in your nigger head?"

He describes his attempts to learn a trade. He finds a position in an optical factory owned by a Northerner, who urges him to watch the two white lens-grinders and learn the trade. These two Southern gentlemen tolerate Richard until he begins to ask questions about the work, whereupon one turns upon him shaking his fist, "This is a white man's work around here." They see in Richard a potential contender for their jobs, and eventually they drive him out.

One day they corner him in the shop. One accuses him of calling the other by his last name, Pease, without using Mister before it.

By this simple trick they put Richard in an impossible situation. In his own words, "If I had said, 'No sir, Mr. Pease, I never called you Pease,' I would in inference have been calling Reynolds a liar; and if I had said, 'Yes, sir, Mr. Pease, I called you Pease,' I would have been pleading guilty to the worst insult a Negro can offer to a Southern white man." To avoid bloodshed, Richard is obliged to leave his job.

Here, in this single incident, is embodied the economic basis for anti-Negro prejudice, and it typifies the economic basis for anti-Semitic prejudice as well. It is fear: fear that the Negro, the Jew or the members of any minority group may aspire to the jobs held by the members of the majority and deprive them of a livelihood.

In the economic world, it must be stated, the Jew enjoys certain advantages over the Negro by virtue of being white and therefore slightly more acceptable. But let there be a depression, unemployment, jobs at a premium, and the first to suffer will be the Jew and the Negro as the majority group acts automatically to safeguard the livelihood of its members. Even when there is no depression, there are still whole areas of enterprise closed to the

Jew, areas in which the Jew has talent to contribute, but which are denied him by college quotas and by discrimination in the bestowal of awards. Recently we witnessed an example of the latter at Harvard University. A prize awarded by a big business enterprise is regularly denied the eligible Jewish students because that business wishes Jews kept out of its industry.

What is the solution to such a condition? Mr. Wright hazards none, nor shall we tonight, other than this obvious conclusion. It is fear, cold fear that paralyzes the finer instincts in man, fear that the Negro or the Jew may rob a man of his job. Remove that fear, shape a society in which there will be opportunities for all, and you have removed the fundamental cause for race hatred and group tensions. Establish an order in which no man fears for his bread and butter, and then no man will fear his neighbor. Until that time, we shall be obliged to echo the words of Amos, "Are ye any better unto me that the children of the Ethiopians, O ye children of Israel?"

Socially, the Negro and the Jew share the humiliation of living outside the area of universal acceptance. In the Northern states, the social barriers are harder to discover, but they are there nevertheless. They are painfully similar for Negro and Jew. Both peoples are gently prevented from dwelling in areas which are tactfully called restricted. Both peoples are denied admittance into hotels and resorts whose clientele is known as selected. Neighborhoods into which Negroes or Jews infiltrate gradually witness the exodus of former residents, and one hears that the neighborhood has become run down. These and many other petty annoyances torment and gnaw at the consciousness of the Negro just as they do at the consciousness of the Jew.

In the South, however, as revealed in Mr. Wright's book, the social ostracism of the Negro is much more open and resembles the ostracism the Jew suffered when he lived in the European ghetto. Indeed, the Negro is ghettoized in the south. The boy, Richard, describes his first realization of the fact. He says on one occasion, "At last we were in the railroad station, and for the first time I noticed there were two lines of people at the ticket window, a white line, and a black line. A sense of the two races had been born in me with a sharp concreteness that would never die until I die. I was aware that we Negroes were in one part of the train and that the whites were in another."

The young man, Richard, is taught the lesson of addressing all white men with the proper respect in the following incident. "One day, while returning from the suburbs, my bicycle tire was punctured. I walked along the hot, dusty road, a car slowed at my side.

"What's the matter, boy?" a white man called.

I told him that my bicycle was broken and I was walking back to town.

"That's too bad," he said, "hop on the running board."

The car started. It was full of white young men. They were drinking.

"Wanna drink, boy?" one asked.

"Oh, no," I said.

The words were barely out of my mouth before I felt something hard and cold smash me between the eyes. It was an empty whisky bottle. I saw stars and fell backwards from the speeding car into the dust of the road, my feet becoming entangled in the steel spokes of the bicycle. The car stopped and the white men stood over me.

"Nigger, ain't you learned no better sense 'n that, yet," asked the man who hit me. "Ain't you learned to say 'sir' to a white man yet? If you had said that to some other white man, you might've been a dead nigger now."

This was indeed a kind, tolerant gentleman speaking.

Perhaps you think Mr. Wright exaggerates? Perhaps things are little better today, for after all, this incident happened in his early youth. Here is an item I chanced to read in the newspaper, and it strengthens his case considerably, as you will agree.

The news item comes from Jackson, Mississippi, the town where Mr. Wright spent his youth. This past Tuesday a group of Negro soldiers, just back from overseas, were passing through Jackson on their way to Camp Shelby. They were waiting in the station and began fraternizing with some white soldiers they had known overseas.

The military police, seeking to preserve Southern customs, informed the men that they could not mingle together in Mississippi, insisting that they divide themselves by race and retire to their respective waiting rooms. The colored soldiers returned to their car and undressed for bed.

News of the incident reached the civilian police, however, and they arrived heavily armed with sawed-off shotguns and rushed into the car, ordered the soldiers out of bed and searched them. While the military police looked on, several of the soldiers were beaten around the head with blackjacks and clubs. Several of the men just back from combat duty were forced to board the train with blood streaming down their faces.

Socially the Negro has a very long road to travel before he will begin to feel at home in this land, and while his position in the South is intolerable here in the North, his position is hardly much better. Dislike and distrust of him has gone underground, just as have dislike and distrust of the Jew. Essentially our problems are the same, and we hear the prophet's ringing question, "Are ye any better unto me than the children of the Ethiopians, O ye children of Israel?"

Psychologically, the Negro shares many of the problems of the Jew. Just as there are Jewish types who try to assimilate, so are there Negro types. The Negro purchases creams for whitening the skin, preparations for straightening the kinky hair, and introduces all the snobbishness, the class distinction, the airs that he believes distinguish the successful white man. Like the Jew, he is sometimes given to self-hatred because he lives and breathes in an atmosphere charged with hatred of him.

Just as the Jew, grateful for someone for whom he may treat as an inferior in a hostile society, is often guilty of hating and maligning the Negro, so the Negro is eager to despise the Jew, who is perhaps the only white man he can despise.

Wright gives us examples of both reactions. He indicates the manner and the cause for Jews harboring anti-Negro feelings in the following penetrating analysis of men with whom he worked on one job.

"I weighed the personalities of the men on the job. There was Don, a Jew; but I distrusted him. His position was not much better than mine , and I knew he was uneasy and insecure. He had always treated me in an off-hand, bantering manner that barely concealed his contempt...his frantic desires to demonstrate a racial solidarity with the whites against the Negroes might make him betray me."

Somewhere along the way, then, the Negro child, the cute little bright-eyed, happy baby, becomes conscious that he is different just as the little Jewish child, sometime in his early days, makes the great discovery. Countee Cullen expresses something of the tragedy a white world makes of being colored when he writes of the gleeful child riding in old Baltimore, Maryland

Now I was eight and very small
And he was no whit bigger
And so I smiled, but he poked out
His tongue and called me "nigger."
I saw the whole of Baltimore
From May until December.
Of all the things that happened there
That's all that I remember.

These poignant, simple lines remind me of my own sixth year of life. Of all those 365 days my only recollection is the day when I was first called a bad name in connection with the word Jew.

Conversely, the Negro can harbor an unhealthy hatred for the Jew. Wright tells us quite candidly about his own childhood prejudices, "All of us black people who lived in the neighborhood hated Jews not because they exploited us, but because we had been taught at home and in Sunday school that Jews were 'Christ killers.' With the Jews thus singled out for us, we made them fair game for ridicule."

And so the Jew and the Negro, each feeling insecure in the face of discrimination, vent their feelings upon each other. You and I have been guilty in our thoughts and acts toward the Negro. You and I have been guilty of sweeping generalizations such as, "All Negroes steal, all Negroes lie, all Negroes are dirty, all Negroes are stupid." Generalizations as vicious as "All Jews are crooked, all Jews cheat, all Jews are dirty, and all Jews are shrewd and sharp." As vicious as the generalization, "Jews are Christ killers."

Certainly some Negroes steal. Wright tells us why very simply: because they couldn't keep alive otherwise. He confesses stealing himself. He confesses working for two dollars a week, washing dishes, chopping wood, scrubbing floors, cleaning the yard and then gulping down glasses of milk behind the kitchen door to keep himself alive. He speaks of the serving girls who were forced to pilfer in order to supplement their inadequate wages. But we Jews, victims ourselves of slanderous generalizations, should take the lead in correcting our own bigoted impressions and educating the public at large to the truth.

Yes, in terms of the personal, psychological problems of victims of prejudice, the Jew and the Negro are virtually in the same boat. Therefore, before we, by slip of tongue or thoughtless act, malign or injure the Negro, let us remember the prophetic words, "Are ye any better unto me than the children of the Ethiopians, O ye children of Israel?"

Perhaps some of you have been thinking, "It is fine for the rabbi to talk charitably about the Negroes, but he doesn't have to work with them, he doesn't have them for employees, he doesn't understand them as well as I do. He doesn't know that they don't know any better, they don't care to advance themselves, they don't want to be educated, they are not conscious of discrimination!"

And I must give the same answer that a good Christian should give his anti-Negro neighbor, "How much do you really know about them? If you read a book like 'Black Boy' or know a man like its author, you will discover you know practically nothing about the Negro. If you have never read a Negro newspaper that gives a true Negro opinion, then do not say you understand the Negro. For the Negro has learned to put on what Wright calls the "laugh like a simpleton because that's what the white man expects from you" type of behavior. Beneath that exterior, put on like a protective shell, are all the longings for freedom, for equality, for beauty, for knowledge, for cleanliness, and for self-respect that you and I have.

We cannot go down South and revolutionize the situation there, but we can applaud and support the legislation which will repeal the poll tax and outlaw discrimination. We cannot force the North to accept the Negro into its innermost bosom, but we can be more understanding in our own attitude. Above all, we should know that his fight and our fight for real democracy in this great republic are one and the same.

We thought of the Ives-Quinn bill outlawing discrimination, recently passed in Albany, as progress for the Jews. The Negro press applauded it just as vigorously as progress for the Negro.

We should carry on the struggle for the rights of all groups to life, liberty and the pursuit of happiness as a religious struggle and feel it an act of worshiping God if we make this earthly existence one fraction more livable for Jew or Negro or Chinese or Hottentot. It is well for us to remember that our mission as Jews is not to labor exclusively for the welfare of the Jews, but to find welfare for the Jews in the welfare of all peoples. It is well for us to remember and act in accordance with the great democratic slogan our Bible has taught the world and which the world must eventually adopt when all the intolerance and the hatred have spent themselves:

הלא אב אחד לכלנו, הלוא אל אחד בראנו
מדוע נבגד איש באחיו לחלל ברית אבתינו

"Have we not all one father, Hath not one God, created us all? Why do we deal treacherously every man against his brother, profaning the covenant of our ancestors?" (Malachi 2:10)

IS LOYALTY A MATTER OF LAW OR OF LOVE?

The early 1950's, sometimes wistfully recalled as an idyllic time in America, were actually a very troubled time. The Cold War was raging between the Soviet Union and the United States. There was growing anti-Semitism behind the Iron Curtain. Jews in America were especially singled out as possible subversives involved in treasonous propaganda, if not actual treasonous acts on behalf of the U.S.S.R. Accusations were made against writers, Hollywood figures, politicians and many innocuous organizations. The leading accuser and veritable symbol of that search for Communists under every bed was Senator Joseph P. McCarthy.

In 1953, as President of the Southern California Board of Rabbis, I was part of a committee investigating several physicians suspected of subversive affiliations whom Cedars of Lebanon Hospital was not reappointing to their staff positions. The proliferation of so-called "Loyalty Oaths" taken by individuals and organizations in order not to lose jobs, tax-exemptions, or even personal freedom for prison reached into the heart of the churches and synagogues.

The following is a sermon delivered as a protest to the wave of fear which engulfed the country and invaded our own synagogue Board of Trustees.

APRIL 2, 1954

Dear Friends:

"The world has never had a good definition of the word liberty and the American people are just now in want of one." Abraham Lincoln made the statement exactly 90 years ago this month. It is no less appropriate today. It is of defining liberty that I speak tonight, defining liberty and three other concepts which begin with the liquid sound of "L:" loyalty, law and love. These definitions are sorely needed, in Lincoln's words, just now, for good Americans who are loyal and loving, who respect our nation's laws, and who believe in preserving its traditional liberty, but are madly confused by the doubts and fears generated since the conclusion of World War II.

Perhaps the most tragic single development in our time has been that all the sacrifices of all the men and women who worked and fought and died in this most recent world-wide struggle, have not purchased peace or victory or security. Our nation, the most victorious of all the victor nations, with none of our soil invaded or our property ravaged, has reaped a bitter harvest of insecurity, suspicion and unhappiness.

The cause? Our justifiable fear of the acts and the intentions of Russia and her satellites, many of which have been rendered all the more fearful by being veiled behind an Iron Curtain of secrecy. This fear is compounded into terror by the armaments race in which we have led, but Russia has followed closely behind so that her destructive potential is horrifying to a degree only slightly less than ours. These have been the causes of our bitter fruits of victory.

And the effects? The effects have been to turn citizen against citizen in suspicion and accusation and produce a gradual erosion of our traditional American freedoms. Since the end of the war, we have watched the policing powers of the Executive branch of government and the punitive powers of the Judicial branch of government taken over by investigating committees of the Legislative branch of both state and national governments. We have seen men and women tried and condemned by innuendo, by newspaper headlines, by being placed upon lists, sometimes on the basis of legitimate evidence, sometimes on the basis of hearsay and highly questionable testimony.

We have seen fear of similar treatment silence American citizens one by one, as the press, the schools, the politicians and even the clergy fell prey to irresponsible and unrestrained attack.

We have seen a proud nation of patriotic citizens insisting by law upon oaths of loyalty, as if the imposing of these oaths could insure our national security. In New York, in order to become a tenant in a publicly financed housing project, one must take an oath that one does not belong to any of the organizations listed as subversive by the attorney general. In California, one must take such an oath in order to hold any office or employment with any county, city, district, political subdivision, authority, board, bureau, commission, or other public agency, including the University of California. There is a proposal that such an oath be required of veterans of the United States Armed Forces in order to receive their veterans' benefits. Some industries have imposed upon themselves a loyalty oath to be taken by all those seeking or holding employment.

The effect of all this has been to change the political climate of our country radically in a very few years. We have learned very rapidly to give up certain rights to express ourselves freely, and we have become suspicious of one another to the point of becoming informers upon one another. We have learned to be very careful and circumspect in what we say, what we endorse, whom we criticize and whom we join.

In fact, the taking of the loyalty oath was finally faced by this and every other religious congregation, as well as every charitable, health and welfare institution in this state. Let me clarify the circumstances. On November 7, 1944, a new section was adopted as part of Article XIII of the California state constitution. This section reads in part, "The Legislature may exempt from taxation all or any portion of property used exclusively for religious, hospital or charitable purposes...not conducted for profit and no part of the net earnings of which inures to the benefit of any private shareholder or individual."

It means that the property our congregation owns, which must be in excess of $200,000 in value could be exempted by the state legislature from taxation, as could the earnings, and was and is so exempted. It means that places like the new Jewish Center building, the Cedars of Lebanon Hospital, and others which could not exist were they obliged to pay exorbitant taxes, may carry on their function enjoying a tax exemption.

Now on November 4, 1952, you and I went to the polls and voted for two propositions which were approved by a majority of the voters and incorporated in the same constitution. I call your attention to part of that Amendment, which is known as Section 19 of Article XX. It reads, "Not withstanding any other provision of this constitution no person or organization which advocates the overthrow of the government of the United States or the state by force or violence or other unlawful means or who advocates the support of a foreign Government against the United States in the event of hostilities shall...(and there is a section (a) which forbids holding of any public office or trust) and (b) receive any exemption from any tax imposed by this State or any county, city, district, political subdivision, authority, board, bureau, commission, or other public agency of this State. The Legislature shall enact such laws as may be necessary to enforce the provisions of this section."

In 1953 the State legislature acted on the strength of the Constitutional Amendment as it was permitted to do. The Revenue and Taxation Code of the State of California now contains a Section 32 which reads, "Any statement, returns or other document in which is claimed any exemption...from any property tax imposed by this state, or any county, city, etc. shall contain a statement that the person or organization making the statement, return or other document does not advocate the overthrow of the government of the United States or the State of California by force or violence or other unlawful means nor advocate the support of a foreign government against the United States in the event of hostilities. If any such statement, return or other document does not contain such a declaration, the person or organization making such statement, return or other document shall not receive any exemption from the tax. Any person or organization who makes such declaration knowing it to be false is guilty of a felony. This section shall be construed so as to effectuate the purpose of Section 19 of Article XX of the Constitution."

On March 15th, our congregation had to file its State return and ask for an exemption, as it has done every year. This year, however, we were obliged to make a solemn declaration that, as you heard, we do not advocate the overthrow of the government by force or violence or any other unlawful means nor advocate the support of a foreign government against the United States in the event of hostilities.

Our alternatives were as follows: If we wanted the tax exemption we had to make our pledge of loyalty. If we wanted to waive our exemption and pay the tax, we did not have to take such a pledge, but by our waiver we would be indicating our objection to the oath. Or, we could make the declaration, claim the exemption, and send along a note of dissatisfaction with the law, which we were obeying.

Our Temple Board of Directors met and had a heated discussion, in which the many facets of the problem were explored. The entire Board was then polled by telephone. The decision was about two to one in favor of signing the oath, asking for the exemption and sending along a note of protest.

All Catholic institutions took the oath and stated it was a privilege to do so. The Protestant institutions, by and large, took the oath, with only the Friends Society, some Methodists, some Universalists and a few Congregationalist churches refusing. All Jewish organizations with one or two possible exceptions took the oath, with many registering a protest.

Now let us see why this should be such a problem. Surely we of this congregation do not advocate disloyalty to our state or nation. Indeed, on page 130 of our prayer book you will find our prayer, read weekly with genuine sincerity, "Our God and God of our Fathers, we invoke Thy blessing upon our country, on the government of this republic, the President of these United States, and all who exercise just and rightful authority."

Deeply impressed upon our people, wherever we have lived in the world, has been the Prophetic teaching: "Seek the peace of the city, for in the peace thereof shall you find peace." Our Talmudic instruction regarding loyalty to the government of the lands in which we dwell, is a simple one of three words "דינא דמלכותא דינא The law of the land is the law" for

Jews in all civil and criminal matters. We are not ashamed of our loyalty. Why not declare it?

Unfortunately my friends, the matter is not quite so simple. First of all, the atmosphere of fear and suspicion I mentioned earlier has, by this new step, been introduced into the houses of worship in this state. Where loyalty has never been questioned, where indeed, loyalty and good citizenship have been taught, where the public morale has been sustained in times of national strife, suddenly it is challenged. Suddenly, religious people are afraid they will be suspected of disloyalty, their tax exemptions will be lost, their institutions will suffer in some way. Suddenly, we have a situation in which men say, "If we do not sign the loyalty oath I will not belong to this congregation because I would be afraid to be identified with it." Others say, "If we sign it, I will not belong to this congregation because it has abdicated its traditional role of leadership." Not in ours, thank God, but in many, many congregations there has been great and heated division of opinion, and there remain wounds which will never heal. The first product is fear and suspicion.

And second, there has followed the inevitable result of fear and suspicion: informing and accusation. Men and women on boards of synagogues and churches are suddenly calling one another reactionaries or communists. There is already detected a tendency to report to someone that the minister or the deacon or the elder has leftist leanings.

Third, censorship of the pulpit must inevitably follow. Let us examine the law again. The president or other lay leader of the congregation has taken an oath that the organization does not advocate overthrow of the government by force or violence or any other unlawful means. Now who advocates in a church or synagogue? The priest or minister or rabbi.

Suppose he does advocate something which is construed as a breach of the oath. Then, if you recall the law, the person who took the oath is guilty of a felony and can be prosecuted. Now, should not the congregational leadership set up some machinery for censorship of the pulpit in order to protect itself? Should not the rabbi, as someone suggested to me in jest, submit his sermon for scrutiny and approval by Wednesday at the latest? And lest he deviate from the script, should not his remarks be recorded as they are actually delivered? And what of his remarks away from the pulpit? Who will monitor them? Who will verify a bad report of his remarks?

I wonder if you share my concern in this matter and see as I do, that freedom of the pulpit, so long a sacred right jealously guarded not only in

America, but in most lands, is in grave danger. How many preachers, earnestly motivated by what they believe is the word of God spoken through them, will either talk themselves into a heap of trouble or else desert the pulpit rather than compromise with their freedom of expression? Unless I am mistaken, the end product of this new development would be censorship of the pulpit and a further loss of freedom.

And fourth, there is the one great problem which darkly colors the other three: the problem of who is to interpret what is disloyal. Who will decide what is meant by the words "advocate overthrow of the government by force or violence or any other unlawful means?" What committee of the state government not yet constituted, will supervise the enforcement of this oath? Is it to be someone of the nature of our own State Senator, Jack B. Tenney? In his red book are such names as B'nai B'rith, Hadassah, Rabbi Max Nussbaum and Rabbi Edgar I. Magnin among those whom he regards as subversive. Is the man who has advocated the reading of the infamous "Protocols of the Elders of Zion," who accuses American Jews of brain-washing their non-Jewish neighbors, is he to be one of the judges of what is disloyal in the pronouncements of a Jewish religious organization?

We do not know who will interpret the law, nor how nor by means of what machinery. We can only look into the future and realize that year after year we shall be obliged to swear not that we are loyal, but rather that we are not disloyal, unless our state constitution is once again amended, or what is more likely, unless our legislature can be persuaded to change the Revenue and Taxation Code once again to eliminate this tragic error of legislative judgement.

Because, my friends, the oath it contains is a futile instrument to test genuine loyalty and devotion to American ideals. If it could save our beloved land, if it could protect our citizenry from sabotage and destruction or from insidious subversive propaganda, I would advise swearing our loyalty every hour of the day.

Unfortunately, however, the loyalty oath has become a kind of magical incantation, intended to make us more secure, but actually making us fearful and less secure. What truly subversive person, what fanatical Communist or Fascist would hesitate to swear loyalty on a stack of Bibles to gain immunity for acts of treason? What avail are repeated oaths which offend and insult the loyal and shield the disloyal? Will the Communist be less dangerous if he does not live in a New York housing project? Will the veteran who has spent his years leaping in and out of foxholes become more patriotic when he takes an oath? Is the State of California now safe from the bomb because the churches and synagogues, of all harmless places, have pledged they will not advocate its use against their own homes?

The present international crisis calls for greater wisdom than is implied in the atmosphere of hysterical investigation, name calling and oath-taking which we are now breathing. It calls for wise legislation by level-headed and wise political leaders.

Happily, I believe that the past several weeks have begun to witness a turning of the tide against irresponsible legislators and legislation which do not protect our nation but do undermine our traditional freedoms. Courage has suddenly become fashionable once again in some quarters, and loyal Americans are reminding us of our great American heritage of freedom. Recently in Washington the Freedom Shrine was dedicated and the Freedom Credo, composed by Don Belding of our city was made its central theme. That credo stresses, among other things "the right to worship God in one's own way; the right to free speech and press; and the right to freedom from arbitrary Government regulation and control."

It is good to hear such a credo these days. It is good to hear the president of Stanford University, Dr. Wallace Sterling, say, as he did last week, "The problem is that controversy has ranged far beyond the communist issue in recent months. It is pointed up by the anxiety of many, including myself lest honest patriotic dissent be regarded as disloyalty. Loyal dissent is both permissible and necessary."

It is good to hear that one may dissent from the opinions of Tenney and McCarthy and Stevenson and Eisenhower and still be a loyal American. It is good to hear men expressing themselves with greater courage and candor and condemning the reign of terror which has been threatening our free land. It will be good to hear the citizens of this state, now that they are alerted to the implications of the loyalty oaths for religious and welfare organizations, raise their voices in opposition to the new laws and, by peaceful and legal processes open to the citizenry, amend or abolish them. It will be good to restore American rugged individualism which speaks its mind unafraid because we can have no wise laws nor free enforcement of wise laws unless there is free expression of the wisdom of the people and, alas, their folly with it.

But folly will die of its own poison and wisdom will survive. And if wisdom survives and freedom with it, then I have no fears for America. Because the people of America love America, and loyalty is not a matter of law but of love. You cannot legislate loyalty to country any more than you can legislate loyalty to husband or wife, to parents or child. Only love can produce that loyalty, and only love for America can guarantee the loyalty of its citizens. Let us never forget it.

I believe in that love. I teach it from the pulpit and shall continue to teach it as long as I am free to do so. I know it is there in the grateful hearts of the overwhelming majority of our citizens. I am confident that if we dissipate the atmosphere of fear and suspicion, the people of our land in all their glorious love for country will protect her from attack and subversion. They will go on to share our traditional freedoms with the free world and work for a united, peaceful and happy life for all the nations of the world.

INTEGRATION OR DISINTEGRATION

In late 1957, the Supreme Court decision holding segregation to be unconstitutional resulted in refusal to uphold that law in Little Rock, Arkansas, and throughout the South. The battle against integration there absorbed the attention of most Americans. Every device, legal and illegal, was used to thwart the spread of integration. Blacks were in flight from the Southern states to the North and whites in the North were in flight as blacks moved near them.

I joined with many activist rabbis around the country in denouncing efforts to thwart integration. This sermon states the Jewish position as I saw it and insists that Judaism stands squarely in support of all persons whatever their color and suggests that the choice facing us was integration or disintegration.

NOVEMBER 8, 1957

Dear Friends:

It is almost exactly 100 years since Abraham Lincoln, speaking at the Republican State Convention in Springfield, Illinois, made his famous address which began, "If we could first know where we are and whither we are tending, we could better judge what to do and how to do it. We are now in the fifth year since a policy was initiated with the avowed object and confident promise of putting an end to slavery agitation. Under the operation of that policy, that agitation has not only not ceased but has constantly augmented. In my opinion, it will not cease until a crisis shall have been reached and passed. A house divided against itself cannot stand. I believe this government cannot endure permanently half slave and half free."

Now that century has passed, and again I wonder if we know where we are and what to do. We are now in the third year since the Supreme Court decisions which marked an official end to policies of segregation in our land and the beginning of a gradual process of integration. Yet, to use Lincoln's words, "that agitation has not only not ceased, but has constantly augmented," and to paraphrase his words, this government cannot endure permanently half-integrated and half-segregated. The choice confronting us at this moment in American history is integration or disintegration.

In a Gallup poll published last week, the public was asked which issue they believed of greatest importance in American political life today. The answer, interestingly and, perhaps, surprisingly enough, was not the issue of national defense or even the current excitement over the artificial satellites. With the intuitive wisdom sometimes possessed by the man in the street, Americans expressed the greatest amount of concern over the problem of integration. To Americans, the battle of Little Rock was of more immediate concern than the international arms race. It may be that the man in the street senses the great challenge to American ideals posed by Little Rock and feels, too, that the choice is integration or disintegration.

Tonight we, as a Jewish congregation, should stop to consider how this choice affects us as Americans, as Jews and as individuals claiming a religious faith.

What does Little Rock mean to us as Americans? It was January 1, 1863 when the final form of the Emancipation Proclamation was signed by President Lincoln. It read in part, "...I do order and declare that all persons being held as slaves within said designated States and parts of States are, and henceforth shall be free; and that the Executive Government of the United States, including the military and naval authorities thereof, will recognize and maintain the freedom of said persons."

That was in 1863. Children born that day grew up, married, had children; their children had children; their children had children; their children had children; their children had children and through these five generations the venom and hatred, the contempt and bigotry have survived and been transmitted. Even this year in Little Rock, Arkansas, as well as in Georgia, and Alabama, and many another states, teenage youngsters are still expressing deep-seated convictions that their Negro contemporaries are somehow different, inferior, less than human.

Meanwhile, their elders are employing every device, legal and illegal, to thwart the objectives of the Supreme Court decisions holding segregation unconstitutional and are defying the law of the realm. The result is, in effect, a state of insurrection, a second Civil War.

That Civil War, currently in the Cold War stage, has been slow in developing. At first the South was somewhat stunned by the Supreme Court decisions. There were even voices of reason lifted up there expressing their acceptance or the law of the land even though they disagreed with it.

Today, three years later, such voices of reason have largely been stilled as tempers have flared hotter and hotter. At first, the average citizen was shocked, but yet unwilling to defy the wisdom of so august a body as the United States Supreme Court. Today the spirit of rebellion is much stronger. Voices of moderation have been hushed, teachers expressing views of acceptance of the inevitable have been dismissed, newspaper opinion has been stifled. Fewer and fewer compromises have been made.

The resentment expressed first against the Supreme Court has spread to include the national government, the North and finally the Negro, himself. Not uncommon these days is the expression, "A war between the whites and blacks is coming as sure as you are standing here." The contemptuous but sometimes good-natured tolerance of the Negro has now been replaced with deep-seated resentment. One Southern editor recalled how easy it was for him to raise funds for a Negro YMCA a while back. "Now," he reports, "I wouldn't get a nickel if I tried to do that."

For the first time the Negro is being encouraged to migrate out of the South. Years ago jail sentences were handed out to people enticing Negroes to move out. Trains were held up and Negroes caught trying to move out of town and go North were arrested and fined. This was when the South needed their labor. It was true even in recent decades. Today, with the South less dependent upon cheap labor, the Negro is being pushed to move out if he doesn't like his environment.

The result is the great migration northward and westward, with over a third of American Negroes living away from the South. Many Southerners point to discriminations that Negroes suffer in the North and say, "Why don't you clean up your own backyard before telling us what to do?"

There is truth in their charge, as we shall soon see, and yet there is a difference, the real difference which makes us at this moment a nation half integrated and half segregated. In the North, the Negro can fight for his rights, using the law to help himself. In the South it is the law of the state itself which is against him. In the North, the Negro suffers in the conflict of groups and at the hands of prejudiced individuals. In the South he suffers from discrimination holding sway by law. In the Biblical words, quoted by Lincoln, America is today a house divided, and a "house divided against itself cannot stand."

I do not speak in alarm but in sober warning: the seeds of division which could split the American union have been planted deeply and fertilized by the segregation issue. There is a real possibility of America choosing between integration or disintegration.

Where shall Jews stand on this issue? In Little Rock itself, Rabbi Ira Sanders has taken his place as one of the leaders of the interfaith effort now underway in the tense community. In Virginia, in the community of Falls Church, Sam Klein refused to sign a pupil placement form for his son

Joel, a device used as an anti-integration measure. Mr. Klein claimed that the anti-segregation stand of his spiritual leader, Rabbi Emmet Frank, had been his guide. In Detroit, Rabbi Morris Adler represented the Jewish community in a declaration denouncing intimidation of non-white persons moving into previously white residential areas.

Now in taking such forthright stands, the Jewish citizen finds himself on the one hand risking a vicious trap. If he chooses to throw in his lot with the white citizen's councils, he finds himself a quick target for boycott of his business by the large Negro population in some Southern communities, and the victim of Negro-sponsored anti-Semitism. If he takes a firm stand for integration, he finds himself attacked as a Jew by his white Christian neighbors.

For each of the rabbis I previously mentioned there is another rabbi who has been forced to resign by his congregation for expressing views such as I am expressing. The most recent case of such a resignation was observed only this week.

On the other hand, the Jew finds himself reacting personally in many places as a creature of prejudice himself. For all our liberal utterances, the American Jewish community is as fearful and antagonistic to the Negro as the American white Christian community. The Jew does not express himself in burning crosses, however, but rather in the no less expressive process of running from the Negro as from the plague.

No one will ever be able to record how many millions of dollars it has cost the American Jewish community to build community facilities and then abandon them because neighborhoods ceased to be Jewish in the face of Negro invasion, The entry of one Jew into an all Christian neighborhood produces nowhere near the panic that is occasioned by the entry of one Negro into an all-Jewish neighborhood. That is regarded as a signal for a new exodus, with "For Sale" signs popping like mushrooms on the lawns. We have seen it happen in community after community: parts of Brooklyn, Philadelphia, Cleveland, Chicago, even Los Angeles.

The West Adams Jewish community thrived for less than one generation before abandoning synagogues, schools and centers and fleeing before the onslaught of the Negro. And now, with 1,700 Negroes a month moving from the South into Los Angeles, we are told in a recent survey that the Beverly-Fairfax and the Wilshire-Fairfax areas will soon be Negro. No Jew will have been ousted from his home, his Jewish shopping, his synagogues and schools, his Jewish center. He will have run. The milk of human kindness and brotherly love for the Negro of Little Rock pumping in his veins, he will pick up his skirts and run before the Negro of Los Angeles. He has ideals and principles about brotherhood and tolerance for himself and the Negro of Little Rock, but the dark-skinned family down the block from him is real, and that is another matter.

And yet, who better than the Jew should understand the need of the American Negro for acceptance? Who better than the Jew, to whom there was given the taste of slavery in Egypt, there was given the lesson of Moses, "Thou shalt love thy neighbor as thyself;" to whom there was hurled the challenge of God through Amos his prophet,

הלוא כבני כשיים אתם לי בני ישראל נאם יהוה

"Are ye any better than the children of the Ethiopians unto me. O Children of Israel," saith the Lord. (Amos 9:7)

Who better than the Jew who has known the isolation of the ghetto, the snarling of the mob, the stigma of the yellow badge, the gas chambers of Hitler? Who better than the Jew, who, himself, has been accused falsely of every imagined blemish now applied to the Negro-a distinctive odor, a dangerous nature, a sub-human status, who better than the Jew should understand the need of the American Negro to be accepted not as a freak but as a fellow human being? If the Jew has himself not yet been thus fully accepted, let him at least not be guilty of the same sin against another man because his skin is dark.

For the religious Jew, his faith imposes upon him certain beliefs, which he must embrace or else, in hypocrisy, reject in practice. Our Bible teaches us that we are all children of God, created in His divine image. That means the Negro bears that heavenly stamp no less than you or I. Our Bible teaches us that we are all essentially brothers tracing back to a common ancestry in Adam.

Our Bible asks us, "Have we not all one Father? Hath not one God created us? Why do we deal treacherously, a man against his neighbor?" It tells us that there shall be one law, not two, for the Jew and for the non-Jew who dwells among us. Our faith recognizes that as human beings, so imperfect, so insecure, we tend to be afraid of that which is unlike ourselves. Therefore it tries to teach us to overcome these prejudices rather than be overcome by them. The Talmud proclaims, "או חברותא או מיתותא... Either brotherhood or death."

Dear friends, this country with its mixture of citizens cannot survive unless its inhabitants learn to live with one another without fear and without prejudice. The white community will not be swallowed up by the Negro community. The Jewish community will not be swallowed up by the non-Jewish community, white or Negro. Not only the people of Little Rock, but the people of Los Angeles, including the Jews, will have to learn that their children may attend a school and sit side by side with a Negro, an Oriental, an alien and be the richer, not the poorer for the experience. We shall have to learn that a Catholic, a Protestant, a Jew, a Negro, a Mexican, a Nisei, can live in the same block without the world coming to an end. We shall have to learn that a principle is a principle no matter to whom it is applied.

In today's Jewish press the big headline was, "Florida Revokes Broker's License for Sale to Jew," and we are incensed. Would we be similarly incensed if it read "for Sale to Negro?" We cannot talk out of both sides of our mouths. It is increasingly clear that the alternatives facing our country are integration or disintegration, "או חברותא או מיתותא." Brotherhood in action, not only in words, or death to the great American experiment in freedom and equality. Our religion, Judaism, is unequivocal in its choice in the matter. It chooses life and brotherhood. It recognizes the worth and the sacredness of every human soul.

It remains for you and for me, before we condemn Little Rock, to look deep within ourselves and see what we discover there. If it is unworthy of the Jew, let us cast it out and replace it with love, understanding and a real determination to make our faith operative in our life and in the life of these United States.

THE VISIT: AN IMMORALITY PLAY

I rarely reviewed books, movies, or plays from the pulpit, leaving this pleasant exercise for a less formal setting. The play, "The Visit," by Friedrich Duerrenmatt, was hailed as the best foreign play by the New York Critics choice. A brilliant stage piece, it espoused a relentlessly monstrous notion of man as utterly corruptible from the highest to the lowest in society, the clod and the cleric, the plebeian and the politician. It said unequivocally that greed is the prime mover in all interpersonal relationships, usurping man's judgment, hardening his heart and blinding him to justice.

The play's popularity and unilateral acceptance cried out for rebuttal of its philosophy. I cannot say that in the heat of my retort I succeeded in giving the lie to its depressing message, but perhaps some who listened had second thoughts about it.

Now, 43 years later, having witnessed the corrupting power of materialism, I am not quite so sure any more that "The Visit" was a false image of society. Materialism and greed can make man utterly corruptible.

DECEMBER 4, 1959

Dear Friends:

"In the beginning God created the heaven and earth. And God beheld all that He had created, and behold, it was very good." (Genesis 1:1,31) So begins the story of creation in the Bible, a picture of harmony very gratifying to its author. Its peacefulness is soon broken, however, with the serpent's temptation of Eve, her temptation of Adam, their vain attempt to hide from God, their banishment from the Garden of Eden, the first murder and the growth of wickedness in human society, culminating in the narrative of Noah. As the Bible says, "And God saw that the wickedness of man was great in the earth…and it repented the Lord that he had made man on the earth." (Genesis 6:5,6)

From that ancient day when man became aware of human wickedness, we have been faced by a great dilemma, the dilemma of a creature, made somehow other than all other creatures, capable of great heights of nobility, created, as it were, in the divine image, and yet capable of terrible corruption. What is man? Little lower than the angels or little more than the serpent?

One answer to that riddle is offered currently on the stage in a play called, "The Visit." It stars Alfred Lunt and Lynn Fontaine, and has been playing since May 5, 1958 in America and before that in Zurich, France, England and Germany. It was written by Friedrich Duerrenmatt, a Swiss playwright and novelist, and adapted in English by Maurice Valency, Professor of Comparative Literature at Columbia University. It was awarded the New York Critics Award for the best foreign play of 1958 and is included among the ten best plays of 1957-1958.

It merits its recognition as a theater piece for it is a remarkably well-wrought script, marching inexorably to its grisly final curtain without a single wasted word, a single extraneous motion. It is brilliantly staged, lighted, directed and acted. But its technical excellence is not what compels me to mention it.

It preaches a doctrine, an evil doctrine, in my opinion, even a dangerous one, which must be discussed, understood and rejected. It is the doctrine previously articulated by Duerrenmatt, who said, "The world for me stands as something monstrous, an enigma of calamity which has to be accepted but to which there must be no surrender."

This doctrine he illustrates with a dramatic fable, shall we call it, this play, "The Visit," in which he answers the question "What is man?" with an absolutely uncompromising, unrelieved indictment, "Man is little more than the serpent, an utterly corruptible and corrupted being in a monstrous world of his own making." My question tonight is, does society accept this indictment with that complete resignation in which the play's chief protagonist accepted his, or does society reject it?

In order better to understand why I am raising this question it is essential we know something about the story. It begins in the dilapidated railway station of a little European town called Gullen where Goethe slept and Brahms once composed a quartet. Now its industries are all closed by some mysterious blight which has plunged all the village into poverty and despair.

Word has come that Madame Claire Zachanassian, who is perhaps the world's richest woman, is coming to be married in the town cathedral. For there, long years ago she had been born and raised until she was 17. It is hoped she will invest a little of her wealth in Gullen and wake it from its economic slumber, and the hopes are pinned on a shabby storekeeper, Anton Schill, who once was her boyhood lover.

She arrives with a strange entourage. In the course of being obsequiously welcomed by the town she makes a remarkable proposal. She will give one billion marks, five hundred million to the town for its development and five hundred million to be divided up personally among the people of the town.

All she wants in return is that Anton Schill, who, when she was 17 refused to acknowledge paternity of her illegitimate child, shall be put to death. To this proposal the mayor of the town responds, "Madame Zachanassian, we are not in the jungle, we are in Europe. We may be poor, but we are not heathens. In the name of the town of Gullen, I decline your offer. In the name of humanity, we shall never accept." Everyone in the town applauds his stand, but Madame Zachanassian rises and says, "Thank you, Burgomaster. I can wait."

The second act sees Anton Schill in his shop, bewildered as the townsfolk begin to buy more expensive items from him, asking him to extend them credit. He observes they have purchased new shoes on credit. Schill begins to feel the clutch of panic. He rushes to the policeman, asking him to arrest Madame Zachanassian for incitement to murder, saying, "All of a sudden my customers are buying white bread, whole milk, butter, imported tobacco, new shoes." To which the policeman replies, holding out his foot which has a shiny new boot, "And what do you have against new shoes?"

Schill sees the policeman is drinking imported beer, not the local brew, and he even has a new gold tooth. Schill rushes off to the mayor's office, where he runs into bland hypocrisy. Observing that the burgomaster has an expensive cigar and a new silk tie, he asks, "And have you also bought new shoes?"

"Why yes," says the Burgomaster, "I ordered a new pair from Kalberstadt. Extraordinary, however did you guess?"

Schill runs to the church, where the pastor assures him he has nothing to fear. Schill seems to find relief from his panic as he kneels before the altar, until suddenly, the bells peal. Then a new bell chimes in. Schill lifts his head, hearing the new bell.

"Yes," says the pastor with pride. "Its tone is marvelous, don't you think? Full. Sonorous."

Stepping back in horror, Schill cries, "A new bell! You, too, pastor? You, too?"

Falling to his knees, the pastor prays, "O God, God forgive me. We are poor weak things, all of us. Do not tempt us any further. Go, Schill, while there is still time."

Schill's fright grows as he is convinced beyond a shadow of a doubt that everyone is incurring debts against the day when he will be killed, and they will get their billion marks. He writes to the authorities in Kaffingen, but the postmaster holds up his letter. He runs to the railroad station to escape the town, but all the townspeople are there and stand between him and the train until it leaves. Utterly defeated, realizing the avenging lady will find him even in Australia and have her way, he turns back to the town, rejecting a passing truck driver's offer of a ride.

The town teacher and doctor make a last stand, appealing to the lady for mercy, the highest form of justice. But she replies, "The highest form of justice has no pity."

And to their pleas that she endear herself forever to the town by buying its industries and setting them working again, she answers, "I cannot buy these plants. I already own them. I bought up this rubbish piece by piece and own it all. Your hopes were an illusion, your vision empty, your self-sacrifice a stupidity, your whole lives completely senseless. I am 'that mysterious blight.'"

The teacher and the doctor give up, feeling themselves hardening against Schill. The burgomaster comes to Schill and offers him a gun to take his own life and spare the town the trouble, but Schill says, "You were my friend, you smiled and reassured me. But day by day, I saw you change your shoes, your ties, your suits, your hearts. If you had dealt frankly with me, perhaps I would feel differently toward you now I might even use that gun you brought me for the sake of my friends. But now I have conquered my fear. Alone. It was hard, but it's done. And now you will have to judge me. And I will accept your judgment. For me that will be justice. How it will be for you, I don't know. You may kill me if you like, but I won't do your job for you, either."

Schill turns finally to home and family. His wife, his son and his daughter come in, all decked out in their new finery, bought "on account." They are going for a ride in their new car, bought "on account." He asks them to take him for a ride, but they refuse, saying, "That wouldn't look very nice."

He says goodbye to them, but they scarcely acknowledge his farewells as they drive off to the next town, to the cinema, so as not to be present for his execution.

The people have a meeting for the benefit of the press, who have come to this little town to cover Madame Zachanassian's eighth wedding and witness her huge gift to the people. When the press is gone, the townspeople, all dressed up, form two lanes, leading to the town athlete, in his sleeveless jersey, who stands waiting. As the policeman shoves him, the burgomaster turns his back, the pastor prays, Schill drags himself to the athlete, who strangles him to death with his bare hands.

When the job is done, the teacher covers him with his academic cloak, the doctor pronounces "heart failure," which the Burgomaster changes to "died of joy," and the avenging woman enters with her butler, who takes a check for one billion marks from his wallet.

I found myself outraged at the total depravity of the human spirit this play presented. It preaches that money and vengeance rule the world. This is sometimes and in some places true, but not always and everywhere. Men are motivated by nobler impulses than greed and hatred, powerful as they may be. Men are motivated also by the need to be of service in this life, by the need for love, by the need for sacrifice.

The same day I saw this play, I read the remarkable story of a little Israeli boy who went with his father on a mission to Ghana, in Africa. There he suffered a brain concussion and seemed doomed to death. His father, unable to move him, unable to find medical help in that isolated place, radioed an S.O.S. for help. His plea was picked up by amateur short-wave operators in four parts of the world. They, in turn sought medical help. Within hours, without knowing of one another, four of the greatest brain surgeons in the world were on planes, at their own expense, flying to Ghana to help this unknown little Israeli boy. Why? For money? For vengeance? Because the world is monstrous?

I grow weary of those who are always questioning the enigma of calamity, which means the problem of pain and evil in the world which often afflict the innocent. This is a problem man has been raising since the dawn of consciousness, the problem of Job, the problem of the wandering Jew. How is it we never challenge the enigma of life and beauty and goodness, never ask why there should be life and health and a new day and kindness and love?

Life is a variety of experiences. The world is a variety of environments. Society is a variety of human actions. Our privilege is to know and experience that variety of pain and joy, of night and day, of evil and good, of hatred and love, of black and white, of love and death. Whoever says it is all pain and night and evil and hatred and blackness and death lies to us, deceives with a cunning half-truth, blinds us to our opportunities for happiness and robs us of our ambition to improve ourselves and our world.

We cannot accept such a half truth. We Jews who thank God of whom we say He is "עושה שלום ובורא רע" creator of well-being as well as evil; we Jews who found there was a Noah worthy of saving even though God saw the wickedness of man was great upon the earth; we Jews who found a Lot worthy of saving even in the wickedness of Sodom and Gemorrah;

we Jews who preached the doctrine of the saving remnant; we Jews who speak of the ל׳ו צדקים, the Lamed Vav Tsadikim, the minimum of thirty-six saintly personalities, in every generation, no matter how corrupt an age may be.

This is why I take exception to the play I described. It gives us not one saving remnant, not one *tsadik*, not one uncorrupted person in all that town, not one ray of hope. I cannot believe that all sparks of decency could be so easily extinguished without a single individual left to protest, just as I refuse to believe that a lynching somewhere in the South tells the whole truth about the South, that the fact there is crime means all men are criminals or the fact that there is war and tyranny and poverty means there will never be peace, freedom and plenty.

The world is neither intrinsically nor unalterably monstrous. It can be as bright and beautiful and humane and benign as the highest ideals to which we cling and aspire. It is only the human imagination, when it becomes sick and despairing, dreams up such fiendish decadence and inhumanity and retreats into immobilized pessimism, that is monstrous.

What is man, little lower than the angels or little more than the serpent? He is both, my friends, he is both. And he lives a lifetime, a commingling of sickness and health, temptation and idealism, evil and goodness in which he has a glorious opportunity to arise from slithering in the mud and slime and lift up his sights to the very stars.

Perhaps no age before ours has been faced with more dangerous pessimism and more breathtaking potentials for progress. It remains for us to pray to be granted the faith and the morale to storm the great heights, discover and appreciate the treasures in each new moment of life and realize the promise of a better future.

THE MARCH ON MONTGOMERY

Thirty-six years ago, at this writing, Dr. Martin Luther King Jr. wired an urgent request to clergy around the country to join him in the Victory Day march on Montgomery, the Alabama state capital. It was to celebrate the successful march from Selma where once he was driven back by state troopers, fire hoses and attack dogs.

I had shared the pulpit with Dr. King in South Central Los Angeles some time before, and that, perhaps, is why he followed up the wire with a phone call. I went and marched. The sights and sounds and emotions of that day were such that I felt compelled to share them with the congregation on the Sabbath eve immediately following my return.

The assassination of Dr. King on April 4, 1968 shocked the world. History took an abrupt turn, but not for the better. The day after the funeral my secretary, Rachel Ferrier told me she, too, had had a dream of America mourning, and its face was both white and black. She asked that I draw it. My drawing follows this address and reflects an idealized image of an America united in mourning. Unfortunately, the image has yet to be realized.

MARCH 25, 1965

Dear Friends:

I have just returned from a brief but extremely vital visit to a foreign country, the capital city of the sovereign State of Alabama; a city whose state capitol flies two flags, the flag of the State of Alabama and the flag of the Confederacy, but not the flag of the United States. I have just returned from the place where Jefferson Davis was sworn in as President of the Confederacy and where, over one hundred years later they still refuse to acknowledge the fact that they lost the war. And if they cannot fight the United States of America, they fight the 34 percent of the population who are descendants of their slaves. I shall try not to repeat the things that you have seen and heard but rather share with you my own vivid impressions.

The first impression was that of deciding to go. Almost everyone said "Don't go! Why you?" And I answered "Why not I? Who is supposed to go? Why is it wonderful for the next man to go, and wrong for me?" There was no good answer, so I went.

My next impression was of departure. Arriving an hour before plane time on Wednesday night I found the 293 men and women who were going. I found dozens of people who were trying to get reservations but couldn't. I found 700 relatives and friends and swarms of photographers and newspaper men jammed into the tiny Burbank air terminal, a space about as large as our temple lobby.

A man from KHJ radio stuck a microphone under my nose and asked, "Rabbi, why are you going?" I answered, and I think in all honesty, "Well, I missed the crossing of the Red Sea. I missed the Boston Tea Party. I was not with the Freedom Riders on the segregated buses. So when Dr. Martin Luther King issued a call to join him on the Victory Day march in Montgomery, I made up my mind that I wasn't going to miss that."

In the crowd, I met my rabbinical colleagues: 13 Conservative rabbis and two Reform rabbis. We stood at the gate together. The dozens of clergymen and the one Catholic nun who were there began to sing Christian religious hymns.

When they paused we looked at one another and spontaneously we broke into singing "HINAY MAH TOV UMAH NA'IM SHEVET ACHIM GAM YACHAD" "Behold, how good and how pleasant it is when brethren can dwell together!" Then we shifted to Hava Nagilla. With pleased smiles the people around us began to pick up the Hebrew words. We repeated them over and over again and they sang them with us. In the chilly, narrow boarding area against the chain-link fence, in that airport, a convivial religious spirit was born and it grew and it did not leave us for the next 40 hours.

The plane was delayed and delayed, and a rumor flew through the crowd, "They think there is a bomb on board!" With that in mind, we eventually boarded the plane and took our seats, weary and drenched in perspiration. Once the plane was airborne, the stewards passed around hot coffee in paper mugs. We had hardly tasted it when the plane took a sudden sustained drop. The coffee flew up to the ceilings, and there was a bit of a panic. I was seated next to the popular singer, Nancy Wilson, who didn't bat a false eyelash, but went on sipping what was left of her coffee.

When the plane touched down in Montgomery, it was 2:45 A.M. our time, 4:45 A.M. their time. We had not yet slept. We entered the air terminal loaded with food, luggage, heavy coats and boots because we had been told it was going to be cold and rainy. We found it hot and humid. We also found no lockers, no check room and no official of the terminal to tell us anything. There were only two Montgomery policemen who refused to answer any questions, not even "Where is the restroom?"

As 43 plane loads swelled our ranks, we awaited the dawn. An Episcopal minister from the North handed out mimeographed instructions which concluded ominously that at the program's end, "All participants are urged to disperse with as much efficiency and speed as possible. Stragglers must not remain in the city." That was not very encouraging.

We bought a copy of the morning newspaper and we read some of the letters to the editor. I quote: "In this gathering of paid professional agitators, pinkos, left-wingers, liberals, beatniks, imitation ministers and brain-washed students, the state of Alabama has, within her boundary, the greatest collection of hypocrites ever assembled. Of course, these are being led by the greatest imitation minister of them all, Dr. Martin Luther King."

Then it went on to add, "I think the above clearly describes the motley gang gathered in Alabama to follow a Judas-goat from Selma to Montgomery." And so on and on and on.

Thus "encouraged," our rabbis jumped over the fence to the landing field, the grassy area, put on tallis and tefillin and davvened Shacharit with greater fervor, I am sure, and sincerity than ever. Our Christian brethren watched us with warm interest and they began to take pictures, and I suspect that they will be back home this weekend telling their congregations of their experiences, and how they saw this marvelous group of Jewish ministers saying their morning prayers, and why didn't they have such a thing?

Wondering what to do with our luggage and reluctant to carry suitcases and packages and bags of food on the long, long march, four of us got the idea of going by cab to the local synagogue. We found that there was no rabbi. We entered through a door which was left accidentally open overnight, which convinced us that there was no rabbi there.

Soon the cantor arrived. He was on his way to a morning minyan. But, like the officers at the terminal, he answered no questions.

I thought it might be a good idea to stand on the steps of the capitol and sound the shofar blast, the traditional ram's horn call to freedom, so I asked the cantor to lend me a shofar. He didn't know of any.

A little discouraged we left our luggage and we went by cab to the so-called City of St. Jude, a large Catholic hospital complex, whose campus was turned into a muddy quagmire by tens of thousands of feet and hundreds of army trucks and jeeps. We felt very much as if we were going into an army camp.

Four thousand people had gathered through the night, and they were just getting up when we got there a little after seven o'clock in the morning. Everywhere there were groups singing and rallying. I met rabbis from all over the country, ministers and priests from everywhere in full ministerial garb spattered with brown mud. I bumped into Dean Sayre, the minister of the National Cathedral in Washington, where the President prays.

Introductions were unnecessary. Every man was every other man's brother. It rained. Nobody noticed it. It stopped. The sun came out, and the ground steamed. Nobody noticed it.

We stood there until 11:05. We were supposed to leave earlier but we heard over the walkie-talkie from the gate leading out of St. Jude's that there were police at the exit who told the head of the line that they could not make a right turn. It was against the law, which meant we couldn't leave the complex.

And then, too, subpoenas were served upon Dr. King and that further delayed us. So it was 11.:05 in the morning when the first marchers left. Dr. King, Dr. Ralph Bunche, James Baldwin, Rabbi Abraham Joshua Heschel and a host of others led the line. It was 11:40 when we got to the gate. We were the California delegation marching behind a California flag held by an Episcopalian minister, loaned by a state senator.

Now for some more impressions: As we marched through the gates of St. Jude's Hospital and out onto the dirt road of the Negro shantytown I had a feeling of leaving safety and getting ready to run a gauntlet. We were instructed to march six abreast. In another ominous instruction we were told that the men should march on the outside of the line and put the women on the inside.

Negro Shantytown was unbelievable - unpainted wooden shacks, three or four generations of Negroes sitting and standing, waving, clapping, singing and blowing kisses, warm smiles from toothless babies to toothless elders.

We felt embraced by humanity, by the marchers all around us, the people in the houses, by the songs that we were singing. Marshaling the lines and keeping us from breaking any city ordinances were the workers. These workers were not what the "Letter to the Editor" described but were mostly ministers, white men in ministerial garb, many with their jackets off and their white sleeves and their white turned collars contrasting proudly with their black vests, running up and back, chanting directions, perspiring, soaking in the rain, smiling.

As we walked along every so often a man stood and held up a little card. It was printed by a Jewish philanthropist out of the middle West, a man who had done a great many wonderful things in this world, a man who had the foresight to print little signs: "KEEP SMILING!" It was a necessary instruction as we trudged those six miles. And wherever we saw it, we did smile.

At one point we reached a hilltop in the road, and I was able to look back behind me at a solid column of chanting humanity at least a half-mile long. Then I looked down the hill in front of us and again I saw a half-mile of solid humanity, united from everywhere by a common concern for other people, for human decency. I must confess as I stood on that hilltop and saw myself and felt myself surrounded by these decent, caring persons, I burst into tears and never really got my eyes dry for hours afterward. They weren't tears of sorrow. They weren't tears of hatred or frustration, but they were tears of pride in the goodness of which man is capable when he tries.

I met many people in the line. Everybody talked to everybody. To my surprise, I found the widow of Sam Zimbalist at whose funeral I had officiated a few years ago. She lives in Malibu and I asked her what religious group she was with. She said, "None in particular." She had heard about the march, phoned the airport, asked if she could get a reservation and just came along.

A tall, heavy set man with a shock of white hair said "Hello, I'm from Iowa." He didn't even have a jacket. He had lost it. He was in shirt sleeves. He said, "You know what happened? I had heard about this march and I said to my wife 'I'm going to Montgomery.' She said, 'You're crazy.' And so I came."

A young man I married eight years ago was in the line and this is how he got there: March 25th was his wedding anniversary. He said, "Remember that date, Rabbi?" I didn't. He said, "It is my anniversary so I said to my wife, 'Honey, would you give me a wonderful anniversary present?' She said, 'Anything you want.' So I said, 'I want to go to Alabama.'" And there he was.

Suddenly we entered the white neighborhood. Lining the road were white faces, faces like our own staring at us in utter hatred.

They had been shouting and jeering for over an hour, but by the time we got there they were tired and silent. Our singing also became quieter. We suddenly felt fear. We felt isolation. An image flashed through my mind. I suddenly imagined, as we ran a few hundred yards to close ranks, that we were a column of prisoners running toward a Nazi concentration camp under the cold eyes of hostile citizens.

This feeling passed again as we entered a Negro section past the shopping district. The Negroes ran out to us with bottles of Coke and ice water and pop and towels for our perspiring faces. Little children ran out to shake hands and somebody made a V for victory sign, and it caught on. From then on, everyone communicated back and forth to the sidewalks with a V for victory sign and the singing revived.

Another impression: The last half mile to the Capitol steps is a broad beautiful avenue between tall buildings at the windows of which and on the pavements of which stood well-dressed white people, screaming at us. You will forgive me if I quote. They called out to us, "Niggers! Bastard Californians!" and other things. But I tell you it didn't hurt at all. I pitied them that they should have to feel that way toward us.

Many windows flew the Confederate flag. One had a huge picture of Dr. Martin Luther King, which said, "A picture of Dr. Martin Luther King at a school for Communists." At one hotel's second-story windows we saw four Negroes, probably waiters, in little white mess-jackets. They were leaning out the window and making the V for victory sign and smiling, and we were smiling and waving back to them from the street.

At the very next window, possibly in the very next room and possibly the dining room, stood a silent, very grim group of well-dressed white diners. They seemed to wonder why we were smiling at them until one leaned out and saw the hand of the Negro waiter in the next window waving at us. We turned to one another and said, "There goes that job."

An impression: In front of the Capitol we were urged to sit down in the streets. There was a soldier every two yards along the pavement, a soldier in United States Army uniform with a Confederate flag patch sewed on his chest. We were surrounded on all sides by a sea of humanity five city blocks long and 70 feet wide, which I am confident was well over 50,000 people singing with Harry Belafonte, listening to speaker after speaker.

Dr. Martin Luther King spoke, stirred us to the core, with his refrain of "Let us march until Brotherhood is more than a meaningless word in an opening prayer, but the order of the day on every legislative agenda."

We could actually feel the sound, the sledgehammer blows of crowd reaction as he said of Alabama since the Civil War, describing the real meaning of segregation, "They had segregated Southern money from the poor whites. They had segregated Southern morals from the rich whites. They had segregated Southern churches from Christianity. They had segregated Southern minds from honest thinking. They had segregated the Negro from everything." And then came an unforgettable climax as he recited the Battle Hymn of the Republic as it has never been recited before, and never received before, until the final refrain with that glorious Hebrew word, "Hallelujah." He repeated it and repeated it four times, "Glory, Glory, Hallelujah, Glory, Glory, Hallelujah, His truth is marching on!"

An impression: The excitement died suddenly and apprehension took over. Our mimeographed instructions said that we were to go three blocks northeast to Patterson Field where buses would be waiting to take us back to the airport. We went over to one of the Montgomery Policemen. We said, "Where is Patterson Field?" He shook his head.

We asked the young soldiers in the United States Army uniform. They were the National Guard. "Where is Patterson Field?" They shook their heads. "Which way is northeast?" They shook their heads.

We felt a growing uneasiness as twilight rushed in, hastened by dark clouds. We began to run in one direction and then in another. Nobody would tell us anything, A rumor spread that the State National Guard which had been nationalized would be de-nationalized in ten minutes and turn from guards to enemies.

We spotted a Negro cab and we took it. We didn't look for any buses, and we raced back to the synagogue for our gear and then down highway 80 to the airport, remembering the warning, "Stragglers must not remain in the city!"

One of our group was in another cab. Suddenly they were given chase by a deputy car, and they were forced slowly off the road, not to the right but to the left. Only by skillful driving on the part of the cabby did they avoid collision with oncoming traffic.

One marcher, as you know, did not make it. Mrs. Viola Gregg Liuzzo was shot and killed as she drove that highway.

Back at the airport, I tried to reach Dr. Martin Luther King and was successful in finding the phone number of the place where he was staying, in absolute secrecy, under heavy guard.

I called him and spoke to him and gave him the good wishes of this community and told him of some financial help which I had along with me. At the end of this incredible day, after having been delayed at the gate, after having marched all those miles, after having spoken and exhausted himself, and after having been turned back from seeing the governor, he was still cordial. He was still warm and friendly: an extremely simple and humble man.

An impression: Utter exhaustion as we awaited our plane for eight long hours, returning home after 42 hours without sleep. Talking it over, one foot-weary rabbi said to me, "You know, it is easier to read history than to be mixed up in the making of it." And that is true.

But I wouldn't have missed it for anything. None of us who went was a hero, and many of us from time to time were afraid of things that might happen. None of us was a hero, but each one of us felt that at least he was, in the fullest sense, a human being. I am glad I went. And as I said, I would not have missed it for anything. And because I was there, you were there. It will get worse before it gets better, but I believe even more now in the goodness of man because I went.

And because I went and saw what I saw and heard what I heard, I believe even more in the goodness of God.

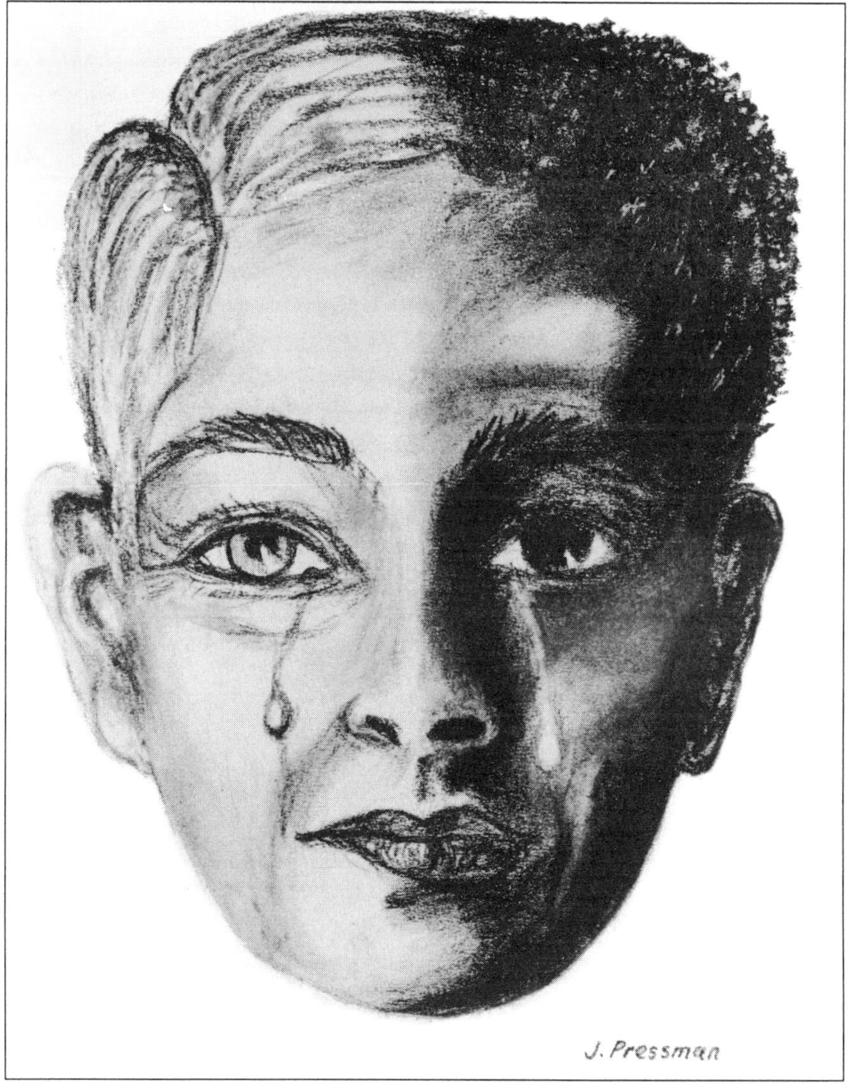

YIZKOR FOR VIETNAM

The winding down of the war in Vietnam coincided with Passover in 1975. The full story of the Vietnamese people who lost over a half-million of their countrymen and the awful truth of the loss of over 65,000 American soldiers blended in with our Yizkor memorial to our Jewish dead and our memories of the Holocaust.

The hot political issues surrounding America's military presence in Vietnam were still being debated, but the human issue of the suffering of the Vietnamese people challenged us. With painful memories of how little the world at large has cared about the successive victimizations of the Jewish people, we asked ourselves if we were much more concerned about the victimization of the Vietnamese. Due to the confusion and the distance of their struggle, it has taken a low priority in our personal agendas. This sermon attempted to heighten our awareness of the interdependence of the whole human race as we recite the Yizkor for those we have known and those whom we have not.

APRIL 3, 1975

Dear Friends:

My head is buzzing with numbers, numbers which rob my days of peace and my nights of sleep. I ask that you share my restlessness and my anguish this day. We have added to our Passover festival of liberation and joy, the solemn Yizkor which evokes memories of people we have loved and lost.

This Book of Remembrance in our hands is crowded with names, thousands of names. To each of us, these names are not cold statistics but warm memories, mixing the pain of our longing for them with the consolation of remembered love for father, mother, husband, wife, son, daughter. Each memory is sharp, special, infinitely important not as a number but as a sacred soul. Heartbreaks of separation cannot be numbered. Things can be numbered. Time can be numbered, but not persons.

Today we read from the Book of Deuteronomy (XVI:9)

"שבעה שבעת תספר לך...Seven weeks shalt thou number unto thee from the time the sickle is first put to the standing corn." This teaches us to number seven weeks from Passover to Shavuot during which the omer of barley was offered daily in the ancient Temple as a sign of gratitude for God's bountiful nature. We call this period the Sefirah, the numbering day by day for 49 days. Days may be numbered. The Psalmist said,

למנות ימינו כן הודע ונביא לבב חכמה

"So teach us to number our days that we may get us a heart of wisdom."

However, persons may not be numbered. In the Book of Exodus when Moses was ordered to take a census, each man was obliged to pay a ransom of a half-shekel for his soul (Exodus XXX:12) "That there be no plague among them when thou numberest them," In a later time, when King David did number his people, we read (Samuel XVIII:) "And there was a great slaughter there that day of 20,000 men." That was pretty scary, I tell you, and so we Jews gave up numbering people. If forced to count, we say, "Not one, not two, not three, etc." It may or may not keep away the plague, but it certainly makes counting interesting.

So we Jews do not number persons. We think of the martyrs of our people immortalized by this memorial wall, inscribed name by name in this black book of the Holocaust victims, as individuals. It may even be wrong to refer to them as the six million. They were Avram and Miriam, Moisheh and Sarah, and Mottele and Shaindele and Leale, and Yankele, 6,000,000 times. They were persons: fathers, mothers, sons and daughters, husbands and wives. Today we ask God Almighty Himself to remember: יזכור אלהים and weep for them along with us.

While the Almighty and you and I weep for them, what of the thousands, alas again a number, who fell to create a homeland for the homeless who survived the Holocaust; the soldiers and civilians of Israel who died in 1948 and 1956 and 1967 and 1973, and all the years between?

And what of the 65,000 American boys and girls, still a depersonalized number, who died in Vietnam, in Quang Tri, and Hue, and Donang, and Kontum, and Pleiku and the Mekong Delta? What of the hundreds of thousands, perhaps millions, of men, women and little children in Indochina who died miserably for reasons as mysterious to them as they are to the American soldiers? I don't know about you, but my Yizkor today will be said in my heart for a suffering humanity in which the familiar faces of my loved ones and the strange faces of people far from me in race and creed are equally precious in the sight of their Creator.

These are not the only numbers which give me no rest today. I am distressed. I am ashamed because 32 years ago at Passover I carried on my life as usual while the Jews of the Warsaw ghetto wrote with their blood a futile but glorious chapter of resistance to tyranny which lasted from Passover to Shavuot. Thirty-one years ago, I carried on my life as usual while the Jews burned in Hitler's crematoria. Thirty years ago, I carried on my life as usual while Jewish survivors wandered across Europe seeking welcome only to meet closed doors except those leading into the displaced persons camps. And 29 years ago, I carried on my life as usual while leaky old boats like the Struma and the Exodus carried my people to ports which turned them back and British gunboats sealed off what was then Palestine,

Now what of this Passover, when the synagogue services in Moscow were forcibly disrupted by uniformed Soviet police; when emigration from Russia is dropping; when Jewish activists like Nashpitz and Taitlionok are sent into exile for five years? What am I doing? What are you doing? What of this Passover when Israel stands holding its breath with constant threat of terrorist attack or with confrontation by a pack of intransigent enemies at Geneva, intoxicated by the smell of oil and blood; or even a sudden undeclared war on one of its borders? What am I doing? What are you doing for Israel bonds, for Welfare Fund pledges, for political action?

To these concerns for my people this Passover, events have added one more torment, elevated from the realm of numbers to the realm of flesh and blood reality and most dramatically illustrated on the cover of *Time* magazine. It shows three Vietnamese mothers, one photographed in 1967, one in 1972 and one last week. In each one, the mother's face is etched with numbed agony holding in her arms the limp, scarred and tattered body of an infant child.

As we sit here, an unknown number, half a million or more...no! Not numbers but Hguyen and Leong and Ngo and Van Chung and Quang and more names strange to us but faces familiar to us, are in flight, in fear, in panic, in hunger, in pain.

Do you know why these slant-eyed brown faces are familiar to us? It is because they are the faces of refugees, the innocent victims of the greed and villainy of others. We Jews know the bitter taste of being refugees. We have had 2,500 years of sad experience at being refugees, of leaving home and possessions and taking staff in hand, putting a pack on our back and eating the dust of unfamiliar roads.

As I watch the tragic, frantic march of the Vietnamese to questionable safety, possibly to starvation, possibly to retaliatory execution, tears of rage and sorrow for the human condition fill my eyes and blur my vision so that I cannot tell whether they are my people or Indochinese people. I can only tell that they are God's people and refugees.

This blurring, this blessed blurring of my vision and my loyalties, is best symbolized for me by identical incidents described in Mr. Nathan Shapell's book, "Witness to the Truth," and in one episode this week in Danang. Shapell tells of carrying little children out of a Polish detention compound in large soup kettles and having mothers with no thought of themselves, thrusting their most precious possession, their children toward him and pleading, "Take mine! Take mine!"

Three days ago at the steps of the last plane out of Danang, jammed with screaming, struggling refugees, Vietnamese mothers unable to get aboard, thrust their babies at arm's length above their heads to those lucky enough to get on board, screaming, "Take mine! Take mine!" Do you think the Vietnamese mother's heart was any less broken than the Jewish mother's? Do you think God weeps any less this week than He wept 30 years ago?

And do you think that the world is any more disturbed about the Vietnamese tragedy and the Vietnamese refugees than it was about the Jewish tragedy and the Jewish refugees? Not at all, my friends. Not at all. Think for a moment and try to measure the extent of your active concern for these newest victims of governmental corruption and stupidity. Look about you at society and analyze the extent of active concern of people in general. What you see is the way it was when the news began to leak out of Europe that Hitler was carrying out his declared intention to murder every Jew in the world! Have you read the dispassionate columns making learned estimates of how many Vietnamese will die in the imminent bloodbath? That is the way pompous commentators spoke of the imminent execution of millions of Jews.

This is what robs me of my sleep: not only the tragedy which is being acted out before our very eyes, but the greater tragedy that we are not half out of our minds with grief and rage and helplessness. The parallel with the Holocaust, a parallel which some Jews resent, saying, "There is nothing like the Holocaust," but is a parallel nevertheless. It instructs today's younger generation and sends chills down my spine because the world cared very little down deep. It was only Jews who were dying.

Today in 1975, the world really cares very little down deep. It is only Vietnamese, only gooks who are dying. Realizing how no progress has been made in the humanizing of man in these past 30 years, I look into the unpredictable future and ask myself in a whisper, "If, God forbid, the State of Israel were ever truly in jeopardy, truly threatened with bloodbath at the hands of a 100,000 Arabs, who would really care and where could we run?"

What to do about Vietnam right now when the possibility of rendering some aid opens up? I am certain that the very first problem would be the problem of starvation. The rice paddies are deserted, the farmers have fled, the distribution chain broken. Already child refugees arriving in the South show the bloated stomachs and spindly legs which are sure symptoms of malnutrition, some beyond hope.

I propose that next Tuesday, Yom Hashoah, the Day of Remembrance of the Holocaust, be declared a day of fasting by every Jew and anyone else who cares to join; and that the money which would have been spent on food be contributed instead to Vietnamese food relief. I estimate a modest ten dollars a day per person for food, and ask that it be sent to me by check made out to Beth Am Vietnamese Relief to be ready for the day when it can be put to use in an organized fashion. I ask that we actually fast as an act of memorial to the Jewish victims of the Holocaust who were our kin so that we can help the Vietnamese refugees who are our fellow human beings, and therefore also our kin. I shall urge my colleagues to ask the same of their congregants.

Unless the tragic experience of the Holocaust sensitizes us to the sufferings of other people, then the one lesson we could have learned from it will be lost, and Hitler will have been handed a posthumous victory.

If there is any lesson we Jews can teach the world, it is the lesson of thinking of all people as sacred souls, children of God, not numbers and of acting toward them all in love and mercy. We, Jews, do not number persons. If forced to count, we say, "Not one, not two, not three, etc." The world will not long survive unless it stops counting its dead by pogroms and pointless wars, and begins to insist, "Not one, not one precious human soul is expendable, not one."

We, especially, are people who understand the truth of John Donne's well-known *Meditation XVII,* written in 1634, a truth the world has yet to learn: "Any man's death diminishes me because I am involved in Mankind; and therefore never send to know for whom the bell tolls; it tolls for thee."

POLITICS AND ETHICS - STRANGE BEDFELLOWS?

In the late summer of 1976, this nation was reeling after the discouraging scandals which resulted in an American president, Richard Milhaus Nixon, and a vice-president, Spiro Agnew, ignominiously being forced out of office.

The misuse of power touched many persons in government. Young people especially were losing faith in politics and politicians.

In re-reading this sermon in the year 2000, I am desolated that many of the ills I described are still with us and have cost the faith and interest of a new generation in their government.

The hotly contested election of the year 2000 and the long, drawn-out court trials and recounts loom large as we review the following sermon with the resigned attitude that the practice of justice and ethics is not compatible with practical politics.

Judaism's long tradition in setting standards for those given authority to lead resounds with striking freshness this befuddled year. It insists that honest government is not an oxymoron, but an ideal for which we must never cease to strive.

AUGUST 20, 1976

Dear Friends,

Believing that you have not heard enough about politics this week, I thought I would talk about it and ask the question, which you will note on the bulletin board outside, "Politics and ethics, compatible?" Is it possible to have the public administration of groups of people compatible with the ethical principles which we attempt to teach in the synagogue and in other religious disciplines.

As we come to each Shabbat we are already thinking about the following Shabbat. It struck me that in the following Shabbat we are speaking of "שפטים ושמרים תתן לך בכל שעריך You shall appoint judges and officers at all thy gates which the Lord thy God giveth thee and they shall judge the people with righteous judgment. Thou shalt not show partiality to persons neither shalt thou take a gift, for a gift shall blind the eyes of the wise and pervert the words of the righteous."

In that context we have the admonition "צדק צדק תרדף –Justice,

justice shalt thou pursue. למען תחיה וירשת את הארץ אשר יי אלהיך נתן לך that thou mayest live and inherit the land which the Lord thy God giveth thee." This pursuit of justice is found in our text in direct connection with the question of political leadership. It is an instruction not only to the people at large but to their leaders. Justice, justice shalt thou pursue.

In the same portion, in the Book of Devarim, the Book of Deuteronomy, in the 17th chapter, there is something unique written about the King. In the Torah, written presumably before we ever had a king, the Lord, through Moses, says to the people, "I suppose, when you come into the land and you become a political entity that you will have a leader."

In those days the only conceivable leader was a king, a monarch. He said, "Only shall he not multiply horses to himself, neither shall he multiply wives to himself, neither shall he greatly multiply to himself silver and gold." In other words, the person in power shall not use that power for his own gain. You have already heard that the judges were instructed not to accept a bribe or a gift for it blinds the eyes and perverts the words of the righteous. Now the king is told, "Look here, I don't care if you're a king. Only don't try to pile up your wealth and multiply your wives and your silver and your gold."

"And it shall be," the Torah says, "that when he sitteth on the throne of his kingdom that he shall write in a copy of this law in a book out of that which is before the priests and the Levites." The king is told that he has to have a copy of the law which is transcribed from the wisdom and the possession of the Levites and the Kohanim to have a copy before him, "And it shall be with him. And he shall read therein all the days of his life that he may learn to fear the Lord thy God to keep all the words of this law and these statutes before him that his heart be not lifted up above his brethren, that he turn not aside from these commandments, neither to the right or to the left hand."

The king is not above the law. He has to have the law always before him. He is even told to read it daily so that he knows what are the moral and ethical principles by which he shall administer the people in order that he shall learn to do these things. He is not exempt from the Mitzvot. He is not exempt from the laws by which everybody lives.

He must do right and not think he is special "...that his heart be not lifted up above his brethren and that he turn not aside from these commandments," that he does not act in any way which is outside the law, "neither to the right nor to the left."

It is interesting that the Torah has a political right and a political left written into it. We read earlier in the Book of Exodus (XVIII:31) that the instruction was given to Moses by his father-in-law Jethro. When he first began his leadership of the people his father-in-law said to him, "You shall appoint out of the people *anshei chayil*," able men *"Yirei Elohim"* such as fear God, *"Anshei Emet"* men of truth, *"Sonei Batzah"* men who hate unjust gain; and place such as them that they may minister over the thousands and the hundreds and the fifties and the tens and let them judge the people at all times." Aren't these wonderful criteria for the selection of leaders? *Anshei Chayil,* able men, capable men. *Yirei Elohim*, men who fear the lord. *Anshei emet,* men of truth. *Sonei batzah,* men who hate unjust gain.

The Torah would not have concerned itself with these instructions were people not, already in those ancient times, long experienced with the corruption of leadership which is somehow inherent in politics. They attempted to give guidelines by which the people should appoint leaders and by which the leaders should conduct themselves. That was a long time ago.

We are modern people; much wiser, more sophisticated, so I guess you and I could assume, therefore, that all of the problems, the bribery, the unjust gain and multiplying gold and silver, perverting justice and turning aside and favoring persons with great partiality and considering one's self as above the law would all be problems of the past.

Unfortunately in recent years, you and I have had considerable exposure to the incompatibility of politics and ethics. It is really staggering to recapitulate what has been happening to this country alone, and this country is fairly uncorrupt.

In this country, only four years ago, the leading nominees who were ultimately elected to office were Nixon and Agnew. And since that time we have had not only the exposure and disgrace of Agnew but shortly thereafter his election to be a spokesman and apologist for the Arab world, expressing himself most unkindly about the Jewish people.

That is all the more disappointing because there was a time during his leadership in Maryland when he was the darling of the Jewish community, the Man of the Year at many a Jewish fund-raising function for Israel and for Jewish education. All this was not very long ago.

In that same time period we have seen the disgrace and departure from office of the president, Richard Milhaus Nixon. We have found in his conduct the violation of the principle which we read in the Torah that a leader may not set himself above the rest of the people, that he must be law-abiding, that he cannot twist the law neither to the right nor to the left. He must be not only one citizen who obeys the law but the prime example of the leader who is law-abiding and ethical in all of his behavior.

In this same time period, we have been treated to the exposure of many of our congressmen and other representatives found guilty of violations of various matters of personal conduct, of personal ethics and misappropriation of federal funds with questionable employees.

In this same time period we have seen the great Lockheed scandal, the payoff that great industries in this country give to leaders, representatives, purchasers and people in sensitive positions in other countries. These payoffs rock the very foundations, the political structure of some other countries, notably Japan.

In the same time period we have seen exposure of principal defense agencies of this country, the CIA and the FBI as acting beyond the law, in violation of the law and in violation of citizen's rights altogether without the due processes of law and not acting according to the will of the people represented by their congressmen and senators and other duly elected representatives.

We have seen the Internal Revenue Service utilized for political purposes, for tormenting and harassing the political enemies of the administration. We have even seen a published list of so-called enemies of that administration, a list, I might add, in which many good people are proud to be included.

We have seen favoritism rampant. We have seen nepotism. We have been witnessing what I would call the Achilles heel of our elective process. We see it in the process of the nominating convention in so many ways.

One of the abuses, and I consider it an abuse and one about which we are going to have to give some thought, is that after all the vast sums to which I shall soon refer are expended in the selection of a president, and people are elected to delegations from each state at great expense, in public elections, in private caucus, people come by the thousands to national nominating conventions. They wrangle and they debate and there are lengthy primary campaigns that are costly and expensive to see who will be nominated for vice-presidency which is a breath away from the presidency and therefore no less important if left to one man.

Nevertheless, the naming of the vice-presidential candidate of whatever party has been left by and large to one man, the man not yet president, the man who is nominated by either party. This is a flaw in our system which at the present moment has provided us two men for the presidency and vice-presidency, neither of whom was the result of that vast and cumbersome nominating process which we have described.

We have seen the national conventions. They are colorful. They are entertaining. They are hard work for the delegates. But the rest of the world sees them as three-ring circuses.

It is hard to explain how, in this very serious matter, there is so much horseplay. It is hard also to realize that in this past week it is estimated the Republican delegates spent about fifteen million dollars in Kansas City. The Democratic convention in New York must have spent as much or more. I think of the millions that were spent on all the primaries and the millions on the elections. I would estimate that before the next president is inaugurated, citizens like you and me will have spent, in contributions, buttons, flags, stickers and political dinners for which we pay and which we attend, a hundred million dollars.

That kind of money is not raised in pennies and nickels and dimes. That kind of money results from just what the Torah was fearful of, the bribe which blinds the eyes of the wise and corrupts the words of the righteous.

People, in order to run for office, must become obligated to other people who give vast sums in one way or another toward a collection pot. It is very difficult to accept thousands of dollars as a political gift for campaigns, and later, when the donor of the gift has a problem either personal or business, to turn that person away and say "I will not help you. I will not listen to your cause. I will not change my vote."

Our elected representatives are virtually the captives of those who contribute so munificently to their support, bringing about a rather peculiar and unethical process of the so-called fat cats supporting all candidates equally so that whoever wins, one has a friend at court.

How is it possible to retain the highest level of ethics in the face of such terrible temptation? Having witnessed the convention process, I see the truth in a reaction to it that "politics is civilization with its pants down." Nevertheless, flawed though it may be, the elective system is still the best possible system for choosing our leaders and representatives. The real tragedy is not only that we have seen a great deal of corruption in politics but that you and I seem to accept with a shrug the idea that there is nothing we can do about it and we shouldn't bother our heads over it.

That is the tragedy, that we do not have a truly developed sense of moral indignation and the impulse to change things, but sit back and say, "What can you expect? This is the way it has been. The rabbi already quoted from the Torah that it's an old problem. I suppose it will always be."

There are two ways of approaching the problem. One way, as suggested by Rabban Gamliel in the *Pirkei Avot,* The Ethics of the Fathers (II:3), states, "הוי זהירים ברשות–Be careful in dealing with the ruling power for they who exercise it draw no man near them except for their own interest, appearing as friends when it is for their own advantage but not standing by a man in the hour of his need."

It is hard to find a more cynical description of politics. I believe there is a more constructive stance than that jaded one; and that it is for the average citizen, for you and for me, not to shrug our shoulders and feel very detached in the presence of political problems and political corruption but to realize that where there is no government, as the Bible teaches us, men would swallow one another up alive. Were there no government, no controlling agency society would be destroyed. Government, especially for populations reaching hundreds of millions such as ours is now, is absolutely essential.

We ask so much from government that our waters be pure, that those who are poor be supported, that those who need schooling get an education, that there be roadways on which to run our cars, that our country be defended against attack by enemies, and so on and so on.

We who ask so much of our government must be all the more impatient with corruption. We must be alert constantly to abuses and vocal and active and concerned whatever our political party. We cannot shrug our shoulders and turn our backs upon it all and say of the great parties: "A plague upon both your houses."

Otherwise we shall be saddled with rulers such as are described by the Torah who multiply unto themselves horses and wives and gold and silver and lift themselves up above all the people. Standards are essential. Good people should be encouraged to enter politics.

Young people should not be disillusioned or disenchanted but encouraged to prepare themselves for just and righteous leadership. They should be taught always a nobler vision of what leadership can be, the kind of people described in the Book of Exodus: "Thou shalt provide for thyselves out of all the people *Anshe Chayil*–able men."

It is time that the most able people, men and women, the people with the most talent and the most skill and administrative ability and leadership be ferreted out and encouraged to lead, and that we not settle for mediocrity, that we not settle for the average man, the good guy, but *Anshei chayil*, the most capable men. We find them in universities, we find them in offices, we find them in businesses. We encourage them, the most able leaders, not the mediocre.

Yiryei Elohim, such as fear God, is a very important criterion. It means people who have great reverence for the moral and ethical principles by which we have been taught to live by the great religions.

Anshei Emet, men of truth. We have been suffering so long by not being told the truth about so many important things including going to war. *Sonei Batzah,* who hate unjust gain. It is interesting that the Torah chose such a strong word as hate. It doesn't just say men who avoid unjust gain. It says men who hate unjust gain with a passion and who resist.

These are the criteria. In the final analysis the strength does lie in the hands of the voter. Sometimes he uses that strength negatively either by voting thoughtlessly or by not voting at all. My friends, this week when we have had the second of the very complex, very colorful and sometimes confusing nominating conventions, it is important for us not to turn our attention now to the summer replacement series but to begin to look to those trying days during which we are going to be barraged by television, radio, newspapers and throwaways, to elect this one or that one to the presidency, to the Senate, to the Congress, to local office, but to realize that this is our job.

The Torah instructed people to set upon themselves leaders of all categories: leaders of thousands, leaders of hundreds, leaders of fifties, leaders of ten, men in high office down to the low office, but to seek out for those offices the most capable people, the most honest people, the most incorruptible people, the most sincere people, and let them lead us.

Why? "למען תחיה–In order that thou shalt live and inherit the land that the Lord hath given thee." I interpret that to mean in order that we shall live and not lose our democracy, not lose our independence to some tyrant, some dictator or through weakness and foolishness to some foreign force.

I said facetiously at the outset I'm sure we haven't had enough politics this week and I ought to add a little more, but what I am discussing is not so much politics as that essential complicated process by which men dare to administer the affairs of other men. And in that administration, you and I will either play our part or get the leaders we deserve by our inattention, inactivity or by being corrupted ourselves.

My hope and my faith lie in the essential good sense of the people. For 200 years now, this land has survived and has thrived and has grown great. You know from our congregation's American Bicentennial Expo I for one am very proud of this land and all it has done for the Jewish people.

I therefore hope and pray that the third century may see America improving in every aspect, but, above all, placing into office an administration which will not give us the shameful, disgraceful stories that we have been witnessing in the past few years. If we have such a future, in the final analysis we shall have no one to blame but ourselves. Our religion teaches us the importance, the responsibility of every single human being. I trust you and I will not shirk that responsibility.

A CENTURY OF FALSE PROPHETS

In reviewing my reactions to the second half of the twentieth century, I realize that, in addition to reacting to the crises of the moment, I was also often making predictions of things to come.

Sometimes I was wrong, as in predicting there would be two billion people by the year 2000, and it turns out that there are six billion. Often I was surprisingly correct, as in predicting the changed role of women in the world in general and in the Jewish world in particular.

It was a century too often misled by false prophets who have brought nothing but alienation and violence and the most horrendous bloodbaths in all human history. My biblical studies had taught me warnings of false prophets. This brief sermon at the end of the century suggests that they had indeed arisen.

JANUARY 9, 2000

Dear Friends:

We have all lustily sung that great prophecy of the Prophet Zechariah (14:9) with which we conclude the Alenu prayer:

והיה יי למלך על כל הארץ.
ביום ההוא יהיה יי אחד ושמו אחד

And the Lord shall be King over all the earth: in that day shall the Lord be One, and His name One. It prophesies a world united and conducted with love.

Twenty-six centuries ago, the Prophet Jeremiah complained, "The prophets prophesy falsely." Undoubtedly in every century since then, there have arisen prophets who malevolently or unwittingly prophesied falsely and those who were duped followed blindly, like the children who followed the Pied Piper of Hamelin to a watery death. The vaunted Twentieth Century may have exceeded all those which came before in the number and the havoc wreaked by false prophets.

The century began when the absolute domination of absolute monarchs held much of the world, East and West, in its grip. Emperors, czars, and kings oppressed, taxed, impressed into military service, tyrannized capriciously, claiming some kind of divine right to impose their will upon their subjects. They uttered a word, and all slavishly obeyed.

To loosen the bonds of oppression prophets arose. In Russia and elsewhere, they took the teachings of Nineteenth Century visionary Karl Marx and prophesied the panaceas of socialism, bolshevism, and communism which powered new dictatorships of Lenin and Stalin. They offered attractive and irresistible slogans of "From each according to his ability; to each according to his needs." What was once a mighty Russia which traumatized half the world during the Cold War and struck fear into the American body politic, is now a splintered shipwreck which has dragged down Eastern Europe.

Kaiser Wilhelm prophesied "Deutschland uber Alles, Germany Over All" and World War I ravaged Europe and left Germany in a shambles, sowing the seeds of World War II. Hitler renewed the promise of German domination of the world, prophesying "A thousand-years Reich." Il Duce of Italy promised his people the revival of a Roman Empire. Hirohito predicted the rising sun of Japanese world domination. These three false prophets left only ruins, tens of millions of dead and smoldering ashes of hopes, which must be monitored lest they ignite again.

False prophets arose in America wrapped in patriotic and/or religious flags. We have had the Elmer Gantrys raising false hopes of salvation and healing, but for a price. We have had television evangelists rise, attract millions and then fall ignominiously because their clay feet showed, disillusioning their hopeful, unquestioning followers. We have had tragic extremes of false prophecy as in the case of the Jim Jones debacle. We have had our home-grown Pied Pipers promising an eager new generation love and peace, out-of-body experiences and the nirvana of psychedelic drugs, leaving behind damaged young lives. Of them, some have made it out and some have fallen by the wayside.

One of the most far-reaching of all the false prophecies of the glorious Twentieth Century has been the episode of Y2K. A sophisticated society, creator and master of the cybernetic world, was hyped into a frightened frenzy by everything from fear of going without water, food or power, fear of the disappearance of all their financial resources, fear of cities plunged into chaos, looting and murder for a crust of bread; to threats of Armageddon, the final war between good and evil or even the end of the world itself. We read that $200,000,000,000 were expended to avoid these problems, $100,000,000,000 in the United States alone! These figures may well be found to be higher. Imagine what those dollars and pounds and francs and marks and yen and pesos could have bought: better schools, more teachers, more housing, more food for the hungry, more opportunities for art and labor and music, and mass transportation, and, and, and!

Then, when the ball fell, the clock struck twelve, the sun came up, and nothing of significance had happened, we began to think that we had been had. Reasonable and knowledgeable people have for some years now warned us to take preventive and remedial measures. Responsible industries and government agencies worked feverishly to bring their equipment in line. Meanwhile, false prophets, in order to peddle their wares, sold their books, chattered non-stop on the air, grabbed their sound-bites on the screen and whipped some of the world into a frenzy. However, there were always the clear-eyed who noticed that the emperor had no clothes. They calmly made remedies, laid in a reasonable amount of extra supplies just in case and went on living. There seems to be a good dose of common sense in the common people.

In the last days of December, I chanced to be walking up a path leading to a local supermarket. Lining the path on the left were ready-made bouquets of flowers to be bought for adding to the celebration of the new year. On the right were cases and cases of bottled water to be bought should something happen with the water supply. People left, carrying bundles of them both.

In the public gathering places of the world, millions came to greet the new millennium joyfully, despite the dire warnings of the pundits. Once again, the false prophets, some deliberately, some innocently, proved to be just that. I wonder what Jeremiah would have said.

What will the Twenty-first Century bring? Hopefully, less false prophecy and more real progress, less hype and more hope, less fright and more flight to the worlds without end in that gorgeous firmament which twinkles tantalizingly all around us.

We Jews shall continue to express our firm belief that that day must come: והיה יי למלך על כל הארץ.

ביום ההוא יהיה יי אחד ושמו אחד

"And the Lord shall be King over all the earth: in that day shall the Lord be One, and His name One."

RIGHTEOUSNESS SAVES JEWS FROM DEATH

Every year since 1951 when Israel floated its first bond issue, it was my privilege to solicit the purchase of such securities by the members of my congregation. Over the years we have purchased approximately $100,000,000 in Israel bonds and treasury notes. Understandably, it became more and more challenging to find a way to convey the same request in a new context. From the time of the Yom Kippur War in 1973, the solicitation was made at Yom Kippur Yizkor. In 1976, my sermon called for expressing our love for Israel by purchasing bonds.

OCTOBER 13, 1976

Dear Friends:

The time has come for the expression of the ultimate form of unselfish love, Yizkor, remembering the dead with tears and tzedakah. Why do I call it unselfish? Because it is an act on behalf of others for which we can expect and want no reward. Our parents, or partners in marriage, or sisters or brothers, or, saddest of all, children who have passed away, can not reciprocate our action. They are beyond the tears and laughter of this world, beyond even remembering. So remembering is left to us and we have fixed special times for especially more intensive remembering: these High Holydays when we try to visit the graves of our loved ones and even more especially, this *Yizkor*.

Between Rosh Hashanah and Yom Kippur my wife and I flew to our hometown, Philadelphia. I went for two kinds of remembering: my fiftieth high school reunion and the visiting of the graves of my family for the first time in 40 years. I went to one of Philadelphia's oldest cemeteries, Montefiore, and walked among the huge, standing grave monuments in search of my people. On the cemetery was a nice, old man, shaking a charity box and saying: "**צדקה תציל ממות**, charity saves from death." I dropped some bills into his box, and he offered to help me find my family's graves and say a prayer for me. I accepted his help, but assured him I could say my own prayers.

There they were, the stones, remarkably new looking: Hyman and Freda Pressman, my dear, dear zayda and boba; and nearby, Benjamin and Zelda Fox, my mother's parents.

I chanted the *El Molei Rachamim* with a lump in my throat. And then we looked for the grave of my little brother. Only after much searching did we find it. A tiny, white unpolished marble stone almost hidden among the tall markers: Irving Pressman, born August 26, 1925, died October 16, 1930. I began to chant the *El Molei Rachamim*, which I have recited so many times, and I could not finish because my tears choked me. After 56 years the love I had had for my little five year old brother welled up inside me and overflowed. It struck me, without the help of that nice old man at the cemetery to whom I had given צדקה and who found my brother's little grave for me, I might not have seen it.

צדקה תציל ממות–Charity saves from death; love saves from death, your love and mine for those we remember.

And soon at Yizkor, I shall recite his name again and remember and rescue him from oblivion. There is no one here who has not someone, somewhere for whom to say Yizkor. Surely all of us can say the prayer for the Jews who were killed by Hitler. Why remember the Holocaust after 40 years? Because it saves those killed from oblivion.

And we shall remember the fallen soldiers of the State of Israel. Why? Because they, in turn, have saved all of Jewish history from oblivion. They have helped make possible the impossible, a State of Israel, for the third time in 3,000 years. Nowhere, at any time, has a nation that was destroyed ever reestablished itself after 2,000 years. Nowhere, at any time has a people who were exiled and dispersed to the four corners of the earth ever returned to the very place where their ancestors had lived. Nowhere, at any time, has a people preserved and revived a language that was dead and renewed it with modern usages. Only the Jewish people has survived, returned to their ancient homeland and revived the Hebrew language as a living tongue. Resurrection is a term we usually associate with mystical happenings. You and I have witnessed actual resurrection in our day. And what wonders we have seen.

Our people, confined to cities, forbidden to own land, squeezed into crowded ghettos became farmers, made the swamps and deserts bloom; produced fruits and vegetables for size and taste the envy of the world; the latest being a tomato with a long shelf life so that it can be exported around the world to join Israel's oranges, cotton and avocados for excellence. Israel has become again the land of milk and honey, exporting not only its products, and her automated hydroponic agriculture and dry irrigation even to America, but its expertise to advise farmers in Africa, Asia and Latin America.

Our people, long confined to being merchants and middlemen, created an economic miracle. The 600,000 original Jewish population in 1948 has absorbed 2,400,000 immigrants, most of them within the first ten years, and found jobs, homes, food, and education for them. Can you imagine what America would be like today if the 200,000,000 in 1948 had absorbed 800,000,000 more immigrants from all over the world and today we were a billion people? Proportionately that is what the State of Israel did. We can be proud to say, some of us helped from here!

What wonders we have seen! Our people restricted from the academic worlds around us, concentrating on our classical texts of Bible, Talmud and Commentaries, swiftly created great universities in Israel, excelling in science, medicine, technology, art and literature, exporting our discoveries to the world.

What wonders we have seen! Our statesmen have been the envy of a world hungering for gifted leaders. No country has had as brilliant a founder as Chaim Weizmann. No country has had a spokesman as eloquent as Abba Eban, an architect of its establishment as David Ben Gurion, as gifted and strong as Golda Meir.

What wonders we have seen! Israel's soldiers have been the bravest and most daring in the world, and yet still compassionate and peace-loving. Who can forget pictures of Israeli soldiers entering the Old City or giving milk to Arab children? Who can forget the daring rescue mission of Entebbe, the operation to save Jews held captive simply because they were Jews?

There have been Yom Kippur days when our memories were overshadowed by current fears. In 1973, when the news of the war cast a pal of anxiety over our prayers. That year we immediately interrupted our Yizkor service and asked our Beth Am people to buy bonds for Israel and they did, four million dollars worth! There have been years of shelling, Jewish children living out their nights in bomb shelters, war in Lebanon and galloping inflation of over 450% in 1985!

This year, I am happy to note, we have causes for rejoicing to share with our concerns. Cause for rejoicing: 1. Israel and Egypt peacefully resolved the question of the Sinai seacoast town of Taba by agreeing to submit it to arbitration. 2. Prime Minister Shimon Peres and President Hosni Mubarak held a summit meeting in Alexandria and issue a joint communique committing themselves to reviving the peace process after five years of strained relations, with the aim of achieving a "just, lasting, and comprehensive peace" and declaring 1987 would be "a year of negotiations for peace."

Cause for rejoicing: Peres and Defense Minister Rabin visited Washington and are warmly received. President Reagan in a White House Rose Garden farewell for Peres called him "a valued friend, a statesman and a spokesman for peace," and leader of a country with which the United States has "deep and special ties."

Rabin, in conference with Secretary of State George Shultz and Defense Secretary Caspar Weinberger, asked that Israel be upgraded as a "major ally" of the United States, which would give her equal treatment with NATO allies and was promised that the request will have their full consideration.

Prime Minister Shimon Peres met with Soviet Foreign Minister Eduard Shevardnadze and discussed steps to arrive at full normalization of relations between Israel and the Soviet Union.

And the underlying cause for rejoicing? Let it never be taken casually for granted that the heads of a tiny Jewish state met as equals in diplomacy with the heads of the two superpowers of the world.

Cause for qualified rejoicing. In 1992, it will be 500 years since the beautiful Jewish community of medieval Spain was brutalized and summarily expelled from what had been their homeland. For five centuries we have repudiated and ignored Spain. This past year relations were tentatively begun between Spain and Israel. Two weeks ago, Spain's foreign minister, Francisco Ordonez arrived in Israel condemning "the recent and savage acts of terrorism," maintaining "terrorism affects us all including Spain not the least." Together, Israel and Spain agreed to study increased cooperation in tourism, science, technology, culture and consumer affairs. Visiting Yad Vashem, he spoke of the "complicity" in the Holocaust of those who had remained silent in the face of carnage. A small step, perhaps, and it only took five centuries, but oh, how different from the savagery of the Inquisition and the ignoring of the Exile.

Cause for rejoicing: Formal relations were renewed between Israel and the African state Cameroon, which can be a key to re-normalizing the ties between the Jewish state and much of the African continent, broken following the Yom Kippur War. In 1982, Zaire resumed diplomatic ties and in 1983 Liberia, then the Ivory Coast. Now several more states are expected to follow suit. (Underlying it all is African awareness of the enormous help Israel has given and can give; and the failure of Arab promises to be fulfilled and of Soviet influence to take hold.) It is good to see the boycott of Israel by such a large segment of humanity slowly being lifted. Better ten friends then one enemy.

The less isolated Israel is, the more the Arab states will realize they must accept Israel as a member of the family of nations.

One more cause for rejoicing: After 12 nightmare years of imprisonment, isolation, of unshakable, unbreakable defiance of everything mighty Russia threw at him, on February 11, Anatoly Scharansky, alighted from a plane at Frankfurt, Germany, embraced his incredible wife, Avital, from whom he was separated on their wedding day and greeted her with the words, "I'm sorry, I'm late!"

And later that day, together they arrived at Ben-Gurion airport in Israel to be greeted by an ecstatic, singing crowd. That night on the shoulders of an excited crowd, clutching the book of Psalms which he had virtually committed to memory during his imprisonment, he was brought to the Kotel, the Western Wall, and gave thanks for his deliverance.

We, who watched all this on television, recalled how on July 14, 1978, the day he was sentenced, Anatoly spoke. I wish you would read one of these two books on Scharansky, by Martin Gilbert and by the *Jerusalem Post.* I shall quote only the end of his courageous statement in the sight of his hostile prosecutors.

"For more than 2,000 years the Jewish people, my people, have been dispersed. But wherever they are, wherever Jews are found, each year they have repeated, 'Next year in Jerusalem.' Now, when I am farther than ever from my people, from Avital, facing many arduous years of imprisonment, I say, turning to my people, my Avital, לשנה הבאה בירושלים–Next year in Jerusalem. And I turn to you, the court, who were required to confirm a predetermined sentence, to you, I have nothing to say."

This past February 11, he kissed the Western Wall. Last month his mother-in-law, Ida Milgrom, was released to join him. Shall we not rejoice? Shall we not laugh with a giddy appreciation of the triumph of the human spirit?

But, let us face it: Scharansky's emancipation could only happen because there is a State of Israel, as was the case with the absorption of 2,400,000 Jews from lands of oppression; as was the case with the rescue at Entebbe; as was the world-wide awareness that the Jews are no longer helpless, stateless, friendless people upon whom any atrocity could be committed with impunity, all only because there is a State of Israel.

The State of Israel is a secure haven and a land to be conjured with because, among other reasons, we as American Jews have put eight billion dollars in investment capital in Israel to build every aspect of its economy.

Our support for Israel has been more than matched by Israel's heroic efforts, not only on the battlefield, but in the economic arena as well. Israel has reduced runaway inflation from that 450% last year to 0% this year, slashing government programs and consumer subsidies, but at the cost of great sacrifices by the Israeli citizens, whose real wages have been cut by one-third.

The most important single source of bond investment has been the synagogue, which last year in a few minutes on the High Holy Days produced $50 million in bond purchases, $5 million in greater Los Angeles alone, of which $2 million was purchased by our little congregation.

This year a new issue is available to us that is both ideologically and economically attractive, the IVRI Bond (Individual Variable Rate Issue). This issue has a guaranteed interest rate of six percent, better than bank pass books, plus 50 percent of the difference between six percent and the average quoted prime rates of three major American banks. Right now IVRI is returning seven and one-half percent. The minimum subscription is $10,000, or, for IRA plans, $2,000. There are all denominations, including the $250, which can by used to buy El Al tickets, to give to charitable organizations or to cash in Israel in five years for $360 which is over 22½% return for the money.

Proud as we may be of her accomplishments, happy as we are this year to rejoice in the brighter signs we see, we must temper our joy with awareness of how precarious her position continues to be.

Our late, beloved teacher, Rabbi Abraham Joshua Heschel spoke prophetically when he said, "There is an error in understanding the situation of the State of Israel. Many people assumed the condition of the State of Israel was absolutely assured, as if the effort of building had ended, the roads cleared, the task completed. People were ready to celebrate a completion rather than realizing that the economic, political and spiritual development is still in a stage of beginning. The achievements are impressive but the tasks are still immense. The creation of the State of Israel was like the miracle of dividing the Red Sea, and the State is still in the dry passages, in the midst of the Sea."

Israel's need of our realistic appraisal of her situation today is brought down to individual human scale by a story. At Auschwitz, when a Jewish woman was discovered to be pregnant, she was put to death immediately. So, if a woman could not abort the fetus her fellow inmates would help her hide the fact that she was pregnant, through harrowing round-ups, selections and searches. When she was about to give birth, the undertaking brigade would put her in a large wagon, cover her with dead bodies and take her out to the fields, where she gave birth.

There was one woman who risked her life daily to help such expectant mothers. It was her horrifying assignment to strangle the newborn infant out there among the dead bodies. This she did many times and saved many women's lives. She eventually got to Israel, married, and had a daughter, now in medical school, and two sons. The older son, was named Rami.

Rami was an athlete, and served in a crack unit of the Israeli Defense Force. Rami finished his service in May of 1982, but in June, 1982, he was recalled on a Friday. The following Monday, the war in Lebanon broke out. There was no word from Rami, Tuesday, Wednesday, Thursday. Then an announcement came over the radio. "The cease fire will be on Friday." No word from Rami, but a friend of his called who had seen him. His unit was in the Golan. No action.

At Shabbat dinner, a sense of relief filled their little house on the kibbutz. Then the doorbell rang. Two officers were at the door, the sight every Israeli parent dreads. Their message: Rami was alive, but ten minutes before the cease-fire, his position was attacked. Rami ran after a wounded officer to help him. Rami was wounded, too. A bullet tore through his body and out the left side. He was alive, but paralyzed from his shoulders down.

Rami has since received physical therapy and learned to swim and ride horseback. The kibbutz has rebuilt facilities for his wheelchair. Rami's parents visited him on the kibbutz. They saw him horseback riding. They saw how the kibbutz accommodated him, how he has become a youth leader. In the middle of this, his father broke into tears and ran out. He was proud of what Rami is doing, but cried at what he might have done, the life he might have led, the wife he might have had, the children he might have raised.

Do you love Rami? Do you sense his pain? Are you with him in his struggle on that far-away kibbutz? His sacrifice multiplied by the thousands cannot be wasted or lost in oblivion. He is but one, but he symbolizes for me all that is meant in the simple but profound phrase, צדקה תציל ממות doing the right thing can save from oblivion.

Yizkor time is here, the time to express the ultimate form of unselfish love, the act that expects no reward. At this hour of remembering, not only our very own, but those who perished and those who survived the Holocaust and those who came and are still coming to Israel "לבנות ולהבנות בה to build and to be built there," we are given the opportunity and the privilege of showing that unselfish love.

By some mystery of the divine clock, we find ourselves with these small pieces of cardstock in our hands by which we pledge our resources four-square behind Israel. By bending over a half-square inch of paper we are assuring Israel that she can expand her power stations, provide additional water for food, for industry, for recovery of the desert; can build telecommunications; explore for oil; construct new roads, parks, airports, harbors and railroads, in short, that Israel can raise the quality of life for the people and ultimately become self-sustaining.

Our Talmud says that one who has the wherewithal to lend to his friend and withholds it is guilty of שפיכת דמים, shedding blood. The Talmud meant it as a figure of speech. I fear that at this moment in Jewish history we can even take it literally.

I stood at my brother's grave and fantasied he had lived and been part of our family life to see Israel reborn and to help in her building; that my grandparents who never saw Israel though they dreamed of her were now seeing her through the eyes of our daughter, Judy, who made *aliyah* 15 years ago and lives there happily. I heard the nice cemetery rabbi remind me צדקה תציל ממות. The righteous act rescues from oblivion. I decided then that I would share my thoughts with you today and urge you to perform the righteous act of building up the Jewish state through your loving investment in her survival by your purchase of bonds.

CHAPTER FOUR
Challenges Old and New

There are times when the pulpit can afford the luxury of examining subjects which offer challenging alternatives. This chapter singles out a few such which generated considerable discussion after their delivery.

The question is still raised from time to time as to whether Christopher Columbus was a Jew or a Christian, a Spaniard or an Italian, a discoverer or a freebooter. I took a firm stand.

Decades before Women's Liberation or Feminism I called for egalitarianism in religious Jewish life as well as in society in general. In a time when so many young people were trying to "find" themselves, a sermon asked whether we live life as refugees or pilgrims, asked "What makes Abraham run?" and tried to define true charity.

In a baccalaureate address at the time of the ordination of our son, Daniel, at the Jewish Theological Seminary, I dared describe that elusive calling known as the rabbinate.

With many people asking questions about the value of their life, questioning whether or not it has meaning, I spent some time suggesting how we survive our failures and how we cope with our sorrows. In each and all Judaism offers illumination.

WAS COLUMBUS A JEW?

The Fall of 1944 was a time of great apprehension in the West, among Jews in particular. The Allied invasion of Europe had not resulted in the rout of Hitler's army and was bogged down in the bloody Battle of the Bulge. We were finally learning the enormous extent of the Nazi atrocities against the Jews and were pessimistic that any might survive. In the United States paramilitary groups were gathering in camps and goose-stepping with wooden rifles, to be replaced with real weapons when Hitler invaded the U.S. Anti-Semitism was more pronounced and more open.

In this gloomy climate, I decided to make a statement about the Jewishness of Columbus and some of his crew to suggest in an oblique way that we had a long-standing right to be at home in America. Research showed me that the current monarchy of Spain strongly endorsed the Spanish birth of Columbus even if it meant that his family was Jewish. The debate is still on, but I believe the following sermon offers much food for productive thought.

OCTOBER 24, 1944

Dear Friends:

The Synagogue Council of America, in cooperation with the Navy Department, has designated this Sabbath as National Navy Sabbath. In the midst of this war, we honor and pray for the men who sail our ships. As we do, our thoughts are carried back, back over four hundred and fifty years to the event which made possible an American Navy, an American people and the American Jewish community.

It was on the morning of August 3, 1492, half an hour before sunrise, when three small caravels sailed forth from the Spanish seaport town of Palos. Once again there was תהו ובהו, darkness and chaos. Darkness lay yet upon the deep, and chaos filled the hearts of the 90 sailors who started out upon an unknown sea for an unknown port.

Further still, darkness and chaos extended. They covered the whole earth, and they ruled the minds of all its people. Not yet had the mighty creative words of "Let there be light!" resounded for the second time. But the break of day was at hand. The experienced eye could already discern along the dark horizon the first faint gleam of dawn. Gutenberg had invented the art of printing, and the presses of Venice, Florence, Rome, Strasbourg and Paris had begun to arouse the people from their long intellectual stupor. Copernicus sat dreaming on his school bench of the earth revolving about the sun. The cosmographers Behaim, Toscanelli and Rabbis Moses, Abraham, and Vecinho were drawing charts and making globes to prove the earth was round and that it was possible to reach India by a westward course.

And now a little fleet was starting out to make the possible real. By its unparalleled achievement it hastened the full break of that glorious day whose first glints darted with roseate promise athwart the New World and whose radiant morning beams wreathe our fortunate brows today.

Seldom has a fleet started on a momentous voyage under such disheartening auspices as did that of Columbus on the first Friday in the month of August 1492. Seldom were there such heartrending farewells, such bitter curses hurled by the men and women on shore. Had not this mad adventurer forced them, by order of the crown, to fit out two of his three vessels, which they never expected to see again? Was he not taking their husbands, fathers and brothers out into a sea of darkness to make them the doomed prey of the elements and of horrible sea monsters? What ill-fated craft had ever returned?

Was it a wonder, therefore, that it took Columbus nearly three months to fit out his fleet? To complete his crew, he was forced to rob the jail of its prisoners in order to make sailors of them.

Yes, Columbus, as you stood at the prow of your little ship and gazed Westward, little did you dream of the glory that would come to you, the riches, and the everlasting honor. And little did you dream, that your success would become a far greater source of pain and disappointment to you. In your lifetime the people would strip you of your hard-earned rights and titles. The monarchs who enriched you would be jealous of your honors. The new world you were to discover would be called by another name, not yours, and you would weep, "The slanders of worthless men have done me more injury than all my services have profited me."

But standing with Columbus were two other men peering Westward. Their attire was Spanish, but their faces and their heritage were Jewish. One was named Rodrigo Sanchez, the Veedor or overseer, of the crew, destined to be the first to behold the new world. The other man was Luis de Torres, the linguist and interpreter, destined to be the first to explore the interior of the newly discovered land. What brought these sons of Israel here, such an unaccustomed place, on the prow of an explorer's ship? Was it choice or was it compulsion or was it destiny?

It is possible that it was their own free will which led them to join the expedition. The Jews at that time and long before were noted as experienced travelers. Being driven from land to land, and obliged to speak the language of the people among whom they resided beside their own. They possessed an extraordinary knowledge of lands, peoples and languages, thus being especially suited for exploration.

Jews had become the most renowned astronomers and cosmographers of the world. Three hundred years before Columbus, the Spanish Rabbi, Benjamin of Tudela, had penetrated as far east as China and explored the islands of southern Asia, recording his adventures in manuscripts preserved principally in Jewish sources.

Three centuries before Columbus dreamed of a shorter route to India, Jewish scholars taught that the earth was a sphere, approximated its circumference and diameter and declared that a journey westward over the sea of darkness must lead to the eastern shore of Asia. And before Columbus could venture out on a wholly unknown sea, the learned cosmographer, Martin Behaim of Nurenberg, had to call on the assistance of the Jewish mathematicians Moses, Rabbi Abraham and the physician Vecinho to construct a globe and perfect the astrolabe, thus lessening the dangers by enabling sailors to measure their distance from the equator and the shore by the altitude of the sun.

It might well have been choice that placed Jews alongside Columbus in his explorer's caravel, but it is also possible that their embarking on that perilous journey was a necessity, rather than a choice. It may be believed that when old and experienced sailors of the seafaring port of Palos feared to enter upon a journey that held out no other promise but infinite suffering and miserable death, these strangers of the Jewish race would never have embarked unless urged by some impending danger, unless impelled by a belief that the sea might afford some chance of escape which the land denied.

We have grounds for such a belief, for was is it not on the day before, August 2, 1492, that scenes were enacted in the whole of Spain, the likes of which but few have transpired in the history of the world, scenes that moved the hands of progress on the dials of civilization back hundreds of years, scenes which have not been duplicated until the atrocities of our own day.

On the day before Columbus sailed, 300,000 human beings, men, women and children, rich and poor, feeble and strong, were driven from the land of their birth, from the land which their industries had enriched and their learning had blessed, driven out and deprived of all, for the great crime of having been born Jews and for adhering to the faith of Israel, driven into strange lands and among hostile peoples or to the seacoast, there to be packed into ships like so many cattle. Wives were torn from husbands, mothers from their babes, sisters from their brothers, to be carried off, to be dropped into the raging sea, to perish through want and exposure, through outrage and cruelty, to be disembarked on uninhabited islands and left a prey to wild beasts and starvation.

There was little chance of escape for the Jews in Spain. Conversion only brought suspicion of secret adherence to the old faith, and that brought the terrible test of the Inquisition. Could a voyage on an untried sea be more horrible? Could the elements be more cruel than their fellow men? What wonder that some Jews in their eagerness to escape found their way to Columbus' fleet? With their backs turned to the country that brutally thrust them out, they heartily thanked God for their escape.

And who can tell whether it was not destiny which guided the steps of the wandering Jews to the ships of Columbus? Who can tell whether it was not the will of Providence that a Jew should be the first to behold the new promised land, to set foot upon the soil that was destined to become a refuge for all the persecuted, a haven for the oppressed, the home of religious and political freedom? Who can tell whether the hand that guided the Jew westward from the Euphrates to the Jordan, from the Jordan to the Nile, from the Nile to the Tiber and from the Tiber to the Guadalquivir, did not lead him across the Atlantic, that he might continue his circuit around the world as teacher of the God of Israel and disseminator of His law? Who can say it was not divine Providence that led us to these shores to insure a place for Judaism to live when extinguished in Europe by the miserable hand of Hitler?

The same hand which signed the edict of expulsion of the Jews, signed the articles of agreement authorizing Columbus to sail! The same day Ferdinand and Isabella banished their loyal Jewish subjects, a fleet manned by Jews stood ready to find a new home for them where a government would arise to grant every man the right of worshiping God according to the dictates of his own conscience. Here was destiny operating. Divine Providence is illustrated by this voyage of Columbus and his men as clearly as in any other event the world has known. Here is illustrated that history is not a matter of blundering chance, but a translation of God's will.

Columbus has been called by various historians, a Spaniard, a native Italian, even a Greek whose real name was Nikolaos Ypsilantis from the isle of Chios. But would it not be the crowning stroke in our story of the operation of destiny, if Columbus himself had been a Jew? History has not yet recorded him as such, but recent findings prove very interesting to me, at least.

In 1921, the King of Spain commissioned Dr. Abraham Shalom Yahuda to investigate the contribution of the Jews to Spain before they were expelled. His work was confirmed by historian Salvador de Madridga. It was the hope of the King of Spain to use the facts in attracting Jews back to that country which has been in a state of eclipse since 1492. Dr. Yahuda presented the following information, sanctioned by the King of Spain. Columbus was Jewish and his name was Cristobal Colon. He was born in Pontevedra, Spain, of Jewish parents. His father was Jacob Colon, a wool weaver, and his mother was Susanna Fontarosa. Among the Jewish families of Spain, Colon and Fontarosa ranked among the highest. Married in Pontevedra in 1447, Jacob and Susanna had three sons Bartolomeo, Cristobal and Diego.

Jacob was a wool weaver who couldn't get along in Pontevedra so he moved to Genoa, the largest free port city on the Mediterranean Sea, where he arrived in 1456. We learn that in 1489, in the auto-da-fe of Torquemada, Jacob's relatives, Andrew, Bianca and Francisca Colon, were executed for manifesting the Jewish faith. Fearing a like treatment someday, Jacob changed his name to Dominic Colombo. Since his son's name was uncommon in Genoa, he changed Cristobal to Christoforo. Thereafter, the Colons lived as Christians, and the children were brought up in ignorance of their faith. They played in the harbor, bought and sold maps and learned navigation.

When Cristobal became a navigator, he bought maps made by the Jewish astronomer Abraham Zacuto of the University of Salamanca. He was impressed by their exactness, and determined then to use them on the great day when he would find the new route to the Orient.

Professor Zacuto, and his friend Don Isaac Abarbanel, chief in King Ferdinand's cabinet, heard of Columbus's reputation as a navigator and came to Cordova, where Columbus set his ideas before them and prevailed upon Zacuto to draw a special chart for sailing by way of India. Zacuto's chart is available to us, and this historic paper is entirely in Hebrew letters.

Abarbanel and Zacuto called upon Susanna to confront her son with the truth about their Jewish nationality for Columbus believed he was a Catholic. Susanna then explained to her son in the presence of these two guests that she wore a black apron with a white cross over her dresses only to avoid suspicion about her Jewish nationality. She confessed to him that he was the son of a Jewish father and mother and that they were from the best Jewish families in Spain, but because of the terrible persecutions against the Jews, she was compelled to hide her faith while remaining a Jew at heart. Zacuto told Columbus he was the only man who could save his Jewish brothers from the Inquisition by discovering new lands where they could find refuge, because all the countries of the world known at that time were hostile to them.

Columbus was presented to King Ferdinand and Queen Isabella by Don Isaac Abarbanel, their Jewish minister; by Don Abraham Zacuto, their Jewish mathematician; Don Abraham Senior, the Jewish farmer-in-chief of taxes; and Don Louis de Santangel, Jewish chancellor of the royal household and controller-general of Aragon. They prevailed upon the monarchs to sanction the trip, and Santangel advanced them a substantial loan out of his own purse to finance the voyage.

And so, financed by Jews, with charts by Jews and sailing with Jewish members of his crew, the Jew Cristobal Colon crossed the Atlantic and discovered America. That this evidence is absolutely trustworthy, we cannot be perfectly certain, although I tend to believe it is. But in the light of all the help he received at Jewish hands, it scarcely matters whether Columbus was or not. What concerns us most is not that Columbus was a Jew, but that the Jew has always been Columbus: the explorer and the practical visionary of the world.

Other peoples have contributed bloodshed and warfare and suffering to the world. We have tried to contribute discovery and innovation and peace. Our contribution took as much courage, if not more than that of our neighbors. It has taken courage to believe the opposite of what the world has believed for thousands and thousands of years.

When the known world believed in many pagan gods, we believed in one, invisible God. When the world believed in one God of cruelty and war, we believed in a God of justice and love and peace. When the world believed in sacrificing human beings and animals, we converted that practice into prayer and synagogue worship. When the world believed the earth is flat, we believed it is round. When the world believes today in fascism and inequality among men, we believe in brotherhood and peace. The world believes we should disappear from this earth, and we stubbornly maintain we have a right to live on it, contribute to it and receive some blessings from it.

Yes, it has taken courage to go against the stream, to think, to explore, even to exist contrary to the beliefs of our neighbors, but as we look at the record we see we have always been right. It took courage, and it took one thing more. It took our insatiable thirst for knowledge and our ability to study—study texts, study nature, study human personality, study the will of God.

With courage and learning, we have conquered every difficulty. We have opened new worlds of science, medicine, letters and even of exploration. Spurred on always by the twin incentives of intellectual curiosity and the need for a friendly home, we have been the world's Columbus. I feel certain that if the day ever comes that man sails from this earth to some other planet, the Jew will have some hand at least even in that enterprise.

There is a beautiful thought offered by the ancient rabbis. When God gave the Torah on Sinai, there came down from the heaven "*Sefer V'sayof,* A book and a sword," bound one against the other as if wrestling to see which would be victorious.

And a heavenly voice was heard to say, "Choose one or the other. If you choose the book, life will be yours. If you choose the sword, death must be yours."

This simple legend tells in clearest fashion the struggle of civilization. It was always the book versus the sword, the mind versus brute force. It is not an accident. It could not have been otherwise that the first act committed by the Nazis after coming to power was to burn books. It was the old struggle of the Sayof, the Sword, against the sefer, the book. The Nazis thought that by burning books you can burn and destroy human thought.

How little they understood the working of history. The Talmud tells of Rabbi Hananya ben Teradion. He was put to death by the Romans. They wrapped his body in the sacred scrolls of the Torah and set fire to both. As the flames were burning and scorching his flesh, the rabbi's pupils asked him, "Master, what do you see?"

He answered, "I see scrolls burning, but I also see the letters of the scrolls flying heavenward." The truth which books teach cannot be burned, cannot be crushed to earth, because it lives in the hearts and minds of men.

Let us, the Jewish inhabitants of this new world, in tribute to the man who discovered it, remain ever courageous and ever faithful to our heritage of the study of and search for new worlds of truth. Let us live and study and teach and explore so that the world will come to recognize us as its Columbus, ever looking up for newer and broader horizons.

AN EARLY CALL FOR EGALITARIANISM

The future status of Jewish women was my concern 55 years ago. It was daring to have women on the pulpit even at the late Friday evening service. It was virtually unheard of at the Sabbath morning or holiday services. To me, this was an embarrassment and called for change.

In the course of the sermon, I outlined what should be the privilege of women equally with men. In rereading it for publication, I am surprised that I had the chutzpah to suggest that women should be admitted to rabbinical school and ordained as rabbis. It is also gratifying that virtually all I predicted at that time has come to pass. I did my part along the way to help the progress take place.

MAY 10, 1946

Dear Friends:

It affords me a great deal of pleasure to honor the ladies of our Sisterhood on this, the concluding late Friday evening service of the year and, incidentally, the last late Sabbath service at which I have the privilege to officiate in Forest Hills. It is good, it is encouraging to me, and I think, to all of us, to hear the current and the future presidents of the Sisterhood express themselves sincerely in support of all those ideals we have been trying to teach.

I suppose it should not surprise us that our ladies are able to express themselves. The Talmud tells us that when God created the universe, the women took nine measures of speech and the men took one.

From another consideration, however, it does surprise some of us, at least, to hear women speaking from the pulpit at a religious service. I might even hazard a guess that the women themselves feel a bit uncomfortable, even though in the case of this congregation, they speak from the same platform as that upon which they preside during the week.

Twenty or 30 years ago, no rabbi would have dared to invite women to speak from or even to sit on the religious platform. Even at this very moment there are literally thousands of synagogues, where the appearance of a woman upon the pulpit would signal an immediate storm of protest by the worshippers. And lest we foolishly condemn others, let us not forget that no woman ever appears upon this very platform here during a Sabbath morning service or on Rosh Hashanah or Yom Kippur.

And let us not forget either that the Jewish woman is not obliged to read the morning or the evening prayers, to put on the tefillin or the tallis, to blow the Shofar or to dwell in the Sukkah during the Sukkoth festival. If there are nine men present in the room of worship, and 1,000 women, under existing laws we still do not have a quorum, a *minyan* for prayer. A woman does not count in the quorum needed to say grace after meals. If a woman, as an expression of pious devotion, should sit down and write out a *sefer Torah*, we could not under existing laws use it at public worship. A woman is not accredited as a witness to Jewish legal documents, including a certificate of marriage.

I shall not bore you with a long recital of dry laws. From these few examples, it is quite clear that the traditional legal status of women has been unequal to that of man.

I wonder if you agree that this inequality in the year 1946 is not fully in keeping with the demands of justice or the progress of civilization. I wonder if it is out of place, on this Sabbath which precedes Mothers' Day, a day when womankind is universally honored, to treat with the problem of the legal status of women.

For there is a difference between the legal status of women and the position of respect accorded them. This weekend will see an outpouring of sentiment in loving tribute to women. I think this sentiment is summed up in a poem by W.R. Wallace, the last lines of which are familiar to everyone:

They say that man is mighty,
He governs land and sea.
He wields a mighty scepter,
O'er lesser powers than he;
But mightier power and stronger
Man from his throne has been hurled
For the hand that rocks the cradle
Is the hand that rules the world.

Beautiful as this poem is, it is part and parcel of a long-term hoax by which man, who actually controls the governments, the economics and the religions of the world, has tried to convince woman that, despite her inferior status, she is actually the real boss. In Jewish life for the past 2,000 years, we have been trying to convince our women of the same idea.

I say for the past 2,000 years, because there was a time before that, when society was more primitive and yet woman enjoyed greater privilege. The very story of Creation in the Bible places the highest kind of estimate upon woman. We read that the Creator proceeded step by step from the crudest form of animal life to the highest, each succeeding creation higher in the scale than the previous. Adam, man, appears as higher than the beast. But the crown creation is not in man, but in woman. Man was dust refined. But woman was dust doubly refined, one more step farther removed from the earth.

In the Bible, the four matriarchs, Sarah, Rebecca, Rachel, and Leah, receive as much emphasis as Abraham, Isaac, and Jacob. Women played a great part in the story of the Exodus from Egypt, and the victory song of Miriam has become a part of our liturgy. No less than seven prophetesses are recorded in the Bible, who take their place along side our great prophets. Deborah, who led the armies of Israel and inspired them, and composed the martial Song of Deborah; and Hannah, mother of the great judge, Samuel; are but two of them. Two great books of the Bible are named after women: the book of Ruth and the Book of Esther.

In the courtyard of the Temple in Jerusalem, men, women and children congregated together to worship the Lord, God of Israel.

So it was in those early days that women as well as men took their place in wars, in writing and in religious practice.

But just as Jews today must by the very nature of things assume many of the practices of their neighbors, the Jews of old began to adopt the point of view of the ancient world. The Roman and the Greek civilizations were operated on a theory of male superiority. The ancient world was man's world. In pre-Christian Germany, as in many other lands, man could with impunity sell, give away, lend and even kill his wife.

In Christianity, Paul taught that it was the duty of woman to be subservient to her husband. In Thirteenth Century Germany, we find the husband was advised to chasten his wife only with a stick, in keeping with his dignity and honor. Toward the end of the Sixteenth Century, the Church was still discussing the question whether the woman was a human being in the full sense of the term.

It was inevitable that parallels should arise in Jewish life and that the legal status enjoyed by woman should decline during the long dark centuries.

In modern civilization, nation after nation has recognized the necessity of granting the woman complete equality with the man. Women can now vote, hold office, plead before the bar of justice or sit upon the judicial bench. They take their place in the halls of Congress, on the assembly line and behind the scalpel. They have even been granted the doubtful privilege of donning the uniform of the soldier and sacrificing their lives upon the battlefield.

If we find that we agree this newly-acquired equality is just and desirable in daily life, then we Jews are confronted with a challenge: Shall we keep, amend or abolish the restrictive laws concerning women in our religious practice?

Already the inexorable march of human events has brought about radical changes. The young Orthodox woman who cuts her hair and retires behind the ritual wig is very rare indeed. The voices of women are heard in the majority of synagogue choirs. Women have been invited to speak from the pulpit, and young girls to participate in the actual service during confirmation on Shavuot.

Most significant step of all, here you are, men and women seated together at worship as in Temple days, although even this practice has not been adopted universally by any means. And I maintain that this practice is good and that the decorum which now enhances our services may be attributed to the seating of men and women together. Under the old conditions, the women gossiped together while the men exchanged their views. Today husbands and wives sit together and find nothing to say to one another, devoting their attention to the service itself.

Times have changed indeed, but the fact is that most of the inequalities still exist and the question remains: What will Judaism do to abolish the legal disabilities of our women?

I am neither the prophet nor the son of a prophet so I cannot predict what Judaism will do. But I can suggest what I believe it ought to do.

It ought to consider seriously that just as Judaism has always been subject to change and to progress, so must it be subject today. And just as Judaism has always vibrated with exquisite sensitivity in harmony with the best in the civilizations in which it has existed, so must it respond to the all too recent advances in the status of women.

Jewish women should count as full-fledged individuals in the composition of the *minyan*.

Jewish women should enjoy the privilege of standing at the Torah and pronouncing the benedictions when it is read.

Jewish women should enjoy the prerogative of witnessing religious documents.

Jewish women should have the right to aspire to office in religious congregations.

Jewish women should be encouraged to continue their religious education through Hebrew college and even into rabbinical schools. And if they demonstrate that they have mastered all the requirements thereof, they should receive the degree of rabbi, teacher and preacher in Israel.

I realize that these modest suggestions will earn for me the title of the extremist radical. Actually I do not deserve the mantle of the radical for what I propose is not something sweepingly new and different, but rather a return to the original mentality of the people of Israel.

The novelty of a woman as rabbi pales a little when one visualizes the prophetess Deborah declaiming to the hushed and awed armies of Israel. The novelty of women receiving higher training disappears when one reads of women in the Middle Ages who were great Talmudic scholars, delivered addresses in public and rendered great social service in rescuing victims of distress.

The fearfulness about calling women to the Torah disappears when one realizes that women actually composed whole sections of the Torah. And the hesitation to count a woman as one significant member of any assembly of living souls who wish to approach the Lord in prayer disappears when one remembers that it is the woman who comes face to face with her Creator in her travail to bring life into the world! It should be true, in life as well as in poetry, that the hand that rocks the cradle, is the hand that shares equally in ruling God's world.

These suggested changes will only come about if women actually want them to and exert effort and initiative to bring them about. Whatever liberal-minded men may do or say is bound to remain but a futile and meaningless gesture. Many men through the ages believed that women deserved the right to vote, but it was not until women demanded that right and fought for that right that it was finally given. So, too, in Jewish life, if women wish to have a greater share of equality in religious matters they must ask for it and demonstrate by their devotion to prayer, Jewish living, education and to all the wonderful ideals you ladies of our Sisterhood have advocated, that they are ready for it.

I urge the women of our Sisterhood to dedicate themselves during the coming years to their real mission as a group: full, sincere, enthusiastic participation in Jewish life and religious worship so that their deserved status as equals in the sight of God and man shall be accorded them. That beautiful *midrashic* interpretation of the creation of Eve, eternal symbol of woman, shall be fulfilled, "that woman was taken out of man, not out of his head to be his superior, not out of his feet to be trampled under foot; but out of his side to be equal to him, under his arm, to be protected, and near his heart, to be beloved."

So be it. Amen.

REFUGEES OR PILGRIMS?

In the years after World War II and the Holocaust, there were a floundering, a loss of focus and mission for people individually, for America and for the surviving element in the Jewish world. The Jewish people were struggling against latent anti-Semitism and the flood of displaced persons into Israel.

All of this created the image in my mind of two kinds of travelers through life: refugees and pilgrims. They suggested to me familiar rabbinic comment on the two times the Lord impelled Father Abraham to leave one place and travel to another, using the imperative, לך לך *"Go!" in each case, once running from and once running toward. I saw the same choice in our personal, American and Jewish lives.*

Echoes of this 1949 prophecy still reverberate today, making the sermon in many ways of current relevance as well as historic interest.

SEPTEMBER 24, 1949

Dear Friends:

Have you ever traveled on a train, a fast express hurtling through the night with the speed of the wind and carrying you from one great city to the next? And have you ever experienced the stopping of the train not at a station, but somewhere in the wilderness for a reason undisclosed? Were you not a little frightened and bewildered when the monotonous progress you had begun to take for granted was suddenly arrested? Did you then begin to think for the first time about the problems of travel, to listen for the sound of the bell and the engine to which previously you had paid no attention?

In a sense, that train is life itself. We speed from day to day, thinking scarcely at all about our destination, our directions, the safety of our course or the problems involved in our travels. But now, at this season of the year, on Rosh Hashanah, we interrupt our headlong rush and in this unaccustomed break in our routine ask ourselves how and why and where we are going.

These are days of *Yom Tov*, of holiday, but they are *Yomim Noraim* as well, days of awe, in which a man must search his soul, analyze his own character, strip bare his heart and discover his motivations, his directions in life, his deepest yearnings and submit them to test and judgment.

Once we speak of travel, we are immediately struck by the recollection that the man whose life is the central theme of our Torah readings on Rosh Hashanah, the first Jewish father of a wandering people, was a traveler himself. It is Abraham of whom we read, Abraham who left his home in Chaldea in answer to God's call and traveled to Canaan, down into Egypt and back to Canaan. It is Abraham who went to Mount Moriah, again at God's request, to be tested by the life of his own son Isaac.

Twice the Lord said unto Abraham, "לך לך Go thy way" and twice Abraham obeyed, posing an interesting problem to the interpreters of the Bible. As Rabbi Levi asked of old,

שני פעמים כתיב לך לך ואין אנו יודעים איזו חביבה

"Twice it is written 'Go thy way' but we know not which occasion was more precious in God's sight." The first time was the occasion of Abraham's leaving his father's home, when the Lord said,

לך לך מארצך וממולדתך
ומבית אביך אל הארץ אשר אראך

"Go thy way from thy birthplace and thy father's house, unto the land which I will show thee." (Gen. 12:1) The second time was the occasion of which we read, the second day of Rosh Hashanah, when Abraham was instructed to take his beloved son Isaac, and told לך לך אל ארץ המוריה "Go thy way to the land of Moriah," (Gen. 22:2) and offer him there for a burnt offering.

The rabbis considered the wording of the two verses and concluded that the second was more precious to God because in it He named the destination Mount Moriah, while in the first He did not name the destination Canaan, but merely said "Unto the land which I will show you." By this choice the rabbis were teaching that a journey with a purpose and a goal is to be preferred over a journey without a known destination and that a flight from a scene is less desirable than a march toward a scene. When Abraham was a pilgrim, journeying with resolution to the altar of the Lord, his behavior was more precious to God than when he was a refugee, fleeing from the idolatrous influence of his father's home in Ur of the Chaldees.

They were teaching a lesson which is pertinent to Rosh Hashanah and our daily lives, for each of us makes the choice between being a refugee in life or a pilgrim, running from life's problems or resolutely marching toward them and overcoming them.

Since we shall be mentioning these two terms over and over again, it would be wise to understand them more fully. The meaning of the term "refugee" is, unfortunately, much more familiar to the Jew of today for many of us have actually been refugees or witnessed their plight through modern means of communication. The refugee does not choose his journey; it is thrust upon him. The refugee has no destination. He wanders on his way hopeless, frightened, with no zest for his travels and with the feeling that there is nothing he can do about his plight.

Not so the pilgrim. The pilgrim willingly chooses his path. He is confident, courageous, purposeful. He is the master of his fate. He takes joy in his expedition. He acts not out of fear or despair but out of love and idealism.

Such are the differences between the refugee and the pilgrim, differences by which we can test our own behavior and the behavior of the groups in which we move so that we may judge whether we are making the best possible use of the life for which we pray today.

To make the most of that life, we must choose to be pilgrims on life's highway and not refugees, pilgrims in our individual lives, pilgrims in our American life, pilgrims in Jewish life.

To make the most of our individual lives, we must make of life a pilgrimage rather than a flight. And yet, a careful analysis of Twentieth Century life would reveal that in the midst of the greatest technological progress in history and the greatest abundance of both - necessities and luxuries, the life of the individual man today is by and large a life motivated more by fear than by love. That this should not be goes without saying.

In this age when the science of psychology has confirmed the great religious insight that love is more wholesome than fear, life should not be moved by fear, and yet we see that it is. Our behavior in the economic world is not an idealistic pilgrimage at all, but a constant flight from fear. Certainly it does not give us much confidence. People are afraid of failure in the economic world. Men are afraid of losing their jobs, making no progress in them or of being discarded in middle age.

The fears of the parents make for the insecurity of the children. For example, recent tests relative to the fears of ten-year old children, have indicated that one of the most dominant fears is that father will lose his job.

Fears and frightened self-interest are exploited to make us want too many things and for the wrong reasons. What we have never seems quite good enough. We are encouraged to discard things before they have outlived their usefulness and become intimate and familiar objects. We tend to believe that the lack of material goods creates all our mental, emotional and social problems.

The most powerful forces beg us, even threaten us, to be careful, to be sure. Insinuating voices instruct us, "Don't be half-safe...," "Your best friend won't tell you...," "Be the first to own one...," "Your friends will envy you...," "Avoid halitosis, falling hair, chapped hands, decayed teeth, abdominal roll, shoes that offend the eye." Hourly, we are offered something to make us beautiful, distinguished, popular, successful, fragrant and slender.

The items that make the headlines are the shock items, the unpleasant, frightening, negative aspects of life. The positive and encouraging items are buried on the back pages or never appear. Our political attention is focused upon the drama of conflict. Political interest is barely aroused unless there are two strong antagonists engaged in knock-down, drag-out electioneering battle. Politicians appeal to our fears and our prejudices: fears for our own group, prejudice against other groups. Labor, capital, white, Negro, Jew, Catholic, farmer, city-dweller often think and vote less in terms of positive goals than out of fright and mistrust of the opposing interest.

For these and many other reasons, we go through life manifesting all the attributes of the refugee: fright, aimlessness, a feeling there is nothing we can do about it all. We are constantly running away, instead of marching toward. And now comes Rosh Hashanah, telling us to stop running away, to stop acting the refugee, to stop dying every day out of fear, insecurity and hatred, and to begin living everyday as pilgrims on the path of life acting out of love, confidence and determination to make the most of this God-given opportunity to walk the face of the earth for a time and make it a better place for our having been here.

Rosh Hashanah says, "Take a moment to catch your breath. Where are you going? How are you traveling toward your goal? Are you living every minute of every day with a purpose in mind or are you dying every day out of fear and aimlessness?" On Rosh Hashanah, we pray for another year of life. To make the most of that life, we must make it a pilgrimage rather than a flight.

We live as individuals first and foremost, but let us not forget that the life of the group is colored by the behavior of the individual. How are we coloring the life of America? Is America still a nation of pilgrims, purposeful and fearless? Or have we begun to be moved by fear and aimlessness in our national life as well?

There was a day when this was in name and in deed a nation of pilgrims. Men and women came confidently to these shores and created a republic dedicated to the cause of human dignity and freedom. They had great problems, internal and external, but they were able to meet them fearlessly because they believed they had a mission in the world.

Where is that sense of mission today? Where is that confidence and love? It is buried under the rubble of the atomic explosions that rocked the world and made refugees of all mankind.

Today we are ridden with doubts and fear as a nation: fears of a coming depression, fears of a coming war, fears that America might find herself facing a hostile world.

For a brief moment we put our trust in a new cause, a new pilgrimage, the United Nations. For a brief moment we followed its proceedings in the press and on the radio with keen interest. Then boredom set in, only the crises made the headlines, and the average man was unaware and uninterested in its slender accomplishments. We have carried into the United Nations the suspicious attitude that if our country yields on any point it is showing weakness; while if any other country fails to yield, it is merely proving its stubbornness and bad faith. We have talked of one world. We have been thinking in terms of winning or losing. We have slipped back with shocking ease into the old conviction that when nations disagree, the thing to do is to start hating and frightening one another instead of understanding and loving one another.

Unless America can recapture the old, clean, positive feeling of being engaged in a great pilgrimage, unless we can make our role in the world the mission of bringing to it our great pilgrim heritage, proclaiming in the name of all nations, "We hold these truths to be self-evident, that all men are created equal, that they are endowed by their Creator with certain inalienable rights, that among those rights are life, liberty and the pursuit of happiness," unless we can achieve such a life-loving national policy, then America and all the world are doomed to become the refugees of a stupid and cataclysmic final world war.

We must think about this choice on Rosh Hashanah, think about it in our personal lives, in our national life and in our Jewish life as well. For all the Jewish refugees are not those now leaving Europe. There are refugees among us here in America as well Jews in flight, acting through fear, without a goal, without a sense of mission, dying a thousand deaths daily as Jews because they have no courage to live as Jews. For many an American Jew, Judaism is not a pilgrimage, but an affliction. As a speaker said in addressing one of our groups this week, "There is nothing I can do about it so I might as well make the best of it. Some people happen to be blind, some people happen to be lame, some happen to be a Jew."

What do we fear most as Jews? We fear anti-Semitism. There is a story in a recent novel which parallels what is happening to us as Jews. It describes a farmer in the hills of Kentucky who is obsessed with hunting down a great red fox nicknamed King Devil. He buys pedigreed dogs, feeds them at great expense while starving his wife and children. His fences, his soil, his farm stock are neglected, and he ends up with an empty cupboard.

What a striking parallel with the way American Jews have neglected our spiritual heritage as a result of our preoccupation with anti-Semitism, neglecting our spiritual lives, the Jewish education of our children, all our cultural and religious possibilities. We are busy hunting King Devil of anti-Semitism instead of building up Jewish life.

In our refugeeism we take strange twistings and turnings. In one town, the Jewish defense agency established a nonsectarian dental clinic used 94% by non-Jews, in the hope, I suppose, of inlaying love for the Jews into the cavities of our neighbors' teeth. In another town the director of the YMHA told how cleverly he worked the project of building a YMHA by the Jewish community. He got the director of the YMCA to write a letter saying that the YMCA cannot accept Jews and therefore they had to build a YMHA.

These days, the first thing we worry about when we read of a crime in the newspapers is whether or not the criminal bears an old Biblical name. The proof that fear obsesses our people lies in the fact that generally the first topic of conversation among us is not religion, but the Jewish weather. Is it sunny or cloudy for the Jews? We stand in a vicious circle and point an accusing finger at one another, trying to fix the blame for anti-Semitism upon other Jews.

Only last week I stood in a local Jewish bookstore and observed the following incident. A shopper was purchasing Jewish New Year's greetings. One card had been moved from the ten-cent box to the five-cent box. When the proprietor quoted ten cents for the card the shopper began to shout. "That's the trouble with us Jews, always scheming and cheating. It is not so in any other stores."

Why she bothered to note the coming of Rosh Hashanah at all I cannot understand for her Jewish self-respect was worth exactly five cents to her, no more.

Even our interest in Israel is frequently colored by fear of anti-Semitism.

Many of you must have read the recent articles in the *Readers Digest* about Zionism, including one by Alfred M. Lilienthal. He wrote a touching letter to his mother pouring out his hurts and troubles which seem to be principally the creation of the State of Israel.

We cannot answer his arguments this morning, but we can point out how clearly the fear of anti-Semitism has motivated this insidious attack against his fellow Jews. He says, "It is Semitism, the constant effort of some Jews to assert themselves as Jews and not their religion of Judaism, which feeds anti-Semitism." The logical conclusion of his statement is that if Jews would only be so kind as to wipe themselves off the face of the earth, anti-Semitism would disappear.

But my friends, to live, a man must assert and have confidence in his own personality, and Jews if they are to live fully must cease to wander aimlessly and fearfully. Have you seen the faces of Jews sitting and lying hopelessly in refugee camps, and have you seen the faces of many of the same people as they disembarked from their vessels upon the soil of the land of their dreams, Israel? Such a touching scene appears in a new motion picture, "Sword in the Desert," in which one sees the refugee shrugging off his old rags and wounds and marching bravely into a future with a purpose in it.

Have you seen this contrast? Then you have seen the decision which each one of us must make here in America, here in this synagogue, today, about his own Jewish future. To make our Judaism a blessing, our life a joy, and our journey a real pilgrimage, we must here resolve to live a Jewish life with a purpose, not because we can't do anything else, not out of fear of oppression, but out of love for everything ennobling and uplifting in Jewish life.

We must here resolve to live as Jews, not one day or three days a year, but every day in the year, to educate our children through schools and home, living in the belief that theirs is a mission in life to be whole, loving and unafraid. Let not this generation be the one to perish wandering aimlessly in the wilderness because it lacks the courage to live courageous Jewish lives. Let this generation be the one to march ahead boldly without fears, to help build Israel across the seas, to reconstruct Jewish life here in America. Let each Jewish family take counsel together, to plan its Jewish living for the next twelve months, including the plan of Jewish education for the children, the plan of Jewish education for the adults, the plan for attending religious services all year round, the plan for dispensing charities judiciously so as to include the positive, creative institutions of Jewish life at home and abroad.

Let each family do this, and its little trip to the synagogue on Rosh Hashanah will have been worthwhile for it will have led to a greater journey, the journey as pilgrims ascending toward the knowledge of what is goodly and what is Godly, even as Father Abraham made his pilgrimage to Mount Moriah, side by side with his beloved son.

We pray today for life, let us have the courage to live it. Let us read and understand what it is for which we are praying. When God has helped us see our course clearly, let us embark upon that course. Here, in the stillness of Rosh Hashanah when we have interrupted our travels through life to reconsider our direction, let us resolve never to permit ourselves to be refugees, but always to elect to be pilgrims in our personal life, in our national life, in our life as Jews. Let us pray, as we shall again and again during these days, in the words of the second of the two *U'v'chen* prayers in the *machzor*, ובכן תן כבוד יי לעמך "And therefore 0 Lord, grant hope to those who seek Thee, and confidence to those who yearn for Thee. Bring joy to Thy land, gladness to thy city, renewed strength to the seed of David, and a constant light to Thy servants in Zion. 0 may this come to pass speedily in our day."

Amen.

NOT BY BREAD ALONE

In 1965 it became apparent, that in these United States, affluence, plenty and comfort were flowing more rapidly into the middle and upper classes and not into the less privileged. The end result of the widening of the gap between rich and poor was beginning to be recognized by the have-nots and overlooked by those prospering.

If, indeed, material rewards flow more readily to some and less to others, the seeds of future confrontation are currently being planted and may very well grow into revolution or something akin. There are no more unwashed hordes camping on our borders to erupt into a nasty struggle for power.

Even as we enjoy our growing prosperity we must remain ever the more careful about conspicuous and wasteful consumption while belts tighten on the other side of the tracks. No great civilization before us ever remained forever immune from the frustrations of those who observe with envy and one day rise in revolt.

AUGUST 21, 1965

Dear Friends,

The Book of Proverbs is traditionally ascribed to King Solomon, which makes the 30th chapter of the Book of Proverbs something of a problem to its interpreters because it begins: "The words of Agur, the Son of Yawkeh." Perhaps there is another author here. Perhaps this is another name for Solomon. But there is a kind of sharpening of the acuteness of the wisdom of Solomon that is apparent in the words of Agur ben Yawkeh. I mention this because, in the 30th chapter of the Book of Proverbs there is a passage which relates with a kind of shocking immediacy to the times through which we are passing now in the American community and in our own local community as well.

Among the things for which Agur ben Yawkeh prays to the Lord are the following: "Remove far from me falsehood and lies. Give me neither poverty nor riches. Feed me with mine allotted bread lest I be full and deny and say 'Who is the Lord?' or lest I be poor and steal and profane the name of my God."

This is the prayer of Agur ben Yawkeh. Surely as I read it, you are acutely aware of its reference to the times in which we are living. The past week has seen extraordinary upheavals, and I am not going to afflict you with another analysis today, any wise and learned, and not-so-wise and not so well thought-out interpretation. But the consensus, it seems, is arising that this is not a racial struggle we have seen in our community. It is not even a struggle for civil rights, but something we thought had disappeared from the American scene, the class struggle between the haves and the have-nots.

Reverend Martin Luther King said it was the hungry reaching out for food. People who never in their wildest dreams thought they would possess some of the beautiful and precious and luxurious things they saw behind the glass windows, broke them and just reached out and took them. The have-nots were trying to get what the haves possess.

It is an attractive explanation. It has elements of acceptability that would rid many of us of some of the feelings we have of perhaps our own failure in one way or another.

Yet I cannot fully accept it. This is the morning in which we read in the Book of D'varim, the eighth chapter, the third verse, Moses tells the children of Israel there in the wilderness "and He, the Lord, afflicted thee and suffered thee to hunger and fed thee with manna which thou knewest not, neither did thy fathers know that He might make thee know that man doth not live by bread alone but by everything that proceedeth out of the mouth of the Lord, doth man live."

There are many passages in the Bible which suffer from our very familiarity with them. We take them for granted, and we repeat them very glibly. We accept them at their superficial meaning. If we were suddenly to hear them for the first time as something novel, perhaps not even out of our Bible, their originality and their pertinence would cause us to ponder over them and to consider their implications and the lesson to be derived from them.

As it is, we welcome them as old friends, and as we do with old friends, we don't analyze them too very deeply. This familiar verse from today's sidra is a perfect example. Who hasn't heard the phrase that man does not live by bread alone? And yet who is there who can say exactly what is its meaning and what are its implications? I should like to reflect upon them with you today.

Apparently from ages past, this verse has been taken at face value. In the great *Midrash Raboh*, there is no explanation of this verse. The commentator did not spend any time at all on Chapter 8, Verse 3 of the Book of *D'varim*. He felt its lesson spoke to the heart of the people. Many of the commentators thereafter have nothing to say. Even Rashi doesn't attack this special verse and have much to tell us.

I found in the commentary of Jacob and Asher of the beginning of the 14th Century, the *B'al Haturim*, the author of the comment that developed into the *Shulchan Aruch*. In his explanation of this verse, "He fed you the manna in order to teach you," he found the significance was in the "in order to teach you." And he says "that through this process of eating the manna they acquired a certain understanding."

The *B'al Haturim* found something especially illuminating in this experience of the children of Israel, the suffering they underwent in the wilderness, "And he afflicted thee and suffered thee to hunger and then he fed thee with manna which thou knewest not and neither did thy fathers know."

Apparently this verse gives us the meaning of the two extremes which we know, even in this modern day, hunger and affliction and suffering and sorrow on one hand, and, on the other hand, a blessed state of not having to want for anything. The manna the children of Israel were fed sustained and supported them there in the wilderness. And they did not lack, but they got their bread from heaven without toil and without anxiety.

So we have these two phenomenon in life: the having and the not having; the suffering and the being fed; and together, the *B'al Haturim* points out, they teach us that affliction and suffering and luxury and comfort instruct us that man does not live by bread alone, that food and material comforts are not everything.

Note the word *"l'vadoh,"* <u>only</u>, man does not live by them <u>only</u>. It implies the Jewish teaching, the recognition that we need the bread, and we need the comforts of life, in order to survive. It doesn't deny that these matters are something. It is just pointed out that they are not everything. Man must eat and man is entitled to comfort and joy and security in life. These things are something, but they are not everything. <u>Man does not live by bread alone</u>.

As we examine this verse we find the little word *"al"* which every elementary Hebrew school student recognizes. It has many meanings. *"Al"* means "on." Here it is translated as "by." It can also mean "for." Man does not live for bread alone. He lives for that which comes out of the mouth of the Lord. It is not what goes into man's mouth that he lives for, but for what goeth out of the mouth of God that he liveth.

It is a kind of ancient answer to a paradoxical question that people ask. You have asked it in jest or in seriousness. "Do we eat to live or do we live to eat?" If we live for that which goeth into man's mouth alone, if we live for bread alone, then we are no better off and no different than the rest of the animal world.

But if we eat for that which cometh out of the mouth of the Lord, eat for the word, for the idea, for the concept, eat for principals and ideals and goals in life, then our physical appetites are there to serve a greater purpose and not mere satisfaction. Our text does not say "man lives for bread alone." Those who say we eat to live, that the purpose of eating is to sustain life, have to ask for what we are living. If there is no answer, then life is barren indeed.

The answer of our Torah is very cryptically given and has to be interpreted. "We live for that which proceedeth out of the mouth of the Lord." We live for certain ideals. We live to propagate and to further those ideals. The burning words uttered on Mount Sinai, the glorious visions of the prophets, the prospects of a better world, of the ultimate establishment through our efforts of what we choose to call "the kingdom of God on earth."

That is the answer to the suffering of the world and to its comfort, to the affliction, the hunger and the plenty. Suffering teaches us that happiness and bodily comfort are not the be-all and the end-all of existence. Sometimes the fulfillment of our ideals is distilled out of the very sufferings and the sacrifices of our bodies.

An easy gratification of our desires teaches us that there is something in life beyond that. Being interrogated the last few days, the people, so many of them, in the troubled area of our city, answered the question that it was not for bread only that they were struggling. It was not exclusively a struggle of the have-nots against the haves. It was for things that did not have to do with bread alone. It was for subtle questions of personal dignity and self-respect.

One young woman quoted in the press said, "I want a job so I can be independent. I hate getting that check from the county. I want to be able to go out and make my own money."

There is the dole. There is relief. The manna keeps falling from heaven without work. The county, the state, the federal government are constantly giving away money.

But man does not live by bread alone. It is not enough. It does not satisfy the inner need. Something more important than bread is to be the independent purchaser of that bread. To have a job, to have self-respect, to be treated with social equality and with deference, these are the things for which people hunger as much, perhaps more, than they hunger for bread. Man does not live by bread alone.

The answer to the needs of the so-called have-nots, the poor and the underprivileged, is not simply to rain manna from heaven. Long ago we were taught that man does not live for that, by that alone. It is not even the answer in the homes of the rich. I know it is an old and an abused lesson, but money does not buy happiness. Many a joke has been made about it, and people have turned it around and said, almost in seriousness, "Happiness can't buy money".

The fact is that money does not guarantee automatically the happiness which is the goal of human life these days. There is not only the problem of broken homes, the problem of anxiety, insecurity and even melancholy, mental depression, mental illness in the homes of the poor. It is everywhere. It does not guarantee the comforts and luxuries, does not guarantee stability of home. The divorce rate is as high among those in the prosperous areas or perhaps higher than in the areas of the poor. Not alone, divorces, but inner happiness, companionship and stability of the marriages that survive are not guaranteed by manna from heaven.

Money cannot guarantee friendship, reputation or character. Friendships are not bought with money. They are bought with the investment of one's self and one's time and one's consideration. The giving of one's self makes for friends. Money attracts a host of acquaintances as honey attracts the flies and the bees. But it does not bring true friends. The test is that when the money flies out the door, such friends fly out the window.

Money does not buy real friendship. It does not buy real reputation. It buys notoriety. It buys attention. But it does not buy reputation. Many a person was courted and fawned upon by the public for his money but is privately reviled and held in contempt.

Reputation cannot be bought. Character cannot be bought. There is a rather cynical Hebrew expression. "Silver purifies the *momzerim.*" It makes good people out of the illegitimate and the suspect but they are still *momzerim* as far as we are concerned. Money does not guarantee immunity from sorrow. Money does not positively guarantee the tranquility of life.

There is something which is a burning necessity in the homes of the poor and the homes of the rich. What is it? "By the word that goeth out of the mouth of the Lord doth man live." What does that mean? On the simplest level it can mean the word itself: education. As hungry as the have-nots of the world are for bread, they are hungrier for knowledge, for the education that can help them be independent and have jobs and climb the ladder of society. We Jews know that from our own personal experience.

There was hunger in the ghettos of Europe. There was hunger in the reestablished ghettos of the East side of New York and every great metropolitan area where poor immigrant Jews gathered. What did they set as their highest goal? Riches, luxury, bread, in effect? It was necessary to sustain life, but they sought something more. They sacrificed not for their counterparts of automobiles and television sets, but they sacrificed to train their children, to give their children the tools of knowledge and education. That was the noblest aspiration of the poverty stricken areas of Jewish immigrants, to have a child who was a college graduate. That was the highest aspiration. Coupled with that, those who were true to our tradition, sacrificed to give and to provide a good Jewish religious training.

In the homes of the poorest, it was not uncommon that one dollar out of every ten (when ten dollars was a good week's wage) would be spent for a melamed, an instructor. Ten percent. Where, in recent experience, has anyone been prepared to spend ten percent not alone for the religious instruction of the child, but for education in general? How many of us do not grumble at our tax bills which do not reach ten percent of our income for education? The simplest interpretation for the words "that cometh out of the mouth of God" is education. Man lives for and by knowledge and understanding. That is what distinguishes him from the animal.

These days, when a man does not have the education, he does not have opportunity. When he does not have opportunity, he does not have social acceptance on the job. When he does not have social acceptance on the job, there comes a day when he riots, when he pillages, and when he burns.

But more than the simple idea of education itself, the word of the Lord is the guidance for living. Moral standards by which to live and ethical principles against which to measure one's life, man needs these.

There is poverty everywhere in our day. We live in an impoverished time when people literally have ceased to know for sure what is right and what is wrong, what is moral and what is immoral, what is good and what is sinful. All of our standards have been turned upside down. The final criterion seems to have been that given us by Ernest Hemingway, "That is moral about which I feel happy after I have done it." There may be some who looted who feel happy, although I suspect there are even more who feel ashamed.

"That which cometh out of the mouth of the Lord" is the standard by which man can raise himself up from the beast and become "a little lower than the angels." What we are searching for in our time is of course for bread. Man needs that in order to live.

But he cannot live in order to eat. He has to live for something higher. In today's Torah portion, we have been given a very simple and much abbreviated answer to what it is for which man lives.

Man lives not for bread, but for the word, for the literary idea and its concepts, for goals beyond his own lifetime. Man lives for elusive, evanescent ideals such as peace for all men, the brotherhood of man, the distribution on an equitable basis of the goods of society. Man lives for these vague, amorphous and yet very real values.

Man lives for the word that has come to him out of the mouth of the Creator. It has been planted within him and spoken to him by inspired prophets and seers in every age. Even today when we tend to oversimplify and we think that the answer to all problems, and this is perhaps the Marxist answer, which has been rejected by Western society, the answer to man's problems is "give him the bread, give him the material things, and that is what he really needs," the answer is found in our text. "Man doth not live for bread alone, but for that which cometh out of the mouth of the Lord, doth man live."

And so, in our prayers, our strivings, in all our yearnings, it is not for great riches that we yearn. Great riches have a way of corrupting a society and causing men to conduct themselves, as Moses said to the children of Israel as they should not conduct themselves. When they have built their houses and established them, they should not say, "My power and my strength has gotten me all these things." And they should deny the Lord. No, what we seek is a golden mean of balance in life: to have sufficient and plenty to keep our bodies strong and our morale high and then go on to live for things beyond and above material things.

This is the balance which we seek. This is the answer to the problem in Watts and in Harlem and in the Puerto Rican section of New York and in the slums of Philadelphia and Chicago and Boston. The answer is not to rain the dole from heaven like the manna. Man cannot live on bread alone. He should bring the word, the word of education, moral standards, instruction, family solidarity, self-respect, dignity and unselfishness. It is this for which man riots. It is this for which the human heart yearns, be it in his castle or in his hovel.

That is why I say that in the prayer of Agur ben Yawkeh, written in the 30th chapter of Proverbs, there is great wisdom. There is a maxim which each one of us could adopt as the slogan of his life's goal: "O Lord, give me neither poverty nor riches. Feed me with the food that is needful to me lest I be full and deny the Lord and say 'Who is the Lord?' or lest I be poor and steal and profane the name of the Lord."

From the twin evils of having too much and puffing ourselves up in arrogance and of being crushed under the burden of poverty so that we are driven like hungry animals to pillage and ravage, save us, O Heavenly Father and enable us to share the bounty of this earth equitably and change it from a cruel jungle to a benevolent paradise.

Amen.

WHAT MAKES ABRAHAM RUN?

After the quiet fifties, life was getting quite hectic and, gradually in the sixties and seventies, became ever more so. By the eighties and nineties, it became increasingly frenetic; and as we begin this Twenty-first Century, it is positively frenzied.

The speed of work-product has been increased dramatically as the ubiquitous computer processes ever faster. Today's latest model is obsolete before it reaches the store shelves. Today's humans, while living longer, are over the hill at a younger and younger age.

So, we are all running, running, running. I asked Budd Schulberg's question then, and I ask it again now. "What makes Sammy run?" What makes me run? What makes you run? And, by the way, where are we running, and why?

NOVEMBER 2, 1963

Dear Friends:

Speed seems to be the goal of our age: haste is the ideal. Have you ever stopped to realize how much of our energy, our substance, our time, and even our health is sacrificed to speed? Man, running, has broken the four minute mile. Man, driving a car, has passed 400 miles an hour. Man, in a plane, has passed 3,000 miles an hour. Man, in a space capsule, has orbited the earth in an hour and a half.

Speed is exciting, but costly. It is costing us billions of dollars for our space program and for the building of airports, highways, freeways and vehicles. It has made ugly and noisy cities, poisoned the air we breathe and cost 40,000 lives in one year in the United States alone, in auto accidents.

And speed has invaded our private lives and taken over our schedules. This is the age of haste and he who hurries faster than his neighbor is deemed superior to his neighbor. A man has to hustle these days more than ever before. Here, in our community, the ultimate question was asked by Budd Schulberg in his book about Hollywood, *What Makes Sammy Run?* The answer was greed, success, luxury, power. And "Sammy" ran, sustaining kicks, degrading and menial treatment and sacrifice of principle and self-respect, in the pursuit of riches and a questionable status. Abraham, our patriarch, **אברהם אבינו**, whom we regard with reverence and accept as the prototype of the Hebrew people, also ran. Today's Torah reading *Vayera* contains a story remarkable for its emphasis upon Abraham's haste. Our *Sidrah* begins with the picture of Abraham sitting in the entrance to his tent in the heat of the day.

Since the last chapter ends with the story of Abraham's circumcision, it is assumed by many commentators that Abraham was convalescing from the resulting indisposition. Nevertheless, we read, "And he lifted up his eyes, and looked, and lo, three men were standing over against him, וירא וירץ לקראתם מפתח האהל וישתחו ארצה and when he saw them, he ran to meet them from the door of his tent, and bowed down to the ground."

He ran to greet them and what is more, when they had accepted his hospitality, we read וימהר אברהם האהלה אל שרה And Abraham hastened into the tent to Sarah, and he said to her, מהרי, quickly, make ready three measures of fine flour and make cakes."

And then we read, ואל הבקר רץ אברהם "And Abraham ran unto the herd and fetched a calf, tender and good, and gave it unto the servant וימהר לעשות אתו and he hastened to dress it."

My goodness, did you ever see such running around? What made Abraham run? Surely, he did not run after riches, this Abraham of whom we read last week that he said to the King of Sodom who offered him goods, the spoils of war, "I shall not take even a thread or a shoelace nor anything that is thine, lest thou shouldest say, 'I made Abraham rich.'" No, Abraham didn't run after the spoils of victory.

Nor did he run to assume power over anyone but himself, not even over Lot who was indebted to him. When they found difficulty getting along together, Abraham let Lot choose his own territory, saying, אם השמאל ואימנה ואם הימין ואשמאילה, "If thou wilt take the left hand, then I will go to the right, or if thou take the right hand, then I will go to the left."

If it was not riches nor power, then what made Abraham run? He ran when the chance to perform a מצוה came his way. He ran to offer hospitality to the three strangers. He ran to save his nephew, Lot. He ran to pray to God to spare the populations of Sodom and Gemorrah. This prototype of the ideal Jew ran to perform a מצוה and is credited as the inspiration for Ben Azzai's teaching over a thousand years later in פרקי אבות, *Ethics of the Fathers* (4:2), הוי רץ למצוה קלה ובורח מן העברה Run to do even a slight precept, מצוה, and flee from transgression, עברה. שמצוה גוררת מצוה, ועברה גוררת עברה for one מצוה draws another, and one transgression draws another.

Now every man runs according to his own values in life. Our generation, so in love, with speed and haste should ask itself, "What makes us run?"

What makes you run? Is it riches for their own sake? For many people wealth is the object of their running. It doesn't matter who gets trampled in the rush, or what principles are compromised. There isn't even a satisfactory goal, a time to cry enough. They run, run, run, and the findings of medical science are confirming every day that their drive is their undoing, undermining physical and mental health and shortening life itself. And all for something that can be lost through chance, accident, illness or a shift in the economic or political winds.

What makes you run? Is it reputation? Glory? As long ago as the Jerusalem Talmud, our Jewish rejection of this goal was also expressed in terms of running.

יבוא מי שרץ אחר כבוד אחר מי שברח מן הכבוד "He who runs after honors will come after the one who runs away from honors."

I never fail to marvel at the seasoned wisdom of these ancient writings which captured the truth of human relations in such brief, pointed phrases. How self-defeating is the pursuit of the bubble reputation, but men will pursue it, Shakespeare said, even into the cannon's mouth. The pursuit of honor is the destroyer of the pursuit of fulfilling the מצוה . It has perverted the time-honored Jewish מצוה of צדקה into an endless round of testimonial banquets, so that no great cause is served these days without a big dinner to praise some individual and, incidentally, to raise money, a spectacle that caused the great speaker Shmaryahu Levine to observe that Jewish philanthropic life in America stands on "chicken legs."

As unstable and fleeting as riches may be, honor is even more so. Nothing is so stale as last year's hero or beauty queen or guest of honor or defeated candidate.

What makes you run? Is it beauty, that fades; or youth, that vanishes; or thrills, that soon pale; or power, that is quickly overthrown? There are so many incentives dangled before us in life, all dazzling and tempting, which shall we pursue? Where is the signpost that tells us in which direction to run?

We have run aimlessly in a thousand directions without finding joy in our flight. Is it not wise to take a second look at the answer that classical Judaism gives to these questions, run, to perform a מצוה , as Abraham ran? A Jew hastens to begin the Sabbath, hastens to the synagogue, hastens to save souls from hunger for bread or knowledge, hastens to make peace between a man and his neighbor, hastens to study, hastens to free the enslaved, to clothe the naked, to see justice done on behalf of the oppressed, to heal the sick, to comfort the bereaved. A Jew hastens to extend hospitality to the homeless, and give the hand of friendship to the lonely, the disheartened, the defeated.

And, he who runs to fulfill the **מצוות** finds zest and purpose in his life. He hastens to arise in the morning because there is so much good to be done in this world. He is busy all day in a wholesome, productive way because מצוה גוררת מצוה, one good deed leads to another. And he sleeps the sound of untroubled sleep of one whose conscience is clear, for no dishonesty, deception, violence or fear bedevil him who runs to perform the מצוה .

What makes you run? What keeps you so busy? Each man and woman must answer this question for himself and herself. Is it what made Sammy run? Or is it what made Abraham run? Is it the self-seeking pursuit of elusive riches, fame, youth, beauty, excitement and power? Or is it the earnest pursuit of God's purpose for you in life, the best possible use of His gifts of body and soul?

Speed in itself is not a vice. Abraham ran in his time. It is the goals of our haste that determine if it be vice or virtue. And a certain test of those goals is found in the famous teaching of Yehudah ben Temah which epitomizes all I have attempted to say:

הוי גבור כארי ורץ כצבי לעשות רצון אביך שבשמים

"Be strong as a lion and swift as the deer, to carry out the will of they Father in Heaven." Amen.

DO IT WITH A SMILE

Almost 35 years after the experience I cite in this sermon, the example of my rebbe, the good-natured, roly-poly, bearded man who had once been a rabbi in Moscow continued to inform my life. His pronunciation of a word, strange to my ears, taught me not only how to give, but how to live: with a smile.

It came to mind again as I thought about the loss of good manners, of good humor, of joyous giving of service and of charity we were experiencing then. It struck me as even more of a problem of the time in which I edited these works. These are the days of rudeness, unsmiling and unhappy human encounters, road rage, family violence, and disrespect for almost all authority: law, parents, politicians, tradition, good taste. A loss of grace in our society has occurred.

Picture, then, the little scene with my rebbe, and if it brings a smile to your face it has served you well.

SEPTEMBER 22, 1967

Dear Friends:

I suppose we still have some people here who remember the difference between a Gallicianer and a Litvak, members of two Jewish cultures with very different styles, even different dialects.

To a Gallicianer, the Hebrew letter ש, a Seen, is pronounced "es." To a Litvak, ש, a Seen, is pronounced "sh." This difference brought about some comic events in the Russian Army when some Jewish Lithuanians were pressed into the Czar's service. They were on the battlefield and armistice had been declared. The captain gave the order to "cease fire!" The only one still shooting was this Litvak. When questioned, he said, *"Du host mir geheson seeson hob ich gesosen."* I cannot possibly translate that but after services someone may explain it.

My rebbe in Philadelphia, when I was studying Talmud privately, was Rabbi Nahum Olinsky, was a wonderful Litvak. Then we came to a subject which occurs very frequently in the Talmud and which occurs in our Torah today, and that is, the giving of the tithe, the ten percent. When I was a neophyte and not too schooled in the language, whenever he said "give maisher" I learned to say "we give my share." I didn't understand what *"maisher"* is, but when beggars would come to the door, he always had pennies on the mantelpiece. He then said, "See, (and he said this with a big smile) *ich gieb 'maisher.'*"

I thought he meant he was giving "his share." It was not until I was halfway to the Seminary that I knew he was saying *ma-asser*, a tenth, a seen but to the Litvak, it was a sheen. But there was some value in the way he said it because giving *my share* with a smile became the slogan for fulfilling *mitzvot.* Doing your share with a smile is the way.

The Torah today speaks of new forms of ritual and sacrifice for when the children of Israel would come into the promised land,

והיה כי תבוא אל הארץ אשר יי
אלהיך נתן לך נחלה וירשתה וישבת בה

"And it shall come to be when thou dost enter into the land and when the Lord thy God giveth thee for an inheritance and doth possess it and dwell therein..." (Deut. 26:1)

There follow rules for offering the first ripe fruits of the new land, a land described here again in our text as **ארץ זבת חלב ודבש**, a land flowing with milk and honey. And the rules are given for the *ma-aser* for the tithe. For the *Ma-aser awnee*, the poor tithe. Every third year, ten percent of one's produce had to be offered for the *ma-aser*. The Jew had to make a declaration before the Lord when he gave his ten percent, just as you do have to make a declaration to the government before you declare your deductions and charity. They had to make this declaration before the Lord. **בערתי הקדש מן הבית** "I have put away all the hallowed things, all the things that are consecrated to these purposes, out of my house," (Deut. 26:21) " **וגם נתתיו ללוי ולגר ליתום ולאלמנה** and I have also given my *ma'asher*, my tenth, my tithe, to the Levites, to the stranger and to the fatherless and the widowed," (Deut. 26:13) **ככל מצותך אשר צויתני** according to all Thy commandments which Thou has commanded me **לא עברתי ממצותיך ולא שכחתי** I have not trespassed against any of Thy commandments neither have I forgotten them." Rashi comments on this expression, **ולא שכחתי** and I have not forgotten, because aren't these one and the same? If you don't trespass a commandment, it means you haven't forgotten the law. Rashi quotes in the *Mechilta* in translating **ולא שכחתי** "I have not forgotten," he says, **ולא שכחתי מלברכך על הפרשת מעשרות** "I have not forgotten to say a blessing before setting aside my ten percent, before separating the tithe." What is so important about not forgetting to say the blessings? Is it not enough that," he says, "I haven't trespassed your commandments, I have not broken any of the laws, I have kept them all?"

What is so special about not forgetting to say a *b'rachah*? The reason is very deeply ingrained in our Jewish concept of how to serve. The *b'rachah* is an expression of willingness and happiness to perform the *mitzvah*, to show joy in the performance of the *Mitzva*h, to have the *simchah shel mitzvah*, the joy of performing something that we are supposed to do. Because the sincerity with which we do a *mitzvah* is in direct proportion to the joy and desire with which we fulfill it, in Jewish life we always recite a *brachah*, a blessing before fulfilling a *mitzvah*, before obeying one of the rules of our faith.

We don't simply do it, grudgingly, offhandedly, but we say "Thank You, God. Blessed art Thou, oh Lord, our God, Ruler of the Universe, Who has sanctified us with Thy commandments and commanded us to do this; commanded us to put a *mezuzah* on the door, commanded us to perform the *brit milah*, commanded us to light the Sabbath candles." The degree to which we have joy in our *mitzvah* is the degree to which we are sincere in its performance so that the *mitzvah* and the *brachah* become one and the same.

In fact, the rabbis teach in the Talmud, in the tractate of *Shabbat*, "Every *mitzvah* which we accept joyfully, we continue to perform joyfully." Think about that. Every obligation that we accept joyfully, we continue to do joyfully. They gave, as an example, the *mitzvah* of *mila*h, the *b'rit*, on the eighth day. This is a *simchah* which everyone enjoys.

I think the best way in life is ever to be mindful of the joy that there is in doing the proper things, the things we have to do. Be happy in performing our *mitzvot* because those *mitzvot* which we accept joyously we never forget. We are able to say **לא עברתי ממצותיך ולא שכחתי** "I have not transgressed Your commandments nor have I forgotten them." I think there is great wisdom in that teaching. It is surprising that teaching is so old, as old as the beginning of the modern era, the era of the millennium. You might imagine that this, our ancient law, would place upon us stern commands, unyielding, unsmiling, rigid, but that is not so. Here we are told to rejoice in the performance of our *mitzvah*.

Witness our situation in the text that I described today. No, it is not true that our religious faith is a solemn and somber business. It isn't true that fulfilling the divine commandment is a process that we must do grudgingly and routinely, without a smile of pleasure. Quite the contrary; it is essential in life that we perform all of our *mitzvot*, all of our obligations with joy, in a happy way. I think that those who come into the synagogue who are strange to the ways of the Jews are sometimes surprised to see the casualness and the informality, to see smiles, greetings and joviality. Those are people who imagine that the service of the Lord is some kind of unpleasantness. It is not true.

One religious philosopher of our day, Alfred Whitehead, said, "I have always noticed that deeply and truly religious persons are fond of a joke, and I am suspicious of those who are not." It is true, those who have heard preachers, Jewish or Christian, know that their religious representative generally sees the humorous side of life. I think if he did not, he could not continue in his profession.

All the areas of life which impose upon us *mitzvot* must be done joyously and must be done with a smile.

Work, even our daily job, our work has to be performed as if it were a *mitzvah*. What ever happened to service with a smile? Have you had any service with a smile lately? In a department store, a gas station, anywhere? I think it is a tragic thing that people go off to work and their professions and feel this is a *mitzvah*, a must, an obligation, but they do not have joy in it. They do not precede their work with a *brachah*. They do not say "Thank God that I am called upon to serve my fellow man in this way and let me rejoice in it."

We are not cheerful to customers, to clients, to an audience. There is bitterness where there should be a real jubilation. The obligation of work is not being accepted with good grace today. I think it is a pity because it robs not only the laborer, the one who serves us, but it robs the one who is served of any pleasure in the life problems.

We have obligations that arise in the course of our day-to-day living and many of us take the problems of life unsmiling, without any joy, as a drudgery, a monotonous routine. Malcolm Muggeridge, that sharp and humorous English social critic and columnist, has this to say: "If only men could be induced to laugh more, they might hate less, and find more serenity here on earth. If they cannot worship together or accept the same laws or tolerate the wonderful diversity of thought and behavior and physics with which we have been blessed, at least they can laugh together."

Many of us proceed about the problems of day-to-day living and there is no laughter at all in our lives. Many of us have lost the quality of optimism and good cheer as we look about us at a world situation which is quite understandably and realistically frightening. And yet, optimism and good cheer in accepting the *mitzvah*, the obligation, of going about the business of life in spite of difficulties should be cultivated. Someone said, "It is optimism which enables a teakettle to sing though it is in hot water up to its nose."

You and I are in hot water up to our nose and yet if only we would cultivate this *simcha shel mitzvah*, this optimism, we could still sing. Our health and hygiene imposes upon us certain *mitzvot*. We have to take care of ourselves.

Many people approach the job of staying alive and well without any joy, without any sense of happy purpose, without a *brachah*. I admit it is a little difficult to recite a *brachah* before going off to the dentist to have a tooth drilled, but it is something that has to be done and it might as well be done with good cheer. The dentist is cheerful as he drills. Why not you?

Things have to be done with a smile or you will cry. Even the things which pertain to our body. Think of them as *mitzvot*. A wonderful columnist of the Eighteenth Century, Joseph Addison had this to say, "Cheerfulness is the best promoter of health and is as friendly to the mind as to the body."

We have *mitzvot* which have to do with family obligations. Too many people take them to be burdens which they perform grudgingly. They have no joy in the fulfillment thereof. Many a husband and wife whose relationship with each other is very dutiful fulfill all the written and implied obligations of marital life but without joy. When years pass and there is no *simchah* in fulfilling the marital vows, the marriage is in jeopardy and threatens to fall apart.

Many parents are most resourceful, most conscientious in the raising of their children. When things sometimes go wrong with their children, some parents will come to me or some other counselor and say, "What have I done wrong? I have given the child everything, the best clothes, the best schools, the best food, the best home, the best care and yet there is a chasm between the child and me. Where did we go wrong?"

Perhaps it is simply that there has been no joy in the fulfillment of the obligations of parenthood. The parent has not enjoyed the child's mistakes, and the child's failures, even the child's rebellion and seen the humor of it all. The parent has forgotten his or her own childhood, youth and has become humorless about it. And so there is forgetfulness of the *brachah*, the blessing that it is to be given children and the opportunity to raise them with all the the pain of rearing children to which the rabbis referred a thousand years ago as nothing new. Unless we see it as a *brachah,* the *mitzvah* is liable to failure.

Our religious commitments, too, have to be performed joyously. As I said before: this is the spirit of the Jewish service, of the *Minyan,* of the *Shabbat,* of the *Yom Tov.* About the only times in the year when we permit ourselves solemnity, sobriety and even a tinge of sadness are on occasions like *Tisha b'Av,* and *Yom Kippur* when we reflect upon the imperfection of our lives and of our history.

All the rest of the time we should be fulfilling our *mitzvot* with joy. Smiles are in place in the synagogue. Max Eastman, a very sharp observer of our times said, "Religion in whatever form is consolation for the pain of life. Humor is the instinct for taking pain playfully. They are both inseparable."

Imagine that, humor and religion inseparable. And so, when in the *Mishnah*, Shammai (that colleague of Hillel of whom we sometimes imagine as straight-laced, dour and humorless compared with the gentle Hillel) is the one quoted in the Pirkei Avot as giving us the admonition, **והוה מקבל את-כל-האדם בסבר פנים יפות** Receive all men with a cheerful countenance" (Pirkei Avot 1:25)

Rashi, in commenting upon the verse which I quoted from today's Torah reading, **לא עברתי ממצותיך ולא שכחתי** "I have not trespassed Thy commandments, nor have I forgotten them" very interestingly understands "nor have I forgotten" to mean: "I am keeping the rules, but I am doing so with a sense of pleasure, with a sense of gratitude, with a benediction and a smile upon my lips."

So you see, my Rebbe, for all his *Litvishe lisping*, had something very lasting to teach me when he took his pennies off the shelf and gave charity. He didn't give it with the grumpiness and complaint with which some of us give our service and our charity today. He gave it with a smile. "My share" with a smile. It is a little maxim I hope you remember as the teaching of this day for it makes life livable and endows it with the joy God meant it to have.

May I quote you in conclusion a little poem which you could easily memorize. It is by Henry Rutherford Elliot, and I think it is more essential in these harried days when we are all getting so grumpy and disagreeable with one another at work and at home:

"*Are you worsted in a fight? Laugh it off!*
Are you cheated of your right? Laugh it off!
Don't make tragedy of trifles.
Don't shoot butterflies with rifles. Laugh it off!
Does your work get into kink? Laugh it off!
Are you near all sorts of brinks? Laugh it off!
If it's sanity you're after,
There's no recipe like laughter.
Laugh it off! Laugh it off! Laugh it off!"

HELPERS OF THE POOR

When our son, Daniel, was ordained a rabbi, the Sabbath before the actual graduation exercises was dedicated to prayer for the well-being of the new rabbis. I was invited to deliver the baccalaureate sermon.

Before a daunting panel of the august faculty of the Jewish Theological Seminary, including its chancellor, Dr. Louis Finkelstein and our son's peers, I chose to challenge the newly ordained with the enormous difficulties and deep satisfactions to be discovered in the process of helping one's troubled contemporaries confront life's hurdles. Drawing upon several years of intense concentration on the texts of the Jewish tradition, on scholarship and erudition, I observed that the new rabbis would find the world outside academia drawing upon their every spiritual resource. I promised them a glory exceeding all others in faithfully fulfilling the charge to be helpers of the poor.

MAY 18, 1974

Dear Friends:

It is almost 30 years to the day since last I stood on this platform. It is reassuring to look around and see that nothing has changed in the Unterberg Auditorium. It is also chastening to realize how much change has taken place in the Jewish condition in some ways and how little in others.

Thirty years ago I stood here during a seminary student body protest, reading a script of agonized outrage over the genocide which was taking place in Hitler's Europe.

Yes, we were painfully aware that three million were already murdered and we were tortured by fears that Hitler would win. American Nazis ranting on street corners in Yorkville were mixing boasts of takeover with sneering accusations that the Jews had murdered Charles Lindbergh's baby and used its ground up flesh in the making of Passover charoset. Every gate in the world was sealed against us, Palestine, especially.

We felt that the forces of darkness were innumerable and in that spirit we assembled in this room and I read from the Psalms, "How long, O God, will Thou be angry forever? Help us, O God of our salvation, and deliver us. Wherefore should the nations say 'Where is their God?' Let the groaning of the prisoners come before Thee. According to the greatness of Thy power set free those that are condemned to death." And when "Who is a Jew?" was the sneering question of the storm troopers casually fingering toward the gas chambers those with even the remotest taint of Jewish identity.

That was 30 years ago and today, although the three million became six and the wound still bleeds, there is a Jewish voice among the nations and a homeland gathering in its newest returnees from Russia this time. "Who is a Jew?" has become a political issue excluding from the Third Jewish Commonwealth those with even the remotest suspicion of non-Jewish identity.

In all these years of protest to prick the sleeping conscience of the world, to care for the displaced persons, to open the gates of Israel, to spearhead the raising of billions of dollars for her defense and her development, to bring home her exiled children, to elevate the quality of Jewish awareness and Jewish observance and Jewish knowledge throughout the Diaspora, no single group of men and women has played a more consistent, more significant role than those who have paraded across this platform, studied within these walls and left here to fill the teachers' rostrums and the rabbinical pulpits of the world.

Today as one of that group, I have been invited back to this platform לא בזכותי, ולא בזכות אבא, אלא בזכות בני to deliver not a senior sermon but a senior citizen's sermon, the old boy returning to the campus full of wise saws, modern instances and cholesterol, but still remembering vividly an old boy's sermon delivered when I was a student. He shall remain unidentified here, but he spent almost two hours on the subject, "The Sermon Is Outmoded."

With that recollection in mind, I searched for a vehicle for conveying to this year's graduates and those soon to follow them, a deep-seated conviction I hold, and to do so in less than two hours, without being patronizing or insulting your intelligence. It is the conviction that the rabbinate affords a man and his wife with him the opportunity to lead a full Jewish life, to realize their human potential to its uttermost and to effect enormous changes for good in individuals and in society. It is the conviction that even more than we are wanted by the Jewish community, we are desperately needed. And to be needed is to experience the ultimate justification for living.

Where does a rabbi search for the proper vehicle? He begins by looking into the Torah portion. Such was the foresight of our biblical and rabbinical ancestors that they invariably prepared for us long ago the thoughts most germane to each week's needs. This morning, the Torah described at length the ways in which a man expresses practical love of his neighbor, laws restoring a man's mortgaged land as well as his personal freedom to him if he must borrow on either because he has become impoverished. The מצוה is incumbent upon every Jew מאחזתו כי ימוך אחיך ומכר. If your brother is impoverished so that he must sell some of his possessions, יבא גאלו קרב אליו וגאל את ממכר אחיו then his nearest kinsman shall come and redeem what his brother has sold.

There follows extensive discussion on ways of preventing increasing disparity in the economic levels of society. The rabbinic commentators were even more specific and detailed in this matter of dealing with the less fortunate, and relate this verse to the passage in Psalm 41:2... אשרי משכיל אל דל ביום רעה ימלטהו ה׳ "Happy is he who deals wisely with the poor, in the day of evil, the Lord will deliver him."

Issi took this literally to mean the financially impoverished, איסי אמר זה שנותן פרוטה לעני. This promise of God's deliverance refers to one who gives a *perutah* to a poor man. But others expanded our understanding of what we mean by the needy brother

אבא בר ירמיה בשם רבי מאיר אמר זה שממליך יצר טוב על יצר הרע

Abba, son of Jeremiah, said in the name of Rabbi Meir, "This refers to one who enthrones the good inclination יצר טוב which is personified as the 'poor man' over the evil inclination, the יצר הרע.

Rabbi Jochanan said, רב יוחנן אמר זה שקובר מת מצוה

This refers to one who buries a מת מצוה – one who has nobody to take care of his burial. For as עץ יוסף puts it, דאין לך דל מן המת none is poorer than the dead. Our Rabbis say that it refers to one who assists a person escaping from tyrants שמבריח ומציל ממי שרודפו להמיתו he assists and saves a man from one pursuing him to kill him;

דאמר רב הונה כל מי שמבקר את החולה פוחתים לו אחד מששים בחליו

Rav Huna said its refers to one who visits the sick (adding the famous medical mathematics) for whoever visits the sick reduces his illness by one sixtieth part of his illness.

And regarding all of these, Rav Levi said in the name of Rav Hama, son of Rav Hanina, "The expression אשרי (happy) is recorded 22 times in connection with some good action and only in this case is recompense mentioned, ת ביום רעה ימלטהו השם "The Lord will redeem him in the day of evil," that is why Moses exhorts Israel saying "If thy brother be waxen poor then his kinsman shall redeem."

So the poor is not solely the impoverished but includes in these varying interpretations all the categories of human need with which every man should deal, but the rabbi has a unique opportunity to serve, to bury the dead, to visit the sick, to feed and clothe the needy, to rescue those in jeopardy of their lives and to carry on the battle to help man strengthen his better inclinations.

This outline only begins to describe the challenges of the rabbinate, which because of its serendipitous nature, make the rabbi the last general practitioner in this over-specialized world.

Over the years, I have heard the derisive sophomoric description of the rabbinic functions to "hatch, match and dispatch" a cliché which flippantly dispenses with those major peaks of human emotion, of human crises which the rabbi is profoundly privileged to share. When people open those jealously guarded and most private locked secret places of their soul and let us in even for that fleeting moment when they are דלים, their own spiritual resources depleted, it is a humbling, precious experience, something like treading on holy ground and just as instructive.

It is no pleasure burying people I have loved, closing the eyes of old friends, children I have named, couples I have married. השם ימלטהו Only God can help me to be simultaneously sensitive and strong in leading the grieving widow or the mother with sagging knees away from the casket. But my friends, in a thousand funeral homes and muddy cemeteries I learned something about life and death the scoffers will never know. Spading the first clods of clay, hearing their hollow thud prepared me to meet the death of my own father with a balance of grief and acceptance.

It is no pleasure standing by the sickbed listening to symptoms or to the sounds of depression and fear, but those nights I paced hospital corridors with anxious relatives, shared with busy doctors the delicate process of a negative prognosis and of being the first face seen by the patient in post-surgical intensive care, have prepared me to occupy my own bed of pain and critical illness with some measure of dignity and courage, and faith.

Dealing with emotional ills is not only to be עוזר דלים but also to be a student of life. The young men and young women who terminated with suicide every therapeutic effort taught me to listen long and hard to the cry of human desperation behind the words. The foolish quarreling over trivia, the unconscionable cruelties I have seen husbands and wives, parents and children commit against one another, have sent me home to loving appreciation of my own wife and greater awareness of my own human imperfection.

Looking into the eyes of 5,000 wedding couples, each one so different, so special; knowing from lengthy interviews or lifelong acquaintance their doubts, their fears and their weaknesses has taught me patience and respect for my own children's determination to let them be themselves.

Please forgive me for personalizing; I can't think of any other way of saying that the Seminary made me a rabbi, but the rabbinate is making me a *mensch*.

Rabbi Meir opined that it was a מצוה to enthrone the יצר טוב over the יצר הרע. It is still a מצוה in the true sense of the imperative, one of the burning imperatives of our day. He was right. Every organ of the human body seems bent on following the יצר הרע except the conscience, and the latter is being derided these days of איש הישר בעניו יעשה every person bent on doing his own thing. Who is there to say לא זו הדרך "This is not the way we were meant to live?" The computer programmers? The porno panderers? The lawyers? The politicians? The President?

The classroom and the pulpit, and personal example are the last trenches in the battle against the return of jungle morality to society. I beg of you: do not sell short the power of the rabbinic teacher. A sick society is ready to believe in the world and follow the counsel of men and women who are zealots for the cause they espouse. Rabbis and teachers who believe deeply enough to make sacrifices for their beliefs, who are enthusiasts, not cynics, who are unshakably convinced that the ills of society can be remedied and roll up their sleeves to heal them.

I have seen people change, turn 180 degrees: ritually, ethically, intellectually, spiritually, because of a rabbi who took his sacred commitment seriously, and believed that the layman is not a benighted enemy or a Philistine, but a person impoverished spiritually and longing for honest nourishment for mind and heart.

Issi took the מצוה literally to mean help to the poverty-stricken. Here, too, the rabbinate presents us with unlimited opportunities to relieve human suffering. We are in the vanguard of every charitable drive, Jewish and general. There is not a single hospital, orphanage, home for the aged, catastrophic disease, here or in Israel, which is not inspired by that original thought, "Now, if we can only get the rabbis to call upon their people our cause is a sure success."

The truth is, they are right. Our judgment, our intentions are trusted and sometimes heeded. But the rabbi's study is also the last haven for those whose needs do not perfectly meet any agency's requirements: the desperate stranger in town, the youngster who needs lodging and a job, the proud man who needs a little stake to start again, the housewife who gambled away the grocery money and needs a loan more than a lecture. Nobody need be too embarrassed to ask the rabbi, and the rabbi is never too busy to listen to a plea, nor should be.

Interestingly enough, the *rabbanim*, the majority of rabbis took the מצוה

to mean המבריח עצמו מן המלכות–to assist a person escaping from tyrants. The rabbinate today spends a substantial portion of time and energy in helping the victims of tyranny find escape and refuge. It has been so for me every one of these 30 years: the call to rise in or outside the synagogue and be the voice of the trapped prisoners of Hitler's concentration camps, of the displaced persons herded, angry and bewildered behind barbed wire fences again, of the Haganah before there was a state and the Israel Defense Forces when the State was declared, and immediately attacked, the voice of the Jews of Yemen, Ethiopia, Morocco and Iraq in their moments of unprovoked agony, and latterly the voice of the Jews of Silence behind the Iron Curtain.

No group of leaders anywhere has mobilized unbidden as rapidly, as universally or as effectively as the rabbinate in the defense of the victims of tyranny and dastardly attack. Witness only last Yom Kippur. Every pulpit in America was turned instantly from atonement to "at-one-ment" with Israel. I mean no play on words. I mean at-one-ment. Millions of dollars were given and loaned in response to the trumpet voice of the rabbis. Even before the dollars arrived the people of Israel knew they were not alone in this hostile world as long as Diaspora Jewry was alive and alert.

Two weeks ago the agony of Kiryat Shemonah was protested if scarcely anywhere else, at least from every Jewish pulpit. This Shabbat again, wherever a rabbi rises to speak, the horror of Maalot will be condemned and *Kaddish* said for the Boy Scouts and Girl Scouts from Safed who were wantonly murdered. A question will rise like a chorus of sighs to Heaven from the lips of the rabbi and the heart of the bewildered and angry kids we have been teaching to love Zion and from 18 fresh graves and millions of old ones: "How long, O God, wilt Thou be angry forever? Help us, O God of our salvation and deliver us...Wherefore should the nations say, 'Where is their God?'"

Tomorrow our voices which have grown hoarse and old with protest will be reinforced by 18 fresh voices, with youthful vigor, updated tools, new insights and old wisdom. To those who may happen to be here, including our son Daniel and his *Eishet Chayil*, Beverly, may I say, "Welcome." Life for you will unroll in triple tense from now on. The past is yours to preserve with your scholarship. The present is yours to man the battlements where the action is. The future is yours to assure by teaching a new generation. May God give you strength for your noble calling.

Amen.

SURVIVING OUR FAILURES

When a dear member was confined at home with a serious illness and expressed frustration at not being able to attend Kol Nidre services for the first time in his life, I decided to make it possible for him to hear the service. We agreed to call him by phone before services and hang the receiver of our back-of-the-pulpit phone in front of our pulpit sound monitor. He heard the entire service, the last, sadly, of his life.

In discussing this broadcast with a synagogue officer, he volunteered to underwrite a radio broadcast of Kol Nidre for all shut-ins the following year. A half-hour service of cantor, choir, and sermon would be taped in advance and broadcast that Kol Nidre eve. This we did for years and continue even to this writing and, from the response, served many people.

My sermon had to be brief, with some comforting message. The following is one of them.

OCTOBER 11, 1978

Dear Friends:

On a night like this it is a privilege to be admitted into your life, even if we cannot see one another. Kol Nidre night we need the company of others to reinforce us as we confess our mistakes of the past and ask God to forgive us and grant us a new start. It is difficult to admit our frailties even in the company of others doing the same. It is even more difficult if tonight we are alone, sick, too old to travel or far from a synagogue. I thought perhaps these few shared moments might be of some help to you.

A great contemporary teacher, the late Abraham Joshua Heschel once spoke to a group of us rabbis about the meaning of this holy day. He said, "We are all failures. At least one day a year we should recognize it."

Tonight let me talk about failures, not to teach you how to fail–we all manage to do that without help–but rather how to look at failure, how to handle it. We Americans set great store on being a success. But life is filled with failures, so much so that one university, the Massachusetts Institute of Technology has initiated a new course called, "Failure as a Dominant Theme in Society."

To fail is an experience we must all understand and handle properly if we are to lead any life at all. The stores are filled with books whose titles begin: "How to Succeed." Helping people avoid failure is big business in the United States. Rabbi Heschel is right. We are all failures. One day a year we should recognize it.

But if we all are failures at times, then we can live with it. There was a book published recently which was immensely popular called, *I'm O.K., You're O.K.*. Commenting on it a great Protestant minister said, "I'm Not O.K., You're Not O.K., But That's O.K." The lesson is: accept ourselves and one another with our strengths and our weaknesses, our occasional small successes and our frequent failures.

Some people are lonely because they are looking for perfection in friends. We mustn't do that because if they were looking for perfection, would they choose us as friends? They tell of a young man who didn't marry because he was looking for the perfect girl. When at long last he found her, too bad for him! She was looking for the perfect man.

Children must learn very early that failure is part of living. You rock and fall over and then one day you can stay sitting up. You crawl and wobble and pull yourself up and fall down, and then one day you can stand! You take steps and fall and fall and fall, and one day you can walk. Failure is human.

And it is partial, like success. Nobody is totally successful. Remember funny Groucho Marx? George Bernard Shaw called him the world's greatest living actor. But, Groucho knew the failure of three marriages and three divorces. He was a vastly complicated fragile human under that funny moustache. He gave us a hint of his inner turmoil when a fan once said to him, "It is such a pleasure for me to know the great Groucho Marx."

Groucho answered, "Madam, I've known him for years and I can tell you, it's no pleasure."

How do you measure success? Once in a play called, "Maker of Men," a bank clerk returns home after being denied a promotion. He speaks dejectedly to his wife, "I see other men getting on. What have I done?"

His wife answers, "You have made a woman love you. You have given me respect, admiration and loyalty, everything a man can give his wife except luxuries, and that I don't need. Shall you call yourself a failure who within these four walls are the greatest success?"

Ladies, would you have responded the same way? The basic lesson of Yom Kippur is that failure need not be final. Much of the greatness in people is manufactured out of the raw material of failure by people who refuse to give failure the last word. Take, for example, a 15 year-old boy who once stood embarrassed before the headmaster of a Munich school who was censuring him for lack of interest and expelling him. "Your presence in the class destroys the respect of the students. Out!"

The boy took an exam to enter the Federal Polytechnic School in Zurich. He failed. He went to another school, graduated and then asked for an assistantship at the Polytechnic, but was refused. He got a job as tutor for some boys at a boarding school but was fired. Finally he managed to get a job in a patent office in Berne. Who was this consistent failure? Albert Einstein, the greatest mathematician and scientist of our time. He refused to give failure the victory.

Or take the story of another man who failed in business in 1831, was defeated for the Legislature in 1832, and failed again in business in 1833. His sweetheart died in 1835. He had a nervous breakdown in 1836. He was defeated for Speaker in 1838, defeated for elector in 1840, defeated for Congress in 1843, defeated for Congress in 1848, defeated for the Senate in 1855, defeated for Vice-President in 1856, defeated again for the Senate in 1858, but elected President of the United States in 1860. His name was Abraham Lincoln, a man whom failure could not defeat because he would not give failure the last word.

Ernest Hemingway once wrote in "A Farewell to Arms," "Life breaks all of us and many are strong in the broken places." Isn't that a great statement? There is a television commercial I see frequently. It is for some fantastic cement product. Two wooden boards are cemented together with it. A karate expert gives the cemented board a tremendous chop and it breaks, but not where glued. You and I can be strongest in the broken places if we mend them with the cement of facing and learning from and growing because of our failure and not becoming embittered nor giving up trying because of them.

Recently I went to console the young wife and parents of one of the young lawyers who died in the PSA plane crash in San Diego. They had survived the Holocaust, and were now bereft of their 29-year-old only son. The mother said, "What is left for me? Life is over."

So I told her the story of my doctor and his wife. They had three little children when we first met. When the youngest, a girl, was about four, she developed a brain tumor and died. Their middle child, a son, developed cancer and died at age 16. Then their oldest son also developed cancer and passed away in his 26th year.

But the doctor continues to treat his patients with skill and great love. His wife continues both to help him in his office and to keep up with their many supportive friends. Together they work very hard for one of the foundations seeking the cure for cancer. They delight in the life of the children of their friends. They refuse to give the last word to the tragic failure of all their parental hopes and dreams.

And come to think of it, to be a Jew is to belong to a people who have known so much failure: slavery, defeat, burnt temples, destroyed homelands, exiles, pogroms, deportation, expulsions, the Holocaust. And yet, did we give in to failure? We survived. We enriched the world with our talents, our gifts of mind and spirit. We have not given failure the last word in over 3,000 years. You are alive. I am alive. You're not O.K. I'm not O.K. But that's O.K.!

It is Yom Kippur, time for erasing the slate full of mistakes and accepting from God for our prayers: forgiveness and a new beginning.

GOOD GRIEF!

Gentle Charles Schulz spent a lifetime cartooning. His thousands of comic strips showed us the world through the eyes of children. When one of his characters wanted to unburden himself of an expletive, the harshest Schulz would allow him was, "Good Grief!"

What that means was up to each character, but to me it touched on an experience with which I have spent much of my career as well as my personal life. Is the expression not an oxymoron? How can grief be good?

I was impelled to reflect upon it, as did many others, and found I had so much to say which might be of help to others that I devoted a sermon to it more than once, and learned, again, that some of life's most profound messages may lie, not so much in elaborate and obscure texts, but in the simple phrases we use daily.

FEBRUARY 19, 1994

Dear Friends:

This morning we read in the portion תצוה, 101 verses devoted to describing in the minutest detail a movable sanctuary, the *Ohel Moed*, glorious in its variety of brilliant colors; its gold, silver and precious stones; the elaborate vestments of the high priest; the drama of its rituals.

And where is all this taking place? In the rocky and inhospitable Sinai Peninsula where ex-slaves lived and died, often thirsty and hungry. Out of their adversity and their homelessness, there developed a religion and a people who have made incalculable contributions to the civilization of the Western world, because they were able to discover and enjoy the good side of every event in life.

This simple but normative facet of the Jewish personality was made clear to me by the antics and the performing skill of a humorist friend of ours named Emil Cohen. He pointed out a wonderful attitude we have, which we have borrowed from the *Ribono Shel Olam*, who on the sixth day of creation surveyed all that He had created, and behold, it was very good. *"V'hinei tov m'od...alles is ba-im sehr gut. Und bei uns yiden is oich alles sehr gut.* With God everything is very good, and with us Jews also, everything is good. *Ehr is gut krank. Ehr is gut farshnushkid. Ehr is gut meshugeh. Ehr is gut uhrim. Ehr hat gut ahrain gefallen. Ehr is gut in d'rerd...*" and so on. *Alles is gut.* Everything is good with us Jews. If the Yiddish escapes you, call a friend.

You may have noticed that in the announcement of the subject for today it read "Good grief." I took the topic from that great theologian, Charles Schulz, creator of the comic strip called "Peanuts," which features a loquacious, precocious dog named Snoopy. In one episode I remember, Snoopy is lying on his back when a flock of birds lights on him, followed by a second and a third, and Snoopy says, "Good grief, I'll be glad when the snow-birds fly home!"

The exclamation caught my attention because it seems such a contradiction in terms. The dictionary defines "grief" as "The pain of mind cursed by loss, misfortune, sorrow, physical suffering, or disease." How can grief be good? And yet, this is a common expression many of us use. I recall being astonished when a waiter in a restaurant where I was eating, dropped a tray piled with hot dishes, and I distinctly heard him say, "Good grief!" which was strange enough for someone reacting to a costly and embarrassing accident but, even more surprising, everybody at my table said, *"Mazal tov"* as if he had broken a glass at the end of a wedding. What is so good about that? *Bei ins Yiden is alles gut.*

I guess it is wonderful that we Jews understand the process of good grief. Is there anyone here who has not known the bitter taste of grief, seasoned with the salt of tears? If it is not bereavement, it may be sin, fear, loneliness, frustration. It may be a dimly remembered heartache out of our childhood. It may be that moment when we know we are getting old and we ask ourselves, "Is this all there is?" Grief is a scarring, agonizing emotion. How can it be called good?

The lines of the English poet, Ernest Thompson, echo in my memory from my college days when I first read them, "Nothing begins and nothing ends that is not paid with moan, for we are born in other's pain, and perish in our own."

In a sense, life does begin with a kind of grief, not only the aching body of the mother, but also the infant, leaving the warmth and security of the womb and being launched on its own with a scream of protest. Never again will that little person have it so good. But there is no turning back, although sometimes some of us would like to.

And yet, it is a good grief because the adventure of life begins. A little child walking shyly into the nursery school room on the very first day, clinging tightly to mother's or father's hand or the youngster leaving on the bus for camp to sleep away from home for the first time, waving to the parents while fighting back tears, is experiencing good grief. The 13-year-old bar or bat mitzvah standing before the congregation with knees knocking, confronting not adulthood but puberty, which is worse, is experiencing good grief. The little girl teetering on her first high heels on that first date is experiencing a delicious pain, good grief. Graduation with its "What do I do now?"...the first business or professional venture, and that day, years later...only let it not be too many...when mother and father escort their offspring down that long, long, wedding aisle to give their child to some undeserving stranger with an awful family...they know what every parent knows at the marriage of a child: good grief.

Indeed, good grief is a little prayer in which we are saying, "Dear God, please turn this grief to some good purpose." The memories of our parents and grandparents take us back to immigrant beginnings when the thing in which we were richest was poverty. Our generations which strives to give our children everything and spare them all grief will be very fortunate if they think of us with half the love and gratitude with which we think of older generations who gave us very little materially because they had very little to give, but gave us so much spiritually that we never knew we were poor or deprived.

The playgrounds were the streets and they were safe. Who would have dreamed of coming to his mother during long summer vacation days and saying, "I'm bored." There was a classic answer for that, *"Geh shlug zich dein kup in vant...*Go bang your head against the wall." Boredom is the disease of the rich, which we couldn't afford.

Yet out of this lack of privilege, out of the grief of poverty, crowding and discrimination came some of America's most gifted entertainers, judges, scientists, doctors, authors and artists.

Last week there were a series of interviews with Art Buchwald, the howlingly funny and insightful columnist about his new book, "Leaving Home." He told of a mentally ill mother he never saw for 35 years, a succession of foster homes, orphanages and depression. Out of this grief came the humor so many of us have enjoyed for so long.

Good grief! Now this is not a plea for poverty. Certainly I don't want it. But it is a reassurance that it is not the greatest tragedy, especially if it is a grief turned to good purposes. For some it sharpens innate talents and compels them to rise to the top surface of society. For others it reminds them of the value of a dollar and leads them to bestow great benefactions upon society because they can sympathize with and understand the grief of society, they have been there themselves.

War has been the worst common grief of modern life, but it could become a good grief. If only we could turn awareness of its blasphemous and tragic waste to the good purpose of abolishing it forever. This purpose we must cling to even as the shells explode in Sarajevo. The memorable phrase of Abraham Lincoln, "That these honored dead shall not have died in vain" must become the imperative of every government in the world. The prophet Isaiah's vision of beating our swords, symbolic of violent death and grief, into plows, symbolic of life and plenty, can turn the grief of war into the paradise of true peace.

Health is a very big concern in our lives. I remember on a previous visit here with my cousin, we went on a Sunday morning to a very Jewish and very large delicatessen. There in addition to prepared meals for one and for two, I saw something else I have never seen before. There was a huge rack, from floor to ceiling, with more bags and varieties of prunes than I had ever imagined. Are prunes the ambrosia of the golden years?

Health is a big concern, and good health is indeed a blessing. Yet rare is the person who can lay claim to being healthy, never one day sick, at all times and in every stage of life. Poor health and catastrophic diseases, these are a common source of grief, but their effect upon us is determined by our ability to turn them to good purposes, to heighten our appreciation of life or even to make us more understanding of the illness of our relatives and friends. To give you an example of good grief, I have a pacemaker. Once I was stopped by a Beverly Hills policeman for not having my seatbelt on. I told him I had a pacemaker and the shoulder strap irritated my incision. He bought it. Besides, he was Jewish, the only one on the force.

Health: how can one know its value until one has suffered its absence? Sir William Osler, once foremost physician in England, told a graduating class, "Gentlemen, you will never be great physicians until you have suffered at least one crushing illness." How many times have I stood at the bedside of a man recovering from a severe heart attack and heard him say he would develop a whole new set of values in his life. Those who do so have experienced a good grief.

For me, one of the most stirring examples of human nobility is someone who turns the grief of a physical handicap into a good grief. Do you remember Eleanor Roosevelt? She said being hard of hearing was a blessing. In the midst of all the hubbub of the hectic world in which she lived, she managed to remain calm and serene. When speeches grew dull and lengthy, she simply tuned them out. "You cannot imagine," I once heard her say, "what an advantage that is!"

Incidentally, I hope I have not lost any of you with that suggestion. Helen Keller once said, "I thank God for my handicaps, for through them I have found myself, my work and my God."

I once had an organist in my congregation, Joseph Leonard, who had been blinded by accident at the age of five, but who, because of it, turned to music, like so many other musical artists. He conducted a choir he could not see and followed the cantor and me perfectly, sensing our every move. He had a great sense of humor, and his only admonition to me was, "Rabbi, don't give me any hand signals!"

One of my heroes is Rabbi Milton Steinberg, of blessed memory. He suffered a massive heart attack. When he recovered he described to the congregation his feelings on the first day he was permitted to go out of doors. He said, "As I crossed the threshold, sunlight greeted me. So long as I live I shall never forget that moment. I looked about me to see whether anyone else showed on his face the joy I felt. But no, there they walked, men, women and children, in the glory of a golden flood and, so far as I could detect, there was none to give it heed. And then I remembered how often I, too, had been indifferent to the sunshine and I said to myself, 'How precious is the sunlight, but, alas, how careless of it are men.'" Steinberg discovered the sunlight only after his attack, even as the Psalmist realized his cup was running over only after he had walked through the valley of the shadow of death.

One of the most common sources of unhappiness is knowing we are growing old. Remember Tevye in *Fiddler on the Roof?* Looking at his adult children, he sang, "I don't remember growing older. When did they?"

Age, many of those little automatic acts we performed unthinkingly must now be carefully considered, sometimes slowly and painfully be performed, sometimes given up altogether.

One day we wake up and realize we are trying to lead a youngster's life with last year's model body. We can't remember when the first hair turned gray, when the steps got higher, the telephone book's type got smaller, the golf holes got farther apart. It is not so much that we fear the end of life is near, but rather that the end of youth, romance, popularity, activity is closer at hand. And it grieves us that we are growing old at the very same time that life expectancy for those born now is getting longer and longer. Is that such a tragedy? Or is it really good grief that modern medicine, hygiene and sanitation have extended our lives far beyond what they would have been a century ago. Aging isn't so terrible when, as Churchill said, you consider the alternative.

Bereavement is the ultimate grief. What can be good about that? Well, it can cripple us or it can ennoble us. Benjamin Disraeli said, "Grief is the agony of an instant. The indulgence of grieving is the blunder of a life." In this connection I think of the great tower of Stanford University which dominates the City of Palo Alto. Leland Stanford, governor of the State of California, had a son, whom he loved, an only child. Before his dreams for his son could be realized, the boy died at the age of nine.

Instead of drowning in his sorrow, Stanford erected and heavily endowed a university, one of the world's great institutions of learning, bearing the name, Leland Stanford Junior. In Israel, at Yad Vashem, a friend of ours, Abraham Spiegel, established "The Memorial to a Million and Half Children" who were murdered during the Holocaust. We never knew that the Spiegels, themselves survivors, had had a son who died in that tragic time. Now we know.

Last week we dedicated a beautiful new Day School building for our congregation. It is called the Pressman Academy, but the building will be known as the Rena Ganzberg Building because the Ganzberg family, who have never really stopped grieving for the bright, pretty Rena who died just as she was entering medical school, gave generously to keep her name alive. And then there was the rabbi of Klausenberg. This pious man witnessed the slaughter of his wife and eleven children by the Nazis. Instead of going mad from his grief, he survived, made his way to Israel and founded eleven schools for underprivileged children, one in the name of each of his dead children.

Another of my dear rabbinical friends was the late Bernard Harrison. He suffered his first heart attack at the age of 49, and when he recovered he wrote this message to his congregation "If I had one more year to live, I would want to live longer, but I would console myself with the hard medicine that no one lives forever. If I had but a short time to go, I would want to live it so that my children would remember me kindly, lovingly and with pride in their hearts for what good qualities I may have been blessed with. And if my parents survived me and my brothers and my sisters, to remember what joy I may have brought them and forgive what hurt I might have done them. If I had a short time to go, I would want to do something I could take pride in: my chosen work. If I were a builder, to build one beautiful, as nearly perfect home as I could. If I were a physician, to bring back to health at last a few who were in mortal danger. And if I could do no more, to console myself in this: that homes were built before me and will be after me; that lives were saved and will be saved.

And if I lived a hundred years I could not build all the houses and bring to health all the ill of the world. And, finally, if I had but a short time left, I would be charitable to all men, irrespective of their creed or color. I would try to do what good I can to my fellow men and leave the world a little the better, the nobler, the happier for my having been in it. And I would want this to be remembered by my beloved, my children, and my family, my colleagues and my friends. 'Remember that I lived. Forget that I died.'"

Dear Barney Harrison died a year later.

Good grief. It is one of those capacities which validate our claim to being in the image of God, for God is capable of grief, the divine pathos, the late Rabbi Abraham Joshua Heschel called it. God was disappointed in man before the great flood and was sorry He had made us. God weeps to see man's inhumanity to man. God renews our chances every time a new soul enters this world and teaches us the value of good grief.

One of the best known and most dramatic stories demonstrating "good grief," turning trial into triumph is the story of the Patriarch, Jacob, whose name I bear. In the portion וישלח, Jacob, who had fled his brother Esau's justifiable anger, is returning home from Haran, where he had worked for decades, established a large family and acquired much cattle and sheep, and is preparing to meet his estranged brother. He is afraid of a possible reprisal, for he had learned that Esau was coming with a large army of men to meet him.

He divides his possessions into two camps, so that in case of trouble, one group would survive. He goes to sleep and is attacked by a mysterious presence with whom he wrestles all night. Jacob is wounded seriously in the thigh, but he prevails. When his adversary begs to be released he says, לא אשלחך כי אם ברכתני "I will not let you go unless you bless me!" Jacob is wounded in battle, suffers the grief of pain, but he says, "I demand that some blessing comes out of all this." This, in brief, is my message today. We all suffer trials and setbacks, wounds, pain and tragedy, but we mustn't let them go without deriving some good out of them.

May our Heavenly Father spare you and me from much grief and sorrow, but if grief be our lot, O Lord, give us the wisdom to behold in it the truths we could never behold in joy and grant us the strength to transform grief into acts of nobility and goodness, for ourselves, for our fellow men, and for Thee.

Amen.

CHAPTER FIVE
Moments to Warm the Heart

While the sermon may be in the Prophetic mode, addressing the ethical and moral issues of the day, it is also a time for lifting the heart with examples of the goodness, kindness and love of which we are capable.

This chapter begins with an eye-witness report and response to the great blackout of New York City in 1965. In a totally unexpected way, this incident brought out the better part of human nature: people helping people, an absence of taking advantage of the opportunity for pillage and violence, a bringing together of strangers.

A tribute to Denmark recalled when that tiny nation became a moral giant in the saving of Jews from Hitler's "final solution." The space adventures suggested that man's unbounded curiosity led him beyond the moon. The faltering falls which lead ultimately to progress, and the kindness of which man is capable were encouraging subjects in discouraging times.

Included is a charming story of how our best childhood dreams can become our adult realities if the child is allowed to remain in us.

For many people, this kind of sermon is what they really yearned to hear when they came to the synagogue. As one man put it, "I need to learn my Judaism, but I need even more to be inspired by it."

THE GREAT BLACK WAY

A full moon was all that illuminated New York City and much of the Northeast region of America on November 9, 1965. By chance, I was there in the middle of it all. For all its eerie atmosphere, there rested upon this roiling metropolis a strange and unfamiliar peace. People responded with warm concern to the problems of others, reassured one another, shared what could be shared and allowed the milk of human kindness and brotherly love to bubble to the surface. What could have been a depressing experience became for me and many others an uplifting one.

The Sabbath eve following my return, I shared with the congregation my impression humanity is stronger than technology.

NOVEMBER 12, 1965

Dear Friends,

On this Sabbath when we read two Biblical stories warm with reassurance of the essential goodness of man, I thought I might share yet another with you, a modern day experience akin to the sweet example of Father Abraham's hospitality and the kindness of the Shunemite woman who sheltered the Prophet Elisha.

So that you may understand how I came to this experience let me explain that I arrived back here in Los Angeles from New York at three o'clock this afternoon. I had gone East to attend the biennial convention of the United Synagogue of America, our federation of 800 Conservative Synagogues in the United States, Canada and Mexico. Its theme was "Except the Lord build the house, they labor in vain that build it." It was an exciting conference and was held at a hotel 100 miles from New York.

On Tuesday evening of this week, I was invited to come to the city to attend the opening night of a new play, "The Zulu and the Zayda." Since I might some day become at least one of these, I took the bus for New York. I sensed something very peculiar on the third floor ramp when I arrived at the Port Authority Bus Terminal.

It was unusually quiet. There were no loudspeaker announcements and there was little talking. I walked to the down escalator and observed that the light was exceedingly dim. The escalators were not moving so I joined the crowd walking down the immobilized escalator steps. On the ground floor, the crush of the people was even thicker than usual, and half running, rather than walking. Soon I was half pushed, half carried through the doors and deposited on the sidewalk. Eighth Avenue was choked with cars and buses and taxis, their headlights lighting the street. There were hopelessly snarled at the intersection of 41st Street and 8th Avenue in a traffic jam that seemed like a slovenly parking lot. The traffic signals were out, the lights were out, the stores were dark.

A trio of teenagers ran past me with flashlights shining in their hands. "Flashlight, mister?" said one, "Only five bucks."

I looked around, up at the tall buildings, and then it struck me at last. New York was blacked out. It was about six o'clock, but the electric clocks dimly visible showed 5:25. I was pushed into the street by mobs pouring out of subway entrances. I asked a policeman who was whistling at the snarled traffic, "What happened?"

"I dunno," he barked. "Move along."

I tried to listen to what people were saying, and I heard, "A bomb dropped on Niagara Falls and wiped out the generators. A Russian bomb." "It's a big civilian defense test!" "The whole East Coast is blacked out!"

My friends, how shall I describe my feelings? Three thousand miles from home, not a familiar face and an unexplained blackout. I headed east toward Times Square one block away. A few feet off Eighth Avenue, 44th Street, a street ordinarily bright with theater marquees, was absolutely black except for an occasional flashlight-bearing pedestrian.

I got to Times Square in a hurry and saw the most extraordinary sight I can recall. The Great White Way had become the Great Black Way. I headed for the theater on 48th Street where the play was to open for a press preview at 7:15. There, at the stage door stood Howard da Silva, the star of the play, in a tuxedo, holding a yahrzeit candle in his hand, in the middle of a little knot of people, including some women in elegant first-nighter long gowns. I went up to him and asked, "Who died, the Zulu or the zayda?"

He gave me a disgusted look and said, "Both."

In the box office two men sat by candlelight and I got my first reasonable explanation of the circumstances. "There is a total power failure from here to Canada, including Massachusetts and almost all of New England. There will be no show tonight."

So, I did what any red-blooded American rabbi would do, I headed for the nearest kosher restaurant, which, luckily, was about a half-block from the theater. Inside, candles burned on every table, and the place was filled with diners. I had dinner and tried to telephone our temple president who was stopping at the Hilton Hotel.

It took 30 minutes to get the call through, although he was only about five blocks away. Sure enough, there he was, on the twenty-seventh floor of the blacked-out hotel, no elevator running, no lights, no dinner. I hated to tell him I had just finished a hearty meal.

Instead, I promised to go to the Hilton lobby and wait there until the power came on. The hotel is brand new and so its stairway is a very tiny inside fire escape, which I attempted to negotiate but gave up after getting up three of the 27 stories. I fought my way back down against people carrying suitcases in both directions in utter blackness on a 30-inch wide stairway.

And so I sat in the lobby, now jammed with people and smelling of human sweat and candle wax. I met and talked with people from all over the country and from out of the country. I sat until three, when it was announced on transistor radio that there would be no lights that night.

I left a note for Mr. Shapell, our temple president who was still on the twenty-seventh floor, since I could no longer get through to him on the telephone. I went out on the street again to head for a haven at the apartment of a friend across town.

As I walked across a paralyzed New York, I felt better and better about my fellow man and here is why: At almost every intersection, traffic was moving. Men in shirtsleeves, for visibility, stood in the 34-degree cold, directing traffic, risking being hit and volunteering to meet emergencies. Private cars stopped and people offered rides. "Want to go to Queens?" "Anybody for Connecticut?"

I walked down Fifth Avenue past windows showing tempting clothing, jewelry, linens and furs. None were touched. There was no looting, no panic, no fighting, no shouting.

People cheerfully talked to strangers passing the news. "They chopped out the wall in the Empire State Building and got them out of the elevator."

"Just heard a hundred people walked five miles through the subway tunnel under the East River and got out O.K."

"Policeman says the crime rate in New York tonight is less than on an average night."

These rumors were all true. In stygian darkness, 14 million New Yorkers acted with restraint, courage, courtesy and even compassion. They helped one another and, with the real possibility that this was a prelude to war, invasion or even annihilation, let the essential morality of the Judeo-Christian tradition shine through.

I tramped along the eerie black canyons of Manhattan. At 4 A.M. a full moon was shining, I felt as if the human race had just been submitted to some cosmic test and looked heavenward at the cheerful white disk up there. The theme of the convention, taken from Psalm 127, rang in my ears, "Except the Lord build the house, they who build it labor in vain." And then its companion verse, "Except the Lord guard the city, the watchman waketh but in vain."

People, fallible and vulnerable to temptation, had remembered the religious lessons this generation sometimes ridicules. For one black night, which might have been civilization's last night since the president's finger was at the red atomic missile button for ten heart-stopping minutes, they became their brothers' keepers, performing countless acts of heroism, hospitality and help. I am not given to overdramatizing, but as I walked, my eyes on the moon, I found they got a little misty. I said aloud, "God is guarding the city, and he is doing it through the human heart."

I reached my destination, got up to my room by the candle I took from the restaurant, lay down and thought about the past ten hours. I thought about Abraham running out of his tent to bring in the weary travelers. I thought of Elisha's hospitable hostess. I thought about the small segment of society trying to teach human values in these highly mechanized days. I thought about how when the miracles of this electric and electronic age black out because of mechanical difficulties, man is still safe and life is still good because of the miracle of the divine impulse in the human heart. I thought about my family, you, my congregation, and this my work, and I said to myself, "It is good!"

As I did, at 5:30 in the dawn, the lights in the room came on and I fell asleep.

WHEN A TINY NATION BECAME A GIANT

Like many congregations, we would celebrate Thanksgiving with a neighboring Christian church, alternating between the synagogue and the church from year to year. When the story appeared of the heroism of the people of Denmark in defying the Nazi occupiers by refusing to join in the betrayal and expulsion of its Jews, which many other occupied nations did so cravenly, it seemed that the inspiring story was not familiar to non-Jews, despite its presence in a growing number of publications.

In 1968, it was our turn to lead the Thanksgiving service, and I chose to use Denmark as an example of the goodness of which people are capable.

NOVEMBER 28, 1968

Dear Friends:

On this Thanksgiving night, when we remind ourselves of some of the marvelous deliverances of our people, we use the words we recite before each new month: "Mi she-asah nissim l'avoteinu... May he who wrought wondrous deeds for our fathers and redeemed them from slavery unto freedom, redeem us and grant our exiled brethren from the four corners of the earth sanctuary. For all Israel is one fellowship."

When we ask ourselves on this Thanksgiving weekend what are some of the things for which we have to be grateful, the newspaper headlines give us scant comfort. Although we are told that in this land and in this community there is great prosperity and great plenty, we are still suffering. We still know of want. Even more than physical want, we are aware of our spiritual thirst. For notes of brightness in darkening clouds at such a time, I find it heartening indeed to look to a little country across the seas, one which it was our happy privilege to visit on two occasions, a little finger of land thrusting northward in western Europe called Denmark.

When we visited a synagogue in Denmark on a Sabbath morning we were able to follow the prayers and then step out into a little courtyard beyond the synagogue. In it there are buildings housing the aged. We were able to communicate in Yiddish and be asked in Yiddish, "Maybe you know my cousin Mr. Cohen in New York?" To which, we were happy to respond, "We may once have met."

In Denmark this year there are signs of an awakening young Jewish community. There are 6,000 Jews now in all of Denmark, about as many as there are now within three blocks of where we are sitting. Yet for a time there has been grave concern over the survival of the Jewish community. It is a good sign that the youngsters who grew up since the War have taken an interest in Judaism. They have been fighting for places on the Board of Deputies, the leaders of the Jewish community. They have been canvassing for votes, publishing leaflets and brochures and organizing groups. Young people increasingly are appearing in the synagogue, asking to conduct the service and read from the Torah. More young couples are keeping kosher homes than was the case with their parents.

These are small changes, but within them there is some hope. Behind that hope there is one of the heartening incidents of the entire period of the Holocaust, perhaps one of the brightest sparks of the entire twentieth century. That spark was kindled by a courageous people, perhaps among the most courageous, the ordinary people of a little nation who by their deeds became giants of our time. They gave life and courage to their brothers at the risk of their own lives.

Hear their story tonight, and hear it well. Let it be known to your friends and neighbors and to your children so that the world will know that out of the worst holocaust known to man there was a beacon of light which still beckons men who yearn to be free, with the message, "Stand up and do not be afraid to stand for the right." Hear the story of these brave people tonight.

On the morning of September 9, 1943, in that Copenhagen synagogue, Rabbi Marcus Melchior arose and addressed the small congregation present at the daily service. He said, "Tomorrow night on the holiest of days, tomorrow, *Rosh Hashana*, there will be no service. Instead, I have very important news to tell you. Last night I received word that tomorrow the Germans plan to raid Jewish homes throughout Copenhagen, to arrest all the Danish Jews for shipment to concentration camps. They know that tomorrow is *Rosh Hashana* and all our families will be at home or in synagogues. The situation is very serious. We must take action immediately. Leave the synagogue now. Contact all friends, relatives, neighbors who are Jewish. By tomorrow night, we must all be in hiding."

It was a hard message for the rabbi to give. He had received his information from German soldiers through some of the Danes. From April 1940, when Germany invaded Denmark until September 1943, those in charge of the occupation of that peninsula had been very unwilling to enforce the same occupation laws and hardships on the Danes, let alone the Jews of that country, because reports flowed back to Berlin that the people of Denmark unlike those of other occupied countries, would not tolerate, would even revolt against persecution of the Jews. And so this was to be the model community. The Germans had always said that the Danes invited the Germans in for their own protection. The Germans wanted to maintain this myth. To avoid stirring up resistance, the Germans actually allowed the Danish Jews to go their way until the fall of 1943. This was not a new thing for the Danes. The tradition of amity for their Jewish brethren went back as far as 1690 when a police chief was fired for anti-Semitic acts. Denmark passed a law against all racial and religious discrimination, not in the Twentieth century, but in 1814.

Denmark, shortly after the German occupation circulated reports of the Danish king's response to the Nazis when the subject of yellow arm-bands for the Jews arose. It is said that he swore that if yellow arm-bands would appear, he and his family would wear them. While there is some question as to the authenticity of this story, there are those, even in the city, who claim that they remember King Christian taking his morning ride with the yellow Star of David prominently displayed on his arm. The atmosphere which could give birth to such a story was important.

There was a student festival in a town outside of Copenhagen. During the occupation, the students asked everybody to join in the singing of two songs at the end of that festival. The Nazis present were not surprised when the first song presented was the Danish National Anthem, but they were shocked when the second turned out to be, not Deutschland Deutschland, but the unfurling of Jewish flags and the singing of *Hatikvah*.

Since the Danes flaunted their patriotism and were not punished because the Jews of that country were let alone, the word from Rabbi Melchior stunned his congregation, but they had to believe. They had to take a chance that this was not just a trick to stir up Jewish activity so as to bring the Gestapo down upon them, but was actually a real threat. So the word was passed, mouth to mouth, family to family, neighbor to neighbor throughout the community and into the surrounding towns on the 29th of September.

The first plan was to go into hiding. Escape would have to come later. First save the Jews from the roundup. Rabbi Melchior had not only the members of his family to save, but the objects of the synagogue, the scrolls of the Torah, the prayer books. He called one of his closest friends who was a Protestant pastor and said to him, "It is kind of you to offer shelter.

Perhaps you will take two of my children and my wife and I will go elsewhere."

And he was told, "No, rabbi. You must come with your entire family. We have room."

"But if you are caught, even though you are a Lutheran minister, you will surely go to jail," said Rabbi Melchior.

The pastor replied, "I am ready for that."

Throughout the day of the 29th, the day before Erev Rosh Hashanah, Christian policeman and postmen, taxi drivers and shopkeepers, teachers and students, gave warning to their Jewish friends. One young ambulance driver ripped a telephone book from a phone booth and drove through the city calling on strangers with Jewish sounding names. He piled many of them into his ambulance and drove them to the hospital to hide. Many individuals like that worked feverishly through the day and through the night.

Meanwhile the Gestapo was preparing to strike and so confident were they that they would find 8,000 Jews in their homes and synagogues that the Gestapo chief had already wired Berlin in anticipation of his success saying it is my duty to clean Denmark of her Jews and when this is achieved, Denmark is Judenrein, clean of Jews, completely purged.

He wanted to be very prompt with his message, but he was a little premature. That night the Gestapo, armed with address lists raided the residents of Denmark's 8,000 Jews, they were not at home, with the exception of 202 Jews, who for one reason or another, decided not to act upon the warning. Nobody was at home. The roundup was a failure. The Nazis realized that the Jews were in hiding and they tried using threats and rewards for turning in Jews. The bribes failed. Reprisals against the church as well as the people met with statements like that of one pastor who said, "Politics must not be discussed from the pulpit because it is punishable. In spite of this I tell you that I would rather die with the Jews than live with the Nazis."

Jews were in hiding everywhere, in the homes of Christian friends, in churches, in summer huts, in warehouses, on farms, and in hospitals. No group was more helpful than the physicians. When word of the Gestapo raids reached the hospitals, Danish Jews with Jewish-sounding names were discharged on the books and then readmitted with Christian-sounding names. Hundreds of Danish students went into the woods in organized search parties to find the Jews who were in hiding there and bring them to safer hiding places. And so the Jews were in hiding.

And now for the second phase, how to get the Jews out of hiding and into safety. The most obvious haven was just across the water in Sweden.

But, would Sweden accept the Jewish refugees because Sweden was neutral? They still had a slight bent in favor of Germany. Certainly they wanted to do nothing to offend Hitler. When two proposals by Sweden to Germany to accept at least Danish children were turned down, they thought it was better to say and do nothing.

In 1943, the Allies wanted the Danish physicist Niels Bohr in the United States to work on the atomic bomb. Bohr was a Jew. And Bohr was smuggled into Sweden from Denmark. He was to leave immediately to England by plane, but he refused to go until he had an audience with King Gustav of Sweden. With King Gustav he insisted on Sweden's insurance of haven for the Jews of Denmark. That insurance was given him, whereupon he left for this country in his part of the creation of that ultimate weapon of destruction.

And so, when it was known that Sweden would offer haven, both Danish Jews and Danish Christians were delighted.

One question remained on how to get the Jews to Sweden. Of course there is only one way and that is by boat. But the Germans had removed all Danish pleasure boats from the water with the exception of fishing boats. And so fishermen and sportsmen, and people with motor boats and row boats loaded their vessels to the gunnels with human cargo. All kinds of devices were used when the Jews burrowed down among the fish under the tarpaulin. They came to the water's edge and spoke to the Danish fisherman always with the confidence that they would not be betrayed. They would sometimes come asking, "Perhaps you could take one of my children."

The response was always, "I'll take them all."

"Perhaps you can take one of my friends."

"I will make trips."

Sometimes as many as 50 people a night were taken by a single fisherman, and his boat made several trips across the waters. When the suspicious Nazis intercepted some of these boats, the Danes stormed and protested and said, "You're supposed to have come here to protect us, not to harass us. Get off our ships. We will report you for harassment." The ruse worked. The Germans let the ships go through.

Out of these acts of saving the Jews, the Danes realized that their sporadic acts of resistance, sabotage here and there, slowdowns in the factories, that they could not act individually. They had to be organized. The saving of the Jews was the catalyst that created a united Danish resistance.

So, they created an underground. That underground was used as a collection point for Jews and other political prisoners various places in Copenhagen. Ambulances and taxis were the best ways of getting people to the boats. Bookstores, dental offices, so many places were used as depots for the collection of refugees. Physicians were especially helpful, tending the sick, giving harmless drugs to babies to prevent them from crying out and giving groups away.

The women of Copenhagen cooked and fed the hundreds who came through their homes and their churches. Their story is one of the most heartening and courageous examples in human history. Unless we think of this as something remote and not having to do with people we know, possibly there are some here who are Danes of either Christian or Jewish background.

There are people of this community whose heroism was not known until recently. Perhaps you read of just one of them. This was a girl named Mussi Tova Hansen, called Mussi or little mouse. A timid girl in 1943, a dental assistant in a large medical building, she suspected that her brother was doing something with the underground, but did not know for sure. Finally she was brought into the underground movement.

Her first task involved the sabotage of a large Copenhagen exhibition hall, the forum which was used as a Nazi barracks. She became involved in the exodus of Jews by providing hiding places in the dental office. When almost all the Danish Jews were rescued, she fell under suspicion. At the urging of her friends, she fled to Sweden in December of 1943, but she could not rest there. She could not stay there. After two months she went back to Denmark and continued until she was arrested, interrogated and jailed for three months. But her captors learned nothing of her activities.

When she was released, she went back immediately to the underground and continued her work. When the underground fighters finally were able to come into the open when victory was achieved in 1945, she continued to work aiding refugees. In 1947, she came to America and married a man with the same second name, Kenneth Hansen.

After becoming an American citizen she settled down to work alongside her husband. I suspect there are some people here who have been in her restaurant, the restaurant that Kenneth and Tova Hansen run on the Sunset Strip called Scandia and did not know that 25 years ago, as a young girl she was busy rescuing our people.

When the war was over, she was asked by reporters why she did what she did. She replied that there was no other way to live as a human being. She was saving, not Jews especially, not Danes especially, but fellow human beings. She was asked what was the happiest moment of her life after those days, was it Nazi defeat, was it seeing the last Nazi truck disappear from the streets of Copenhagen.

She said, "No," her most rewarding experience was when she saw 8,000 Jewish Danes able to come home safely. When the Jews of Sweden returned and became once again the Jews of Denmark and those who had been in camps and had been kept alive simply because of the insistence of the Danish Red Cross, and they came home, they all wondered, who would have won, the Nazis or the Danes. Whose influence would have rubbed off on whom? They found that some of the Danish humanity had rubbed off on some of the German occupying forces.

Would the Jews be welcome back in Denmark? They were welcome. The government tried in every way to restore them to the conditions that they had held at the time of their departure. There were many Jews who returned to find that their homes had been cleaned, spic and span. There was food in the icebox. Their lawns were freshly mowed. Even their pets were fed and healthy. This was a glorious chapter in a very dark period in human history. Now a new generation of Danish Jews has grown up, free of the fear that drove their parents across the waters to Sweden, inspired by the freedom of that land and deciding in part to return to the traditions of their fathers.

It is very interesting because in many Western Jewish communities, Jewish life is diminished, even dying away in lands where the people collaborated and betrayed them. Perhaps it is understandable there is one bright spot and that Scandinavian Jewry, while small in numbers, is beginning to return to good health. This bright spot, my friends, is for me as I hope it is for you, a beautiful oasis in the desert of man's inhumanity to man. And I would ask you on this day, 25 years later, to pay tribute to that proud little people who alone extended that hand of friendship to rise and hear their national anthem.

Det land endnu er skønt,
Thi blå sig søen bælter,
Og løvet står så grønt;
Og løvet står så grønt;
Og ædle kvinder, skønne mø'r
Og mænd og raske svende
Bebo de danskes øer,
Bebo de danskes øer.

And still that land is fair,
So blue the seas that belt her,

So green the woodland there;
So green the woodland there;
And noble women, comely girls
And men and lads of mettle
Dwell in the Danish isles,
Dwell in the Danish isles.

This is the national anthem of Denmark. When you hear it, remember the story. The story of heroes with names that are strange to us, names of Knudson, Bohr, Hansen, Staffels. Thousands of Danes have proved that at least one time in our century there was meaning to the phrase, "I am my brother's keeper."

BEYOND THE MOON

On July 20, 1969, man put his footprint on the moon. It was one of the most exciting moments in history and gave astronomers and theologians new challenges. It was impossible to address the congregation on the eve of Rosh Hashanah and ignore this incredible achievement. I could not fail to discuss with the congregation my own feelings about the event nor what I believed were its implications for the future. In August I had informally asked the question, "Space or heaven, where are we heading?"

Over 30 years have passed, we have been back to the moon and beyond and are even building a platform in space where people can sojourn and work, but still the question remains: space or heaven, where are we going?

SEPTEMBER 12, 1969

Dear Friends:

It is the year 5730 in our Jewish calendar. It is the year תשל, tav, shin, lamed, the letters which symbolize the number of this new year, and which also begin the words תהה שלום לעולם "May there be peace forever."

How do we know it is the beginning of a new year, *Rosh Hashanah*? We know by looking into the heavens at our nearest celestial neighbor, the moon, of which we sing between the *Shema* and the *Amidah*: תקעו בחדש שופר "Sound the shofar on the new moon." Since Biblical days we Jews have blessed the new moon, ordered our calendar by its phases and marveled unabashed at its beauty. Its white light ruled the night and added to our awe-struck reverence for its Creator.

Somehow we always measured ourselves against the moon in speculations which reached their most eloquent expression in the eighth Psalm of David:

O Lord, our God, how glorious is Thy name in all the earth.
When I behold thy heavens, the work of Thy fingers,
The moon and the stars which Thou hast established,
What is man that Thou art mindful of him,
And the son of man that Thou thinkest of him?
Yet Thou hast made him but little lower than the angels
And hast crowned him with glory and honor."

A new glory and honor crowned man and the son of man on July 20 of this year when our old earth-bound era came to an end and the age of the moon began. Since time immemorial when someone wanted the impossible, we would say, "He wants the moon." We have lived to see the impossible accomplished. Two men have done the most unlikely thing ever conceived: they have stepped on the moon. Almost as unlikely, you and I witnessed it one-and-a-third seconds after it happened. The door to the universe has been opened, and we are destined to explore and explore and probably eventually to colonize.

This Rosh Hashanah of which our prayers say, היום הרת עולם "This day celebrates the birthday of the world," is for us the birthday of a world expanded. Reactions to this giant step for mankind have, as one might expect, been mixed. On the one hand there was the reaction of exultation, national pride and extravagant enthusiasm typified by President Nixon's description of it as "the most important event since the creation of the world." At the Century Plaza Hotel, in what seemed to be a political academy award of space, our national leadership exuded a heightened sense of national confidence. After so many crises and unresolved problems, which have dogged American efforts and dampened our national spirit, it was good to have a real victory and a peaceful one, at that.

On the other hand there were many deep and searching questions raised in the very hour of exuberance. "Is this trip necessary? Was it worthwhile in terms of thousands of man hours of labor, the preoccupation of tens of thousands of highly educated men and women and billions of dollars spent?" Sober and sage voices charged that in view of the tremendous unresolved problems here on earth it would have behooved us far better to spend those billions and all that human energy on more urgent problems bedeviling society, on welfare and education, on purifying and beautifying our environment, on achieving a peaceful and prosperous humanity; in short, solving all the terrible vexations which cheat life of its joy and tranquility.

There are some critics who cynically compare our flight to the moon with the biblical Tower of Babel when man conceived the same exciting human goal: to storm the heavens, to reach the skies. They said, "Come let us build...a tower with its top in heaven and let us make ourselves a name."

Is it possible that our motives in reaching for the moon were less than unselfish? Did it all begin in response to the challenge of the Soviet Union to shore up our sagging national prestige when the first Sputnik circled the globe? Was it only to make ourselves a name?

Other critics gleefully point to a symbolic coincidence. The astronauts left behind on the moon, or in a sense transplanted to the moon, two major problems the world has to solve. They left the American flag which symbolizes the nationalism which not only triggered the space race but is at the core of war itself. Also they were litterbugs, leaving millions of dollars of space garbage behind, symbolizing what is perhaps the greatest emerging problem we have, the problem of our environment.

Would it not be better, people ask, to have spent all those billions in attacking hunger and poverty, disease and pollution here? With a world crisis threatening land, air and water pollution, experts tell us we are rushing toward global suicide. Our lakes are dying. Our air is not fit to breathe. Our food supply will not suffice to feed the exploding world population. Our cities are decaying under our feet. And yet more billions were spent on providing pure air and water and disposal of waste for the astronauts in ten days than for all the other two hundred plus millions of Americans this year.

The controversy over the merits of the moon shot will undoubtedly rage on for years. What concerns us here is not which side is right, but rather which will make for the greatest human good?

In addition to those billions of dollars spent on the race for space, there are even more billions of dollars which were spent on war, the tools of war and the destruction of man rather than on the enhancement of his life. We spend a billion dollars or more every week on military matters which destroy nature as well as man. The real choice is between what makes for life and what makes for death, the very stuff of which our Holy Day reflections are made: מי יחיה ומי ימות "Who shall live and who shall die."

Historian Salvador de Madriaga, a Spanish-born historian and something of a philosopher, whom I first met with great excitement when I read his documentation of the fact the Columbus was Jewish, has something to say again. "The discovery of the new world of space may change modern civilization and provide a new life so that our supreme aim may become clear: the intelligent organization of life on this planet. Our supreme aim may be given additional life even through these new discoveries." It is a very interesting expression which he uses: "The supreme aim of man, the intelligent organization of life on this planet." In other words the supreme aim of man is not to reach the moon but to use the knowledge gained thereby to make this a better world.

If we understand that scientific achievements can neither help us solve the real problems of life nor help us escape them by going elsewhere, then we need not make a choice between extolling or damning our space adventures. It has been suggested that perhaps we can get away from it all by living on the moon inside a plastic bubble, dining on algae cultures and recycling our human waste from breathing and digesting, straining and purifying them and using them over and over. But I ask you, "Das heist gelebt...do you call that living?"

No, even though the scientists promise us that if we go far enough in the solar system and beyond, if we spend enough time and money, we may eventually learn the answer to the questions, "Where did life come from, and how did it all start?" That may prove very exciting when it happens, but in the meantime it is far more important for us to be able to answer the questions, "Where is life going, and where will it end?"

You see, the extraordinary change in our thinking leads inevitably to the theological aspects of the adventure. Rabbis, too, not only scientists are asked questions about space flight. We are asked, "Is this proper? Is it God's will? Does it go against nature? What does it do to our beliefs about heaven and about God himself?"

Regarding heaven, our people have always been Heaven-intoxicated. Psalm 19, part of which is quoted on our Ark, reads earlier, "The Heavens declare the glory of God. The firmament showeth his handiwork. Day unto day uttereth speech, and night unto night revealeth knowledge. There is no speech, there are no words, neither is their voice heard."

The Psalmist declared long ago that the message communicated to man by the very sight, the very awareness of Heaven comes to us without the need for words nor for sound nor speech. The heavens themselves speak to us regarding the glory of God. Best known is Psalm 8,

"When I behold Thy Heavens, the work of Thy fingers,
The moon and the stars, which Thou hast established.
What is man that Thou art mindful of him,
And the son of man that Thou takest knowledge of him.
Yet Thou hast made him but little lower than the angels,
And hast crowned him with glory and honor."

Or hear Psalm 139, saying so long ago what is the theme of this weekend: "Whither shall I go from Thy spirit or whither shall I flee from Thy presence? If I ascend up into heaven, Thou art there. If I make my bed in the nether world, behold! Thou art there."

The Jew and those who take inspiration from the Jewish scriptures have always been excited and attracted by the heavens, and I am sorry that the spaceships are named after pagan gods. I wonder if there is some kind of secret suspicion that somehow space exploration drives the last nail in the coffin of God. I think the exact opposite. I maintain that the space exploration might better have taken their inspiration from our spiritual searching and groping and reaching upward.

Of all the trips in the course of history into the unknown this trip has been the least opposed by fearful theologians. There have been no excommunications, no trials for heresy of the space explorers, have there? And isn't that interesting because this is the most audacious of all of our trips. Theologians recognize that man is a searcher, from Abraham's instruction by God to leave his father's house, to the Exodus from the security of the flesh pots of Egypt into the uninviting wilderness, to Columbus, to the Apollo man who has demonstrated that there is something within him which makes him yearn and reach; or, as Robert Browning put it, "Ah, but a man's reach should exceed his grasp, or what's a heaven for?"

Remember the Psalmist's words, "When I behold the moon and the stars, what is man that Thou art mindful of him?" On the one hand, we have a glimpse of man's almost unspeakable insignificance. This little speck of dust whirled across those hundreds of thousands of miles of space in a thimble, what is he? "What is man...?" Sometimes we become over-impressed with our importance in our piddling day-to-day concerns such as: "What neighborhood is most prestigious, or what honor are we going to receive or is this the best table?"

But our space flight puts us in our place more than ever before, doesn't it? "What is man?" Yet on the other hand, "Thou hast made him but little lower than the angels and hast crowned him with glory and honor." This trip also underscores the special nature of man, the audacity of his dreams and the intellectual and physical courage of which man is capable.

Not only have we heightened and deepened our understanding of man in both directions, I think we have also broadened our concept of heaven. We have shot rockets into space and haven't pierced heaven or killed any angels.

Our Jewish concept long ago broadened beyond the narrow picture of pink clouds, an impressive pearly throne, and a bearded, beautiful old man who was the god of the primitives. For those who have clung to such childish images the flight into space shattered them for all time. We have now reached a distinction between space and heaven. Space we are now exploring. Heaven is an ideal, a state of being, the symbol for that perfect condition to which man aspires. Salvador de Madriaga's supreme aim: the intelligent organization of life on this planet, that's Heaven.

The moon shot also changes our understanding of the nature of God. God becomes not less but more grand, greater than that bearded old man on the pearly throne beyond the clouds. We must now embrace a greater concept of God: God in the pulsing purpose of all energy and matter, including the quivering heart and questing mind of man.

Moreover, this flight draws a line under the "if" in life, the great and beautiful "if." If we can fly to the moon, age-old symbol of the impossible and the unobtainable, then we can also clean our air, purify our water, house the homeless, clothe the naked, feed the hungry, educate the ignorant, love one another and live together here or anywhere.

Then why have we not done so? In 1961 President Kennedy predicted that before the end of this decade an American would set foot on the moon. His goal has been reached ahead of schedule. On the other hand, thousands of years ago Moses, Amos and Isaiah projected the goal of Heaven on earth, that marvelous world of peace, love and harmony.

Why are we still so far removed from these ancient goals? There are two reasons: the first and the most obvious is that we gave our moon flight top priority, the best we had to offer in men and means. We have never given top priority to the projects of our prophets. We have given them only lip service at best. Even more basic is the difference in the nature of the two projects, the attainment of space and attainment of Heaven.

To reach the moon we had only to know the laws of the nature of the universe and apply them to the task at hand. To create a Heaven on earth we must not only understand the nature of man, but we must teach ourselves not what comes naturally but the opposite: namely, to turn our competitiveness into cooperation, our innate greed into generosity, our hostility into harmony. We really have less choice in the second than in the first. We can choose to fly to the moon or stay at home, but unless we tame the beast in man, we shall destroy ourselves. It is to understand our nature and tame the beast within us, to become "a little lower than the angels," not geographically but spiritually, that our religion is all about. In the laboratory of life, the experiment called Judaism brought us here tonight to begin our annual ten-day flight to the highest self each of us can possibly reach by exploring our own inner space.

During this coming year, I suspect we shall hear much about appropriations for expeditions to Mars and beyond, as well as platforms in space where humans can live and work. The most audacious dreamers have suggested that we could even reach the nearest star in a few thousand years at the speed of light by establishing a family in a space ship where they could reproduce over and over again in the hope that their future descendants might reach that star.

A rabbinical colleague made the following observation: the likelihood is that even if that were possible, when those descendants arrive they would have forgotten two important things: where their ancestors came from and why they started out in the first place.

It is the year 5730 in our Jewish calendar, the year "Tashal," the year we shall call: "May there be peace forever." As we assemble for our agonizing reappraisal of our lives and our goals may we not forget who our ancestors were and why they started out in the first place on the great adventure called Judaism. Together let us thank God for sustaining us on our journey through life and implore His help to enable us to reach the destination of our prophets, a destination beyond the moon: our Heaven on earth.

Amen.

MOSES NEVER MADE IT

Moses has been acknowledged by many as one of the greatest, most influential men who ever lived, a man whose personal sacrifices, charisma, self-sacrifice and faith are unparalleled. His story has inspired admiration and adulation for millennia. However, it also proves that it is given to few of the great men of the world to realize the utmost of their ambitions and actually enter their promised land and see their dearest hope realized.

From one point of view, we might regard the life of Moses as a failure inasmuch as he didn't complete the task which he had set for himself. If it was a failure, it was a glorious failure. His greatness lay not in what he achieved but in what he attempted. His example should inspire those who doubt themselves to attempt and become more than they ever dreamed.

SEPTEMBER 3, 1976

Dear Friends:

This morning after the last song of Moses, we read the account, "The Lord said unto Moses, 'Get thee up into this mountain of Abarim, Mount Nebo, and behold the land that I have given unto the children of Israel. When thou hast seen it thou shalt also be gathered unto thy people as Aaron thy brother was gathered.'" "כי מנגד תראה את הארץ You will see the land from afar off, from across the way,

ושמה לא תבוא אל הארץ אשר אני נתן לבני ישראל

and there you will not go, to the land which I give to the children of Israel."

To me, this is the most pathetic event in the Bible. If ever there was a man who deserved to reach the promised land, wasn't it Moses? Moses really sacrificed everything and devoted his whole adult life to one purpose: that of leading his people out of the land of slavery and into the land of promise.

As a young man in the household of Pharoah, a princeling raised by the daughter of Pharaoh, Moses certainly had every opportunity, every advantage, every luxury. And yet he turned his back upon the potential of Pharaoh's court to throw in his lot with the poor and downtrodden and despised people whom he knew were his kinsmen. Moses, in the king's palace, did not try to divorce himself, did not try to sever his ties from his less fortunate brothers. He felt deep in his very marrow that he was flesh of their flesh and bone of their bone. He proved that when he went out of the palace on that occasion which every school child remembers - to observe the construction in which the slaves of Pharaoh were engaged. He heard the groans, the yearnings, he saw the crush of their burdens, and the sight must have made him vow to dedicate his life to the rescue of his fellow Hebrews.

As you know, he had to go into exile because he took the part of a beaten slave and, in resisting the overseer of that slave unfortunately killed him. He had to flee and spend the next 40 years in exile from his country. It was his country, the land of his birth and the place in which he had been raised to maturity with the opportunities and the splendor of Pharaoh's court.

Then, after 80 years he set himself the task of rescuing the Hebrews from slavery. He succeeded.

When the Red Sea was crossed there confronted him yet another 40 years with the most difficult kind of leadership. The people in what you call a newly emerging nation, an undeveloped people with all of the conflicts and all of the difficulties of leading such a people. His time with them was tremendously difficult. More than once Moses felt himself being crushed beneath the burden of his responsibility leading the ragtag multitude of ex-slaves in the wilderness, in the most unpromising place as anyone who has been in a wilderness of Sinai can testify.

More than once, and Moses is described as an *Anav*, a humble man. He was driven to call out to the Lord, "How can I bear with the burdens of this people; how can I bear their strife, their encumbrance, their difficulties?"

These people, just released from slavery, didn't know how to accept or use their freedom. They had been accustomed to the dole. They had been accustomed to being given their food, however meager. Now they had to fend for themselves. They didn't know where their security was, where their next encampment was.

They had given up the relative security, the dependability of being a slave, being a prisoner. When you are in prison, you know where your next meal is coming from and where you are going to sleep. The Hebrews complained at every difficulty which blocked their path and oh, the difficulties were tremendous.

One would gather from the text that the people he was leading displayed very little consideration. He, on the other hand, displayed tremendous consideration and sensitivity to them. There is a touching explanation given of the incident in which Moses encouraged the people in the war against the Amalekites. His young lieutenant, Joshua, led the army against the Amalekites who, in a cowardly way, were harassing the weak flank of his people.

Moses went up a hill and he held up his arms to encourage the people and he grew weary. As you know, he was supported by Aaron on one side and Hur on the other. Finally, when he grew excessively tired, they placed a stone under him upon which he could sit.

In this story about Moses, the Rabbis asked, "Why was this man, so advanced in years, well over 80, why, if he was so tired, holding up his hands to encourage the people as a symbol for them, why didn't they get him a cushion or something soft to sit upon?" And they answered that Aaron wanted to do so. He offered him a pillow. But Moses refused, saying, "While my people are in danger and distress how can I be in comfort? How can I have it easy when my people are having it so difficult?" This was the leadership that he offered, according to the Bible and the legends that have grown up around him.

Surely, amidst these endless trials and challenges, one after another, rebellion in the ranks, and famine, the difficulty of getting water, etc., one thing and one thing only could have given him the courage to persist. That would have been the dream of someday crossing the Jordan and walking at the head of his people into the promised land.

But at the end of his life, when his dream was within sight, it was denied him. He was told, as I read from the text this morning, that his foot would never touch the soil of the promised land. Another would have the privilege of leading the Israelites.

He had to be satisfied with a distant view of his destination of his 40 years in the wilderness. From the top of Mount Nebo, he would look across the Jordan opposite Jericho and see the goal of his hope stretching out before him and there he was to die. He could not have failed to be disappointed.

But the text offers no word of complaint, no murmur of disappointment escaping from his lips, and the text is very detailed in giving the emotions of each of the events. One may even suppose or hope that he died happy although his greatest wish had not been fulfilled because he must have felt that he hadn't lived for nothing or striven for nothing and that the work that he had begun was sure to be completed.

The final scene in the life of Moses which we read in the Torah this morning has a great deal to teach each and every one of us. Not only does it point out the hard lot of the pioneer, the leader, the pathfinder, the thanklessness of the task, the lack of appreciation and the abundance of criticism that anyone must expect when he engages in something new and daring and revolutionary, but the text also indicates what has so often been proved true: that it is given to few of the great men of the world to realize the utmost of their ambitions to enter the promised land and see their dearest hope realized.

From one point of view, we might regard the life of Moses as a failure inasmuch as he didn't complete the task which he had set for himself. If it was a failure, it was a glorious failure. His greatness lay not in what he achieved but in what he attempted. It is the men who don't have great ambitions, men who aim low, who stand a chance of accomplishing all of their desires. But most times men and women who aim high, are bound to fall a little short of those high expectations.

The poet Browning has one of his characters declare "Better have failed in the high aim as I, than vulgarly in the low aim, succeed as, God be thanked, I do not."

The work of one man may be infinitely greater and more beneficial to humanity than the completed task of another man. So reflection on the life of Moses helps us better to understand the meaning of success and failure. Even his brother Aaron, the high priest, a man elevated to high station from the depths of slavery, suffered the tragedy of seeing his sons, Nadav and Avihu, die, untimely in their youth, and could not pass on the mantle of leadership to them. It remained for Moses to put the mantle of leadership on another, Elazar, and finally to see the grandson, Pinchas, elevated to the priesthood. Aaron had his disappointments.

So to accomplish what we set up for ourselves as a goal is not the true criterion of success. If that were the only test of success then some of the most respected men in the world were dismal failures.

Not only did Moses fail, and Aaron fail, but in his greatest ambition, David failed as well. He wanted to build a temple in Jerusalem. He conquered Jerusalem in order to make it the religious seat of a united Israel and Judea. But it wasn't given to him to build the temple. He was told, as Moses was told, "You won't do it! Your son who follows after you, Solomon, he will do it."

Elijah failed to bring the people back to the true service of the Lord. Ezra and Nehemiah, who engaged in the reconstruction of the Temple after the first exile out of Babylon, failed. They didn't see their efforts realized.

Judah the Maccabee, the great hero of the Hanukkah story, who rededicated the temple was killed. He never saw the whole land of Israel free, but his successors did. Rav Ashi spent 30 years completing the Babylonian Talmud and died before the work was finished.

In our modern day, in Jewish ranks, who is more exemplary than Theodore Herzl, a man who had a vision of a third Jewish commonwealth. He dreamed of the new Jewish state, described it, worked for it, convened congresses for it and died without ever beginning to see the fulfillment of his dreams. Chaim Weizmann, one of the architects of Zion restored, died before seeing it firmly established, and who knows how many of the great leaders will pass away long before Israel sits in peace and security among her neighbors?

We can turn to illustrations in the lives of other peoples around us: Galileo, the great astronomer, languishing in prison. Rembrandt, one of the greatest artistic geniuses of all time, died in poverty and neglect. This week one of his canvases was bought by Armand Hammer to be contributed to the Los Angeles County Museum of Art, for millions of dollars. Was he a failure because he died in poverty? Because he never saw the real popularity of his work while people all over the world would pay fortunes for his paintings and would try to steal them? Was he a failure? John Keats, one of England's greatest poets, died with his potential scarcely scratched, died as a young man. On his lips was the lament, "My name is writ in water" meaning nobody will ever remember me.

Our American-Jewish composer, George Gershwin, died without ever seeing the full popularity of his work or realizing the full potential of his talents. Was he a failure? The names of these people are not writ in water. They live in the admiration of humanity yet they didn't quite reach their goals.

To reach the goal is not our Jewish way of gauging a career. Judaism proposes, לא עליך המלאכה לגמור ולא אתה בן חורין להבטל ממנה "It is not your duty to complete the work but neither are you free to desist from it." (Pirkei Avot 2:21) Before undertaking some important job, if we would ask ourselves if we can fully accomplish it, most of us would never even begin to attempt it. The right course to adopt is to start and do our best to make as much progress as we can and leave a little bit to the *Rebono shel olam,* leave the rest to God and to the future. And the bigger the undertaking, the less is the likelihood of our ever completing it but the greater is our credit for making the venture. All that should concern us from the beginning is that we started. We cannot be responsible for the finish.

As one of my favorite poets, Robert Browning said, in his poem, Andrea Del Sarto, "Ah, but man's reach should exceed his grasp, or what's a heaven for?" The greatest hero is not he who can point to the greatest success, as the world understands success. The greatest hero is one who, having a clear and worthy project before him, having striven with all his might and main, with every fiber of his being, to attain it, fails in his achievement, yet returns to his task uncomplaining and unembittered by failure, and continues as long as God grants him the privilege of doing so.

From this standpoint we can appreciate the superb grandeur of the career of Moses. It was an unfinished life. The actor left the stage before the final culmination, the final denouement of the play, but his life was anything but a failure. The test we should apply to it is not "Did he do all he wished to do?" but "Was his life in vain? Did he labor to no purpose?" There could be no doubt as to the answer. He lived to see the promised land. He lived to see people on the shores of the Jordan within sight of the promised land. His life had brought the goal appreciably nearer. That is all that one can hope for.

We are taught by our rabbis **אין אדם יוצא מן העולם וחצי תאותו בידו** "No man dies with half of his desires fulfilled." *(Kohelet Raba)* Very few of us have the privilege of entering our promised land, the land of our desires. Most of us have to be contented with a far-off glimpse.

I think that especially fitting in this synagogue, conceived over 40 years ago by men and women no longer alive. In their time they labored against great difficulties. They worshipped in very unprepossessing and modest quarters. They struggled with pennies to give an education to their children. Were they a failure? Without them we would not have what we have and be what we are as a congregation. In that sense they were a great success.

If we end our life with our face turned toward the "land of promise," as Moses did, the sight upon which we gaze will be reward enough for our labors. So, as we begin a new year and set before ourselves new tasks, look back upon the past and realize we haven't completed all that we have undertaken, it is good to read the story of the greatest man in our history, the story of Moses, and realize that this apparent failure was the greatest success of all.

A CUP OF KINDNESS

Living in two civilizations, as Rabbi Mordecai M. Kaplan insisted we do, I am blessed with not one but two New Year Days. Perhaps I should not have, but while thinking about Rosh Hashanah, the melody of "Auld Lang Syne" sounded in my head along with the words "Let's take a cup of kindness yet for Auld Lang Syne."

But what was a cup of kindness? The Scotch poet, Robert Burns, was thinking of malt liquor! Obviously, that was not for me, but "a cup of kindness," true kindness, ah, that was something to pray for on Rosh Hashanah.

Then I remembered that once the great historian and philosopher, Will Durant, was asked what piece of wisdom he would select from a lifetime of reading and reflection. He said, "If you insist on the brief answer, I say kindness." W. Somerset Maugham, when asked to report the essence of what he had learned in all his years, also concluded that the most important thing in life is kindness.

If giant figures like these could say that out of all the myriad possible things the world needs most it is kindness, who was I to argue with them? And so I spoke of kindness that day.

SEPTEMBER 12, 1980

Dear Friends:

How strange, how remarkable it is that the story of an incident that took place on a rocky hill in a tiny, pastoral land at the easternmost shore of the Mediterranean Sea some 3,200 years ago can still fire our imagination on this westernmost shore of this great, modern country of ours! In a land and a time when primitive tribes tried to bribe or appease their pagan gods by slaughtering their own children in bloody rituals of sacrifice, Abraham, newly migrated from Ur of the Chaldees across the Fertile Crescent in Mesopotamia, walked with his son, Isaac, to an altar of stones to perform such a ritual.

Abraham believed this is what his God demanded of him. Isaac, old enough to appreciate the peril to his life, accompanied his father nevertheless. That ancient tableau was the setting for a marvelous piece of news to be revealed to the human race, called kindness.

When the angel of the Lord called out to Abraham from heaven and said, אל תשלח ידך אל הנער ואל תעש לו מאומה "Lay not thy hand upon the lad, nor do anything unto him," a new chapter was begun in the history of human relations and a new kind of God was revealed to man. After countless eons of religions based on mortal fear of cruel and capricious deities that made man's days on earth a nightmare of superstition and terror, those nine short words taught us of a God who wished us not to be cruel, but to be kind; not to take life, but to spare life.

The Bible stories we read on the first day of Rosh Hashanah use the account of the birth of little babies to teach us that God has implanted within us an irresistible impulse to preserve life. The Bible stories we read on the second day teach us that life is still worthless if it is not blessed with mercy and kindness.

There are not too many analogies between the Christian and the Jewish observance of the New Year, but there is one accidental resemblance that intrigued me long ago. What is the song which has become a must at midnight on December 31? It is the Scotch poet, Robert Burns' famous "Auld Lang Syne," which means "for old time's sake." Now, for years, I sang the last line, "We'll take a cup of kindness yet for auld lang syne," believing it really had to do with finishing the old year and looking forward to a new year with cup filled to overflowing with kindness until I learned what he really meant was a cup of whiskey, of which he drank too many in his short 37 years until they did him in. But I still cling to my mistaken understanding of it because it is such an appealing thought: a cup of kindness to begin a new year, the lesson we learn from the *Akedah* story, the drama on Mount Moriah when the angel of the Lord cried out, "Lay not thy hand upon the lad."

On *Selichot* night and again several times on *Yom Kippur*, we chant the 13 attributes of God which are found in the 34th chapter of the Book of Exodus in response to Moses' plea to know the nature of God. It begins יי יי אל רחום וחנון "The Lord, the Lord is a compassionate and gracious God." Of the 13 attributes, only the virtue of *"chesed"* is repeated. God is called רב חסד "abounding in loving-kindness" and again, נצר חסד לאלפים "preserving loving-kindness for the thousands."

A cup of kindness, רב חסד, is a quality I find being squeezed to less than a thimbleful in today's brutalized, dehumanized and self-centered society. And so I wish to share with you the hope that this Jewish New Year experience we are having may serve to emphasize our desperate need for a fuller measure of chesed, of kindness, in our lives.

Our tradition is abundant in the call for kindness. Just leaf casually through our prayer books and you will come upon "*chesed*, loving kindness" on almost every page. Whenever we read the 145th psalm, the *Ashrei Yoshvei Veitechah*, we declare again, חנון ורחום יי ארך אפים וגדל חסד, "The Lord is gracious and full of compassion, slow to anger and abundant in kindness." Or when we read the *Amidah*, מכלכל חיים בחסד, "Thou sustainest the living with loving-kindness."

One of the greatest of all Biblical passages is the famous message of the prophet Micah, "It has been told ye, O man, what is good and the Lord doth require of Thee, but to do justly, ואהבת חסד and to love kindness, and to walk humbly with thy God. The whole complex of what our religion requires of us distills down to these three simply stated demands: justice, kindness and humility. These three are still not outmoded today. On the contrary there are many who believe there is too little justice, kindness and humility in the world right now.

Let me share a testimonial to that need as told by a venerable scholar who stood at that center lectern four years ago and graciously accepted Temple Beth Am's Bicentennial award. I am speaking of that prolific scholar and writer, author of the history of man called *The Story of Civilization*, Dr. Will Durant. On his 94th birthday, he was asked what piece of wisdom he would select from a lifetime of reading and reflection. He said, "If you insist on the brief answer, I say kindness. And that is, in my opinion, the finest, most successful method of behavior, not merely successful method of behavior, not merely of a man to his wife and vice versa, but of a man to his neighbor, of any individual to the individuals he meets."

Can it be that this simple and obvious virtue, kindness, is the delusion of old philosophers? Let me cite the opinion of a somewhat younger man, the famous writer W. Somerset Maugham. When interviewed and asked to report the essence of what he had learned in all his year, he, too, concluded that the most important thing in life is kindness. Then he apologized for reaching so commonplace a conclusion. He said he would have preferred to leave his readers with some startling new revelation or some sparkling new epigram, but, he says, "I have little more to say than can be read in any copybook or heard from the pulpit. I have gone a long way round to discover what everyone already knew."

Perhaps kindness is reserved for the theoreticians of this world and has no place in the rough-and-tumble of daily life. Let me go way out into left field, literally, and quote the late Branch Rickey, the Brooklyn Dodgers manager who is perhaps best remembered for having signed Jackie

Robinson, the first black athlete to play major league baseball. Rickey wrote, "The most important single qualification a man should have to marry one of my daughters is infinite kindness. Infinite kindness will sustain a marriage through all its problems, its disappointments, its storms, its tensions, its fears, its separation, its sorrows. Out of infinite kindness grows love that is real, and understanding, and tolerance and warmth. Nothing can take the place of such an enduring asset."

And what do little children have to say about such a sissy thing as kindness? There sticks in my memory an incident in a barber shop when I took our son, Daniel, for one of his first haircuts. The barber was a little annoyed at having to trim the hair of a seven-year old and pushed and twisted Danny's head rather sharply as he rushed through the cutting.

Danny finally looked around at him and in the piercing treble of his tender years filled the whole shop with the words, "You're not very kind, are you?" I do not know if the barber learned anything from that day, but I did. And from his congregants, I hear that Rabbi Daniel did, too.

And what of grandchildren? A colleague of mine, Rabbi Sidney Greenberg of Philadelphia, writes a daily column in the *Philadelphia Inquirer*. Of all his learned religious observations, the following received the greatest and warmest response from readers: He described a sweet moment with his six-year old granddaughter after school, one day, when he asked her, "What did you do in school today?"

She answered, "We made warm fuzzies."

"What are warm fuzzies?"

"Well," she said, trying to find words to explain matters to a silly old grandfather, "Warm fuzzies are things that you say to make people feel good." And then, reaching into her school bag, she pulled out some scraps with big crayoned awkward letters printed on them. "Here are some of the warm fuzzies I got."

They read, "You ar my best friend."

"Yu are veree prittee."

"You I lik."

"I liek the prezint you gave mee."

Words were misspelled, but what a lesson the teacher had taught her class. What a beautiful life this would be if all of us would spend less time thinking of mean, cruel and aggressive things to do and spent more time handing out warm fuzzies. Mark Twain once said that he could live on a good compliment for two months.

From Durant to Daniel, the opinion seems the same: We all desperately need kindness and too few of us are getting it or giving it. A psychiatrist, Doctor William McGrath, reports, "Ninety percent of all mental illness that comes before me could have been prevented or cured by ordinary kindness."

What a terrible condemnation of our society! All around us there is emotional starvation and we do not have the time or the thoughtfulness to speak a kind word, perform a gracious act, pay a visit, drop a line or give a compliment. Kindness is not something reserved for the brilliant or the well-educated. The person who has not learned kindness remains ignorant no matter how many diplomas hang on his or her wall.

I cannot imagine how a gruff and insensitive doctor can really heal me better than one who seems to care about me personally and is extremely kind and gentle, not only with my body but with my feelings. The kind teachers and professors I have had during my schooling stand out in my memory and with many of them I established an ongoing friendship that they seemed to appreciate as much as I.

When I was in the hospital many years ago, I noted a study in contrasts. My private nurse on one occasion was abrupt and self-centered. She pushed and pulled me around like Danny's barber. My whole being tensed up when she was around. On the other hand, there was an older woman who came in to empty the waste baskets every morning. She could hardly speak English but her smile, her inquiry after my health, her concern, her tidying up my flowers, the kindness that had stamped itself on her face years before in some distant land did more for my recovery, I think, than did my nurse.

A person's formal schooling may be meager and his or her book learning not the best, but the person who has learned how to bring a ray of light where there is darkness, a touch of softness where life has been hard, a word of cheer to lift a depressed spirit, that person is better equipped to live life as it should be lived.

Rabbi Solomon Freehof, a great preacher of our time, wrote, "People once felt that ignorance was the only bar to social happiness. Now, having seen mass murder in an age of culture, we know that human happiness is barred by active evil in human character, callousness and cruelty. There is so much man-made misery in the world that one begins to long for a little consideration and a little patience. ...I know that I have come to prefer a different kind of person. I once liked clever people. Now I like good people."

Our Jewish tradition has given us so many vehicles for acting with kindness. We have made *mitzvot*, divine commandments, out of such simple things as visiting the sick, burying the dead, marrying off the poor bride, making a free loan and a host of other things.

We have been given phrases to use in case we were not eloquent by nature. Everybody can say "*Mazal Tov*" to someone celebrating an important moment of life. Everybody can say, "*Yasher Koach*" to the person who has had an *aliyah*, read a *maftir*, given a talk, or received a promotion on the job. Everybody can say "*Fur gezindt und kum gezindt*" when a friend leaves on a trip. Everyone can say, "*Titchadesh*" when a friend shows off a new dress or a new suit or "*Trug ess gesindt*...Wear it in good health." Our whole Jewish literature is saturated with instructions and opportunities for kindness.

Read your own *mahzor.*

What are the principal sins we confess on *Yom Kippur*? Acts of unkindness, beginning with על חטא שחטאנו לפניך באמוץ הלב "For the sin which we have committed before Thee by hardening our hearts."

And what is the whole point of our fasting and our praying on the great Day of Atonement? We are told in plain, unequivocating words what religion is all about by the Prophet Isaiah, in the *haftarah* reading of *Yom Kippur* day: "Is not this the fast that I have chosen? To loose the fetters of wickedness, to undo the bands of the yoke and to let the oppressed go free. Is it not to deal thy bread to the hungry, and that thou bring the homeless to thy house? When thou seest the naked, that thou cover him, and that thou hide not thyself from thy fellow man?"

Kindness! Our religion prescribes it for all the ills of man and fills the prescription with words and customs and practices to help us perform it. My friends, I had so wanted to bring you some profound and earth-shaking new message to match the solemnity of these holy days, but I just couldn't do better than Will Durant, Mark Twain, Danny Pressman, the prophet Isaiah or, for that matter, the Lord Almighty among whose divine attributes, *chesed*, kindness, is accorded twice the importance of all the others.

One last little incident. My colleague, Rabbi Irwin Groner of Detroit, was recently invited to the White House for a briefing of Jewish leaders. After the meeting, there was the usual receiving line with photographs taken of each person with the president and a chance for a few words of greeting.

Rabbi Groner says he asked himself, "What should I say? Give President Carter advice? Ask help for Israel? Move the American embassy to Jerusalem?" If you have one minute to speak to the president of the United States, what do you say?

He decided to ask for something small. He said to the President, "This is a double *yontif* for me. Being here, and also it is my father's 90th birthday. He came from Poland at the age of 14 and to have his son here with the President of the United States is the greatest honor of his life. Would you take another picture with me and autograph it for my father?" The President said, "Of course," and he sent a picture to the father properly inscribed.

When the rabbi walked out, he felt badly for a moment. Did I make the right request? Should I have asked for something bigger? Then he remembered a story in the Talmud. When Jerusalem was under attack by Rome, Rabbi Yochanan ben Zakkai stood before the Emperor Vespasian and was told he could ask for something. What? For Jerusalem? He would be turned down. To save the Jewish State? He would be turned down. So he asked for the little town of Yavneh to open a school and he got it. Vespasian thought it was a small thing. It turned out to be a big thing. It saved Judaism. So who knows what a big thing is and what a small thing is? To Rabbi Groner's father it was a big thing. It meant that he had a son who thought of him while enjoying his big moment in the White House.

Why do I tell this story? Because this is our *yontif* and we shall be asking for many things in our prayers. In such a short time, what should we ask for? I suggest three things that seem small, but are really big...from God, from others and from ourselves.

From God, should we ask for an easy life, for security? There is no such thing. Ask instead for the strength to survive the troubles that life brings and the wisdom to appreciate the joys life gives us, just a little kindness from the רב חסד, the God so abundant in kindness.

From each other should we ask enormous piety, tremendous generosity, perfect behavior? That's unrealistic. Let's ask for a little kindness... a tender word, a smile, an encouraging pat. Those are big things.

From ourselves, should we ask great accomplishments 100 percent perfection all the time? Solve the world's problems? Of course not. Let's settle for the ability to keep trying when we fail, do the best we can and not to be too hard on ourselves.

What did Rabbi Groner give Carter? The solution to all his problems? No, just the example of a Jew who fulfills the Fifth Commandment, no small thing to teach a president, and he did it in one minute.

And what should we wish God, who has everything? A little *naches* from his children.

And what do I wish you? I will settle for a cup of kindness from me to you and from you to me.

A CHILD'S PRAYER

My first High Holiday sermon after officially retiring from the pulpit I had held for 35 years reveals a discernibly more relaxed and casual approach to communicating with the congregants assembled. It inaugurates a time of opening up my innermost thoughts and feelings and sharing them because I had learned over the years that these are the thoughts and feelings of the people before me.

This revelation enabled me to turn from the sermon of crisis to an airing of our common, often unspoken, innermost emotions and reactions to life's challenges. In a subtle way, retirement enabled me to grow even closer to the people to whom I had been preaching for a good portion of our lives. It also helped me understand myself much better and accept myself more charitably. I owe my inspiration for this sermon to Rabbi Haim Asa, a very effective preacher and pastor.

SEPTEMBER 17 , 1985

Dear Friends:

Fellow survivors, I salute you. Despite the freedom to worship we all enjoy in this blessed land, many Jews are unable to observe the second day of *Rosh Hashanah*, and many simply choose not to come to the synagogue. So you and I have a double duty today. We have to pray for ourselves and for the absentees as well.

And so, for a few moments, let us roam together. What are you asking? What am I? We may not be asking the same specifics, but, in general, for what do we yearn so that we could say we are grateful and happy? Our *mahzor* is full of such prayers, but I am afraid we do not often relate them to the simple needs of our own life. They seem too grand, too lofty for us, as if God can only respond to four syllable words and old fashioned phrases and passages which are too difficult for us to understand. So, let me bring our thinking down to earth without losing sight of Heaven by repeating a moving little story told by my colleague, Rabbi Haim Asa, of Fullerton, California.

Haim told of being at the Kotel, the Western Wall of the Temple, in Jerusalem on *Yom Ha-atzma-ut*, Israel Independence Day, last April. Someone had given him a *kvittel*, a little paper prayer, to put in one of the crevices in the great stone blocks of that wall. As he tucked his *kvittel* in, another fell out and unfolded so that when he picked it up, he could not help noticing what it said.

As he read it, he tells us, tears came to his eyes, and he copied the words and deposited the original back in the wall.

The writer must have been a boy about bar mitzvah age, Haim assumes, and he had written as follows:

בעזרת השם With God's help
שכלנו נהיו בריאים May all of us be healthy.
שאבא יקנה אופנים May *Abba* buy me a bicycle.
ושאני אהיה תלמיד טוב May I be a good student,
שטלי תאהב אותי May Tali love me,
ושטלי תראה שאני אוהב אותה And may Tali see that I love her.
שנשב על אותו ספסל And may we sit on the same school bench.
ושכל החיילים יחזרו בשלום הביתה And may all the soldiers return home safely in peace.

When I heard this story I thought of the Biblical phrase, "Out of the mouth of babes." This youngster taught me what I should ask this *Rosh Hashanah.*

First of all, he prays for health, not his health alone, but everyone's health. Isn't it natural that this should be the first request because health is our first concern. What is the universal greeting of two people, even at the first meeting? מה שלומך "How are you?" If we are closer friends we may even add, "How are you feeling?"

It doesn't matter that the greeter isn't really listening to the answer. Sometimes, for fun, I answer, "Miserable, thank you," and the person who asked how I am often replies, "Oh, that's nice." I would hope that when we tell God how we really feel, He pays better attention, for if we were really writing a *kvittel,* I suspect most of us would ask for health first, before money, before success.

And if we are wise, as this boy was instinctively, we would ask, שכלנו נהיו בריאים "May all of us be healthy."

On this relatively tiny, enclosed space capsule called Earth, physical and mental health are not exclusively our personal concern. We are affected and infected by the health of the community. Famine in Africa has made millions vulnerable to diseases. Refugees are bringing those diseases with them elsewhere, witness the evidence from Israel regarding some of the Ethiopian Jews.

Tuberculosis, long since considered conquered, has reappeared locally as a result of the entry from south of the border of some people infected with the disease. The growing epidemic of AIDS, Acquired Immune Deficiency Syndrome, threatens to become a devastating plague and appears to have come from Africa via the Caribbean. The conquest of this killer disease is not just the concern of those suffering with it. It is your concern and mine that a crash program fueled by unlimited funds be mounted to stop its spread and find its causes and its remedies. The toxic wastes, the pollution of our air, our water, our very food by carcinogenic chemicals, these are not someone else's problems. They are yours. They are mine. The boy's words on his *kvittel* are deceptively simple, but they express our first desperate need, our first fervent prayer this *Rosh Hashanah* שכלנו נהיו בריאים "May all of us be well: our family, our friends, our neighbors, the whole family of man."

And then the boy asks, שאבא יקנה אופנים "May *Abba*, Daddy, buy me a bicycle." It's a childish request, yet sophisticated enough since the boy doesn't ask God to give him a bicycle, nor even some mythical Santa Claus, but *Abba*, Daddy. After health, he asks for material blessings from realizable sources. Why not? Somewhere along the line you and I ask for material things. Look in the *mahzor* and you will find prayers for פרנסה "for goodly sustenance."

Judaism is not opposed to the material in life. We're a practical people. As Tevye says in *Fiddler on the Roof*, "It's no disgrace to be poor, but it's no honor, either." Or, as that wonderful Yiddish truism puts it, "*Az me darf schon sein urem iz gut tsu haben a bissel gelt.* If you have to be poor, already, it's good to have a little money."

The problem with material appetites is being able to strike a sensible balance and not making acquisition our top priority. Sure, most people here can name something they really want, their own kind of bicycle. It may be a bigger home, a more comfortable home, a second home, cars, clothes. Some of us are lucky and get what we desire only to find that we are not necessarily happier because of that bigger or better whatever. The Talmud teaches אין אדם מת וחצי תאותו בידו "No man dies with even half of his desires fulfilled."

There has to be a sensible balance. We have to make our possessions work for us, rather than work ourselves to death for our possessions without enjoying them. How many widows have told me that they were going on a trip or a cruise because as each one puts it, "My husband and I planned this trip or this visit to Israel for years. He was always promising to take it easier or to retire, but kept postponing it, and we never did go. So now I'm going because that is what he wanted for me, but it just won't be the same. I would rather stay home, and he were there alive by my side." Personally, I am retiring because I didn't want my dear wife, Margie, to have to say that, ever.

I guess each of us has some symbolic bicycle he or she wants Daddy to buy. We may have it in our personal prayers somewhere today, and I hope we are answered. But let us make sure it really matters enough to make the quality of life substantially better.

The next request of our unknown writer of the *kvittel* is not unexpected for a child. **ושאני אהיה תלמיד טוב** "May I be a good student." In his youthful innocence he asks for success in the world in which he moves, the school. But his words open up the question of when learning stops. In Jewish life we are vigorously addressing the challenge of Jewish illiteracy among our children, more and more each day.

Here at Beth Am we have made afternoon school free to children of members and membership more financially accessible to young parents. We have built an all-day Jewish academy which has now reached the stage where some classes must be closed because they are full, and we are out of room. Children are being put on waiting lists.

That is tragic, because Judaism is not some kind of snooty club where we restrict membership and are proud of turning people away. We are not proud, but ashamed and frustrated that any child who could receive the intensive Jewish background which day school can give must be turned away and perhaps lost to ignorance and indifference because we think we can't afford it. Listen, dear friends, we cannot afford to turn anyone away.

I recently read with great chagrin the story of Jordan Gollub, 26 years old, Jewish, and Grand Dragon of the Christian Knights of the Ku Klux Klan in the State of Virginia. Son of a prominent Philadelphia physician, Gollub recently told an interviewer, "I was never Jewish. My parents are Jewish. I never had any Jewish religious background. My parents...don't actually attend religious services of any kind."

How much grief and mischief can such a child of an indifferent Jewish family cause us in the role of leader in a cult community committed to hating Jews and blacks, among others? How much more will he cost us ultimately than if someone had taken him in for an intensive Jewish education, even if his parents who could afford it, refused to pay?

We here at Beth Am Academy, now called Pressman Academy, offered thousands of dollars in scholarships and yet we lost several excellent and eager students because their parents either could or would not pay their remaining share to us. I wonder how many of them will ever be able to write a *kvittel* in Hebrew ושאני אהיה תלמיד טוב May I be a good student.

You may say, "Well it all starts with the parents." If so, adult Jewish illiteracy is even more tragic today. With more leisure time than ever before, adult Jews should be able to find some time to develop some Jewish knowledge. Just knowing the difference between egg bagels and water bagels won't do. Knowing a few Jewish *bubbe-meisahs* and some Yiddish jokes won't do. Insisting on circumcision and rejecting a *brit milah* won't do. Insisting on a Bar Mitzvah and serving the world's biggest shrimp, crab and lobster hors d'oeuvre won't do. Flaunting our ignorance and vulgarizing our Jewish practices and belligerently saying, "I'm as good a Jew as the biggest rabbi," while drooling "chazer-fat" won't do. An ignorant Jewish people will ultimately be a non-existent Jewish people.

Nor is learning the total end in itself. The Talmud teaches:

טוב תלמוד תורה עם דרך ארץ "It is good for the study of Torah to be combined with worldly pursuits."

Education, juvenile and adult, must lead ultimately not simply to remembered data but to the formation of good character. Ask a student, "What did you learn today?" and, invariably you will hear some collection of facts if you hear anything. How often do we hear, "Today I learned respect for elders? Today I learned tenderness, sympathy, charity, justice, patience, love of my fellow man."

Last Thursday I stood at the grave of a grand lady who worshipped among us and died at the age of 83. Two remarkable things were said about her by those closest to her. One was, "I never heard her say 'I' or 'me'. It was always 'you'. It was you for whom she cared.

And the second was, "She never stopped learning until the day she died." Good students come in all sizes and all ages. How wonderful it would be if we never stopped learning.

And then in a burst of candor and self-revelation unusual in adults, let alone in a child, the boy of the *kvittel* wrote to God about a very personal matter:

שטלי תאהב אותי "May Tali love me",

ושטלי תראה שאני אוהב אותה "And may Tali see that I love her."

שנשב על אותו ספסל "And may we sit on the same school bench."

Simple, basic, and yet, how fundamental, how desperate is this need: "May Tali love me." Everybody needs somebody, somewhere to love him or her… a spouse, a parent, a child, a brother, a sister, a friend. The little boy and little girl in each of us looks across the schoolroom called life and wants to be loved, and wants the object of love to know it and wants to be close, together with that person.

I just wish you could have sat where I have sat all these years and heard how many people have *nobody, not one single soul who loves them.* Rich people and poor people, famous people and vagrants, beautiful people...tycoons and movie stars, and derelicts on skid row...rabbis and cantors and executive directors and temple presidents and custodians.

It is interesting, that in the *Los Angeles Times* article I mentioned before, Sherry Lansing, former 20th Century Fox productions president, head now of her own production company, has everything in the world. Right? What does she say? Her mother died a year ago. She says, "It was a year of sadness. I really missed her every day." And then, "I'm not married, you know, so as I approach a new year I have a real desire to have a meaningful relationship. I'm interested in loving someone."

שטלי תאהב אותי It is "May Tali love me." We all share the same silent prayer. Only the names and faces change.

Even that is not enough.

ושטלי תראה שאני אוהב אותה "And may Tali see that I love her." He wants his love to be noticed, remembered, valued. He wants to be credited with the capacity to love. And then, unlike Don Quixote de la Mancha, this wise little boy knows it is...yes, quixotic "to love pure and chaste from afar." He asks God to arrange it so that they share the same school bench, share each other's company. It is such a tender picture to conjure up, these two adolescent kids in their innocence, touching knees and elbows and knowing for that first, unique, never-to-be-equaled time, something precious called love.

We all need it, but many of us won't allow ourselves to become vulnerable by exposing our feelings and risking rejection, So we never tell Tali of our love. Maybe, like the little boy, we expect God to do it. Eighteen years ago, I was hospitalized with a mysterious ailment which almost finished me. When I recovered, I promised myself that whenever I was moved by sentiments of love I would tell that person. Until then, too often I had reserved my compliments for funeral eulogies. Ever since then, I tell people how I feel about them, hug them and kiss them, men, women and children.

Sometimes out of nowhere the thought of a particular person pops into my head, and then and there I pick up the phone and say something good I feel about them. The fact that often such a call is greeted with surprise and suspicion only proves we all do not express ourselves enough. Here is something worth asking of the Lord, honestly, fervently, unashamedly. We'll each put in the names we wish...May that person love me, and may that person see that I love, too; and, may we share the same bench.

Yes, dear friends, health is primary. A little "*parnassah*" helps. Material sustenance helps. Learning is basic and love validates life. We could stop here in our prayers this Rosh Hashanah, having asked quite enough of God. But our little master of the *kvittel* adds something without which all the others could become utterly pointless. He asks, **ושכל החיילים יחזרו בשלום הביתה** "And may all the soldiers return home safely in peace." It is probable that he has brothers in the Israel Defense Force, that his *Abba* goes on *miluim*, reserve duty; or the house next door has an empty chair for a boy or girl who lies in a military grave. But notice, he doesn't say "May my soldiers, my *Abba*, my brothers return home safely. He says it of all soldiers. That means Arab and Israeli, the millions of men wearing the army uniforms of Russia, Afghanistan, Iraq, Iran, San Salvador, Cuba and the U.S.A. May they all return home in peace.

His plea is not surprising. Children seem to understand what the world really needs better than their elders. May I remind you of a little girl named Samantha Smith, who perceived the consequence of a nuclear war and loved peace more than the old political and military leaders of the United States and Russia. She wrote a letter and touched the heart of the man in the Kremlin for one brief moment before her untimely death.

Or remember Anne Frank who wrote, "I still believe in the goodness of man," while hiding to save the life she ultimately lost. And our anonymous little boy who loved Tali so, but didn't forget to ask God to send the soldiers home in peace. I get a pain in my heart when I realize that unless his prayers are answered, and all the soldiers everywhere come home, and there is real *shalom*, real peace, then this boy, too, in a few years will be in the uniform of the Israel Defense Force, victim of a sniper's bullet or terrorist's bomb, and will join Anne Frank and all the kids who die too young because old men won't make peace; and Tali will never sit at his side, never.

So, my friends, I have no preachment, no reproach, only an overwhelming love for the human race and a hope that you will indeed "*Beit sich ois a gut yahr*," that you'll pray for yourself a good year...a year of health, material blessings, learning, love, and real peace for Israel and all humanity.

And, oh yes, remember how the boy's *kvittel* began? As every Jewish message should: **בעזרת השם** "With the help of God." And when I remembered, I suddenly realized that this child had unknowingly paraphrased the prayer with which we end today's service and most of our services on these *Yamim Noraim*, singing it lustily and fervently, the very same idea which he expressed in prose on a piece of paper stuck into a crack in the Western Wall:

**בספר חיים ברכה ושולם ופרנסה טובה נזכר ונכתב
לפניך אנחנו וכל-עמך ישראל לחיים טובים ולשלום.**

In the Book of Life, blessing, peace, and good sustenance may we be remembered and inscribed before Thee, we and all Thy people, the House of Israel, for a happy life and for peace.

And, **בעזרת השם**, with the help of God, may all our prayers be answered, if not in a year, at least in our own lifetime.

Amen.

CHAPTER SIX
There Were Giants in the Land

In a century of false prophets and enormous evil it was a privilege to share the years with certain figures whose greatness makes me refer to them as giants. I note, to my embarrassment, that editorial choices left me with six male figures and only one woman, Golda Meir; and did not include my sermons on Henrietta Szold, Anne Frank, Hannah Senesch, among others. Perhaps they merit their own collection.

I eulogized some of our American presidents, among them Franklin Delano Roosevelt, Harry Truman, and John F. Kennedy, and in all cases indicated my disappointment in retrospect in some of their less commendable actions.

The brightness of the figure of Israel's first president, Chaim Weizmann, has already faded, which is a great loss. His role in the issuing of the Balfour Declaration and in enhancing the armaments of the Western Allies in World War I should be remembered.

Among the many brilliant and distinguished rabbis of the last century, I had the honor of personal contact with several of them. Here I cite my eulogies of Rabbi Stephen S. Wise, Rabbi Louis Finkelstein, Rabbi Mordecai M. Kaplan, and my mentor, Rabbi Simon Greenberg. Each in his way taught me great lessons and inspired generations of rabbis who served the Jewish people well.

PRESIDENT FRANKLIN DELANO ROOSEVELT, IN MEMORIAL

The sudden death of President Franklin Delano Roosevelt was devastating for a nation which had just elected him to an unprecedented fourth term. Many, like me, had never really known any other president. What would happen now with a world war in progress, with the peace to follow, with the reforms he had effected in the economic and social fabric of the nation?

In my youthful enthusiasm and lack of retrospection, I likened him to Moses and virtually beatified him. Somehow, despite my fears, the nation survived, the war was won, the peace was organized. It turned out he was no Moses!

It was only in later years I learned of his calculated failure to respond to our pleas for forcing open the sealed gates of Palestine and stemming the carnage of our people which was going on to his knowledge in Nazi Europe. The more sober hindsight of our understanding of the man revealed this and many other failings, political and moral. However, this sermon is a faithful reflection of the sorrow the people of America, we Jews among them, felt deeply that Sabbath.

APRIL 20, 1945

Dear Friends:

With that unerring fitness with which all the pieces of life mesh with one another, we assemble on that Sabbath when the Torah reading is entitled, **אחרי מות קדשים** "After death; sanctified." We have gathered after the death of our revered friend and leader, President Franklin Delano Roosevelt, to sanctify his memory.

All this past week, with hearts of lead, we thought about this man. A million words have poured from the heart of all mankind in loving tribute. A billion tears have welled up afresh as each new mention of the blow brought them from just beneath the surface of reddened eyes. Even as we read and listened to the news of the sudden death, the White House service and the Hyde Park burial, we could not bring ourselves to believe what was happening nor grasp the enormity of the loss which had befallen us. Now that a week has elapsed, we believe, we understand and we mourn.

Tomorrow morning, as we begin our Torah portion and read, "And the

Lord spoke unto Moses," we shall, remember how many, many times those who eulogized our friend compared him to Moses. One and all remarked that just as Moses was not permitted to lead the children of Israel into the promised land, so was the privilege of enjoying the final victory denied him who died last week. But they should have gone further in their comparison than merely noting the coincidence of the circumstance. They should have compared the man himself with Moses of old, with the saga of his life as well as the giant stature of his leadership. Let us so compare him for there is no greater tribute we, as Jews, can pay any mortal.

The Book of Exodus records the extraordinary circumstances of the childhood of Moses. Unlike his fellow Israelites, Moses was not reared in the poverty of slavery but in the very house of Pharaoh himself; for, as you know, Moses was found in the bulrushes by the daughter of Pharaoh, who adopted him and made him her son. In the words of Rabbi ibn Ezra, "Deep are the ways of Providence! It was His inscrutable intention that Moses should be reared in a palace, that his spirit might remain uncurbed by the oppressive and enervating influence of slavery." The Israelites, their spirits crushed by cruel bondage, could never have emancipated themselves. It required the strength, diplomacy, and princely pride of a Moses to lead them out of their misery.

Could the birth and the education of our late president have been any less providential? He was born on January 30, 1882, a date certain in to rank with the outstanding anniversaries of history, into a family of wealth and assured social position. His early education, he received at home from tutors, and then he went to Groton and Harvard. At Harvard he edited the campus magazine and was elected to Phi Beta Kappa.

While in his first year at Columbia Law School, he married Anna Eleanor Roosevelt, the favorite niece of Theodore Roosevelt, then president. The President himself gave the bride away.

And so, in these circles of position and means were welded the self-confidence and the pride which later enabled him to carry the burdens of an entire nation on his shoulders at a time when that nation was tormented with its most discouraging problems.

Here, too, he acquired the faculties which enabled him to treat with kings, ministers and statesmen the world over; and to defy the frightening power of dictators and tyrants.

A humbler man might not have been able to stand up to the giants of the earth as he did in those dark days. A lesser man would have broken much earlier under the weight of the world's cares these 12 years.

"Deep are the ways of Providence. It was His inscrutable intention that Moses should be reared in a palace." Moreover, when Moses began to lead the Israelites in the wilderness, they were without bread and hungry. They cried out to return to slavery if only to receive the food from the flesh pots, the bread doled out by Pharaoh. But through the initiative of Moses, the Lord provided the Israelites with manna and with the flesh of fowl to eat.

The lot of the president of this nation in 1933 was no easier than that of Moses when he first led his starving people. There was famine in this land, famine which the bread lines scarcely kept away. The hungry masses were desperate. One spark might have ignited the frantic nation in revolution.

Men were ready to sell their souls, their very liberty, for a morsel for their children. Like the Israelites of old, they were ready to return to the flesh pots of slavery, to sell their American freedom for a totalitarian crust of bread.

A demagogue could easily have arisen and swept the nation in Hitlerian fashion. Do you remember those days? Many of you have told me your own hardships then. Remember the homes without gas or electricity, the tables without food, the threadbare clothing, the heart-rending lines of idle men. The people cried out.

Then this man came into office, rolled up his sleeves and, with a burst of inspired energy, began the Herculean task of providing the manna to tide us over the desert period. And he did! Not single-handedly, but with the help of God and man, he succeeded mightily. We began to hope again, to look upward again and, best of all, to work again.

Yes, it was made work, but work had to be made. The farmers were paid for food they could not sell in our crippled system of distribution. The youth were aided by the Civilian Conservation Corps. Many students completed high school or attended college only because they were assisted by the National Youth Administration.

Private homes were saved for their owners by government loan. And as for the made work, somehow the men who labored for the Works Progress Administration and who are supposed to have done nothing but lean upon their shovels managed to build miles of superhighways now facilitating the war effort, hundreds of public buildings to which we now point with pride as they house the machinery of democracy, and dozens of dams whose electric power has been fashioning the tools of the arsenal of democracy.

All the while, these same men ate, their families ate and their children regained the privileges of youth. Despite the pessimism of the alarmists, these men did find jobs of their own and are today completely restored to a position of self-respect. Verily, through the initiative of Moses, the Lord provided the Israelites with manna in the desert.

Not only did Moses lead the Israelites out of bondage and starvation, but he was also the great law-giver. Indeed, the burden of the five books of Moses is principally the Mishpatim, the laws and ordinances which Moses conveyed to the people in the name of God. In our own day, the last 12 years have seen the passage of more laws than ever before in the history of democracy, laws guaranteeing the rights of man and dignifying his position on the earth. Not the least of these laws, of which some were written and some merely spoken, has been the repetition of Moses great injunction, "Thou shalt love thy neighbor as thyself." Only this time it was worded "I would dedicate this nation to the policy of the good neighbor, the neighbor who resolutely respects himself, and because he does so, respects the rights of others." This modern desert period has seen the pronouncement of a whole new Torah-ful of statutes and ordinances, which imposed new responsibilities upon us but have nevertheless given us greater freedom.

Even Moses, great leader that he was had his detractors and his enemies. So responsible a position could not be held without exciting envy and opposition. There was the rebellion of Dathan and Abiram of the tribe of Reuben, the tribe which had once held the leadership in Israel, but had lost it when Moses arose. There was the rebellion of Korach, who told Moses "You take too much upon yourself." Even Miriam and Aaron, Moses' sister and brother, spread evil gossip about him.

Apparently, one of the penalties for greatness is the presence of enemies. Our late president had that quality which engenders not only great esteem, but also violent hatred and opposition among his antagonists. His foes were many, and even some of his early friends turned upon him in open hostility as time went by: men like the late Al Smith and Hugh Johnson, James Farley, John Garner, and John L. Lewis, to mention a few.

Nor were his enemies always at fault like any other mortal being, he was subject to human frailty. Even Moses of old was not without blemish, and the Bible reveals his great error when he disobeyed the Lord's command and smote the rock in the wilderness to bring forth water for the thirsty Israelites.

A startling parallel in the lives of these two great men reveals itself at once when we read Moses own admission, כבד פה וכבד לשון אנכי "I am slow of speech and heavy of tongue!" Moses, the great leader, suffered under a serious physical handicap, doubly serious for one who would be a statesman and a leader. He suffered to such an extent that he was obliged to lean upon his brother Aaron to be his spokesman.

How odd that even as Moses suffered a physical impediment, so did the man we now mourn. At the age of 39 after having achieved national prominence in politics, business, and philanthropies, he was felled by infantile paralysis and hung for many months in the balance between life and death. Only his indomitable courage and his unyielding optimism brought about his recovery. Even thereafter he never regained the use of his lower limbs but walked always with the assistance of leg braces and canes. Where most of us, suddenly crippled, would have resigned ourselves to a miserable old age, he actually began to carve out a new political career with a vigor seemingly born in the midst of his terrible illness. His rise is history from the governorship of New York state to the presidency of the United States for over three hectic terms, to world leadership as the greatest of the Big Three.

The sheer magnificence of will and the courage of the man are almost inconceivable: to dare to fight for the highest offices in the world while laboring under such a handicap. It baffles the imagination! Perhaps the most dramatic of all the demonstrations of his courage was made on that day not so long ago, when he came to Congress, before many of his most critical foes, and wheeled himself in, seated in his chair, all the pretense of the steel braces left behind at home, unashamed and unafraid to appear to be exactly what he was, a crippled old man. I heard the thunderous applause even his enemies set up for him, and I wept out of admiration.

Yes, and as one and all remarked, like Moses, he was not permitted to taste the joy of final victory. We read of Moses, "And Moses went up unto Mount Nebo...and the Lord showed him all the promised land, And Moses, the servant of the Lord, died there."

Startling it was to hear suddenly, last Thursday evening that our own great leader had gone to the little white cottage atop Pine Mountain in Georgia and, before he could taste the joy of final victory, had quietly passed away there. This has been the cause of added grief this notion that he was cheated of his triumph just when it was about to come.

But is it really true that to him who led us has been denied what we the unworthy shall soon enjoy? I cannot believe so. Rather would I believe that to him it was given atop that hill, as he lingered those two hours neither in this world nor in the next, to him it was given as a reward to behold first what we shall some day see: the world of peace he, above all other men, has helped to build. "He went up unto the mountain, and the Lord showed him all the promised land...and the servant of the Lord died there."

And so we close the books of Moses and open the book of Joshua, his successor. And we read words of encouragement and high purpose. "And God said unto Joshua, Moses, my servant, is dead. Now therefore arise go over this Jordan, thou and all this people. As I was with Moses, so shall I be with thee. Only be strong and very courageous to do according to all the law which Moses my servant commanded thee; turn not from it to the right hand nor to the left."

And Joshua gave the people three days in which to get ready to continue on the path Moses had set for them, and the people answered Joshua, saying, "According as we hearkened unto Moses in all things, so will we hearken unto thee; only the Lord thy God be with thee as He was with Moses. Be strong and of good courage."

אחרי מות קדשים After death, sanctified. So may it be with the great man we mourn. We shall carry on, and with God's help we will succeed. But we cannot be condemned for missing him. I know I shall miss him. I only saw him once, last October 21st. It was on a Saturday noon, you may remember, and I concluded Sabbath services early and hurried with my wife to Queens Boulevard where he was to pass. It was alternately raining and snowing, but the pavements were crowded. Some of our children were there: the Levy twins with their older brother; Seymour Entin and others, all decked out in buttons bearing F.D.R.'s name.

And then the line of cars began to pass us and finally his car came along, the top down, the rain beating against that wonderful face. When he was alongside, he waved his hand and smiled. I know he smiled at me. I suppose that was the greatest element in him: he made everyone everywhere believe he was smiling at him.

Now that smile is still. It lives only in the heart of those who loved him. That dear, dear familiar voice rings only in our memories. Of all the words he spoke, the most significant for us as we march to meet the future are those he uttered early in this world crisis: "Some generations take all, some generations give all. But this generation has a rendezvous with destiny."

All who mourn his passing may rise and, in the words of the Kaddish, hallow the memory of Franklin Delano Roosevelt.

A third honor roll has been added to the long list of names of young men and women from Forest Hills who are serving our country in the armed forces. We dedicate that roll tonight and place at the top of the list in letters of gold the name of their commander-in-chief who laid down his life for his country. May his soul be bound in the bond of life.

We humbly pray in the words Franklin Delano Roosevelt used in his lifetime when he led the nation in prayer: "God of the free, we pledge our hearts and our lives today to the cause of all mankind. Grant us victory over the tyrants who would enslave all free men and nations. Grant us a common faith that man shall know bread and peace, that he shall know justice and righteousness, freedom and security, and equal opportunity, and an equal chance to do his best not only in our own lands but throughout the world. In that faith let us march toward the clean world our hands can make."

Amen.

RABBI STEPHEN SAMUEL WISE, IN MEMORIAL

There was a time when American Jews had a voice, stentorian, courageous and militant for peace and freedom. Rabbi Stephen Samuel Wise battled from the pulpit for clean politics, human rights and especially for the survival of the Jewish people and Judaism. He did it from the speaker's platform when he railed against any unacceptable human condition, from the sweatshop, to strike-breaking, to the corruption in New York's Tammany Hall. He did it in the Oval Office of the White House, arguing and pleading for greater efforts to save the remnant of European Jewry from genocide.

He established the necessity for freedom of the pulpit and rejected Temple Emanuel's rather restricted pulpit to found the Free Synagogue where the pulpit was indeed free. He founded his own rabbinical seminary, the Jewish Institute of Religion, and was emulated by generations of its graduates.

A Reform rabbi, he was accepted by all as the spokesman for American Jewry. I spoke of him on the first anniversary of his death.

APRIL 14, 1950

Dear Friends:

Tomorrow evening in our synagogues, we begin again the wonderful custom of reading from the *Mishnah* the tractate called *Pirke Avot*, The Ethics of the Fathers, from which we read one chapter each Saturday afternoon between the *Mincha* and the *Ma'ariv* Services. The second sentence of the first chapter teaches the lesson of Simon the Just, who used to say: על שלשה דברים העולם עומד על התורה ועל עבודה ועל גמילות חסדים "Upon three things does the world stand: upon Torah, upon worship and upon the showing of kindness."

I mention this line, not only because I would like to have many of you present tomorrow evening for our lesson together, but because of the man whose y*ahrzeit* we observe this week, Dr. Stephen Samuel Wise, who died one year ago on April 19, shortly after his 75th birthday. Stephen Samuel Wise did more than one man's share in sustaining this world of ours: he made *Torah, Avodah* and *Gemilut Chasadim* function in vibrant, living terms.

This coming Wednesday evening, at Temple Israel in Hollywood, a great mass memorial meeting will be held in memory of Rabbi Wise. At that time, I imagine, much will be said about the tremendous organization, accomplishment and the incredible volume of activity this man packed into one lifetime. Tonight, however, in the worshipful atmosphere of the synagogue and the Sabbath, I should like to dwell with you for a few minutes upon some aspects of the man which may tend to be overlooked in evaluating him.

There are some, among them those who were his enemies because they envied him, who would challenge including the element of Torah in an appraisal of Rabbi Wise's accomplishments. Let me put the simple story before you, however, and see if you do not agree that Rabbi Wise not only cherished Torah and studied it, but spread it far and wide. He was the son of a rabbi, the grandson of a rabbi, Chief Rabbi of Hungary Joseph Hirsch Weisz. Indeed, he was a product of seven generations of rabbinical leaders. At his father's knee, he acquired the training and from his father received the *semichah*, the ordination, which sent him into the rabbinate as a young man.

In his youth Stephen Wise prepared several articles for the great Jewish Encyclopedia. The translation of the Book of Judges in the Jewish Publication Society Bible is also his work.

In New York City he was the spokesman before the public school authorities on behalf of introducing the study of the Hebrew language into the curriculum. If, today, thousands of Jewish and Christian young people are studying Hebrew in high schools there, it may be credited largely to his efforts. Other thousands of Jewish scholars, writers, students and struggling rabbis in America and elsewhere owe him debts of gratitude for the assistance, financial and otherwise, which he gave readily because of his respect for the *talmid chacham,* the learned student.

The crowning scholarly achievement of his life was a privilege which is granted or sought by few men: the founding of his own rabbinical seminary, the Jewish Institute of Religion, in 1922. There he trained men for the rabbinate, including some of the men here in Los Angeles, Rabbi Bernard Harrison and Rabbi Julian Feingold, just to mention our neighbors. He brought to his faculty scholars and luminaries from many lands.

Emphasis was placed in his seminary upon freedom of religious thought, and thorough knowledge of the Hebrew tongue. His graduates have brought something of his personality to every principal city in this country.

His very gestures were imitated lovingly by his disciples. Some of his men relate that even the bald-headed among them developed the habit of tossing the shock of hair out of their eyes which used to fall into his. Many a rabbi in America has ruined his voice in vain attempts to make it echo the deep, resonant, forceful tones of Stephen S. Wise.

The same chapter of *Pirkei Avot* we shall read tomorrow begins with a sentence which includes the suggestion, "Raise up many disciples." He did so, and rendered a great service to Jewish scholarship and the American rabbinate in so doing. He was not the greatest scholar of our day, but in the midst of his battles for freedom and justice, it is noteworthy that he did not neglect scholarship, but promoted it, believed in it, respected it and practiced it.

Stephen Wise also knew the value of *Avodah*, of worship. I believe it is important to point out to those who choose to remember him largely in terms of his organizational work that he was an active rabbi all the days of his life, leading the services as well as preaching sermons which fired not only his listeners, but often kindled fires which consumed men of evil with their wrath.

There is one element about his ministry that has always been a source of inspiration to me, and should be to freedom-loving men everywhere. It would be impossible to compress the details of 53 years in the rabbinate into 53 days, or 53 minutes, but this one episode is perhaps the most famous and the most significant, even though it happened when he was only 31. After six years of activity in Temple Beth Israel of Portland, Oregon, the largest and richest congregation in America, perhaps the largest and richest that ever existed, invited this brilliant young man to assume the post of rabbi. This meteor out of the West came to New York and addressed the congregation there. I shall let him speak to you in his own words regarding what happened.

"One who preaches trial sermons lays himself open, as no man with self-respect should, to harassing experiences. After five years of free and independent preaching to a most friendly and indeed forbearing, as well as generously appreciative, congregation, I was greeted after preaching at Emanu-El by men and women, meaning to show their approval, with such exclamations as 'We were very much impressed,' 'We were very well pleased,' as if I had wished to please, when in truth I had sought solely to awaken. For the first time I came to understand the term trial sermons, as I had to listen to such expressions as 'Doctor, it was a fine sermon.' It was my soul that was tried; I had poured it out in earnest and unafraid appeal to these people to be single-minded and great-hearted Jews. They responded to me as if I had been delivering a high-school prize oration. I was chilled and disheartened to the last degree. Above all, it prepared my spirit for the great refusal, to which I was inexorably bound to rise after some days.

"'Gentlemen, I name two minor conditions and one major...I must have part in the religious services and the services of a private secretary.' The answer was there could be no objections.

"I said, 'You are calling me to be rabbi of Emanuel. I am not a preacher or scholar of note, but you have heard that I gained for my temple, Beth Israel, my people throughout Oregon, and their rabbi, the respect, and for the most part, the good will of the entire Northwest community. If I have achieved that, it has been because in my inaugural sermon at Beth Israel, September, 1900, I declared, 'This pulpit shall be free.'

"Mr. Marshall, perhaps to his credit be it said, without a moments hesitation, said rather testily, 'Dr. Wise, I must say to you at once that such conditions cannot be complied with; the pulpit of Temple Emanuel has always been and is subject to and under the control of the Board of Trustees.'

"My answer was clear, immediate, unequivocal: If that be true, gentlemen, there is nothing more to say. And that would have been the end had not one of Mr. Marshall's colleagues, all of whom seemed surprised by the finality of Mr. Marshall's statement and the immediacy of my reply, interposed the question, 'What do you mean by a free pulpit?'

"I replied fully and deliberately, putting my worst foot forward. 'I have in Oregon been among the leaders of a civic-reform movement in my community. Mr. Moses, if it be true, as I have heard it rumored, that your nephew, Mr. Herman, is to be a Tammany Hall candidate for a Supreme Court judgeship, I would if I were Emanu-El's rabbi oppose his candidacy in and out of my pulpit.' I continued, 'Mr. Guggenheim, as a member of the Child Labor Commission of the State of Oregon, I must say to you that, if it ever came to be known that children were being employed in your mines,' [having reference to his presidency of the famous copper mines] 'I would cry out against such wrong. Mr. Marshall, the press stated that you and your firm are to be counsel for Mr. Hyde of the Equitable Life Assurance Society. I would in and out of my pulpit speak in condemnation of the crimes committed by the insurance thieves.'

"I added that I could not and would not under any circumstances accept a call to be the rabbi of a congregation under such, as I saw it, humiliating conditions. The interview terminated...My wife, bravest and finest of spirits, waiting for me in the adjoining room, met me with a simple but infinitely heartening greeting: 'You had no other choice.'"

In a subsequent letter to the congregation, the young Wise summarized his attitude toward freedom of the pulpit, in words which, were I able to phrase them as beautifully, would certainly be my own:

"The chief office of the minister, I take it, is not to represent the views of the congregation, but to proclaim the truth as he sees it. How can he serve a congregation as a teacher save as he quickens the minds of his hearers by the vitality and independence of his utterances? But how can a man be vital and independent and helpful, if he be tethered and muzzled? A free pulpit, worthily filled, must command respect and influence; a pulpit that is not free, howsoever filled, is sure to be without potency and honor The minister is not to be the spokesman of the congregation, not the message-bearer of the congregation, but the bearer of a message to the congregation. What the contents of that message shall be, must be left to the conscience and understanding and loyalty of him in whom a congregation places sufficient confidence to elect him to minister to it."

I wonder if we can all appreciate fully the importance of his move. This man relinquished wealth, power of a certain kind and the comforts that a great, established synagogue can offer in order to found the Free Synagogue in New York, because he refused to be shackled to the discipline of fearful and petty minds. The fact that freedom of the pulpit, freedom for a rabbi or minister to express his beliefs, to teach, to try to mold and influence his congregants for good, the fact that I, tonight, can speak freely from this pulpit, unafraid of censorship, is the result of Stephen Wise's sacrifice almost a half century ago. To the thousands who flocked to Carnegie Hall every Sunday to hear him, to the thousands who crowded Clinton Hall every Friday night on the lower East Side to hear him, he was a prophet in Israel, a rabbi worthy of the title.

The world rests, the rabbi said, upon Torah, upon worship, and upon *Gemilut Chasadim*, the showing of kindness to one's fellowman. Stephen Wise was a man who practiced *Gemilut Chasadim* from its traditional sense of helping those who needed a helping hand, to the broadest possible interpretation of working for social reform for the good of all men.

As early as his Oregon days he was appointed Commissioner of Child Labor for that state. In New York City, he attacked the corruption of Tammany Hall, and what he said from his pulpit was repeated in editorials, political cartoons, magazines and from the public rostrum. During Mayor Walker's regime, he wired Governor Franklin Delano Roosevelt protesting against the mayor and the district attorney. He sent a copy to the press, causing Roosevelt to answer, "Rabbi Wise, it wasn't cricket of you to give to the press the telegram calling upon me to act upon the case of the magistrate and Mayor Walker."

Rabbi Wise mentions another, more humorous incident: "I recall that in the course of Mayor Hylan's second term, somebody who should have known both of us better turned to Red Mike and insisted on presenting me to him. The Mayor's response, spoken in surly fashion and in gruff tones, was, 'I ought to know Rabbi Wise. He has attacked me often enough.' Humbly I offered the Mayor this apology, 'Mr. Mayor, I may have attacked you often, but not often enough!'

"In rather more friendly and witty fashion, Mayor LaGuardia once said, having reference to Mayor Walker's not unhurried trip to England, 'When Rabbi Wise talks about mayors, there is usually a run on Atlantic steamship accommodations.'"

But Rabbi Wise talked not only about mayors, he talked against exploitation in sweatshops, against strike breaking, against discrimination and against any act which violated the prophetic teachings of Israel, no matter who was involved. When, in recent years, Hitler came to power, his voice was raised almost as a solo in protest. He was instrumental in organizing the boycott of German goods, which some timid American Jews considered unwise. He sent a mission to Germany, and the reply of German Jewry was, "Say to Rabbi Wise that he need not concern himself with Jewish affairs in Germany...since Hitler will never come to power."

This was the same Rabbi Wise who, in 1942, released to a press conference the first official confirmation of the slaughter of 2,000,000 Jews and the danger of death to 4,000,000 more. This was the Rabbi Wise who went to President Roosevelt on July 22, 1943, and told him that 70,000 Jews in France and Rumania could be rescued if we could get funds to Switzerland, to be put in escrow until after the war. "We'll beat the Nazis anyway," he said, "and never have to pay the pirate's ransom."

Roosevelt gave him immediate approval, saying, "Stephen, why don't you go ahead and do it," and called Morgenthau, who agreed. But the State Department delayed action for five crucial months and the chance was lost.

There is a story told by Rabbi Joachim Prinz, which sums up what Stephen Wise has meant to world Jewry as a friend, and a giant among men:

"During the 1946 Zionist Congress in Basel, a meeting was arranged at which concentration camp survivors reported on some of their past experiences...Dr. Wise and I...sat together and listened to the reports. For the first time we heard the voices of those who had suffered so much and who, without artificiality, spoke simply and movingly of their experiences.

"Suddenly one of the speakers, a young red-headed boy, used the word 'Stephanim.' He must have sensed that many of his listeners did not follow him, so he added by way of explanation: 'You must know that when we spoke of America we spoke of 'Stephania' and when we spoke of dollars, we called them 'Stephanim.''" In the language of the concentration camps, America was "Stephania," being identified with Stephen Wise. He bent over to me and with tears in his eyes, he whispered, 'This I do not deserve.'"

Indeed, there are those who will extol him for his fantastic organizational achievement, for being at the first Zionist Congress, for being one of the founders and first officers of the Zionist Organization of America, for founding the American Jewish Congress and the World Jewish Congress, for leading the fight for the restoration of Israel and taking it to the very doorstep of the White House and the halls of Congress.

But for me, as a rabbi, and for each of you, as individuals who, given one lifetime, are trying to use it most wisely, to become better people and make the world a little better, too, there was a man who was an inspiration, who knew the values of *Torah*, of *Avodah*, and of *Gemilut Chasadim*, who dared to speak the truth and led his life a slave to no man.

GOLDA MEIR, IN MEMORIAL

In retrospect it becomes clear that the outstanding Jewish woman of the Twentieth Century was a schoolteacher from Milwaukee, Wisconsin. She was born in Kiev in 1898, made aliyah to Palestine in 1921 and took in washing to pay her son, Menachem's, school tuition. During World War II, she was a member of Britain's War Economic Advisory Council for Palestine, and she traveled to America to raise money for the hoped-for Jewish state and returned with the unprecedented sum of $50,000,000 making her suddenly a luminary recognized world wide. Her visit to Moscow in 1948 was a watershed experience for that beleaguered Jewish community.

Her role as one of the architects of the new state was enormous. She became foreign minister and eventually prime minister, the first and only woman ever to occupy that post. A compassionate but iron-strong leader, ever humble and down to earth, she was just plain Golda. There is really no similar personality in all of history. Her death was mourned by Jews everywhere, and although she insisted on no eulogies, we used her own words to speak of her. I take no credit for those words of Golda Meir's, but I include this eulogy in this collection of my sermons because of what this amazing woman meant to me, to the Jewish People and to the world.

DECEMBER 15, 1978

Dear Friends:

As we all know, the request of the late Golda Meir was for no eulogies and no monuments. I do not propose a eulogy tonight and indeed most of the words spoken will be hers.

As we reflect on her words over an incredible lifetime, over and above our sadness at her passing away, we find this hour disappointing for her in that she did not realize a primary objective of almost all of her adult life: to witness the signing of firm treaties of peace with Israel's neighbors. As we are assembled tonight, that signing is still quite elusive.

And a new element has been added in that our American government seems to be underscoring criticism of Israel for the failure to have the signing of a treaty between Israel and Egypt by Sunday the 17th. Statements such as that made by Jody Powell on behalf of President Carter, "If the Israelis accept the proposal approved by Egypt, we will have peace; if they do not, I frankly don't know what will happen."

Senate Majority Leader Robert Byrd warned Israel's officials that the new Congress will be extremely reluctant to grant new aid to Israel while Israel continues the proliferation of new settlements on the West Bank. There is also the most recent press remarks of our president himself.

In the failure of all to point out that on November 25, Israel accepted the treaty as it was at that time, Egypt rejected it but there was no Administration criticism of Egypt.

But Egypt has introduced changes from the agreements of Camp David. The first of these is that there will be an automatic review after five years of the treaty's military and security provisions, a review that had been previously abandoned. Egypt also asked that the moment of exchange of ambassadors be postponed until after elections are held on the West Bank. The Camp David mandate asks for full diplomatic relations following Israel's withdrawal from the Sinai, which Israel is in the process of doing. And third, there is the suggestion that if other Arab states become involved in hostilities with Israel, Egypt could abrogate its treaty obligations.

These three measures are calculated to give a great sense of insecurity, and Israel has said they are not what was agreed upon on November 21, has refused to accept them and is now being condemned for the failure of a peace treaty. So that even if Golda had lived another week, she would have been bitterly disappointed.

Tonight however is a night for celebrating her life, and what an incredible life that is to celebrate. She was an active Zionist as a young girl, but we have known her mostly as an older woman. We do her an injustice if we do not constantly recall the image of a Golda Meyerson who was elected to office in the Zionist movement in a day when both Zionism and female participation in political Zionism were unusual. In the book, "As Good As Golda," she is quoted saying, "Zionism and pessimism are not compatible."

Once in Palestine, she wrote of her new life, so different from that of the teacher in America, "The kibbutz made me an expert in growing chickens. Before that, I was afraid to be in a room with even one chicken." On the early days of the children's' immigration to Israel, she wrote, "We have seen children who didn't know how to smile, children who came to us from the camps of Germany, the few who were left after a million children went to the gas chambers. They didn't know how to sing. They didn't know what a rose was. They had never seen one grow. And now in Israel in the North and in the South, these children have made things grow on sand and on rocks, where nothing has grown for centuries."

Golda was, as they say, a curiosity as a woman activist. She has conceded that there is a heavy price to pay for that and reflected upon herself and some of her experiences and sacrifices. She said there is a type of woman who cannot remain at home. In spite of the place her children and family fill in her life, nature demands something more. She cannot divorce herself from the larger social life. She cannot let her children narrow her horizons. For such a woman there is no rest.

The Israeli cabinet was trying to deal with a series of assaults on women. One minister suggested that women should not be allowed on he streets after dark. Golda protested, "Men are attacking women, not the other way around. If there is going to be a curfew let the men be locked up, not the women."

Characteristic of straightforward Golda Meir, when people asked her if she felt handicapped at being a woman minister, her answer was "I don't know, I've never tried to be a man."

Together, just before Israel wanted and won its independence, Golda went to see King Abdullah dressed as an Arab woman. He asked her not to hurry the proclamation of the State. She rejoined, "We have been waiting for 2,000 years...is that hurrying?" In the course of that adventure, she tells of carrying a veil, a veil which she would wear when going to King Abdullah, and in trying to explain her carrying a veil to the customs officials.

Our first encounter with her was on her return to the States in 1948 when she performed a most extraordinary feat. The winter of 1948 found the situation in Israel quite bleak. Ben-Gurion reluctantly agreed to let Golda come to the United States in his stead. She came with just the one dress she had been wearing at the meeting. She did not even have time to pack a bag with a winter coat to cover that dress to shield her from the cold.

Her first speech was in Chicago on January 21. Part of it read as follows: "The Jewish community in Palestine is going to fight to the very end. If we have arms to fight with, we will fight with them. If not, we will fight with stones in our hands. My friends, we are at war. There is no Jew in Palestine who does not believe that finally we will be victorious. That is the spirit of the country. But that valiant spirit alone cannot face rifles and machine guns. Rifles and machine guns without spirit are not worth very much. But spirit without arms can in time be broken together with the body. Our problem is time. The question is what we can get immediately. And when I say immediately, I do not mean next month, I do not mean two months from now. I mean now. I have come here to try to impress Jews in the United States that within a very short period, a couple of weeks, we must have in cash between 25 and 30 million dollars. In the next two or three weeks we can establish ourselves. Of that we are convinced.

"We are not a better breed. We are not the best Jews of the Jewish people. It so happens that we are there and you are here. I am certain that if you were in Palestine and we in the United States you would be doing what we are doing there and you would ask us here what you will have to do. I want to close by paraphrasing one of the greatest speeches that was made during the second World War. The words of Churchill, 'I am not exaggerating when I say that the Yishuv in Palestine will fight in the Negev and will fight in the Galilee and will fight on the outskirts of Jerusalem until the very end.' You cannot decide whether we should fight or not. We will. You can only decide one thing: whether we shall be victorious in this fight or whether the Mufti will be victorious. That decision American Jews can make. It has to be made quickly, within hours, within days, and I beg of you, don't be too late. Don't be bitterly sorry three months from now for what you failed to do today. The time is now."

Golda continues in her memoirs, "They listened and they wept. They pledged money in amounts that no community had ever given before. I stayed in the United States about six weeks. And the Jews all over the country listened, wept and gave money. And when they had to, took loans from banks in order to cover their pledges. By the time I came back to Palestine in March, I raised over fifty million dollars which was turned over at once to the Haganah's secret purchase of arms in Europe. But I never deceived myself. Not even when, upon my return, Ben-Gurion said to me, 'Some day when history will be written it will be said that there was a Jewish woman who got the money which made the State possible.' I always knew that these dollars were not given to me but to Israel."

A fighting speech from a woman who was destined to be involved in wars but one who was passionate for peace. "There is nothing Israel wants so much as peace. There is nothing Israel needs so much as peace. Many people have lost wars and many peoples' countries have been occupied by foreign powers. Our history is much more tragic. Hitler took care of 6,000,000 Jews. But if we lose a war that is the end for ever and we disappear from the earth.

She had the keen insightful economy of language that makes great quotations. To her they came naturally. Golda is always telling people "Don't be so humble. You're not that great." When her chief of cabinet suggested something for her to say to waiting journalists, Golda rejoined, "You can't improve on saying nothing."

Just before the 1967 War, Premier Levi Eshkol delivered a radio address to his nation and was criticized because he stumbled over his words. Golda said, "A leader who doesn't hesitate before he sends his nation into battle is not fit to be a leader." She added, "If only political leaders would allow themselves to feel as well as to think the world might be a happier place."

In 1948, there was a great confrontation between Golda and the people of these United States. I was there and some of you were there. There was another extraordinary confrontation the same year between Golda and a Jewish community that we had thought was lost forever: the Jewish community of Russia.

The first Shabbat after Golda and the Jewish-Israeli delegation arrived in Moscow, they went as a group to the main synagogue in Moscow to be met by a meager 100 or 125 Jews. This was shortly before *Rosh Hashanah*, however, and Golda decided that the entire group would again make an appearance at the synagogue on *Rosh Hashanah* when, they were told, approximately 2,000 Jews would be there.

Two days or so before this *Rosh Hashanah*, a great writer in the Soviet Union, who happened to be a Jew, Ilya Ehrenberg, wrote in Pravda that there was no such thing as a Jewish people and Israel had no meaning for the Jews in the Soviet Union because there was no anti-Semitism in the Soviet Union and only Jews who cared about anti-Semitism or had to flee from capitalist anti-Semitism were interested in Israel.

Golda had this to say. "As we had planned, we went to the synagogue on *Rosh Hashanah*. All of us...the men, women and children of the delegation dressed in our best clothes as befitted Jews on a Jewish holiday. But the street in front of the synagogue had changed. Now it was filled with people packed together like sardines. Hundreds and hundreds of them of all ages, including Red army officers, soldiers, teenagers and babies carried in their parents arms. Instead of 2,000 odd Jews who usually came to the synagogue on the holiday, a crowd of close to 50,000 people was waiting for us. And then it dawned on me. They had come, those good brave Jews, in order to be with us to demonstrate their sense of kinship and to celebrate the establishment of the State of Israel. Within seconds they had surrounded me, almost lifting me bodily, almost crushing me, saying my name over and over again. Eventually they parted ranks and let me into the synagogue. Every now and then in the women's gallery someone would come to me, touch my hand, stroke or even kiss my dress. Without speeches or parades, without any words at all, really, the Jews of Moscow were proving their profound desire and their need to participate in the miracle of the establishment of the Jewish state. And I was the symbol of the State for them. I couldn't talk or smile or wave my hand. I sat in that gallery like a stone without moving with those thousands of eyes fixed upon me.

"No such entity as the Jewish people," Ehrenberg had written earlier that week. "The State of Israel meant nothing to the Jews of the U.S.S.R.?"

But his warning had fallen on deaf ears. For 30 years we and they had been separated. Now we were together again. I felt as though I had been caught up in a torrent of love so strong that it had literally taken away my breath and slowed down my heart. I was on the verge of fainting, I think. But the crowd still surged around me, stretching out its hand and saying, 'Nasha Golda, our Golda,' and 'Shalom, Shalom,' and crying. Out of that ocean of people I can still see two figures clearly. A little man who kept popping up in front of me saying *'Goldele, leiben zolstu...shana tova'* and a woman who just kept repeating *'Goldele, Goldele'* and smiling and blowing kisses at me. It was impossible for me to walk back to the hotel. Someone pushed me into a cab. But the cab couldn't move either because the crowd of cheering, laughing, weeping Jews had engulfed it.

"I wanted to say something to those people, anything, to let those people know that I beg their forgiveness for not having wanted to come to Moscow and for now having known the strength of their ties to us, for having wondered in fact whether there still was a link between them and us, but I couldn't find the words. All I could say, clumsily, and in a voice that didn't even sound like my own was one sentence in Yiddish. I stuck my head out the window of the cab and said, *'A dank eich vos yir zeint gebliben Yidden.'* Thank you for having remained Jews. And I heard that miserable inadequate sentence being passed on through the enormous crowd as though it were some wonderful prophetic saying. In the hotel, everyone gathered in my room. We had been shaken to our very depths. Nobody talked; we just sat there. It had been far too great a revelation for us to discuss it but we needed to be together. Ida, Lou and Sarah were sobbing as though their hearts would break. And several of the men held their faces in their hands. But I couldn't even cry. I just sat. My face drained of color, staring in front of me. That was how we stayed for hours, flooded with emotions so powerful that we couldn't even communicate them to each other. I can't pretend that I knew for certain then that within 20 years I would see many of those Jews in Israel. But I did know one thing. I knew that the Soviet Union had not succeeded in breaking their spirit, that Russia with all its power had failed. The Jews had remained Jews."

This is a moment in Golda's life that has slipped into the back of our memory because of all that has happened since. It is good to be reminded of it and here is what she said when reminded of the great emotional response of Soviet Jewry to her arrival in Moscow in 1948, "If you had sent a broomstick to Moscow and said it represented the State of Israel, it would have received the same welcome."

This was a strong woman, defiant and articulate. She said, "We have our back against the wall. We don't even have a wall. We have a sea. The only friendly neighbor we have is the Mediterranean." And then she said, "We intend to remain alive. Our neighbors want to see us dead. This is not a question that leaves much room for compromise." And in that famous and very telling statement of hers, that I think is not a professional opinion but the Jewish philosophy that we hold it against Nasser, "Not only the killing of our sons, but forcing them for the sake of Israel's survival to kill others."

She told us, "We owe a responsibility not only to those who are in Israel but also those generations who are no more. To those million who have died within our lifetime. The Jews all over the world, and to generations of Jews to come we hate war. We do not rejoice in victories. We rejoice when a new kind of cotton is grown. And when strawberries flourish in Israel."

She was a great interpreter of her people. She said, "The great heroes of the present generation are not only the soldiers, but their wives, their mothers who are forced to say good-bye to them so often.

"In Israel we do not hide facts. Each military death is recorded. Each one who falls defending his country, his story is told. His picture is in the daily press. We count each one. And each sorrow is not only of the mother but of all mothers, of everybody in the country. They are everybody's sons. If we have a choice between being dead and pitied and being alive with a bad image, we would rather be alive and have the bad image." Something for us to remember right now.

"We refuse absolutely to be the one people in the world which consents to having its fate decided by others.

"The fact that Jews have survived, the fact that we have been privileged to live in a generation in which Israel has been reborn is due to one thing, something which many in the non-Jewish world have never understood. We are a stiff-necked people. We are a people who does not bow, a people which stands erect to face its tragedies. If we are criticized because we do not bow, because we cannot compromise on the question to be or not to be, it is because we have decided that come what may, we are and we will be."

Then she said, "Again we won a war. The third in a very short history of independence. We want peace, but our neighbors must learn this lesson. Those who were gassed in the gas chambers by Hitler were the last Jews to die without defending themselves."

But no matter how serious things became she never lost her sense of humor or optimism. Her often-quoted response to her age tells of that. "Being 70 is not a sin. It is not a joy either."

Another quote that is telling is, "People coming here have been asking us about our situation. How long can we hold out? For 2,000 years, the Jews have lived under a barrage of distress. If someone would have asked our forefathers how long will you be able to hold out, I don't know what the answer might have been. But one thing can be said. I fully believe that not only the young generation but I as well will live to see the day when Israel will be free, independent, safe, developed and democratic, proud of having created the kind of society the Jews should create and living in peace with its neighbors and the entire world." The sadness in our hearts is that she did not.

In her memory let us rise and say the *kaddish.*

CHAIM WEIZMANN, In Memorial

In a modest grave in the garden of the world-famous institution which bears his name, Chaim Weizmann, the first president and one of the primary architects of the State of Israel, lies buried. He was one of 12 children, in pogrom-wracked Czarist Russia. His life carried him to cheder, *where, of all places, he encountered the world of chemistry and also came to the conclusion that Zionism was the only solution to the oppression his people suffered.*

Chemistry and Zionism would take him to the highest realms of science and world diplomacy. He was creator of or party to the various institutions and negotiations, including his key role in motivating the Balfour Declaration, which resulted ultimately in the establishment of the Third Jewish Commonwealth.

When he accepted the presidency of the state, his was one of those rare cases in which the man gives credibility and honor to the office which he holds, rather than vice-versa. This sermon records and reacts to his life and his loss.

NOVEMBER 14, 1952

Dear Friends:

At 5:55 last Sunday morning, November 9, death came quietly to Dr. Chaim Weizmann, the first president of the reborn State of Israel.

Attended only by his wife and lifelong companion, Vera, President Weizmann ended 78 years of struggle and triumph which have taken him from the hinterland of Russia to the great capitals of the world, from the *cheder* to the private chambers of presidents and kings, from a hopeless ghetto to dynamic new Israel.

What shall we say of this man, whose name we have known all our life, whose activities have been as familiar to us as those of some distant relative? How shall we express in our sorrow the objective truth of his importance to the history of the Twentieth Century?

Perhaps it will help to think of him as a kind of symbol of Jewish strivings these last three-quarters of a century. His life was the epitome of the existence of all the millions of Jews during this era. They felt their homelessness most keenly and awakened to wrestle with their own destiny and wring from it a blessing.

Like so many of our people, Chaim's life began in 1874 in a backwoods area of Russia in a little village in the province of Minsk called Motol, or to the Jews, familiarly, Mottelle, a marshy "metropolis" of some 700 souls. There in the primitive *cheder* his early childhood was spent at the rebbe's knee. There, too, his teacher in Bible also introduced him furtively to the world of science, by means of a book in Hebrew on natural science and chemistry, the kind of work forbidden in the ghetto and smuggled in by the early *maskilim*, the self-styled "enlightened ones."

His family made their modest living cutting and transporting lumber down the river to Danzig. At the age of 11, Chaim went to school in Pinsk during the days of the oppressive May laws, when Russian Jewry was beginning to stir with tremendous uneasiness after the pogroms of 1881.

He saw the restriction of educational opportunities and he saw the variety of reactions to this by the Jews of his generation. Some buried themselves deeper in traditional Judaism finding a kind of refuge in not permitting it to change one iota. Some sought refuge by assimilating into their Russian environment through baptism. Some believed that in the revolutionary movements of the day, in a non-Czarist Russia they would find personal freedom as Russians. Some felt that only in a Jewish state in Palestine would they achieve a solution to the problems of the Russian Jew. Chaim's own home, in which he was one of 12 children, reflected some of these differing opinions. He, of course, chose in early childhood to believe in Zionism, and he never deviated for one moment of his long life.

From those childhood days, two concerns occupied his life: chemistry and Zionism, an unlikely pair which he succeeded in endowing with relevance one to another. He pursued them both wherever he went - in Darmstadt, Germany, in Berlin, and finally, in Freiberg, Switzerland, where he pursued his university studies and received the degree of doctor of science in the year 1900. From 1900 to 1904, he taught organic chemistry at the University of Geneva. He also attended the early conferences of the World Zionist Organization.

In Geneva, he met Vera Chatzman, a Russian-born medical student, whom he married and of whom he says, "I had found in her not only my future wife, but a helpmeet, comrade and support throughout the vagaries of my rather complicated existence. It was my wife who so organized things as to give me a stable and tolerably safe background. If I have been able to carry on to give my whole mind to my work without taking much thought for financial or other practical matters, it has been entirely due to her forethought, her devotion and her savoir-faire." Indeed, only his death severed a relationship which ennobled their lives for 52 years.

In 1904, Weizmann went to England, a land he loved most dearly of any outside Palestine. There, in the University in Manchester, he began his lectureship in a new tongue, English, and developed an academic career which was to bring him international importance in not too many years. He achieved a certain degree of financial independence, and then turned his attention again to the Zionist Congresses and the development of the Zionist movement.

Like so many of our people then, Weizmann left Russian oppression to find a greater welcome in one of the enlightened lands of the West and proceeded to make his contribution to that land and to the welfare of his people. His home life, made stable by the calm hand of his wife, was enlivened by the passage through it of many of the greats in the world of science, international politics and Zionism.

Yet again and again, at considerable personal sacrifice, he left home and studies to tread the highways of the world in the interest of Zion. He went about selling shares in the Jewish Colonial Trust, making Zionist talks in the little synagogues in Russian villages and stirring the people to self emancipation. He traveled to Palestine and conceived the idea that Mount Scopus should be crowned by some building worthy of the Jewish people.

He fought against the Uganda proposal when it was submitted by Theodore Herzl and held out stubbornly for Palestine and Palestine alone as the place where a Jewish state must rise.

He discussed his ideas with Lord Balfour, Baron Rothschild, Lloyd George, Winston Churchill, General Smuts, Leon Blum, Orde Wingate, Chaim Nachman Bialik, Felix Warburg, Louis Marshall, Stephen S. Wise, Louis Lipsky - almost every great figure in England and the United States one can name.

He was there when some of the most significant acts in Jewish life in this century took place: when the Jewish National Fund and the Keren Hayesod, the Palestine Foundation Fund, were created. As long ago as 1902, Weizmann, Martin Buber and Berthold Feivel wrote the first pamphlet on the subject of a Jewish university in Palestine, in which young Jews, barred from higher learning by the quotas in force in European universities, might be prepared to make their contribution to the world. It was Weizmann who organized the University Committee and in 1913 asked Baron Edmond de Rothschild for the funds to create the institution. Rothschild agreed if Weizmann could get the great medical research scientist, Dr. Paul Ehrlich, to head the university committee. Weizmann succeeded.

It was Weizmann who in July 1918, within sound of the guns of World War I, laid the foundation stones for the Hebrew University on Mount Scopus in the presence of General Allenby.

It was Weizmann who, on April 1, 1925, seated with his wife and his mother, observed the opening of that university. At dinner that night Vera Weizmann asked General Allenby, "Did you think my husband completely harebrained when he asked your permission for the laying of the foundation stones in 1918?"

Allenby thought for a moment and then replied, "When I project my mind back to that day, and I often do, I come to the conclusion that that short ceremony inspired my army and gave them confidence in the future."

It was Chaim Weizmann who was largely responsible for the Balfour Declaration, the turning point in the realizable hopes of our people for a state. We tend to oversimplify that great milestone and say it was a reward by the British government to Weizmann for his contribution to the war effort in World War I. It is true that the Admiralty placed him in charge of their laboratories to create a manufacturing process for the acetone necessary for the cordite used in explosives and that he served patriotically and successfully, and did not choose to capitalize personally on his great achievement, but the Balfour Declaration came as a result of years of work with the leaders of Great Britain. In that work, Weizmann occupied a leading position. As early as 1906, he held his first conversation with Lord Balfour. When they met again in 1915 to discuss the matter, Balfour said to Weizmann, "You know I was thinking of that conversation of ours, and I believe that when the guns stop firing you may get your Jerusalem."

The true story of the issuing of the Balfour Declaration is a heartbreaking tale of opposition to it by the Jewish leaders in top British circles. Claude Montefiore and Edwin Montague, secretary of the state for India, both Jews, violently assailed their Majesty's government's intentions.

Weizmann prowled the corridors of the war cabinet while they debated the issue. It was he who suggested to Balfour that the declaration be addressed to Lord Rothschild rather than to him, and it was to Chaim Weizmann, waiting outside that Sir Mark Sykes brought the final document on November 2, 1917, while the Cabinet was still in session and exclaimed, "Dr. Weizmann, it's a boy!"

From that day until the creation of the state, Chaim Weizmann negotiated the choppy seas of international diplomacy, retrenchment, commissions, white papers and disappointments, which were our common lot. In office or out, he was the giant leader on the Zionist scene, still vigorously serving during World War II with its threat to the Jews.

This time, President Roosevelt issued a call to Weizmann to come to America and work on the problem of synthetic rubber. Weizmann and his wife prepared to fly to New York on February 13, 1942, in answer to Roosevelt's plea. Early that day, they were in the car which was to take them to the airfield when they received a call from London with the terrible news that their son, Michael, was missing in action. He had been flying with the Royal Air Force and had come down somewhere off the coast of France on the night when the German warships, Gneisenau and Scharnhorst, made their dash through the English Channel. Until the end of the war, the Weizmanns continued to hope that perhaps Michael had been captured by the Germans and was safe.

With the end of the war, that hope died. Heavy with sorrow, Weizmann came to America and worked against the vested oil interests to create synthetic rubber from farm products rather than from petroleum which was scarce. Of his efforts, then Vice-President Wallace wrote, "The world will never know what a significant contribution Weizmann made toward the success of the synthetic rubber program at a time when it was badly bogged down and going too slowly."

The greatness of the man and his battle for science and for Zion cannot be compressed into a few brief moments. His people recognized it, however, when four days after the State of Israel was born, they elected him president and reelected him last year. As a fitting climax to that long pilgrimage begun in 1874 in Mottelle in the ghetto, the first official act of the first President of Israel, an act which brought new dignity and happiness to you and to me, Chaim Weizmann came to exchange greetings with the president of the United States. He came bearing a *Sefer Torah* as the most fitting token of his people and what they represent. He rode in a car down Pennsylvania Avenue, and the blue and white flag of Israel fluttered from every post and flew atop the pole opposite the White House as is the case when any visiting chief executive is welcomed. You and I wept for joy at the quiet triumph of this great old man and the great old people he led through the wilderness.

For, my friends, not out of excessive enthusiasm, but out of quiet reflection, we have come to realize that here was the Moses of the new Israel. Like that first Moses, he led our people from the house of bondage in which he was born, back and forth, for 40 heart-breaking years across the wilderness of disappointment, dissension and darkness to the shores of the promised land.

But unlike Moses of old, who was obliged to view Palestine from afar, to die while yet in the wilderness and to lie buried in an unmarked grave, Chaim Weizmann lived to see through his failing eyes the land itself and to have the great joy of leading his people on their soil to die there and to be buried there with the greatest of tenderness in the garden of his home in Rehovoth.

This is a grave which will be visited by graybeards and by little children, by troubled leaders longing for his strength and by young people seeking inspiration. It is not a grave which will be forgotten for he not only molded the history of our generation, he lived that history in his own life. And he has left us, in his own words, a kind of blessing for the future, which I deem most appropriate for the closing of our reflections upon his life, and a prophecy of the future which it now remains for us to shape.

"Whether prophets will once more arise among the Jews in the near future it is difficult to say. But if they choose the way of honest and hard and clean living, on the land in settlements built on the old principles, and in cities cleansed of the dross which sometimes has been mistaken for civilization; if they center their activities on genuine values, whether in industry, agriculture, science, literature or art; then God will look down benignly on His children who, after a long wandering have come home to serve Him with a psalm on their lips and a spade in their hands, reviving their old country and making it a center of human civilization." (*Trial and Error*, pages 465-466)

THE EYES OF DR. LOUIS FINKELSTEIN

At the age of 96, one of the giant intellects, ideologues and innovators of the middle of the Twentieth Century passed away after a long bout with Parkinson's Disease. Ordained at the Jewish Theological Seminary in 1919, he became its provost in 1937, its president in 1940 and its chancellor in 1951.

He transformed the Seminary into a veritable university not only as a scholar, writing major works on Rabbi Akiva, the Pharisees and Saadiah Gaon as well as a compendium of essays on the Jews, but as a pioneer in the field of ecumenism with the founding of the ecumenical Institute for Religious and Social Studies and the ongoing Conference of Science, Philosophy and Religion.

I was fortunate to have him as my professor of theology and later as a father figure and a friend. He was eulogized by some of the leading figures in Jewish and Christian life, but I saw him differently and spoke of him from my heart to my Conservative colleagues at a conference in Palm Springs.

JANUARY 7, 1992

Dear Friends:

The eyes! The eyes on the obituary page, the eyes, I remembered were set deep in a haggard, suffering face, fixed and flashing fierce energy, piercingly conveying dearly purchased ancient wisdom at me and through me for time yet to come...the eyes of Dr. Louis Finkelstein ז״ל.

The words on the obituary page spelled out a sparse outline of the labors of 96 years. To this gathering of grieving disciples, that outline needs no repetition for we have been witnesses to the story. Each has his or her own encounters with this spare and Spartan father, teacher, chief executive officer of the syncretism of the historical, *halachic* and dynamic streams of Judaism we call Conservative.

Permit me to eulogize the man behind those eye from this disciple's viewpoint. I saw a driven, lonely man who lived never in the present but rather in the past and the future simultaneously, not in a world in which he was comfortable, but in the world as he believed it had to become.

Examples: He labored in the most volatile of all centuries, yet the era of scholarship he elected to explore was confined to the period between the Pharisees and Gaonim.

He was 19th-century Orthodox by birth, training and preference, yet he labored in the milieu called Conservative Judaism.

He was basically a teacher by preference. As he said in an interview in 1972, "I think the most rewarding time in my life was when I realized I could teach." Yet he found himself in an administrative position which left little time for teaching. He set high goals for himself and the Seminary. Yet he found himself with limited time for scholarship during most of his working life, when he led a complex structure which he made even more complex with the politicizing which inevitably follows in institutions.

In his religion he was a religious supernaturalist, yet he found himself making common cause with religious naturalists in many aspects of his work.

He was devoted to the rabbinic texts in which he did his chief works: the Sifra on Leviticus and the Rabbinic figures, the Pharisees, Rabbi Akiva, and Saadiah Gaon, yet he founded the Conference on Science, Philosophy and Religion.

He was staunchly chauvinistic about the Jewish faith, insisting on many occasions that what we were doing was the single most important thing in the world, that the survival of the world hung upon the survival and promulgation of Judaism. Yet he pioneered in ecumenism, establishing the Institute for Religious and Social Studies which brought generations of Protestant and Catholic scholars to the Seminary for theological discussions.

He was not an active Zionist zealous for a Jewish state. He maintained that nationalism is at the root of the wars, genocides and general misery of the Twentieth Century, yet he found himself the titular leader of the fountainhead of the staunchly Zionist Conservative movement.

He admitted rarely listening to the radio, yet pioneered in that medium by establishing the Eternal Light program, which was widely acclaimed for its weekly dramatization of spiritual and cultural themes for a broad spectrum of the American public. The same is true with television to which he paid little attention personally, but for which medium the Seminary produced superior programming.

Born in Cincinnati, he was nevertheless a confirmed, provincial New Yorker. No jet-setter he, yet he thought in global terms. In 1945 he said to me, "The Jewish world in the future will rest upon three foundations: New York, Los Angeles and Jerusalem." He backed that prophecy by making common cause with Rabbi Mordechai M. Kaplan ז״ל, and Rabbi Simon Greenberg ז״ל in establishing the University of Judaism in Los Angeles and the Penimiah in Jerusalem.

Personally he was a modest man, little concerned with appearances, always smoothing down his rebellious hair, insisting he only needed two suits: one to wear and one to spare. His office was a converted student dormitory suite, bare and austere. Still his work threw him together with urbane tycoons, with the worldly Reform American Jewish Committee, even secularists and assimilationist types, including Supreme Court justices and national presidents.

He was shy, reserved and soft-spoken, yet when called upon to address crowds or defend a cherished policy, he became a tiger bent on having his way. His eyebrows flew up, his eyes flashed, his voice rose in passionate hoarseness, his mouth sometimes lifted in a smile which intimated, "You know I'm right. Admit it." He was a loner who had to deal with multitudes, a reserved man, forbidding at times and private, who wanted to be loved, a take-charge man who ended up condemned to a wheelchair.

My memories of him extend over 50 years from my first introduction to him by my rabbi, Morris Goodblatt ז״ל who wanted me to enter the Seminary to a precious Shabbat in our home with his face beaming as our infant son, Daniel, pulled at his beard, to his eyes before me in the front row of the Seminary Baccalaureate service in 1974 when that baby was being ordained a rabbi. In those Finkelstein eyes, there was a tear.

My humble belief is that he was rarely at home or comfortable in ישיבה של מטה this earthly academy in which he lived and worked; nor do I believe he was very satisfied with this world. Still, he was one of the giants of the Twentieth Century, effecting so much change within it and setting so many trends which will endure beyond it. I only wish that in the innermost privacy of his personal life he could have been happier. Let us pray that in ישיבה של מעלה the Heavenly Academy, he has found a greater measure of peace.

RABBI MORDECAI M. KAPLAN IN MEMORIAL

If anyone was a prophet in the Twentieth Century, it was Rabbi Mordecai M. Kaplan. He was a prophet in both senses of the term: an unrelenting critic of the social and spiritual society in which he lived and a seer who foresaw great changes in that society but also lived to see them take place and to have a hand in the metamorphosis.

He could not abide the superficiality of the scholarship emerging in this country nor the obscurantism of what passed for its theology. He posited the alternative of religious naturalism in a day when super-naturalism was having a revival, and Jews were making excursions into the occult in Judaism and in many Eastern religions.

Mordecai Kaplan saw the modern synagogue as a center of Jewish civilization, not simply a prayer house, founded the Jewish Centers Movement and saw it flourish while the Reform and Orthodox establishments followed suit. He conceived a movement called Reconstructionism, founded its first synagogue and opened the pulpit and Jewish belonging to the female half of our society.

I left in the actual text of this sermon which I gave when one Margery Jacobs was bat mitzvah, who is now a rabbi ordained at the Reconstructionist seminary which his movement created. In his 102 years, Mordecai M. Kaplan saw his ideals become real, a rare privilege. As my teacher, he helped me learn to think, not merely to learn by rote. He was obliged to fight all his days to have his innovations accepted, and they were.

NOVEMBER 12, 1983

Dear Friends:

This past Tuesday, November 8, Rabbi Mordecai M. Kaplan died at the age of 102 years and five months. It is fitting that we reflect upon his life today not only because of the many new values he added to enrich Jewish life, not only because he was my teacher and mentor, but also because he was one of the few giants in a century strikingly lacking in great rabbinic leadership.

A fire burned in this man, a fire of fierce and unwavering passion for truth, a fire that torched away the sham, the superfluous and the obscurant. This fire seems to have kept the spark of life alive far beyond the life expectancy even of our times. That fire scorched hypocrites, ignited clear thinking and warmed the courage of those who dared to challenge time-worn notions that had become frigid and rigid. It is a fire that still burns in the work of his disciples, of whom I am proud to be one, and in the millions whom he and they have influenced.

Somewhere deep in Lithuania, in a *shtetl* called Svencionys, Mordecai Kaplan was born on June 11, 1881. His family and his early training was steeped in East European orthodoxy. At the age of nine he came with his family to New York, where he encountered a new world of thought, iconoclastic, infinitely varied and, to him, challenging.

The challenge was whether simply to duplicate exactly the Judaism he knew in the shtetl, to reject it as inappropriate for the new world, to recast it in a totally new mold or to reconstruct it using the basic blueprint of classical Judaism and the materials of the new time and place.

Kaplan chose reconstruction and that was the name he gave to his philosophy and his movement. The nursery of these ideas was the young institution called the Jewish Theological Seminary of America, headed by a great scholar, Rabbi Solomon Schechter.

Rabbi Kaplan's first pulpit after ordination was an Orthodox congregation called Kehilath Jeshurun. Even as a pulpit rabbi, he began a life-long career in the Jewish academic world. In 1909, when he was all of 28 years old, he was called back to the Seminary and appointed dean of the newly established Teachers' Institute. A few months later he was asked to teach homiletics, the art of preaching, to the rabbinical students. Soon he was teaching Midrash and philosophies of religion in the rabbinical school, courses which he taught there for the next 50 years.

Teaching those subjects never became tedious for him because his probing, questioning mind kept reconstructing his ideas and he was always bursting to share them with this students.

I happened to be in his class when he had gone to what was then Palestine, now Israel, and decided he would switch from the Ashkenazic to the Sephardic pronunciation of Hebrew. That was already when he was in his sixties. It took real concentration to change the habits of a lifetime. He was trying so hard, however and he told us about the *Mitzvot* of *Pesach* pronouncing it "Petach" in his earnestness to change the "s"s to "t"s. Some of us were rude enough to burst out laughing. When he realized his error he laughed louder than all of us. Incidentally, it was one of the few times I ever heard him laugh.

For example, one evening, Margie and I were attending a movie on upper Broadway, a double bill including a Warner Brothers anti-Nazi film and an Abbott and Costello comedy. Who was sitting next to us? Dr. Kaplan! He sat rigidly through the anti-Nazi film, and at the intermission turned to me and asked, "What did you think of the film?" His tone was exactly as stern as when he was asking some searching question in class.

Flustered, I answered, "Terrific!"

He said angrily, "What do you mean 'terrific'? Define the word 'terrific.' How does 'terrific' apply to this film at this time?"

I guess I flunked the test because after my stammering explanation, he settled back and said nothing until the Abbott and Costello comedy came on. We were laughing heartily, but he sat glumly. After a few minutes he got up to leave saying only, "This is silly." I never did ask him to define "silly."

But that was Dr. Kaplan. He insisted on clarity, as he unfolded for us and compelled us to examine the meaning and mystery of Midrash, as he tore our student sermons apart and demanded we reject shoddy and half-baked ideas, avoid the obscure and clarify, illuminate and apply the wisdom of our tradition to the real world today. I still construct my sermons and utilize the texts and the Midrash as he taught us and, I suspect, deep down I am still trying to please my teacher and avoid his wrath against mediocrity.

All the while he was teaching, he was functioning in the pulpit and in the community. He was the man who spoke of the organic Jewish community and organized the first *"kehillah"* or total community in New York, in which he tried to unite all Jews Orthodox, Conservative, Reform, secular, Zionist, whatever, under a common banner.

He defined Judaism as "the evolving religious civilization of the Jewish people," and put that definition into practice by creating the idea and the first example of the synagogue-center, a place where worship was combined with the cultural, political, social even athletic and recreational life of the Jew. He founded a congregation called The Jewish Center, the first to have athletic facilities in it and was its rabbi from 1917 to 1922. Eventually the Jewish Welfare Board, casting about for something to do after serving the Jewish military men in World War One, created the Jewish Center movement. It all began with Dr. Kaplan.

In 1922, he founded the synagogue known as The Society for the Advancement of Judaism, the S.A.J., which became the testing ground for his new movement, Reconstruction. The philosophy of Reconstructionism is embedded in his master work, "Judaism as a Civilization," published in 1934. In it, he maintained that Judaism is not simply a religious communion like Lutheranism or Methodism, but a civilization having a homeland, Israel, a history, literature, art, music, and dance as well as religion. To Kaplan, religion is a wrestling with God, whom he conceives in non-personal terms and clarifying what are the purposes and values and meaning of human existence. In Kaplan's words, "God is the power that makes for salvation."

Kaplan insisted that this religious civilization is constantly evolving and that tradition must guide but not dictate the forms it takes in response to new times and circumstances. In keeping with this idea, he edited Reconstructionist prayer books, which began as loose-leaf volumes in the hands of the worshipers at S.A.J., and the New Haggadah, which led to a host of other expanded haggadahs.

In 1945, I was privileged to be among those in the Seminary dining hall who heard Kaplan issue a trumpet call for the establishment of a University of Judaism. In 1947, he came to Los Angeles with Dr. Louis Finkelstein, and I was delegated to help generate opportunities for them to invite local leaders to create the University of Judaism, the West Coast branch of the Jewish Theological Seminary. I addressed gatherings large and small of educators in various fields of art and synagogue leaders to join in the creation of the project. Kaplan traveled West many times thereafter during its organization and subsequently as a scholar in residence. It stands as another monument to the realization of Kaplan's many dreams.

As mentioned earlier, he was one of the first champions of women's rights in Judaism. That is what led to his daughter Judith becoming the first bat mitzvah in 1922, to having the Reconstructionist Rabbinical College he founded in 1968 ordain women and eventually, to having the Conservative movement come to grips with the issue of women's equality under Jewish law and to having the rabbinical seminary faculty vote to admit and ordain women as rabbis, only a matter of days before Dr. Kaplan died.

This was a man who introduced new and radical ideas into Jewish life and lived to see them accepted and taken for granted and applied unconsciously even in Orthodox settings where his notions of Jewish cultural and ethnic activities are to be seen in practice.

His disciples are everywhere applying varying areas of his teaching to their pursuits. His Teachers' Institute created the Ramah Camp movement, trained the educators who staff the Solomon Schechter Day School movement and created Bureaus of Jewish Education in major cities. For example, his student, Dr. Samuel Dinin, helped establish the Los Angeles Bureau of Jewish Education on a firm footing.

What was the secret of Rabbi Kaplan's longevity? Was it exceptional genes? Was it that he walked the two miles to and from the Seminary summer and winter for half a century? Was it that in his nineties he moved to Jerusalem to fulfill his concept of Israel as the hub of Jewish life and trudged up and down its hills until he was almost one hundred? Was it the reinforcing satisfaction of seeing his seminal ideas become the norms in his own time? Or was it that fire I described, that fire of fierce and unswerving passion for truth which burned away the dross of lazy thinking and unquestioning pursuit of time-worn, rigid notions?

The answer to these questions and others he was still asking went to the grave with him two days ago, but the fires he kindled in so many others, including many who do not know his name will continue to glow for the foreseeable future.

I acknowledge with gratitude today my debt to my teacher, my master, Rabbi Mordecai M. Kaplan. With sadness, I contemplate a world in which, though his ideas and institutions persist, we shall never see this person again.

זכר צדיק לברכה The memory of a righteous man is an enduring blessing.

DR. SIMON GREENBERG, IN MEMORIAL

Rabbi Simon Greenberg ז״ל was my first and always hero. I was a pre-teen in Philadelphia when I first heard this lean, blond, vigorous man rise to enlist us all in the cause of Zionism. In the following years he was one of the rabbis who suggested that I enter the rabbinate. He provided tutors to help me with certain textual specialties.

His congregation adored him. His colleagues looked up to him. He was the eloquent voice of Conservative Judaism who advocated its causes with unshakable loyalty. He left his congregation to become vice-chancellor of the Jewish Theological Seminary, found our institutions in Jerusalem and serve as first president of the University of Judaism. Humble and modest, he was my exemplar of a true Conservative Jew, a fervent Zionist, a scholar, activist and humane person. I was privileged to eulogize him as follows at the 44th Commencement of the University of Judaism.

MAY 8, 1994

Dear Friends:

In the Spring of 1991, the annual convention of the Rabbinical Assembly dedicated a loving tribute to Dr. Simon Greenberg on his 90th birthday. The privilege of saluting him was given appropriately to Dr. David Lieber, who lovingly recited the unparalleled record of his achievements. After sustained applause from the rabbis assembled, Dr. Greenberg spoke with humor and humility and said the following, "As I draw up the account of today, (Ps. 35:10) every fiber of my being joins me in declaring (Ps. 16:6) 'My lot has been a pleasant one.' Hence, morning after morning, as I put on *tallit* and *tefillin* (his voice broke) and thank Him who has enabled me to reach this day, I ask why He has been so kind to me. I have not as yet received a response."

With some trepidation and considerable chutzpah, I offered my response in the form of a letter I addressed to him after the convention. I wrote:

Dear Dr. Greenberg,

The formality of the salutation bespeaks the lifetime of awe and respect I hold for you. I write to add what I might have contributed to the encomiums heaped on your protesting head at the recent Rabbinical Assembly Convention.

While you were visibly moved by the warm, extended applause of those assembled, virtually all of them your juniors, I thought: how much you must miss your contemporaries, all gone, with whom to share this moment of adulation and gratitude, made sweeter were they present.

You, who over these 66 years have praised so many others, surely must be inured to praise and suspicious of flattery. Nevertheless, you must have realized that you were the object of pure, unadulterated respect and love that day at the convention.

I first heard and saw you, a fiery, blond, ramrod straight young Zionist rabbi in 1934. For 57 years since I have observed your life with awe and wonder.

I gratefully recall your suggestion to me that I enter the rabbinate. Clergy speak of "receiving the call." Well, for me, "the call" came loud and clear from Heaven in your voice. After all, you were the Jewish voice of Philadelphia, its most distinguished and successful rabbi. I marveled at your intimate involvement with the daily report of your religious school principal which kept you in touch with every student's progress.

I can relive the shock I experienced when you told me you were leaving the congregation you had built into the strongest spiritual force in the community, Har Zion, at the peak of your effectiveness to take a subordinate role at the Seminary. When I questioned this move you said, "When Dr. Finkelstein calls, I have no choice but to answer."

I speculate on what the Seminary might have become with you at the helm.

I benefited from your instruction as my teacher at the Seminary. You taught! You did not perfunctorily repeat scraps of your scholarship. You reached out to us and shared yourself, unlike so many other professors. You continued to think and write seminal monographs on Judaism in general and Conservative Judaism as a movement "in Israel," to use your phrase. I maintain that no other writer has a truer grasp of the meaning and the potential of the movement.

I watched as you came to beg and plead with an indifferent Los Angeles community to establish a University of Judaism. I cringed as you humbled yourself to persuade the local leaders who often stonewalled you, refused your calls and failed to show at meetings called to create and sustain this institution. I thrilled to see the seeds you had planted finally take root. I had the privilege of serving under you as registrar during the 15 years you were president of the fledgling school when you were commuting between here and New York at enormous strain on Betty and yourself.

I learned *rachmanut* from you, and courage, too, one dark night on the way from the Los Angeles airport, when you made me stop my car on deserted Stocker Street at 3 A.M. to lend an automobile jack to a stranded motorist. I witnessed your master-minding of the *Penimiah* in Jerusalem, your nurturing it for years, and later your assuming the burden of raising funds for the Masorti movement at the age of 80 because no younger man had the vision or the daring to undertake it. I marveled as you proudly strode the streets of Jerusalem, silver-blond now but still ramrod-straight, looking a little more lonely with each passing year.

Had I the chance, I would have spoken of the success you achieved in training your brilliant sons, and of your being an absolute role model as a husband, partner and protector to Betty. She would probably agree that despite years of physical pain and illness her longevity must be attributed directly to your tireless, attentive and uncomplaining loving care. And what was going on within my strong, optimistic, undaunted hero? I found some hint thereof in the depth, sensitivity and honesty of your poetry.

Were there time, I would have reminisced about an evening when, with my infant son, now a rabbi, on your knee, and I, banging on the piano, our voices blended shouting old songs in Hebrew and Yiddish. But, then, so many other people have stories of sweet, intimate moments spent in your company.

My grandmother, Zelda, would say of someone, "I didn't tell the halft." Well, my cherished teacher and true friend, I didn't tell the halft. Nobody could, not even you, because you would demur and try to minimize the extent of your contribution to raising the quality of this troubled world. Only the *Ribono Shel Olam* Himself can recite the whole story of what you have meant to me, to the Jewish people, to this country and to Israel. As for me, I have written this because I wanted you to know some of the things I would have said on that wonderful evening at the convention.

Your faithful student,
Jack

Early in 1992, Betty Greenberg passed away, and a few months later, Erev Tisha b'Av, Dr. Greenberg followed her. I was moved to write a post-script to my earlier letter. It reads:

Dear Simon,

The barriers of protocol have been removed by your passing, and I can call you Simon, the paradigm of the complete Conservative Jew and, even more, the paradigm of the complete human being. I wish the young people coming up could have known you in person.

Instead they will know you through the many institutions which are your extended shadow: Har Zion, the Seminary, the World Council of Synagogues, the Penimiah, Mercaz, Kibbutz Hanaton, this University of Judaism.

But should they ask, "Who was this man who struggled and created in three parts of the world? What was he like? We can describe you to them in the words of Rabbi Meir, (Pirkei Avot 6:1). "Whosoever labors in the Torah for its own sake, merits many things; and not only so, but the whole world is indebted to him. He is called **רע אהוב אוהב את המקום אוהב את הבריות** friend, beloved, a lover of God, a lover of mankind."

Simon, **רבי** my rabbi, **מורי** my teacher, **רע אהוב** beloved friend, on this very spot where we first broke ground for the University of Judaism, I still feel your vital presence, and so do so many others who had the privilege of knowing you. For the first time, though I have quoted it often, I understand the verse in Talmud *Berahot* (18a-b) "The righteous are called living even when they are dead."

Whenever I long for your presence, I can come here to the University and stroll along its paths, and you and Betty, young and strong, will be with me. Together, we will rejoice over the fruit of your labors.

Jack

CHAPTER SEVEN
Hope in the Face of Terrorism

This is the chapter I never expected to include in this book. Never in my life did I anticipate having to preach about events such as the terrorist attacks on America on September 11, 2001.

Everything in my life in the rabbinate and nothing in my life in the rabbinate prepared me to address the congregation on *Rosh Hashanah*, barely a week after that terrible day, just two weeks before sending this volume to print.

COPING WITH TRAGEDY

On September 11, 2001 the unthinkable and the unspeakable happened: terrorists hijacked four U.S. jumbo passenger airplanes and succeeded with three of them to demolish the twin towers of the World Trade Center in Manhattan, and part of the Pentagon Building in Washington, D.C. Using jumbo-jets loaded with huge tanks full of fuel as if they were missiles, the hijackers took over the controls and aimed the planes precisely killing themselves, the passengers, and the thousands of occupants of the towers, plus firemen and other rescue workers crushed when the buildings crashed upon them.

Americans and sympathetic millions elsewhere were simply devastated. Rage, depression, fear, confusion and despair reigned. A week later, on September 19, I preached the following sermon, offering a note of hope and comfort which was well received.

September 19, 2001

Dear Friends,

The topic of my talk today, agreed upon with Rabbi Joel Rembaum weeks ago, was "Coping with Tragedy."

My text for today was from our Haftarah reading from the Prophet Jeremiah, קול ברמה נשמע, נהי בכי תמרורים, רחל מבכה על בניה, מאנה להנחם על בניה, כי איננו

Thus saith the Lord, "Hark: a voice is heard in Ramah: lamentation., and bitter weeping, Rachel weeping for her children. She refuseth to be comforted for her children, because they are no more."

A great tragedy has struck since our meeting. Last Friday on the national day of mourning proclaimed by President Bush, the Memorial Service held at the National Cathedral in Washington was opened by its Dean, Reverend Nathan Baxter, with the words:

"God said to them through the Prophet Jeremiah 'A voice is heard in Ramah, lamenting and bitter weeping. Mother Rachel weeping for her children. She refuseth to be comforted for her children, because they are no more.'"

How bitter! How ironic! The title remains the same. The Biblical text remains the same. Only I am changed. Only you are changed. Only history is changed. Only the future is changed.

You and I have watched in shocked disbelief how our world seemed to collapse moment by moment as the twin towers of the World Trade Center collapsed, story by story, incinerating with the fury of hellfire the bodies, the lives of thousands of souls unprepared for cremation on the eleventh of September. Those images are indelibly engraved upon your souls and mine, so there is no need for me to dwell upon it.

But I cannot stop there, nor must you. My message is called, "Coping With Tragedy." And the reading from Jeremiah does not stop there. In the name of the Lord he says to Mother Rachel, "You cannot go on forever like this, refusing to be comforted, wallowing in your grief. Thus saith the Lord: Refrain thy voice from weeping, and thine eyes from tears; for thy work shall be rewarded, saith the Lord; and they shall come back from the land of the enemy. ויש תקוה לאחריתך נאם יהוה And there is hope for thy future, saith the Lord."

There it is, on page 112, from which the Haftarah was chanted: There is always hope. We cope with tragedy by never abandoning hope. Jeremiah is talking to a people in exile who had every right to be depressed and defeated, and hopeless. Yet he predicts that they will return, as he says, "With tears of joy..." with dancing and merriment. What cockeyed optimist could promise such things in the face of tragedy? Only a clear-eyed Jewish optimist.

How can we learn how to cope with this present tragedy? We have been taught in the Jerusalem Talmud (Berachot, 9:1) "As long as man breathes he should not lose hope."

Could you and I have a more powerful example than the way the Jewish people fought back from the pit, from ground zero, from the death camps of Hitler to establish the most successful country to be recognized since World War II, a scant 18 years later?

Our experience has been a most costly lesson, in lives, in communities destroyed, in wisdom and talent lost. We must learn from it the lesson that there is always hope in our future and we must not give up our Jewish optimism.

May I share an incredible story out of the Holocaust: "In the ruins of the Warsaw Ghetto a most remarkable document was discovered. It is a scientific report of some 22 Jewish doctors who together with their wives and children were systematically and slowly starved to death by the Nazis. When the physicians realized the fate that awaited them they determined to make a study of the effects of starvation on the human mind and body. With incredible objectivity they recorded the pathological changes, the emotional reactions, the speed of reflexes in their starving wives and children and in themselves, As each doctor in turn met his own inescapable fate the manuscript was passed along to the next one. The last surviving physician buried the manuscript in the flaming ruins of the crumbling ghetto in the hope that someday this study would be unearthed and the scientific findings which it contained might contribute to the store of human knowledge. None of the physicians survived, but what they did collectively was an enduring testament to their belief, in the face of the most crushing evidence to the contrary, that life has a meaning and a purpose which even the bestiality of the Nazis could not destroy."

Did you catch the phrase that they did what they did "in the hope"?

The first answer to coping with tragedy is hope. What did the firemen and volunteers have while digging with machines and bleeding hands in the so-called "pit" at "ground zero" where hundreds of tons of steel and concrete collapsed on thousands of people? All they had was hope, the "maybe," perhaps one live survivor, who himself or herself was lying there still hoping. Without that hope they would have stopped.

In these days of awe when we are thinking about ourselves, our own imperfections, when we read with trepidation the words of U'n'taneh Tokef, "Who shall live and who shall die? Who shall become poor and who shall wax rich?" and some of us are wondering even as we pray, "What is going on in the stock market?" it might be useful to wonder how we cope with the tragedies, the serious problems of our individual lives, health, family, death. No one is immune. How shall we cope?

Talking about health, let me tell you about myself, my physical health. How many people get to talk about their symptoms with so many others? If God lets me I shall be 82 next month. To people who say, "Rabbi, you look marvelous!" I say, "You should see me on the inside."

Except for my health, I am well. If somebody asks how I am, if he is Jewish I say, *Baruch Hashem*, which tells him nothing except that I know the words. If he is not Jewish, I give him an organ recital about every symptom I enjoy from my head, where my ears ring with tinitus day and night, to my chest where my pacemaker is beating merrily along, to my neuropathy in my feet, which makes me walk funny; with eleven specialists keeping me patched up in between. Otherwise I am in good health. Anybody care to sell me some insurance? And do you know what? I am happy, which means I may also be crazy.

Why do I dare say these things from the pulpit? If I were employed I could get fired! I share these things to show we are all vulnerable. We live in an ocean of bacteria and viruses, not to speak of automobiles and planes, and the *Un'taneh Tokef* is right, who knows what tomorrow will bring? Ralph Waldo Emerson put it so well, "There is a crack in everything God made." What is important is how we deal with our cracks and our imperfections.

I think it is wise, that unlike previous generations we are quite open and communicative about our flaws. Not long ago everyone was ready to tell you at the drop of an hors d'oeuvre, "I see my psychiatrist twice a week," and be green with envy when the next person said, "That's nothing. I see my shrink every day."

Well, today there is a new aristocracy in the land, the aristocracy of the handicapped, with our red and blue cards on our windshields. We can park when there isn't a spot for a line of drivers cussing us. Today it is fashionable to be flawed. We wear our "Handicapped" label proudly!

But...our worst flaws are not the visible ones. I was persuaded of this by a carefully worded modern Un'taneh by my colleague, Rabbi Sidney Greenberg, in his book, *Saying Yes to Life*. He wrote, "To be human is to be handicapped, to be flawed. Some of us are handicapped by a disturbing sense of inferiority and inadequacy. Some of us carry childhood scars inflicted by constant criticism and bitter rejection.

"Some of us feel unworthy of being loved; others cannot give love. Some of us are burdened by guilt; others are filled with rage. Some of us are consumed by envy; others are driven by greed.

"Some of us have forfeited our self-respect; others never acquired it. Some of us are battered by fear; others are buffeted by frustration and failure. Some of us are imprisoned by selfishness; others are enslaved by alcohol or pills. Some of us suffer heartaches because of our children; others are tormented by our parents. Some of us carry within us the gray ash of burned-out dreams; others are haunted by fractured hopes and unfulfilled promises."

Our mid-Twentieth Century picture was of an America of happy families, living in their little bungalows with the white picket fence: a lovey-dovey husband and wife, and a darling son and daughter who romp and play and get all A's.

Well, something has smashed into our happy homes and they are crumbling: single parent families, married couples accounting for less than half of all households, child abuse, porn, infidelity

The family structure has been hit hard by infidelity. How do people cope with it? Some, including whole families, are destroyed by it. Some make it through, scarred but intact. Forget politics. Before the prying eye of the world, our immediate national past president, Bill Clinton, and his wife, Hillary and daughter Chelsea endured years of unabated ridicule, satirized by every comic and editorial cartoonist, threatened with impeachment. Tragedy? Yes. Theirs and ours, but, we all came through. The country survived, Hillary is United States Senator from New York, Chelsea has gone through Stanford with flying colors and is now in Oxford; and Bill has fulfilled every man's dream: he has moved to Harlem. They never abandoned their hopes for a better tomorrow and they have reached it.

I don't suggest theirs is the answer to every case of infidelity or incompatibility, but rather that people can survive the interpersonal tragedies if they do not lose faith that they can do it.

Every day brings its challenges, great or small from termites and backed-up drains to blackouts and earthquakes. When a quake struck this neighborhood only a few weeks ago, our condo was also plunged into stygian darkness. I got out of bed, totally disoriented, and clutching Margie's hand crept baby step by baby step toward where we had a night-light which goes on when power goes out. I felt helpless and fearful. I thought, as we shuffled, of Helen Keller, who lived her life in such a blackness, and I recited to myself her words which I memorized long ago, "I thank God for my handicaps, for through them, I have found myself, my work and my God." The lights came on after not too long, and I made up my mind that if ever I lost sight, God forbid, I could still cope, with someone's hand in mine..

It started me thinking of others who coped with what could only be called little tragedies.

I thought of Joseph in the Bible, seized by his jealous brothers, thrown into a pit, sold into slavery betrayed by his master's wife and cast into the Egyptian prison, from which he was eventually released and elevated to the position of Grand Vizier, second only to Pharaoh...a millionaire by thirty. How did he manage it? He dreamed ambitious dreams, he believed in himself, he let nothing get him down.

I thought of King David, the shepherd boy who when the Philistine giant Goliath had thoroughly demoralized the Israelites, stepped out and slew the giant with a slingshot. He had his tragedies...a public adulterous scandal with Bathsheba, the death of their baby.

The baby fell ill and David was inconsolable, fasted, a wreck. When the baby died he rose up, the Bible says, washed, dressed up, worshipped, ate and drank. To his amazed courtiers he said, "Can I bring him back again. I shall go to him, but he will not return to me." Tragedy did not destroy him. He believed deeply in himself and his mission in life,

I think of Jeremiah, who witnessed the conquest of Judea by Nebuchadnezzar and the exile of his people to Babylon 2500 years ago. How did the Judeans cope with exile? We created a great community in Babylon, which was the true center of Judaism for the next 1200 years, and produced the Babylonian Talmud. We coped by refusing to be demoralized. We stayed our course and survived.

Almost the same thing happened in the days of the Roman occupation of Judea and the siege and conquest of Jerusalem. Many will remember that Rabbi Yochanan ben Zakkai got himself carried out of the walls of Jerusalem in a coffin, accosted General Vespasian there and asked for one small favor. When Jerusalem fell, and it was certain to do so, he wanted the Romans to allow the Jews to teach their Torah and practice Judaism in the little town of Yavneh. In that little school Judaism survived, produced the Jerusalem Talmud; and Torah has been taught in that little land of ours, conquered by so many, until today. They coped by holding fast to their principles.

Our history is full of such examples, leading to that old story of three men in a sinking boat, British, French, and Jewish. When drowning seemed inevitable, the Briton cried, "There will always be an England!" and jumped. The Frenchman: "Vive la France!" and jumped. The Jew learned to live under water.

And so we have, down to the Twentieth Century, when, all but wiped out by the Nazis, the Jewish people reestablished the Third Jewish Commonwealth called Israel, and other survivors achieved great heights in many lands.

These few lessons gleaned from the Jewish experience of the past suggest various ways in which we shall cope with this latest attack.

On a more individual level, there are people who have also taught us how we must cope.

I still remember my shock as a child of eight on seeing human flesh and blood shredded by an accident. A tiny tot was crossing our street oblivious to the street car racing toward him. A boy of eleven, our local athlete, leaped at the tot, pushing him out of the way, but leaving his own legs crushed beneath the steel trolley wheels. He became my hero, and eventually went on to play ball on artificial legs, and become a success in business. He coped by never ceasing to train what was left of his body.

I think of a student in my college class in French, clicking with his

Braille writer and taking class notes. A member of the Penn varsity wrestling team, he went on to success in the practice of law. He coped by courage, determination, and a great self-image.

I learned a lesson in coping from the unsinkable Doctor Jerri Nielsen, the forty-seven year old doctor, research scientist at the Amundsen-Scott South Pole Research Station. In deepest winter, the 47 researchers stationed there lived in a dome of snow and ice during this period, with no transportation able to reach it or leave from it in the minus 60 degree temperature.

It was in that forbidding atmosphere that Dr. Nielsen discovered a lump in her breast which was life-threatening unless treated. With no one else available to do so, and no outside help able to reach her, Dr. Nielsen must have faced a terrifying dilemma: give up, or fight for her life as best as she could. By radio she asked for a parachute drop of medical supplies so that she could initiate chemotherapy on herself. I have thought many times about what it must have been like for her, in the blackness of the Antarctic winter, in the total isolation of the ice dome in which she lived, in fear because her knowledge enabled her fully to understand the gravity of her situation, the down-side of chemo, how slender the thread of hope that her life might be saved.

I wept with joy last October 11th when the big plane landed on a runway carved out of ice, and carried her swiftly aloft and back to America. and, we pray, to total recovery. She showed the world how precious is the gift of life and how hard we must fight against all odds to stay alive.

I learned a lesson from a slender young T.V. reporter, Vivian Alpert, who in a freak accident on the job was virtually electrocuted when her hands touched a live power wire and suffered destructive burns. Did she go into hiding with her bandaged hands? No, I saw her doing a broadcast, with her arms mostly behind the table, but refusing to yield to a huge tragedy.

And then there is Superman, Christopher Reeves, that gorgeous hunk of man who thrilled audiences for years until tragedy struck in 1995 when he was thrown from a horse and had his spinal cord severed. In his hospital bed, totally immobile and unable to breathe without a pumping machine, he looked into eyes of his wife Dana and mouthed the words, "Maybe we should let me go." She had a choice, pull the plug, or live with a helpless burden. She unhesitatingly responded, "You are still you and I love you."

The whole world has watched his determined struggle to find a way to retrain or even reconstruct those nerves which once made him every child's dream of Superman. Using Dana's words, he wrote a book, *Still Me*. Someday, I promise you, he will walk. He coped when he realized that tragedy or no, he was still himself. (John Shepler in *A Positive Light*)

Whatever cracks I have, whatever cracks you have, remember: God makes us strongest in the broken places.

Well, back to the tragedy of September 11. Huge. Monstrous. But it will do no good to wring our hands and say, "Lower Manhattan will never be the same. The stock market is in trouble. America will lose its world leadership. We are doomed to insecurity and isolation."

I have given so many examples of the resilience of the human spirit individually that I should have made my case that it is not the end of our world. Let me now point out to some glaring examples of coping with tragedy.

In World War II, during the German blitz of England, London was burning and wreckage was everywhere. London today is one of the world's wonder cities.

In World War II, in the Allied Armies' saturation bombing of Germany her cities lay in ruins. Germany today is rebuilt and one of the world's superpowers.

In World War Two the United States dropped two bombs on Hiroshima and Nagasaki, and Japan was on the ropes. Almost a half-million people died miserably. Could she ever recover, ever rebuild? She did and is now one of the world's great powers.

We, the U.S.A. with our Marshall Plan and other assistance helped those countries rebuild. Do you think we can't do the same for ourselves when our numbers, our resources, our technology are even far greater than they were fifty years ago? The world did not come to an end last Tuesday. We won't let it!

How do we cope with tragedy?

We cope by never abandoning hope.

We cope by never losing faith in ourselves and in God.

We cope by doing constructive things which cancel out the destructiveness of the tragedy.

We cope by accepting the fact that life at best is not perfect, that neither we nor the rest of humanity are perfect.

We cope by learning from the example of others, how they came through small or great tragedies, how they survived despite accident, pain, handicap, disaster. History teaches us. Survivors teach us.

We cope by joining with other people in mutual sympathy and consolation. *Shivah* is infinitely better than solitude for the mourner. Wordlessly holding the warm hand of another human being is better than wringing our own. People need people is not a silly cliché. The gatherings vast and small these past days when people lit candles and sang and wept together were the greatest antidote to despair. Can you imagine singing the *Hatikvah* all by yourself and being inspired? Can you imagine singing *The Star Spangled Banner* all by yourself, alone, and feeling patriotic? Impossible. We cope by joining together.

Let us indeed mourn for the innocent lives lost, and the larger circle of relatives and friends grieving and bewildered. But, as individuals and as a nation let us remember we have the capacity to cope with and overcome this situation. Like Mother Rachel, we weep for our children because they are not. But we also have to listen to God's promise, ויש תקוה לאחריתך "and there is hope for thy future."

Did anybody notice what seemed to survive those terrible explosions In New York: paper. There was a blizzard of papers floating down and covering the ground. Papers survived, could you believe it? It caused me to remember the story we read in the Martyrology on *Yom Kippur* afternoon, the story of the ten greatest rabbis tortured and executed by the Romans in the second century. One, Rabbi Hananyah ben Teradyon they wrapped in the parchment of a Torah and set him on fire so that the parchment would make his torture last even longer. He asked his weeping disciples standing helplessly by, "What do you see?" and they said, "The parchment is burning, but the letters are flying heavenward."

I watched those fluttering papers and I thought that there must be some with hastily scrawled last messages of "Darling, I am not afraid. Take care of the kids. I love you! Carry on."

Whether someone ever finds such messages or not, the letters have flown heavenward on the winged souls of those whose bodies perished. I feel they speak to us from Heaven and say, "Do not grieve forever. Do not give the ultimate victory to the enemy, Carry on and love life. Do not waste it in refusing to be comforted. Life is too precious."

May I ask you to help me demonstrate the power of sharing our common grief and our common hope.

Please rise and join me in two songs of hope for Israel and for America, both written by Jews. Join hands with your neighbor, friend or stranger, and you will realize you do not hope alone.

(All sing) Hatikvah and God Bless America.

EPILOGUE
For All We Know

One of the last sermons I preached before this publication was a heart-to-heart chat with people I have loved for over 50 years. I opened myself to them quite completely, and their response was warm and deeply moving.

I spoke of what we all know and feel: the uncertainty of life and the enormous value of every precious moment we walk this earth. Sadly, since preaching it our congregation has lost some of the most beautiful souls I have ever known, and, indeed, we shall not meet again…until, for all we know…

FOR ALL WE KNOW

This is tentative valedictory by a rabbi who has known his congregation for over 50 years and wishes to share his innermost feelings and understanding of life with these good friends.

Unabashedly intimate and sentimental, this sermon deals with the Untaneh Tokef *prayer. Year after year as I planned my remarks for* Rosh Hashanah, *I would give some thought to the unpredictability of the future. "Who shall live and who shall die" resonated in my head louder and louder with every passing year.*

Looking out at the congregation as they looked up expectantly to me for words of reassurance, I noted with a pang that there were new faces in some of the pews occupied by good friends one short year ago. Yes, we were hopeful that God would favor us with forgiveness and long life, but for all we know, this year could be our last. Rather than leading us to morbid thoughts, we are moved to a fuller and deeper appreciation of what we have now.

This year, in the ninth decade of my life, I opened my heart to the congregation and found a responsive chord in return. Some thought I was predicting my immediate demise. Others thought about their own expectations. Many of us wept at the realization of our own mortality. More persons requested a copy of this sermon than any other I have ever preached.

OCTOBER 2, 2000

Dear Friends:

Shana Tova, I wish each of you a wonderful year, including those whom I haven't seen in *shul* since the last millennium.

Never in my wildest dreams, and I have had some wild ones, did I ever dream that I would be preaching in the Twenty-first Century. In my childhood I thought the Twentieth Century would go on for ever, and I would never have to worry about a Twenty-first. In my golden years, which have been, maybe, 14 carats at most, I thought I would be lucky each year just to survive the assorted things which go wrong from ingrown toenails all the way up to falling hair and every malfunctioning organ in between.

And so, this year I wrote a wonderful sermon called, "But We're Here." It is 12 single-spaced computer-typed pages, rich in Jewish intellectual phrases, historical detail and Hebrew quotations. I decided against it, but you may have it upon request if you are perishing to know what I was going to say.

You see, I asked myself, "Did these wonderful people come to the synagogue because they were desperate to hear how brilliant I think I am?" The fact is, half the current Beth Am membership joined since I retired, and probably half of them aren't sure I'm alive. So I beg your indulgence if I reminisce a bit, since I've reached the age called anecdotage. After all, at almost 81, there is so much more to look backward upon than there is to look forward to.

It has been a long road. While yet in the Seminary, I was foisted upon a congregation of 1,000 sophisticated New Yorkers in Forest Hills. With the majority of them twice my age and more I tried to dazzle them with my erudition, my research, my command of big and obscure words, the books I had read. I tried to disguise my youth under a homburg hat, a vest piped in white and a velvet-collared chesterfield coat.

I realize now I wasn't fooling anybody. They were probably saying, "Let sonny boy speak. He'll grow out of it." I still have a picture, taken of the Forest Hills Board of Trustees with me sitting front and center, and when it hung on the wall in my study here, people would ask, "Who is the *bar mitzvah* boy in the middle?"

Today, 57 years later, I am keenly aware that for all we know, I may not be preaching next year. So, I want to chat with you, person to person. I think now, that if you got anything from my millions of words it was probably what I had learned about life and about myself because, in the final analysis, that is what I know best. Gradually I have opened myself up to you and let you into the deepest corners of my heart, which is only fair, since so many of you and those who have gone before you, have let me into yours. And so I end up with the one thing I alone know, and the only thing unique I have to give: myself, me.

Along the way, I confess, I have never been revolutionary, but rather, evolutionary, setting a pattern for this congregation which Rabbi Joel Rembaum has chosen to follow. There has not been a moment of contentiousness in our congregation, to the point that when I retired, the Jewish editor of the *Westside Los Angeles Times* refused to write up a farewell story. He said, "There is nothing controversial about you or Beth Am under your leadership." What a shame. No scandals here, no big, foolish fights.

I could never forget a story my own rabbi, Morris Goodblatt of blessed memory, told over and over again. It was about a congregation where, when the *Shema Yisrael* was read, half the congregants would stand and half would sit. The ones sitting would yell to those standing, "Sit down!" And those standing would yell, to the sitter, "Stand up!"

A new rabbi came to the congregation. He knew that either custom is acceptable, but he had to iron this thing out for once and for all. So he went to see one of the founders of the congregation, now 98 years old, who lived in a retirement home.

The rabbi took one of the *Shema* sitters and one of the *Shema* standers with him. The *Shema* sitter asked the old man, "Isn't the tradition to sit during the *Shema*?"

The old man said, "No, that is not the tradition."

"So," said the *Shema* stander, "the real tradition is to stand for the *Shema*, right?"

The old man said, "No, no! That's not the tradition!

The young rabbi said, "I don't know what to do. The congregants fight all the time, yelling at each to sit or to stand."

The old man interrupted, exclaiming, "That's our tradition!"

We managed to have a non-controversial, non-politicized congregation. The proof for me came when our son, Daniel, who had surely observed everything said and done in our home and in the congregation, was thinking about his profession in life. At first he thought it would be medicine so we introduced him to our doctors and books on medicine but exerted no pressure. One day he came to us and said, "Mom and Dad, would you be upset if I didn't go in for medicine?"

We said, "Of course not. What would you rather do?"

He said, "I think I want to become a rabbi."

"Wonderful," we said, "any special reason?"

"Yes. There's too much politics in medicine."

He never saw it here. What he saw was a congregation in harmony. Margie and I were able to be ourselves and lead with love and understanding. Feeling that love coming back to us, I allowed myself to do some audacious things: ...singing and dancing from our first show in 1954 to my 80th birthday where I did the same, playing Jerry Lewis, Lawrence Welk, Belafonte, Elvis, Liberace (which almost got me thrown out of the Rabbinical Assembly), Moshe Dayan, Anwar Sadat, and Ronald Reagan at *Simchat Torah* on this *bimah*. I also lay on the floor hammering fixtures for our great expositions and designed three Holy Arks. Most outrageous of all, I asked one *Kol Nidre* night, "Could I stand before you and preach stark naked?" I concluded that I could, because it was not the robe or the homburg which made me the rabbi. I was just one of you, who studied a little more and was honored by being called "Rabbi." Since I was stripped of all pretense, what you saw is what you got.

And so, today I stand before you, a naked 80-year old man. Not actually, just figuratively, because my figure would make us all laugh. I ask myself, what do I really have to say to you at this stage in life, and what concerns do you really have on these solemn days?

And because every sermon still needs a text, I asked myself, "Out of the three days of prayers which fill 499 pages of our heavy *machzors*, what really, really touches us to that innermost heart? I want you to think for a second, of what three special sections grab your *neshamah* and deal with the realities of life?

Mine are: *Kol Nidre*, which asks for forgiveness for all our broken and unfulfilled promises and dreams; *Yizkor*, when we stand silently pronouncing the names of people we have lost; *Untaneh Tokef* which begins by asking, "Who shall live and who shall die?"

Do you notice something unique about these three? They are not part of what we call the **מטבע התפילה**, the matrix of the prayers, the basic core of the prayers. They were created outside the time-honored order of the *Mahzor*, and from time to time were actually fought by this group of authorities or that, with demands that they be removed as not authentic: the old reactionary cry of "It's not our tradition."

The real emotions and the common sense of the people prevailed. They all stayed in. And I wonder how many people over the ages, dutifully recited the entire *Mahzor*, but found their hearts were most deeply touched by *Kol Nidre*, *Yizkor* and *Untaneh Tokef.*

One prayer not in the **מטבע התפילה**, the basic official *mahzor*, is the *Kol Nidre*. Nothing else seizes and holds our rapt attention as does *Kol Nidre*, a brief ritual for nullifying oaths we may have made and failed to keep. It has come to mean so much more to us: the shame over promises not kept, the wail of the Jew driven underground by persecution, the realization of our mistakes, wasted chances. When we hear the words, chanted softly, **כל נדרי ואסרי וחרמי וקונמי**, which some of us may or may not even be able to translate, but we see the Torah scrolls clutched proudly by panels of Jews free to express their faith in a way impossible when the *Kol Nidre* was composed, we are moved as at no other moment in the Jewish year.

Then we begin to realize what we are doing. We are admitting that neither in the past year nor in the year ahead are we able to lead perfect, unblemished lives. We admit we cannot live up to all we promised to ourselves and vowed to the Almighty. We are imperfect, we are human, and that's all right. When we have done all we can do, we need not be ashamed or afraid.

We just have to make things right with people we have wronged. We have to rid ourselves of grudges we have been nursing for silly reasons we hardly remember, get rid of the garbage of wounded pride, of "he said" and "she said." Then, *Kol Nidre* sings, "Perhaps this year we can wipe the slate clean and start again." And we chant, ויאמר יהוה "And the Lord said, סלחתי כדברך I have forgiven, according to thy word."

Kol Nidre draws us like a magnet because we all yearn for that blessed state we call "innocence." No stuffy, insensitive, self-righteous authorities have been able to silence *Kol Nidre*.

And then there is *Yizkor*. For a week the synagogue telephone rings off the hook with people wanting to know precisely, "When is *Yizkor*, precisely?" And then we open the doors and admit all who are drawn like a magnet by it. The walls are lined with people standing and weeping as half-hidden sorrows come poignantly to the surface.

Yizkor is so short, a few minutes of remembrance, and yet holding a message so powerful: life is short. That is what makes every day so important. Where are the years flying until our names appear in the Book of Remembrance? We must do something worthy, something beautiful, something kind and decent and honorable with the years which remain. Nobody said it better than Rabbi Tarfon in the Pirkei Avot, (II:20) היום קצר "The day is short, the work is great, the workers are lazy, the reward is much, ובעל הבית דוחק and the master is urgent."

But *Yizkor* is not morbid. It should not get us down. It should lift us up. Let me share with you the picture it conjures up for me. If you close your eyes you will see it more vividly. When I begin to recite the *Yizkor*, I think of the Twenty-third Psalm, "The Lord is my shepherd, I shall not want." And I hear, "He maketh me to lie down in green pastures." I close my eyes and I am transported to a green meadow, the valley of the shadow of death. And even in the midst of the deadly hills "He spreadeth a table before me."

And so at *Yizkor* time, I sit at a bountiful table of sweet memories in the green valley, and as I mention their names, my loved ones come and sit around me at the table, my dear mother, Dora; and father, Sol; and Margie's parents, Rose and Isidore; my precious *baba*, Zelda; and *zayde*, Chaim; my little brother, Irving...sitting together as once we were. We are happy to see one another.

Around the valley I see thousands of souls at whose funerals I officiated. Over the years forcing myself not to cry because I was the rabbi there to comfort them. Beyond them on the sides of the shadowy hills sit the 6,000,000 whom this Holocaust memorial wall recalls, reproaching us for not having saved them from the monsters who rampaged across Europe under the banner of the Crooked Cross. They are at peace at last because they know they have not been forgotten and the Jews cheated Hitler out of his final victory.

We spend these few precious moments together. And then because life goes on I leave them behind, as I must, and they remain, tranquil and at ease in the green pasture, at the table God has set before them. I say *El Mole Rachamim* for them and *Kaddish*. And even though my eyes are a little moist, somehow I feel uplifted by the thought that not even death has truly separated us. I look around the room at you and at the people standing around the room, some teary-eyed, and I know again why the authorities were never able to remove *Yizkor* from the prayers.

Most moving of all, I believe, is *Untaneh Tokef*. Why do we come here today in the first place?

I don't care how cynical, how skeptical, how far removed someone may be when we chant **בראש השנה יכתבון וביום צום כפור יחתמון** "On Rosh Hashanah it is written down and on the Day of Atonement it is sealed; who shall live and who shall die." That striking metaphor of a book, spread before the author of the Universe, those crucial alternatives we face, they really reach us where we live.

"How many shall pass away, and how many shall be born." **מי יחיה ומי ימות** "Who shall live and who shall die. Who shall attain the measure of man's years and who shall not attain it." The hazards of life: fire, flood, earthquake, plague; and its alternatives: rich, poor, tranquil, disturbed. We are talking here about real life, and its uncertainties, the things we really worry about.

Our spirits, which could be depressed by it all, are lifted by the promise we are offered. We are not totally helpless about everything, victims of a cruel and heartless fate, but we are offered the challenge that there are sometimes things we can do: **ותשובה ותפלה וצדקה מעבירין את רוע הגזרה** Repentance, prayer, and righteousness avert the severe decree. Some say that means we can actually do things which change the undesirable decree, and some say it means we can live so that we can cope with the severity of the decree. There is truth in both, and that's the tradition.

Untaneh Tokef is a passage we just can't mumble through. I can't read them without praying to God in my heart for people I know and about whom I care. I will mention a few of the many whom I know. I am not violating their privacy because we have made a *mishaberach* for the sick every week and spoken their names. I am praying for my faithful former secretary, Marilyn Grobeson, victim of the rarest of illnesses; of sweet Deanie Levine, struggling against a number of painful and debilitating illnesses; for George Konheim, that once dynamic and hugely successful builder, lying on the hospital bed in his bedroom for months and years scarcely alive.

I think of David Zerner, profound thinker, sponsor of so many scholars-in-residence here, now languishing at home for months; I think of Dr. Sigi Ziering, our past president, a Holocaust survivor, a scientific and business giant, whose family name appears on this very building, but is even more deeply engraved in our hearts, lying helpless and speechless on his bed at home.

Every *Shabbat* people line up to pray for sick family members and friends. *Untaneh Tokef* is like a universal lineup of all of us, calling on us to face those uncertainties in life which we all experience; reassuring us we are not alone in trying to deal with questions of life and death, economic ups and downs, unexpected catastrophes of nature which change lives in a minute. We are all in it together, facing the unpredictable human condition.

Perhaps we can draw strength to face the future, rubbing shoulders with our fellow worshipers, being taught that by our collective prayer, *Tefillah*; or by changing our ways with *Teshuvah*, spiritual or physical; or by *Tsdakah*, righteousness. We can cope with whatever this new year may bring, or even modify the so-called "evil decree," roll with the punches and learn how to be grateful when blessings come our way.

Let me share a true story with you about how righteousness can modify the severe decree. It happens that our son, Daniel, took off a year from the rabbinical seminary for more intensive Bible study. To make some money he drove a taxi on the night shift, finishing his run at three o'clock in the morning. I can tell you, that Margie and I didn't sleep until he got home because driving a cab in the darkest hours of night can be dangerous. So I know the value of the following story, related by a cabby who also drove late at night.

"Because I drove the night shift, passengers climbed in, sat behind me in total anonymity and told me about their lives. None touched me more than a woman I picked up late one August night in a dangerous part of town. When I arrived at 2:30 a.m., the building was dark except for a single light in a ground floor window. Under these circumstances, many drivers would just honk once or twice, wait a minute, then drive away. But unless a situation smelled of danger, I always went to the door.

"So I walked to the door and knocked. 'Just a minute,' answered a frail, elderly voice. I could hear something being dragged across the floor.

After a long pause, the door opened. A small woman in her eighties stood before me. She was wearing a print dress and a pillbox hat with a veil pinned on it like somebody out of a 1940's movie. By her side was a small nylon suitcase. In the corner was a cardboard box filled with photos and glassware she was leaving behind. That is all there was.

"'Would you carry my bag out to the car?' she said. I took the suitcase to the cab, then returned to assist the woman. She took my arm and we walked slowly toward the curb. She kept thanking me for my kindness.

"'It's nothing,' I told her. 'I just try to treat my passengers the way I would want my mother treated.'

"'Oh, you're such a good boy,' she said. When we got in the cab, she gave me an address, then asked, 'Could you drive through downtown?'

"'It's not the shortest way,' I answered quickly.

"'Oh, I don't mind,' she said. 'I'm in no hurry. I'm on my way to a hospice.'

"I looked in the rearview mirror. Her eyes were glistening. 'I don't have any family left,' she continued. 'The doctor says I don't have very long.'

"I quietly reached over and shut off the meter. 'What route would you like me to take?' I asked.

"For the next two hours, we drove through the city. She showed me the building where she had once worked as an elevator operator. We drove through the neighborhood where she and her husband had lived when they were newlyweds. She had me pull up in front of a furniture warehouse that had once been a ballroom where she had gone dancing as a girl. Sometimes she would ask me to go slow in front of a particular building or corner and would sit staring into the darkness, saying nothing.

"As the first hint of sun was crossing the horizon, she suddenly said, 'I'm tired. Let's go now.'

"We drove in silence to the address she had given me. It was like a small convalescent home. Two orderlies came out to the cab as soon as we pulled up. They must have been expecting her. I opened the trunk and took the small suitcase to the door. The woman was already seated in a wheelchair.

"'How much do I owe you?' she asked, reaching into her purse.

"'Nothing," I said.

"'You have to make a living,' she answered.

"'There are other passengers,' I responded. Almost without thinking, I bent and gave her a hug.

"She held onto me tightly. 'You gave an old woman a little moment of joy,' she said. 'Thank you.'

"I squeezed her hand, then walked into the dim morning light. Behind me, a door shut.

"It was the sound of the closing of a life. I didn't pick up any more passengers that shift. I drove aimlessly, lost in thought. What if that woman had gotten an angry driver or one who was impatient to end his shift? What if I had refused to take the run or had honked once, then driven away? Great moments often catch us unaware," he said, "beautifully wrapped in what others may consider a small one. People may not remember exactly what you did or what you said but they will always remember how you made them feel."

A sensitive cab driver's act of instinctive righteousness, a small moment of **צדקה**, made the worst moment of an old woman's life bearable. You have to believe that **תשובה ותפלה וצדקה מעבירין את רוע הגזרה** and that you can help or be helped to soften the impact of even the worst moments in life. These three prayers I cited today teach us to be the best persons we can be, because human life is but a fleeting moment between two eternities, a chance to allow God's image to shine in us. How? By the way we treat one another.

That is why I shared with you just a few instances of what your fellow congregants are going through. If, belonging to a congregation, we cannot take an interest in what is going on in the next person's life, then we are in the wrong place. Do we really love one another?

There is a little parable which goes like this, "Do ye love me, brother?"

"Aye, that I do."

"Do ye know what pains me, brother?"

"Nay, I do not know what pains thee."

"If ye do not know what pains me, ye cannot love me." *Untaneh Tokef* alerts us to the uncertainties of life and our need to care for and about one another.

Nothing thrills me as much as when I see families among us who are caring, "*zisseh neshumes,*" sweet souls who put meaning into our name, *Adat Bet Am,* The Congregation of the House of the People. And all I wanted to say today is "Thank you for letting me and my family dwell in your house."

When I began to speak today I used the term, "For all we know." In Yiddish, "*Ver vehst?*" I learned it from my Baba Zelda, who used it more and more as she got older. When I moved away from Philadelphia, she was still alive, but every time I visited and was saying goodbye to return back here, she would take me by the hand and say, "Who can know whether we shall ever see each other again?" We did that many times, until at last, she wasn't there any more to say it. I think some of you have had the same experience.

I have lived a great life with an incredible partner, Margie, and wonderful children and grandchildren, lived it joyfully and optimistically, but somewhere, deep down, I was haunted by the thought each time we were together, "*Ver vehst?* Who knows? For all we know, we may never meet again."

On my 80th birthday I ended my program of songs with those words, and I sing them again now, hoping I shall sing them many times more, but....

For all we know, we may never meet again
Before we go, make this moment sweet again,
We won't say goodbye until the last minute.
I hold out my hand, and my heart's always in it.
For all we know, this may only be a dream.
We come and go like the ripples in a stream.
So love each other today.
Tomorrow may be good for some,
But, tomorrow may never come, for all we know.